Bali
& Lombok

Tony Wheeler
James Lyon

Bali & Lombok – a travel survival kit

4th edition

Published by
Lonely Planet Publications
Head Office: PO Box 617, Hawthorn, Vic 3122, Australia
Branches: PO Box 2001A, Berkeley, CA 94702, USA and London, UK

Printed by
Colorcraft Ltd, Hong Kong

Photographs by

Glenn Beanland (GB)	Colin Kerr (CK)	Tom Smallman (TS)
Mary Coventon (MC)	James Lyon (JL)	Phil Weymouth (PW)
Greg Elms (GE)	Pauline Lyon (PL)	Tony Wheeler (TW)
Sue Graefe (SG)	Lachlan Piece (LP)	Tamsin Wilson (Tass)

Front cover: Besakih, Jim Hooper, Scoopix Photo Library

First Published
January 1984

This Edition
February 1992

Although the authors and publisher have tried to make the information as accurate as possible, they accept no responsibility for any loss, injury or inconvenience sustained by any person using this book.

National Library of Australia Cataloguing in Publication Data

Wheeler, Tony 1946–

Bali and Lombok, a travel survival kit.

4th ed.
Includes index.
ISBN 0 86442 133 8.

1. Lombok (Indonesia) – Description and travel – Guide-books. 2.
Bali Island (Indonesia) – Description and travel – Guide books. 1.
Lyon, James. II. Title.

915.98604

text & maps © Lonely Planet 1992
photos © photographers as indicated 1992

All rights reserved. No part of this publication may be reproduced, stored in a retrieval system or transmitted in any form by any means, electronic, mechanical, photocopying, recording or otherwise, except brief extracts for the purpose of review, without the written permission of the publisher and copyright owner.

Tony Wheeler

Tony Wheeler was born in England but spent most of his youth overseas. He returned to England to do a university degree in engineering, worked as an automotive engineer, returned to university to complete an MBA then dropped out on the Asian overland trail with his wife Maureen. They've been travelling, writing and publishing guidebooks ever since, having set up Lonely Planet Publications in the mid-70s. Travel for the Wheelers is now considerably enlivened by their daughter Tashi and their son Kieran.

James Lyon

James is by nature a sceptic, by training a social scientist, and by trade an editor at Lonely Planet's Melbourne office. He first visited Asia in the '70s, and has been back on several trips. He has travelled in Bali with his wife, Pauline, and their two young children, but returned by himself to update this book and to explore the boondocks of Lombok. A keen gardener, he found the flowers and landscapes of Bali a special delight. He also enjoys walking, which is another attraction of Bali and Lombok, and skiing, which isn't.

From the Authors

From James For information, moral support and friendly advice, my thanks to Ketut Artana of Denpasar; low budget traveller Debbie Cullen; Richard, Tini and Nancy of Lovina; and David Hardy, from the Australian consulate. On Lombok, Ikhsan Chan of Ampenan was an invaluable help, and Hadji Radiah showed me the same wisdom and warmth which I'm sure he shares with every traveller. At home, sincere thanks to my colleagues at Lonely Planet for their support and friendship, and to Pauline, Michael and Bennie.

From Tony Thanks to Ketut Suartana, who runs Ketut's Place in Ubud, for his hospitality, help and the loan of his motorcycle.

This Book

For this edition of *Bali & Lombok - a travel survival kit*, Tony was responsible for updating south and east Bali while James covered the rest of Bali and Lombok. Credit must also go to earlier authors: Mary Covernton for her research on Lombok in the first edition and Alan Samagalski for updates on both Bali and Lombok in the second edition.

Michael Sklovsky provided extra information for the Arts & Crafts colour section and generously allowed Lonely Planet artists and authors to photograph items from his Ishka Handcrafts stores in Melbourne.

Additional material for this book was contributed by Maureen Wheeler, who wrote the Take the Children section, and Kirk Willcox, who wrote the Bali Surfing section. The cycling information is based on Hunt Kooiker's now out of print *Bali by Bicycle*.

From the Publisher

This edition of Bali & Lombok was edited by Miriam Cannell and Kay Waters. Thanks to Tom Smallman for editorial guidance. Tamsin Wilson drew the maps and illustrations, handled the design work for the cover and the new Arts & Crafts colour section, and designed and laid out the book.

Thanks also to those travellers who took the time and energy to write to us with corrections and additions – apologies if we've misspelt your names:

Captain Paul Ake (USA), Ann Aldershof (USA), Sarah Anggarayasa (In), J Armstrong (Aus), Dave & Jim Arnold (USA), Tracey Barrett (UK), Regula Keller Binzegger (CH), Paolo Borsoni (It), Coco Brandon (UK), Jan Brown (Aus), Kathleen Burgess (USA), Steve Cuff (Aus), Dean Decker (USA), Mrs Dhewi (In), Michael Dillon (C), N Dixon (Aus), Megan Donnelly (Aus), Ole Dybbroe (Nl), L Eddy (Aus), Tammie Egerton (NZ), Sarah Erwin, Valerie Ferris (USA), Leigh Fox (USA), Don Frank (USA), Scott Frazier, Lone Frederiksen (Dk), Matthew Frost (UK), Denise Gardiner, Diana Harcourt (UK), Fran Hopkins (Aus), Trishna Horvath (USA), Steve & Bev Hunt (Aus), Louise Jade (Aus), Thomas Karlsson (Sw), Darren Kerr (UK), Stephen Kirkpatrick (UK), Brian Kliesen (USA), Andrei Koeppen (Aus), David Lennie, Camilla Leroy, Chris Lund (USA), George Majoros (C), Louise Marshall (UK), George Melekin (USA), Miko (In), Yasuko Morikawa (J), Tom Mort (Aus), Rianda Mulder (Nl), Joanne Murphy (Aus), Zapheria Nomicos (USA), Denise Norman (UK), Bill & Laura O'Connor (UK), David O'Keefe (C), Joanne Obermaier (J), Mieko Oki (J), Elizabeth Parsons (UK), I Ketut Ena Partha (In), I Made Patera (In), Daniel Pawl (USA), Stephen Pelizzo, Raymond & Pat Peters, Mark Pettit (Aus), Ingrid Pinter (USA), Elizabeth A Post (USA), Anni Poulsen (Dk), Hanne Rasmussen (Dk), Tom Rigby (Nl), Neil Rugg (UK), C T Sartain (USA), W A Schippers, Wendy Schulze (Aus), Leon Sebek (C), Ruth Shepherd (Aus), Rebecca Shields (UK), Greg Smith (C), Shona Snedden (NZ), Peter Stevens (Aus), J Stitfall (NZ), Kirsty Sword (Aus), Deborah Taylor-French (USA), John Triton (UK), Eric & Maggi Turner (HK), Merril Uhlhorn (Aus), Jacqueline van Haaften, Jenny Vanderfelt, Margaret Victor (USA), Margaret Victor (USA), Patricia Wall (USA), Shannon Warwick (Aus), Tim Webb (UK), Sheldon Weeks, Zero Wilaya (In), Noni Wilson (NZ)

A – Austria, Aus – Australia, B – Belgium, C – Canada, CH – Switzerland, D – Germany, Dk – Denmark, Fr – France, HK – Hong Kong, In – Indonesia, Ire – Ireland, It – Italy, J – Japan, Nl – Netherlands, NZ – New Zealand, Phil – Philippines, Sp – Spain, Sw – Sweden, Thai – Thailand, UK – United Kingdom, USA – United States of America

Warning & Request

Things change - prices go up, schedules change, good places go bad and bad places go bankrupt - nothing stays the same. So if you find things better or worse, recently opened or long since closed, please write and tell us and help make the next edition better!

Your letters will be used to help update future editions and, where possible, important changes will also be included as a Stop Press section in reprints.

All information is greatly appreciated and the best letters will receive a free copy of the next edition, or any other Lonely Planet book of your choice.

Contents

INTRODUCTION 9

FACTS ABOUT BALI 11

History 11
Geography 13
Climate 14
Flora & Fauna.........................14
Government 16
Economy 16
Population 17
Music & Dance.......................17
Wayang Kulit 24
Culture & Customs 24
Religion.....................................28
Language – Balinese................34
Bahasa Indonesia 34

FACTS ABOUT LOMBOK.. 42

History 42
Geography 44
Climate 44
Flora & Fauna.........................44
Economy 45
Population & People................45
Arts..47
Culture & Customs 49
Religion.....................................52
Language 54

FACTS FOR THE VISITOR 55

Visas & Embassies 55
Documents................................57
Customs 57
Money..57
When to Go 61
What to Bring 62
Tourist Offices 62
Business Hours 63
Holidays & Festivals – Bali 63
Holidays & Festivals –
Lombok......................................64
Post & Telecommunications 65
Time...66
Electricity..................................66
Laundry.....................................67
Weights & Measures.................67
Books & Maps 67
Media 70
Film & Photography 70
Health..71
Women Travellers.....................77
Dangers & Annoyances 77
Taking the Children 79
Surfing.......................................83
Diving 88
Language Courses.....................89
Other Activities........................89
Accommodation.......................90
Food 93
Drinks..96
Entertainment...........................98
Things to Buy............................98

GETTING THERE & AWAY 99

Bali 99
Air 99
Sea 104
Leaving Bali 104
Lombok.............................. 105
Air 105
Sea 105

GETTING AROUND... 107

Bali 107
Bemo.......................................107
Tourist Shuttle Bus 108
Motorbike 109
Car Rental 111
Hitching 112
Bicycle 112
Lombok.............................. 118
Bemo & Bus 118
Motorbike 119
Car Rental 120
Bicycle 120
Dokar/Cidomo 121
Prahu & Sampan 121

DENPASAR 124

SOUTH BALI 133

Kuta & Legian 133
Sanur.......................................147
Pulau Serangan 154
Jimbaran Bay 155
Benoa Port 155
Benoa Village 156
Nusa Dua.................................156
Ulu Watu 158

UBUD & AROUND.. 160

Denpasar to Ubud............ 160
Batubulan.................................160
Celuk..161
Sukawati 161
Batuan 162
Mas 162
Blahbatuh.................................162
Kutri 163
Ubud 163
Around Ubud 178
Goa Gajah 179
Yeh Pulu..................................179

Bedulu 179   Pejeng 181   Ubud to Batur 183
Around Bedulu 181   Tampaksiring 181

EAST BALI 184

Gianyar 186   Padangbai 190   Tulamben 201
Bona 187   Balina Beach (Buitan) 192   Tulamben to Yeh Sanih 202
Lebih & the Coast 187   Tenganan 193   Amlapura to Rendang 202
Sidan 187   Candidasa 194   Bangli 203
Klungkung 187   Amlapura 198   Besakih 204
Kusamba 190   Tirtagangga 200   Gunung Agung 205
Goa Lawah 190   Tirtagangga to Tulamben 201

SOUTH-WEST BALI 207

Sempidi, Lukluk & Kapal 207   Marga 208   Tabanan to Negara 210
Tanah Lot 207   Sangeh 209   Negara 211
Mengwi 208   Tabanan 209   Gilimanuk 211
Blayu 208   Around Tabanan 209

CENTRAL MOUNTAINS 212

Penelokan 212   Gunung Batur & Lake Batur .. 216   Routes through Pupuan 222
Batur & Kintamani 214   Lake Bratan Area 219
Penulisan 216   Gunung Batukau 221

NORTH BALI 223

Singaraja 223   West of Singaraja 233   East of Singaraja 236
Lovina 225   Bali Barat National Park 234

NUSA PENIDA 238

Nusa Lembongan 238   Nusa Penida 240

WEST LOMBOK 244

Ampean, Mataram,   South-Western Peninsula .. 252   Suranadi 257
Cakranegara & Sweta 244   Senggigi 254   Sesaot 258
Gunung Pengsong 252   Narmada 256
Lembar 252   Lingsar 256

CENTRAL, SOUTH & EAST LOMBOK 259

Central Lombok 259   Rungkang 261   Kuta Beach 264
Kotaraja 259   Sukarara 262   **East Lombok** 265
Loyok 259   Penujak 262   Labuhan Lombok 265
Pringgasela 260   Lenang 262   North of Labuhan Lombok 266
Tetebatu 260   Rembitan (Sade) 264   South of Labuhan Lombok 267
Lendang Nangka 261   **South Lombok** 264

NORTH LOMBOK 268

Sira 268   Senaru 270   Gunung Rinjani 271
Bayan 268   Sembalun Bumbung &
Batu Koq 268   Sembalun Lawang 270

THE GILI ISLANDS 275

Gili Air 278   Gili Meno 278   Gili Trawangan 278

GLOSSARY 280

INDEX 284

Maps 284   Text 284

Map Legend

BOUNDARIES

—— — · — · —— · .... International Boundary
—— · — · —— · .... Internal Boundary
+++++++++++++++ .... National Park or Reserve
- - - - - - - - - - .... The Equator
· · · · · · · · · · · · · · · .... The Tropics

SYMBOLS

⊙ NEW DELHI .... National Capital
● BOMBAY .... Provincial or State Capital
● Pune .... Major Town
● Borsi .... Minor Town
■ .... Places to Stay
▼ .... Places to Eat
▲ .... Post Office
✈ .... Airport
i .... Tourist Information
◖ .... Bus Station or Terminal
66 .... Highway Route Number
☾ ✝ ✝ ...... Mosque, Church, Cathedral
∴ .... Temple or Ruin
✚ .... Hospital
✴ .... Lookout
Å .... Camping Area
⊓ .... Picnic Area
⌂ .... Hut or Chalet
▲ .... Mountain or Hill
.... Railway Station
.... Road Bridge
.... Railway Bridge
.... Road Tunnel
.... Railway Tunnel
.... Escarpment or Cliff
.... Pass
.... Ancient or Historic Wall

ROUTES

—————— .... Major Road or Highway
- - - - - - - - - - .... Unsealed Major Road
——————— .... Sealed Road
- - - - - - - - - - ..... Unsealed Road or Track
════════ .... City Street
+++++++++ .... Railway
—●— .... Subway
· · · · · · · · · · · · · .... Walking Track
- - - - - - - - - - .... Ferry Route
+++++++++ .... Cable Car or Chair Lift

HYDROGRAPHIC FEATURES

.... River or Creek
.... Intermittent Stream
.... Lake, Intermittent Lake
.... Coast Line
.... Spring
.... Waterfall
.... Swamp

.... Salt Lake or Reef

.... Glacier

OTHER FEATURES

Park, Garden or National Park

.... Built Up Area

... Market or Pedestrian Mall

.... Plaza or Town Square

.... Cemetery

Note: not all symbols displayed above appear in this book

Introduction

Bali, a tropical island in the Indonesian archipelago, is so picturesque and immaculate it could almost be a painted backdrop. It has rice paddies tripping down hillsides like giant steps, volcanoes soaring up through the clouds, dense tropical jungle, long sandy beaches, warm blue water, crashing surf and a friendly people who don't just have a culture but actually live it. In Bali spirits come out to play in the moonlight, every night is a festival and even a funeral is an opportunity to have a good time.

A curious mixture of position and events accounts for Bali's relative isolation from Indonesian history and religion, and the amazing vitality of its culture. Six centuries ago Indonesia was still a Hindu nation but when the Islamic religion swept across the islands the Majapahit, the last great dynasty on the island of Java, retreated to Bali with their entire entourage of scholars, artists and intelligentsia. Bali's fertility and the extraordinary productivity of its agriculture meant enough spare time and energy was available for the development of a complex culture, with distinctive movements in art, architecture, music and dance; a culture with a vitality which has hardly faltered to this day.

The Balinese are a most unusual people. Unlike most islanders they are not great seafarers. In fact they shun the sea as the abode of demons and evil spirits, and look toward the holy mountains which rise up in the centre of the island. They're also an unusually friendly and outgoing people – particularly once you get away from the south coast tourist enclaves. Few people manage to spend a week or two in the village of Ubud without falling in love with it.

Although Bali is, for many of its Western visitors, simply a place with cheap living and pleasant beaches, it's much, much more than that. Festivals, ceremonies, dances, temple processions and other activities take place almost continuously in Bali and they're fun to watch, easy to understand and instantly accessible. It's the great strength of Bali's culture that makes the island so interesting

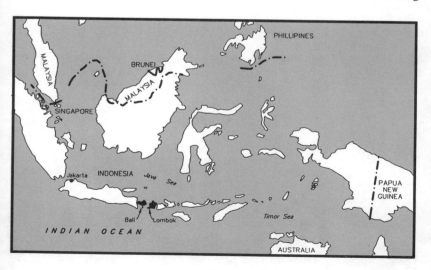

and also ensures that it will stay that way. 'Has tourism ruined Bali yet?' is the question every visitor is asked. It may not have done Kuta Beach a lot of good but the answer has to remain 'no, it hasn't'. If it's any consolation, Covarrubias, whose pre-war guide to Bali remains the classic book on the island, was worried about the effects of tourism at a time when the number of visitors was not 1% of what it is today.

The island of Lombok, Bali's eastern neighbour, has both the lushness of Bali and the starkness of outback Australia. It's an island of contrasts, rimmed with toothpaste-white beaches and tropical coconut palms, dominated by a towering volcano and patchworked with perfect paddy fields. Parts of Lombok drip with water while pockets are chronically dry, parched and cracked like a bleached crocodile skin. The unpredictability of the rainfall can cause severe hardship. Droughts can last for months, rice crops fail

and people have starved to death in their thousands. As recently as 1966, 50,000 people perished in a famine, but water management and irrigation, as well as improved agricultural techniques, have reduced the dependence on rainfall and made life on Lombok much less precarious.

Lombok's indigenous people, the Sasaks, are predominantly Muslim. Though elements of the ancient animist beliefs survive, what the visitor will notice is the raucous sounds of today's muezzin, the loudspeaker, calling the faithful to prayer. Lombok also has an intact Balinese culture with all the splendour and colour of its processions and ceremonies and a number of magnificent, though rather neglected, temples. While you shouldn't be taken in by the stories of black magic that the Balinese like to affect about Lombok, it does have a special magic of its own that in some ways is more powerful than the fairy-tale unreality of Bali.

Facts about Bali

HISTORY

There is no trace of the Stone Age in Bali although it's certain that the island was already populated before the Bronze Age commenced there about 300 BC. Nor is much known of Bali during the period when Indian traders brought Hinduism to the Indonesian archipelago. The earliest records found in Bali, stone inscriptions, date from around the 9th century AD and by that time Bali had already developed many similarities to the island you find today. Rice was grown with the help of a complex irrigation system probably very like that employed now. The Balinese had also already begun to develop the cultural and artistic activities which have made the island so interesting to visitors right down to the present day.

Hindu Influence

Hindu Java began to spread its influence into Bali during the reign of King Airlangga from 1019 to 1042. At the age of 16, when his uncle lost the throne, Airlangga fled into the forests of western Java. He gradually gained support, won back the kingdom once ruled by his uncle and went on to become one of Java's greatest kings. Airlangga's mother had moved to Bali and remarried shortly after his birth, so when he gained the throne there was an immediate link between Java and Bali. At this time the courtly Javanese language known as Kawi came into use amongst the royalty of Bali, and the rock-cut memorials seen at Gunung Kawi near Tampaksiring are a clear architectural link between Bali and 11th century Java.

After Airlangga's death Bali retained its semi-independent state until Kertanagara became king of the Singasari dynasty in Java two centuries later. Kertanagara conquered Bali in 1284 but the period of his greatest power lasted only eight years until he was murdered and his kingdom collapsed. However, the great Majapahit dynasty was founded by his son. With Java in turmoil Bali regained its autonomy and the Pejeng dynasty, centred near modern day Ubud, rose to great power. Later Gajah Mada, the legendary chief Majapahit minister, defeated the Pejeng king Dalem Bedaulu in 1343 and brought Bali back under Javanese influence.

Although Gajah Mada brought much of the Indonesian archipelago under Majapahit control this was the furthest extent of their power. In Bali the 'capital' moved to Gelgel, near modern Klungkung, around the late 14th century and for the next two centuries this was the base for the 'king of Bali', the *dewa Agung*. As Islam spread into Java the Majapahit kingdom collapsed into disputing sultanates. However, the Gelgel dynasty in Bali, under Dalem Batur Enggong, extended its power eastwards to the neighbouring island of Lombok and even crossed the strait to the western end of Java.

As the Majapahit kingdom fell apart many of its intelligentsia, including the priest Nirartha, moved to Bali (see the Ulu Watu section in the South Bali chapter and Tanah Lot in the South-West Bali chapter). Nirartha is credited with introducing many of the complexities of Balinese religion to the island. Artists, dancers, musicians and actors also fled to Bali at this time and the island experienced an explosion of cultural activities. The final great exodus to Bali took place in 1478.

European Contact

Marco Polo, the great explorer, was the first recorded European visitor to Indonesia back in 1292 but the first Europeans to set foot on Bali were Dutch seamen in 1597. Setting a tradition that has prevailed right down to the present day, they fell in love with the island and when Cornelius Houtman, the ship's captain, prepared to set sail, half of his crew refused to come with him. At that time Balinese prosperity and artistic activity, at least among the royalty, were at a peak and the king who befriended Houtman had 200

11

wives and a chariot pulled by two white buffaloes, not to mention a retinue of 50 dwarves whose bodies had been bent to resemble kris handles! Although the Dutch returned to Indonesia in later years they were interested in profit, not culture, and barely gave Bali a second glance.

Dutch Conquest

In 1710 the capital of the Gelgel kingdom was shifted to nearby Klungkung but local discontent was growing, lesser rulers were breaking away from Gelgel rule and the Dutch began to move in using the old policy of divide and conquer. In 1846 the Dutch used Balinese salvage claims over ship-wrecks as the pretext to land military forces in northern Bali. In 1894 the Dutch chose to support the Sasaks of Lombok in a rebellion against their Balinese rajah. The rajah capitulated to Dutch demands, only to be overruled by his younger princes who defeated the Dutch forces in a surprise attack. Dutch anger was raised, a larger and more heavily armed force was despatched and the Balinese overrun. Balinese power in Lombok finally came to an end with the loss of their stronghold at Cakranegara – the crown prince was killed and the old rajah was sent into exile.

With the north of Bali long under Dutch control and Lombok now gone, the south was not going to last long. Once again it was disputes over the ransacking of wrecked ships that gave the Dutch the excuse they needed to move in. A Chinese ship was wrecked off Sanur in 1904, Dutch demands that the rajah of Badung pay 3000 silver dollars in damages were rejected and in 1906 Dutch warships appeared at Sanur. The Dutch forces landed against Balinese opposition and four days later had marched the five km to the outskirts of Denpasar.

On 20 September 1906 the Dutch mounted a naval bombardment on Denpasar and then commenced their final assault. The three princes of Badung realised that they were outnumbered and outgunned and that defeat was inevitable. Surrender and exile, however, was the worst imaginable outcome so they decided to take the honourable path of a suicidal *puputan* or fight to the death. First the palaces were burnt then, dressed in their finest jewellery and waving golden krises, the rajah led the royalty and priests out to face the Dutch with their modern weapons.

The Dutch begged the Balinese to surrender rather than make their hopeless stand but their pleas went unheard and wave after wave of the Balinese nobility marched forward to their death. In all, nearly 4000 Balinese died in defence of the two Denpasar palaces. Later, the Dutch marched east towards Tabanan, taking the rajah of Tabanan prisoner, but he committed suicide rather than face the disgrace of exile.

The kingdoms of Karangasem and Gianyar had already capitulated to the Dutch and were allowed to retain some of their powers but other kingdoms were defeated and their rulers exiled. Finally, the rajah of Klungkung followed the lead of Badung and once more the Dutch faced a puputan. With this last obstacle disposed of, all of Bali was now under Dutch control and part of the Dutch East Indies. Fortunately, the Dutch government was not totally onerous and the common people noticed little difference between rule by the Dutch and rule by the rajahs. Some far-sighted Dutch officials encouraged Balinese artistic aspirations which, together with a new found international interest, sparked off an artistic revival. Dutch rule over Bali was short-lived, however, for Indonesia quickly fell to the Japanese after the bombing of Pearl Harbor in WW II.

Independence

On 17 August 1945, just after the end of WW II, the Indonesian leader Sukarno proclaimed the nation's independence but it took four years to convince the Dutch that they were not going to get their great colony back. In a virtual repeat of the puputan nearly half a century earlier a Balinese resistance group was wiped out in the battle of Marga on 20 November 1946 and it was not until 1949 that the Dutch finally recognised

Indonesia's independence. The Denpasar airport, Ngurah Rai, was named after the leader of the Balinese forces at Marga.

Independence was not an easy path for Indonesia to follow at first and Sukarno, an inspirational leader during the conflict with the Dutch, proved less adept at governing the nation in peacetime. The ill-advised 'confrontation' with Malaysia was just one event that sapped the country's energy.

To Sukarno, British involvement in Malaysian federation meant the consolidation of British military power on its own doorstep and the threat of Western imperialism. In 1963 his decision to embark on a 'confrontation' led to military action between Indonesian forces and 50,000 British, Australian and New Zealand soldiers along the Kalimantan-Malaysia border. Though the confrontation was never a serious threat to the survival of Malaysia, the military expense caused severe economic problems for Indonesia.

In 1965 an attempted Communist coup led to Sukarno's downfall, and a wholesale massacre of suspected Communists throughout the archipelago, events which Bali was in the thick of. General Suharto took control of the government and Sukarno disappeared from the limelight.

GEOGRAPHY

Bali is a small fertile island midway along the string of islands which makes up the Indonesian archipelago, stretching from Sumatra in the north-west to Irian Jaya, on the border of Papua New Guinea, in the south-east. It's adjacent to Java, the most heavily populated island, and is the first in the chain of smaller islands comprising Nusa Tenggara. Bali has an area of 5620 sq km, measures approximately 140 km by 80 km and is just 8° south of the equator. It's dramatically mountainous: the central mountain chain which runs the whole length of the island includes several peaks approaching or over 2000 metres and Gunung Agung, known as the 'mother mountain', is over 3000 metres.

Bali is volcanically active and extravagantly fertile. The two go hand in hand

because eruptions contribute to the land's exceptional fertility and the high mountains provide the dependable rainfall which irrigates Bali's complex and amazingly beautiful patchwork of rice terraces. Of course, the volcanic element is a two-edged sword – Bali has often had disastrous eruptions and no doubt will again in the future. The huge eruption of Gunung Agung in 1963 killed thousands, devastated vast areas of the island and forced many Balinese to accept resettlement in other parts of Indonesia.

The central mountain chain reaches its highest point in the centre. Balinese mythology relates that the Hindu holy mountain, Mahameru, was set down on Bali but split into two parts – Gunung Agung and Gunung Batur. These two holy mountains, both active volcanoes, are respectively 3140 metres and 1717 metres high – at least Gunung Agung was 3140 metres prior to its eruption in 1963. The other major mountains are Batukau, the 'stone coconut shell', at 2278 metres, and Abang, at 2152 metres. Apart from the great central range, there are other, lesser, highlands in the lower plateau region of the Bukit Peninsula in the extreme south of Bali and in hilly Nusa Penida.

South and north of the central mountains are Bali's fertile agricultural lands. The southern region is a wide, gently sloping area where most of Bali's abundant rice crop is grown. The south-central area is the true rice basket of the island. The northern coastal strip is narrower, rising more rapidly into the foothills of the central range, but the main export crops – coffee, copra and rice – are grown here. Cattle are also raised in this area.

Despite the fertility of these zones Bali also has arid and lightly populated regions. These include the western mountain region and its northern slopes down to the sea – an area virtually unpopulated and reputed to be the last home of the Balinese tiger. The eastern and north-eastern slopes of Gunung Agung are also dry and barren while in the south, the Bukit Peninsula and the adjacent island of Nusa Penida also have a low rainfall and support little agriculture.

CLIMATE

Close as they are to the equator, Bali and Lombok have climates evenly tropical all year. The average temperature hovers around the high 20s°C (mid-80s°F) year-round. There are distinct dry and wet seasons – dry from April to September and wet from October to March – but it can rain at any time of year and even during the wet season rain is likely to pass quickly. In general May to August are the best months in Bali. At that time of year the climate is likely to be cooler and the rains lightest.

The climate is a gently tropical one: around the coast, sea breezes temper the heat and as you move inland you also move up so the altitude works to keep things cool. In fact, at times it can get very chilly up in the highlands and a warm sweater or light jacket can be a good idea in mountain villages like Kintamani or Penelokan or if you climb Rinjani in Lombok. Air-conditioning is not really a necessity in Bali – a cool breeze always seems to spring up in the evenings and since insects are rarely a problem, the architecture can make the most of the breeze with open bamboo windows to encourage air circulation.

FLORA & FAUNA

Bali has an interesting collection of animal and plant life. The orderly rice terraces are the most common everyday sight in Bali, particularly in the heavily populated and extravagantly fertile south. There are, however, a variety of other landscapes to be seen – the dry scrub of the north-west, the extreme north-east and the southern peninsula; patches of dense jungle; forests of bamboo; and barren and scrubby volcanic regions. Some of the most interesting Balinese plant life includes the banyan and frangipani.

The *waringin* (banyan) is the Balinese holy tree and no important temple is complete without a stately one growing within its precincts. The banyan is an extensive shady tree with an exotic feature: creepers dropped from its branches take root to propagate a new tree. Thus the banyan is said to be 'never-dying' since new offshoots can always take root.

The shady frangipani trees with their beautiful and sweet-smelling white flowers are almost as common a tree in temples as the banyan.

Balinese gardens are a delight. The soil and climate can support a huge range of plants, and the Balinese love of beauty, and the abundance of cheap labour, mean that every space can be landscaped. The style is generally informal, with curved paths, a rich variety of plants and usually a water feature. You can find almost every type of flower, though some varieties, such as hydrangeas, are restricted to the cooler mountain areas. Orchids are a special attraction, and orchid fanciers should see the collection at the botanical gardens near Bedugul. (See the Lake Bratan section in the Central Mountains chapter for details.)

There are various animals you might come across around the island. Chickens are kept both for food purposes and as pets. A man's fighting cock is a prized possession, more so given it's liable to come to a swift end at the next bout.

Balinese cattle are nearly as delicate as Balinese pigs are gross. They're graceful

animals which, as visitors have often commented, seem more akin to deer than cows. Although the Balinese are Hindus they do not generally treat cattle as holy animals, yet cows are rarely eaten or milked. They are, however, used to plough rice paddies and fields and there is a major export market for Balinese cattle to Hong Kong and other parts of Asia.

To some people, the mangy, horrible mongrels which roam every village on the island are the one thing in Bali which isn't perfect. In fact, some have even said that the dogs are there simply to provide a contrast and to point out how beautiful everything else is!

Ducks are another everyday Balinese domestic animal and a regular dish at feasts. Many families keep a flock of ducks which are brought out of the family compound and led to a convenient pond or flooded rice paddy to feed during the day. They're led using a stick with a small flag tied to the top which is left planted in the pond. As sunset approaches the ducks gather around the stick and wait to be led home again. The morning and evening parade of ducks is a familiar sight throughout the island and is always one of Bali's small delights.

Bali has plenty of lizards and the small ones, hanging around light fittings in the evening, waiting for an unwary insect to venture too near, are a familiar sight. Geckoes, on the other hand, though fairly large lizards, are often heard but rarely seen. The loud and regularly repeated two-part cry 'geck...oh' is a nightly background noise, though you'd be lucky if it's repeated seven times!

The Balinese pig is the animal of the family compound – it cleans up all the garbage and eventually ends up spit-roasted at a feast. The Balinese pig is a most peculiar creature with some relation to the wild boar. It's black and bristly and has a sway-back that droops so low its stomach almost drags on the ground. But what a delicious taste!

Bali certainly used to have tigers and although there are periodic rumours of sightings in the remote north-west of the island, nobody has proof of seeing one for a long time. Hickman Powell in *The Last Paradise*, his tale of Bali in the 1920s, tells of an unsuccessful tiger hunt.

There are also other animals including, of course, the sea turtle (see below). Bats are quite common and not only in well-known haunts like the Bat Cave (Goa Lawah) near Kusamba. They materialise at sunset to start their nocturnal hunt. The little chipmunk-like Balinese squirrels are occasionally seen in the wild, though more often in cages. The Balinese have a variety of caged birds kept as pets. Cats are often kept as domestic animals but are nowhere near as familiar a sight as the miserable dogs.

Bali Barat National Park

The Bali Barat (West Bali) National Park covers a large area which includes most of the western end of Bali. The management of

Sea Turtles

Sea turtles are marine reptiles. They are found in the waters around Bali and throughout Indonesia and are a popular delicacy, particularly for feasts. In several places they are herded before being slaughtered. In fact, Bali is the site of the most intensive slaughter of green sea turtles in the world. Green sea turtles are killed mainly for their meat, and the shells of the hawksbill turtle are used to make jewellery, haircombs and other trinkets, which are sold to tourists. It's estimated that more than 20,000 turtles are killed in Bali each year.

The environmental group Greenpeace has long campaigned to protect Indonesia's sea turtles. It appeals to travellers to Indonesia not to eat turtle meat or buy any sea-turtle products, including tortoiseshell items, stuffed turtles or turtle-leather goods. In any case, it's illegal to export any products made from green sea turtles from Indonesia (see the Customs section in the Facts for the Visitor chapter). And in many countries including Australia, the USA, the UK and other EC countries it's illegal to import turtle products without a permit. ■

the area is to be integrated with a conservation and environment plan for the whole island. For more information, see the section on the national park in the North Bali chapter.

GOVERNMENT

Indonesian government is centralised and hierarchical. Executive power rests with the president of the republic. Under the national government are 27 *propinsi* (provinces) of which Bali is one. Within Bali there are eight *kabupatens* or districts, which under the Dutch were known as regencies. They are, with their district capitals:

District	Capital
Badung	Denpasar
Bangli	Bangli
Buleleng	Singaraja
Gianyar	Gianyar
Jembrana	Negara
Karangasem	Amlapura
Klungkung	Klungkung
Tabanan	Tabanan

Badung in the south is the most populous district. Each district is headed by a government official known as a *bupati*. The districts are further subdivided into the subdistricts headed by a *camat*, then come the *perbekels*, headmen in charge of a *desa* (village) and, finally, an enormous number of *banjars*, the local divisions of a village.

ECONOMY

Bali's economy is basically agrarian: the vast majority of the Balinese are still simple peasants working in the fields. Coffee, copra and cattle are major agricultural exports – most of the rice goes to feed Bali's own teeming population. Although the Balinese are an island people, their unusual tendency to focus on the mountains rather than the sea is reflected in the importance of fishing. While there are many fishing villages and fish are part of the Balinese diet, fishing as an activity is not on the scale you might expect, given how much ocean there is around the island.

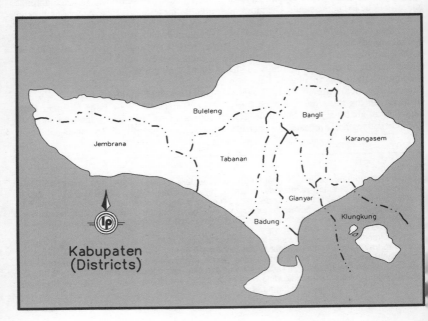

Kabupaten
(Districts)

Top: Children, Candidasa, Bali (GE)
Bottom: Cremation Mask, Ubud, Bali (GE)

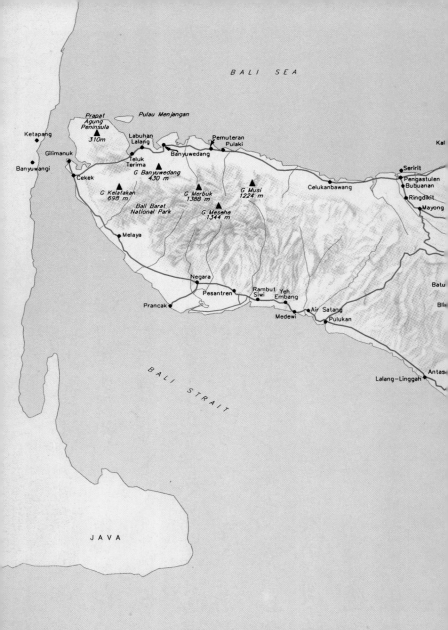

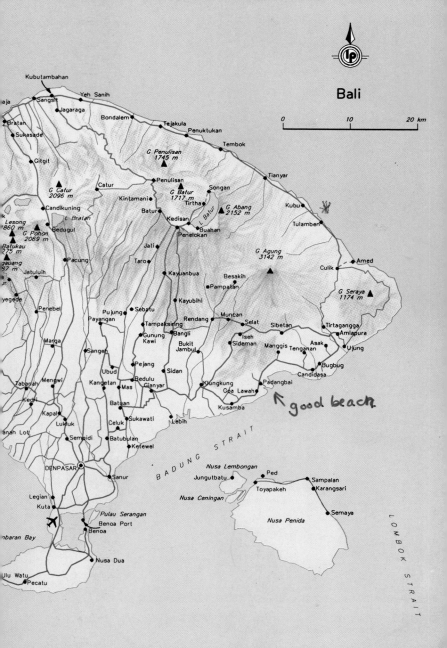

Bali

0   10   20 km

Kubutambahan
aja
Sangsit   Yeh Sanih
Bratan   Jagaraga   Bondalem   Tejakula
Sukasade   Penuktukan
Gitgit   Tembok
                        G Penulisan
                        1745 m   Tianyar
        G Catur   Catur   Penulisan
        2096 m   G Batur   Songan   Kubu
                Kintamani   1717 m   Tulamben
        Candikuning   Batur   Tirtha   G Abang
k Lesong   L Bratan   Kedisan   2152 m
1860 m   Bedugul   Penelokan   Buahan
    G Pohon   Amed
2069 m   Jati   G Agung   Culik
Batukau   Taro   3142 m
275 m   Pacung   G Seraya
rawang   Kayuanbua   Besakih   1174 m
37 m   Jatuluih   Pampatan
yegede   Kayubihi
        Penebel   Pujung   Sebatu   Muncan
                Payangan   Rendang   Selat   Sibetan
        Marga   Tampaksiring   Iseh   Tirtagangga
                    Gunung   Bangli   Sideman   Asak   Amlapura
        Sangeh   Kawi   Bukit   Tenganan   Ujung
                    Pejang   Jambul   Manggis
    Tabanah Mengwi   Ubud   Bugbug
    Kedri   Kangetan Bedulu Sidan   Klungkung   Candidasa
        Kapal   Mas Gianyar   Goa Lawah   Padangbai
anah Lot Lukluk   Batuan   Kusamba
        Sempidi   Celuk Sukawati   Lebih   good beach
            Batubulan Ketewel
        DENPASAR   BADUNG STRAIT
            Sanur   Nusa Lembongan
    Legian   Jungutbatu   Ped   Sampalan
    Kuta   Toyapakeh   Karangsari
        Pulau Serangan   Nusa Ceningan
            Benoa Port   Semaya
nbaran Bay Benoa   Nusa Penida   LOMBOK STRAIT
        Nusa Dua
Ulu Watu
    Pecatu

Top: Getting ready for a procession, Bali (MC)
Bottom: Cidomo (horse and cart), Lombok (JL)

Of course, tourism plays a considerable role in the Balinese economy – not only in providing accommodation, meals and services to the many visitors but also in providing a market for all those arts and crafts!

Rice

Although the Balinese grow various crops, rice is by far the most important. It's not just that rice is such a staple crop, the whole landscape has been moulded to rice growing. There are at least three words for rice in Indonesian – *padi* is the growing rice plant (hence padi or paddy fields), *beras* is the uncooked grain, and *nasi* is cooked rice, as in nasi goreng and nasi puti. There can be few places where people have played such a large part in changing the natural landscape yet at the same time made it so beautiful. The terraces trip down hillsides like steps for a giant, in shades of gold, brown and green as delicately selected as an artist's palette.

The intricate organisation necessary for growing rice is a large factor in the strength of Balinese community life where the *subak*, the rice growers association, has to carefully plan the use of irrigation water. The Balinese use irrigation so successfully that they are reputed to be some of the best rice growers in the world. They manage two harvests a year although there are no distinct times for planting and harvesting the rice.

A legend relates how a group of Balinese farmers promised to sacrifice a pig if their harvest was good. As the bountiful harvest time approached no pig could be found and it was reluctantly decided to sacrifice a child. Then one of the farmers had an idea: they had promised the sacrifice *after* the harvest. If there was always new rice growing, then the harvest would always be about to take place and no sacrifice would be necessary. Since then the Balinese have always planted one field of rice before harvesting another.

The process of rice growing starts with the bare, dry and harvested fields. The remaining rice stalks are burnt off and the field is then liberally soaked and repeatedly ploughed. Nowadays this may be done with a Japanese cultivator but more often it will still be done with two bullocks or cattle

pulling a wooden plough. Once the field is reduced to the required muddy consistency, a small corner of the field is walled off and the seedling rice is planted there. The rice is grown to a reasonable size then lifted and replanted, shoot by shoot, in the larger field. After that it's easy street for a while as the rice steadily matures. The walls of the fields have to be kept in working order and the fields have to be weeded but generally this is a time to practise the gamelan, watch the dancers, do a little woodcarving or painting or just pass the time. Finally, harvest time rolls around and the whole village turns out for a period of solid hard work. Planting the rice is strictly a male occupation but everybody takes part in harvesting it.

The rice paddies are home for much more than just rice. In the early morning you'll often see the duck herders leading their flocks out for a day's paddle around a flooded paddy and, at night, young boys heading out with lights to trap tasty frogs and eels.

POPULATION

With 2½ million people, Bali is a very densely populated island. The population is almost all Indonesian, with the usual small Chinese contingent in the big towns, a sprinkling of Indian merchants, plus a number of more-or-less permanent visitors amongst the Westerners in Bali.

Population control is a priority of the Indonesian government, and the family planning slogan *dua anak cukup* ('two is enough') is a recurring theme in roadside posters and statuary. It seems to have been quite successful, as many young families are limiting themselves to two children, or sometimes maybe three, but certainly not the seven or nine children common two or three generations ago. Yet, there are still many families where women continue bearing children until they have a boy.

MUSIC & DANCE

Music, dance and drama are all closely related in Bali – in fact drama and dance are synonymous. Some dances are more drama and less dance, others more dance and less drama but basically they can all be lumped together. The most important thing about Balinese dances, however, is that they're fun and accessible. Balinese dance is definitely not some sterile art form requiring an arts degree to appreciate – it can be exciting and enjoyable for almost anyone with just the slightest effort.

When our daughter Tashi was 2½ we took her to see a Kechak (monkey dance) one night. I spent half an hour beforehand telling her the story behind the dance and she was entranced by the dance – she knew the characters, knew what to expect, understood (as well as a 2½ year old can) what the story was all about and thoroughly enjoyed it. The story of Rama and Sita, which is what the Kechak is based upon, became one of her favourite bedtime stories.

Tony Wheeler

Balinese dances are not hard to find: there are dances virtually every night at all the tourist centres – admission is generally between 1000 and 3000 rp for foreigners. If you're in Bali long enough, you're bound to stumble upon a dance; they're open to anybody, so just wander in. Dances are put on regularly at the tourist centres to raise money but are also a regular part of almost every temple festival and Bali has no shortage of these. Many of the dances put on for tourists offer a smorgasbord of Balinese dances – a little Topeng, a taste of Legong, some Baris to round it all off. A nice introduction perhaps but for some dances you really need the whole thing. It will be a shame if the 'instant Asia' mentality takes too strong a grip on Balinese dance.

The dances take various forms but with a few notable exceptions – in particular the Kechak and the Sanghyang trance dance – they are all accompanied by music from the gamelan orchestra. Some are dances almost purely for the sake of dancing – in this category you could include the technically precise Legong, its male equivalent the Baris or various solo dances like the Kebyar. Mask dances like the Topeng or the Jauk also place a high premium on dancing ability.

Then there are dances like the Kechak, where the story is as important as the dancing. Or dances which move into that important area of Balinese life where the forces of magic, of good and evil, clash. In the Barong & Rangda dance, powerful forces are at work and elaborate preparations must be made to ensure that the balance is maintained. All masked dances require great care as in donning a mask you take on another personality and it is wise to ensure that the mask's personality does not take over. Masks used in the Barong & Rangda dance are treated with particular caution. Only an expert can carve them and between performances the masks must be carefully put away. A rangda mask must even be kept covered until the instant before the performance starts. These masks can have powerful *sakti* (spirits) and the unwary must be careful of their magical, often dangerous, spiritual vibrations.

As Covarrubias pointed out, the Balinese like a blend of seriousness and slapstick and this also shows in their dances. Some have a decidedly comic element, with clowns who serve both to counterpoint the staid, noble characters and to convey the story. The noble characters may use the high Balinese language or classical Kawi while the clowns, usually servants of the noble characters, converse in everyday Balinese. There are always two clowns – the leader, or *punta*, and his follower, the *kartala*, who never quite manages to carry off his mimicry.

Dancers in Bali are almost always ordinary folk who dance in the evening or their spare time, just like painters or sculptors who may indulge their artistry in their spare time. Dance is learnt by doing and long hours may be spent in practice, usually by carefully following the movements of an expert. There's little of the soaring leaps of Western ballet or the smooth flowing movements often found in Western dance. Balinese dance tends to be precise, jerky, shifting and jumpy. In fact it's remarkably like Balinese music with its abrupt changes of tempo and dramatic contrasts between silence and crashing noise. There's also virtually no contact in Balinese dancing, each dancer moves completely independently.

To the expert, every movement of wrist, hand and fingers is important; even facial expressions are carefully choreographed to convey the character of the dance. Don't let these technicalities bother you though – they're just icing on the cake; basically, most Balinese dances are straightforward 'ripping yarns'. Don't give the dancers your complete attention either – the audience can be just as interesting, especially the children. Even at the most tourist-oriented of dances there will be hordes of local children clustered around the stage. Watch how they cheer the good characters and cringe back from the stage when the demons appear – how can TV ever win against the real thing?

The Gamelan

Balinese music is based around an instrument known as the gamelan – in fact the gamelan is such a central part of Balinese music that the whole 'orchestra' is also referred to as a gamelan. Gamelan music is almost completely percussion – apart from the simple *suling* flute and the two-stringed *rebab*, there are virtually no wind or string instruments. Unlike many forms of Asian music the Balinese gamelan is accessible to ears attuned to Western music. Though it sounds strange at first with its noisy, jangly percussion (there are none of the soothing passages found in some Western music) it's exciting and enjoyable.

The main instruments of the gamelan are the xylophone-like *gangsa*, which have bronze bars above bamboo resonators. The player hits the keys with his hammer with one hand while his other hand moves close behind to dampen the sound from each key just after it is struck. Although the gangsa make up the majority of the instruments and it is their sound which is most prevalent, the actual tempo and nature of the music is controlled by the two *kendang* drums – one male and one female.

Other instruments are the deep *trompong* drums, the small *kempli* gong and the small *cengceng* cymbals used in faster pieces. The whole orchestra is known as a *gong* – an old fashioned *gong gede* or a more modern *gong kebyar*. There are even more ancient forms of the gamelan such as the *gamelan selunding* still occasionally played in Bali Aga villages like Tenganan.

A village's gamelan is usually organised through a banjar. The members of the banjar will meet to practise; the banjar owns the instruments, which are stored in the *bale gong*. The musician's club is known as a *seksa*. Gamelan playing is purely a male occupation and all the pieces are learnt by heart and passed down father to son; there is little musical notation or recording of individual pieces. The gamelan is also played in Java and Javanese gamelan music is held to be more 'formal' and 'classical' than Balinese. A perhaps more telling point is that Javanese gamelan music is rarely heard, apart from at special performances, whereas in Bali you seem to hear gamelans playing everywhere you go! In *The Last Paradise* Hickman Powell tells of the cremation of a Rajah of Ubud where as many gamelans in the Ubud area as possible were asked to attend. No fewer than 126 gamelans turned up!

Kechak

Probably the best known of the many Balinese dances, the Kechak is also unusual in that it does not have a gamelan accompaniment. Instead the background is provided by a chanting 'choir' of men who provide the 'chak-a-chak-a-chak' noise. Originally this chanting group was known as the kechak and was part of a Sanghyang trance dance. Then, in the 1930s, the modern Kechak developed in Bona, a village near Gianyar, where the dance is still held regularly.

The Kechak tells a tale from the *Ramayana* about Prince Rama and his Princess Sita. With Rama's brother, Laksamana, they have been exiled from the kingdom of Ayodya and are wandering in the forest. The evil Rawana, King of Lanka, lures Rama away with a golden deer (which is really Lanka's equally evil prime minister who has magically changed himself into a deer). When Rama fails to return, Sita persuades Laksamana to search for him and, once she is alone, Rawana pounces and carries Sita off to his hideaway.

Hanuman, the white monkey god, appears before Sita and tells her that Rama is trying to rescue her. He brings her Rama's ring to show that he is indeed the prince's envoy and Sita gives him a hairpin to take back to Rama. When Rama finally arrives in Lanka he is met by the evil king's evil son Megananda – this story is full of goodies versus baddies – who shoots an arrow at him, but the arrow magically turns into a dragon and ties him up. Fortunately Rama is able to call upon a garuda for assistance and thus escapes. Finally, Sugriwa, the king of the monkeys, comes to Rama's assistance with his monkey army and after a great battle good wins out over bad and Rama and Sita return home.

Throughout the dance the surrounding

Barong dancer

circle of men, all bare-chested and wearing checked cloth around their waists, provide a nonstop accompaniment, rising to a crescendo as they play the monkey army and fight it out with Rawana and his cronies. The chanting is superbly synchronised, members of the 'monkey army' sway back and forth, raise their hands in unison, flutter their fingers and lean left and right, all with an eerily exciting co-ordination.

Barong & Rangda

The Barong & Rangda dance rivals the Kechak as Bali's most popular dance for tourists. Again it's a straightforward battle between good, the *barong*, and bad, the *rangda*. The barong is a strange creature, half shaggy dog, half lion, propelled by two men like a circus clown-horse. It's definitely on the side of good but is a mischievous and fun-loving creature. The widow-witch rangda is straightforward, bad through and through and certainly not the sort of thing you'd like to meet on a midnight stroll through the rice paddies.

Barongs can take various forms but in the Barong & Rangda dance it will be as the *barong keket*, the most holy of the barongs. The barong flounces in, snaps its jaws at the gamelan, dances around a bit and enjoys the acclaim of its supporters – a group of men with krises. Then rangda makes her appearance, her long tongue lolling, human entrails draped around her neck and her terrible fangs protruding from her mouth.

The barong and rangda duel, using their magical powers, but when things look bad for the barong its supporters draw their krises and rush in to attack the rangda. Using her magical powers the rangda throws them into a trance and the men suicidally try to stab themselves with their krises. But the barong also has great magical powers and casts a spell which stops the krises from harming the men. This is the most dramatic part of the dance. As the gamelan rings crazily the men rush back and forth, waving their krises around, all but foaming at the mouth, sometimes even rolling on the ground in a desperate attempt to stab themselves. There often seems to be a conspiracy to terrify tourists in the front row!

Finally, the rangda retires, defeated, and good has won again. This still leaves, however, a large group of entranced barong supporters to bring back to the real world. This is usually done by sprinkling them with holy water, sanctified by dipping the barong's beard in it. Performing the Barong & Rangda dance is a touchy operation – playing around with all that powerful magic, good and bad, is not to be taken lightly. Extensive ceremonies have to be gone through, a *pemangku* (priest) must be on hand to end the dancers' trance and at the end a chicken must be sacrificed to propitiate the evil spirits.

Legong

The Legong is the most graceful of Balinese dances and, to sophisticated Balinese connoisseurs of dancing, the one arousing most interest and discussion. A *legong*, as a Legong dancer is known, is a young girl – often as young as eight or nine years, rarely older than her early teens. Such importance is attached to the dance that even in old age a classic dancer will be remembered as a 'great Legong' even though her brief period of fame may have been 50 years ago.

There are various forms of the Legong but the Legong Kraton (Legong of the Palace) is the one most often performed. Peliatan's famous dance troupe, who visitors to Ubud often get a chance to see, are particularly noted for their Legong. The story behind the Legong is very stylised and symbolic – if you didn't know the story it would be impossible to tell what was going on.

The Legong involves just three dancers – the two legongs and their 'attendant', the *condong*. The Legongs are identically dressed in tightly bound gold brocade, so tightly encased that it is something of a mystery how they manage to move so rapidly and agitatedly. Their faces are elaborately made up, their eyebrows plucked and repainted, their hair decorated with frangipanis. The dance relates how a king takes a maiden, Rangkesari, captive. When Rang-

Legong dancer

kesari's brother comes to release her, Rangkesari begs the king to free her rather than go to war. The king refuses and on his way to the battle meets a bird bringing ill omens. He ignores the bird and continues on to meet Rangkesari's brother and gets killed.

That's the whole story but the dance only tells of the king's preparations for battle and it ends with the bird's appearance – when the king leaves the stage it is to join the battle where he will meet his death. The dance starts with the condong dancing an introduction and then departing as the legongs come on. The two legongs dance solo, in close identical formation and in mirror image, as when they dance a nose-to-nose 'love scene'. The dance tells of the king's sad departure from his queen, Rangkesari's bitter request that he release her and then the king's departure for the battle. The condong reappears with tiny golden wings as the bird of ill fortune, and the dance ends.

Baris

The warrior dance, known as the Baris, is traditionally a male equivalent of the Legong – femininity and grace give way to energetic and warlike martial spirit. The Baris dancer has to convey the thoughts and emotions of a warrior preparing for action and then meeting an enemy in battle. It's a solo dance requiring great energy and skill. The dancer has to show his changing moods not only through movement but also through facial expression – chivalry, pride, anger, prowess and finally a little regret (well, war is hell, even in Bali) all have to be there. It's said that the Baris is one of the most complex of the Balinese dances and requires a dancer of great skill and ability.

Ramayana Ballet

The *Ramayana* is, of course, a familiar tale in Bali but the dance is a relatively recent addition to the Balinese repertoire. Basically, it tells the same story of Rama and Sita as told in the Kechak but without the monkey ensemble and with a normal gamelan gong accompaniment. Furthermore, the *Ramayana* provides plenty of opportunity for improvisation and comic additions. Rawana may be played as a classic bad guy, Hanuman can be a comic clown, and camera-clicking tourists among the spectators may come in for a little imitative ribbing.

Kebyar

The Kebyar is a male solo dance like the Baris but with greater emphasis on the performer's individual abilities. Development of the modern Kebyar is credited in large part to the famous prewar dancer Mario. There are various forms of Kebyar including the Kebyar Duduk, where the 'dance' is done from the seated position and facial expressions, as well as movements of the hands, arms and torso, are all important. In the Kebyar Trompong the dancer actually joins the gamelan and plays a percussion instrument called the trompong while still dancing.

Barong Landung

The giant puppet dances known as Barong Landung are not an everyday occurrence – they take place annually on the island of Pulau Serangan and a few other places in southern Bali. The legend of their creation relates how a demon, Jero Gede Macaling, popped over from Nusa Penida disguised as a standing barong to cause havoc on Bali. To scare him away the people had to make a big barong just like him. The Barong Landung dances, a reminder of that ancient legend, feature two gigantic puppet figures – a horrific male image of black Jero Gede and his female sidekick, white Jero Luh. Barong Landung performances are often highly comic.

Janger

The Janger is a relatively new dance which suddenly popped up in the '20s and '30s.

Ramayana Ballet dancer

Both Covarrubias and Powell commented on this strange, almost un-Balinese, dance. Today it has become part of the standard repertoire and no longer looks so unusual. It has similarities to several other dances including the Sanghyang, where the relaxed chanting of the women is contrasted to the violent chak-a-chak-a-chak of the men. In the Janger, formations of 12 girls and 12 young men do a sitting dance, and the gentle swaying and chanting of the girls contrasts with the violently choreographed movements and loud shouts of the men.

Topeng

Topeng means 'pressed against the face', as with a mask, and that is what the dance is – a mask dance where the dancers have to imitate the character represented by the mask. The Topeng Tua is a classic solo dance where the mask is that of an old man and the dancer has to dance like a creaky old gentleman. In other dances there may be a small troupe who dance various characters and types. A full collection of Topeng masks may number 30 or 40.

Jauk

The Jauk is also a mask dance but strictly a solo performance – the dancer plays an evil demon, his mask an eerie face with bulging eyes and fixed smile, long wavering fingernails complete the demonic look. Mask dances are considered to require great expertise because the dancer is not able to convey the character's thoughts and meanings through his facial expressions – the dance has to tell all. Demons are unpleasant, frenetic and fast-moving creatures so a Jauk dancer has to imitate all these things.

Pendet

The Pendet is normally neither a major performance nor something that requires arduous training and practice. It's an everyday dance of the temples, a small procedure to go through before making temple offerings. You may often see the Pendet being danced by women bringing offerings to a temple for a festival but it is also sometimes danced as an introduction and a closing for other dance performances.

Sanghyang

The Sanghyang trance dances originally developed to drive out evil spirits from a village. The Sanghyang is a divine spirit which temporarily inhabits an entranced dancer. The Sanghyang Dedari dance is performed by two young girls who dance a dream-like version of the Legong but with their eyes closed. The dancers are said to be untrained in the intricate pattern of the Legong but dance in perfect harmony, with their eyes firmly shut. Male and female choirs, the male choir being a Kechak, provide a background chant but when the chant stops the dancers slump to the ground in a faint. Two women bring them round and at the finish a pemangku blesses them with holy water and brings them out of the trance. The modern Kechak dance developed from the Sanghyang.

In the Sanghyang Jaran a boy in a trance dances round and through a fire of coconut husks, riding a coconut palm 'hobby horse'. It's labelled the 'fire dance' for the benefit of tourists. Like other trance dances (such as the Barong & Rangda dance) great care must be taken to control the magical forces at play. Experts must always be on hand to take care of the entranced dancers and to bring them out of the trance at the close.

Other Dances

There are numerous other dances in Bali, some of them only performed occasionally, some quite regularly but not often seen by tourists. Of course, old dances still fade out and new dances or new developments of old dances still appear. Dance in Bali is not a static activity. The Oleg Tambulilingan was developed in the 1950s, originally as a solo female dance. Later, a male part was added and the dance now mimics the flirtations of two *tambulilingan* (bumblebees).

One of the most popular comic dances is the Cupak, which tells a tale of a greedy coward (Cupak) and his brave but hard-done-by younger brother Grantang, and their adventures while rescuing a beautiful princess. The Arja is a sort of Balinese soap opera, long and full of high drama. Since it requires much translation of the noble's actions by the clowns it's hard for Westerners to understand and appreciate. Drama Gong is in some ways a more modern version of the same romantic themes.

WAYANG KULIT

The shadow puppet plays known as wayang kulit are popular not only in Bali but throughout Indonesia. The plays are far more than mere entertainment, however, for the puppets are believed to have great spiritual power and the *dalang*, the puppet master and storyteller, is an almost mystical figure. He has to be a man of considerable skill and even more considerable endurance. Not only does he have to manipulate the puppets and tell the story, he must also conduct the musical accompaniment, the small gamelan orchestra known as the *gender wayang*, and beat time with his chanting – having long run out of hands to do things with, he performs the latter task with a horn held with his toes!

His mystical powers come into play because the wayang kulit, like so much of Balinese drama, is another phase of the eternal struggle between good and evil. You don't leave that battle to amateurs. The endurance factor comes in because a wayang kulit performance can last six or more hours and the performances always seem to start so late that the drama is finally resolved just as the sun peeps up over the horizon.

Shadow puppets are made of pierced buffalo hide – they're completely traditional in their characters and their poses, so there's absolutely no mistaking who is who. The dalang sits behind a screen on which the shadows of the puppets are cast, usually by an oil lamp which gives a far more romantic flickering light than modern electric lighting would do. Traditionally, women and children sit in front of the screen while men sit behind the screen with the dalang and his assistants.

The characters are arrayed right and left of the puppet master – goodies to the right,

baddies to the left. The characters include nobles, who speak in the high Javanese language Kawi, and common clowns, who speak in everyday Balinese. (The dalang also has to be a linguist!) When the four clowns (Delem and Sangut are the bad ones, Twalen and his son Merdah are the good ones) are on screen the performance becomes something of a Punch and Judy show with much rushing back and forth, clouts on the head and comic insults. The noble characters are altogether more refined – they include the terrible Durga and the noble Bima. Wayang kulit stories are chiefly derived from the great Hindu epics, the *Mahabharata* and the *Ramayana*.

CULTURE & CUSTOMS

Each stage of Balinese life from conception to cremation is marked by a series of ceremonies and rituals known as Manusa Yadnya. They contribute to the rich, varied and active life the average Balinese leads.

Wayang kulit puppet

Birth

The first ceremony of Balinese life takes place even before birth – when women reach the third month of pregnancy they take part in ceremonies at home and at the village river or spring. A series of offerings are made to ensure the wellbeing of the baby. Another ceremony takes place soon after the birth, during which the afterbirth is buried with appropriate offerings. Women are considered to be 'unclean' after giving birth and 12 days later they are 'purified' through another ceremony. The father is also *sebel* (unclean) but only for three days. At 42 days another ceremony and more offerings are made for the baby's future.

The first major ceremony takes place halfway through the baby's first Balinese year of 210 days. Then, for the first time, the baby's feet are allowed to touch the ground. Prior to that babies are carried continuously for the ground is impure and babies, so close to heaven, should not be allowed to come into contact with it. The baby is also ceremonially welcomed to the family at this time. Another ceremony follows at the end of the 210-day year when the baby is welcomed to the ancestral temple.

It's said that the Balinese still regard boy-girl twins as a major calamity although according to Covarrubias it has only ever really applied to ordinary people, not the nobility. The reasoning is that boy-girl twins are said to have committed a sort of spiritual incest while in the womb and that this is dangerous for the whole village. Extensive and expensive rituals and ceremonies must be performed in order to purify the children, the parents and the whole village. Same-sex twins, however, are quite OK.

Names

The Balinese basically only have four first names. The first child is Wayan, the second child is Made, the third is Nyoman and the fourth is Ketut. And the fifth, sixth, seventh, eighth and ninth? Well, they're Wayan, Made, Nyoman, Ketut and Wayan again. It's very simple and surprisingly unconfusing although it actually doesn't make their names any easier to remember. Now was he another Made or was she that other Ketut seems to be the order of the day! The only variation from this straightforward policy seems to be that first-born boys are sometimes also known as Gede and first-born girls as Putu.

The Balinese have a series of titles which depend on caste: the Brahmanas have the prefix Ida Bagus; the Wesia, the main caste of the nobility, are Gusti; the Satria caste are Cokodor; but the poor Sudra, the general mass of the Balinese people, have no prefix at all.

Childhood

If ever there was a people who love children it must be the Balinese – anybody who visits Bali with their children can attest to that. You'd better learn how to say how many *bulan* (months) or *tahun* (years) old your children are because you'll be asked 1000 times! The Balinese certainly love children and they have plenty of them to prove it. Coping with a large family is made much easier by the policy of putting younger children in the care of older ones. One child always seems to be carrying another one around on his or her hip.

Despite the fact that Balinese children are almost immediately part of a separate society of children they always seem remarkably well behaved. Of course you hear kids crying occasionally but tantrums, fights, screams and shouts all seem to happen far less frequently than we're used to in the West. It's been said that parents achieve this by treating children with respect and showing them good behaviour by example.

After the ceremonies of babyhood come the ceremonies marking the stages of childhood and puberty, including the important tooth-filing ceremony. The Balinese prize even, straight teeth. Crooked fangs are, after all, one of the chief distinguishing marks of evil spirits, just have a look at a rangda mask! A priest files the upper front teeth to produce an aesthetically pleasing straight line. Today the filing is often only symbolic – one pass of the file.

Marriage

Every Balinese expects to marry and raise a family, and marriage takes place at a comparatively young age. Marriages are not, in general, arranged as they are in many other Asian communities although strict rules apply to marriages between the castes. There are two basic forms of marriage in Bali – *mapadik* and *ngorod*. The respectable form, in which the family of the man visit the family of the woman and politely propose that the marriage take place, is mapadik. The Balinese, however, like their fun and often prefer marriage by elopement (ngorod) as the most exciting option.

Of course, the Balinese are also a practical people so nobody is too surprised when the young man spirits away his bride-to-be, even if she loudly protests about being kidnapped. The couple go into hiding and somehow the girl's parents, no matter how assiduously they search, never manage to find her. Eventually the couple re-emerge, announce that it is too late to stop them now, the marriage is officially recognised and everybody has had a lot of fun and games. Marriage by elopement has another advantage apart from being exciting and mildly heroic – it's cheaper.

The Household

Although many modern Balinese houses, particularly in Denpasar or the larger towns, are arranged much like houses in the West, there are still a great number of traditional Balinese homes. Wander the streets of Ubud sometime: nearly every house will follow the same traditional walled design. Like houses in ancient Rome the Balinese house looks inward; the outside is simply a high wall. Inside there will be a garden and a separate small building or *bale* for each function. There will be one building for cooking, one building for washing and the toilet, and separate buildings for each 'bedroom'. What there won't be is a 'living room' because in Bali's mild tropical climate you live outside – the 'living room' and 'dining room' will be open verandah areas, looking out into the garden.

Covarrubias compared traditional Balinese house design to the human body: there's a head – the ancestral shrine, arms – the sleeping and living areas, legs and feet – the kitchen and rice storage building, and even an anus – the garbage pit. There may also be an area outside the house compound where fruit trees are grown or a pig may be kept. Usually the house is entered through a gateway backed by a small wall known as the *aling aling*. It serves a practical and a spiritual purpose, both preventing passersby from seeing in and stopping evil spirits from entering. Evil spirits cannot easily turn corners so the aling aling stops them from simply scooting straight in through the gate!

Men & Women

Social life in Bali is relatively free and easy and, although Balinese women are not kept cloistered away, the roles of the sexes are strictly delineated. There are certain tasks clearly to be handled by women, and others reserved for men. Thus running the household is very much the women's task. In the morning women sweep and clean and put out the offerings for the gods. Every household has a shrine or god-throne where offerings must be placed, and areas on the ground, such as at the compound entrance, where offerings for the demons are derisively cast. While the women are busy attending to these tasks the men of the household are likely to be looking after the fighting cocks and any other pets.

Marketing is also a female job – both buying and selling – although at large markets, cattle selling is definitely a male job. For the average Balinese peasant the working day is not a long one for most of the year. Despite their expertise at producing large rice crops, rice growing doesn't require an enormous labour input. Again there's a division of labour based on sex roles: although everybody turns out in the fields at harvest time, planting the rice is purely a male activity.

In Balinese leisure activities the roles are

also sex differentiated. Both men and women dance but only men play the gamelan. The artistic skills are almost totally left to men although today you do see some women painters, sculptors and woodcarvers.

Community Life

The Balinese have an amazingly active and organised village life – you simply cannot be a faceless nonentity in Bali. You can't help but get to know your neighbours as your life is so entwined and interrelated with theirs. Or at least, it still is in the small villages that comprise so much of Bali. Even in the big towns, however, the banjar ensures that a strong community spirit continues.

The village is known as the desa and village plans generally follow a similar pattern. In the centre, usually at the crossroads of the two major streets, there will be the open meeting space known as the *alun alun*. It's actually more than just a meeting space because you will also find temples, the town market, or even the former prince's home. The *kulkul* (warning drum) tower will be here and quite likely a big banyan tree. If you're staying in Ubud notice how, in the street by the bemo stop in the centre of town,

the palace, the banyan tree with its kulkul drums and the temple are all close to one another and right across from the market. In Bangli see how the Artha Sastra Inn, in the family compound of the local prince, looks right out on the main square.

Although village control by the desa authorities is no longer as strict as it once was, there is still detailed and careful organisation of land ownership because of the necessary interrelation of water supply to the rice fields. Each individual rice field is known as a *sawah* and each farmer who owns even one sawah must be a member of his local subak (rice growers association). The rice paddies must have a steady supply of water and it is the subak's job to ensure that the water supply gets to everybody. It's said that the head of the local subak will often be the farmer whose rice paddies are at the bottom of the hill, for he will make quite certain that the water gets all the way down to his fields, passing through everybody else's on the way!

Of course, Bali being Bali, the subak has far more to do than share out the water and ensure that the water channels, dykes and so forth are in good order. Each subak will have

Family Compound

Typical layout of a Balinese family *pekarangan*

1 Sanggah Kemulan (Family Temple)
2 Uma Meten (Sleeping Pavilion for the family head)
3 Tugu (Shrine)
4 Pengidjeng (Shrine)
5 Bale Tiang Sanga (Guest Pavilion)
6 Natar (Courtyard, with frangipani or hibiscus shade tree)
7 Bale Sikepat (Sleeping Pavilion for other relatives)
8 Fruit trees & coconut palms
9 Vegetable Garden
10 Bale Sekenam (Working & Sleeping Pavilion)
11 Paon (Kitchen)
12 Lumbung (Rice Barn)
13 Rice Threshing Area
14 Aling Aling (Screen Wall)
15 Lawang (Gate)
16 Apit Lawang (Gate Shrines)

its small temple out amongst the rice fields where offerings to the spirits of agriculture are made and regular meetings held for the subak members. Like every temple in Bali there are regular festivals and ceremonies to observe. Even individual sawahs may have small altars.

The subak is not the only organisation controlling village life. Each desa is further subdivided into banjars, which each male adult joins when he marries. It is the banjar which organises village festivals, marriage ceremonies and even cremations. Throughout the island you'll see the open-sided meeting places known as *bale banjars* – they're nearly as common a sight as temples. They serve a multitude of purposes, from a local meeting place to a storage room for the banjar's musical equipment and dance costumes. Gamelan orchestras are organised at the banjar level and a glance in a banjar at any time might reveal a gamelan practice, a meeting going on, food being prepared for a feast, even a group of men getting their roosters together to raise their anger a little in preparation for the next round of cockfights.

Death & Cremation

There are ceremonies for every stage of Balinese life but often the last ceremony – cremation – is the biggest. A Balinese cremation can be an amazing, spectacular, colourful, noisy and exciting event. In fact it often takes so long to organise a cremation that years have passed since the death. During that time the body is temporarily buried. Of course an auspicious day must be chosen for the cremation and since a big cremation can be a very expensive business many less wealthy people may take the opportunity of joining in at a larger cremation and sending their own dead on their way at the same time. Brahmanas, however, must be cremated immediately.

Apart from being yet another occasion for Balinese noise and confusion it's a fine opportunity to observe the incredible energy the Balinese put into creating real works of art which are totally ephemeral. A lot more than a body gets burnt at the cremation. The

body is carried from the burial ground (or from the deceased's home if it's an 'immediate' cremation) to the cremation ground in a high, multi-tiered tower made of bamboo, paper, string, tinsel, silk, cloth, mirrors, flowers and anything else bright and colourful you can think of. The tower is carried on the shoulders of a group of men, the size of the group depending on the importance of the deceased and hence the size of the tower. The funeral of a former rajah or high priest may require hundreds of men to tote the tower.

Along the way to the cremation ground certain precautions must be taken to ensure that the deceased's spirit does not find its way back home. Loose spirits around the house can be a real nuisance. To ensure this doesn't happen requires getting the spirits confused as to their whereabouts, which you do by shaking the tower, running it around in circles, spinning it around, throwing water at it, generally making the trip to the cremation ground anything but a stately and funereal crawl. Meanwhile, there's likely to be a priest halfway up the tower, hanging on grimly as it sways back and forth, and doing his best to soak bystanders with holy water. A gamelan sprints along behind, providing a suitably exciting musical accompaniment. Camera-toting tourists get all but run down and once again the Balinese prove that ceremonies and religion are there to be enjoyed.

At the cremation ground the body is transferred to a funeral sarcophagus – this should be in the shape of a bull for a Brahmana, a winged lion for a Satria and a sort of elephant-fish for a Sudra. These days, however, almost anybody from the higher castes will use a bull. Finally up it all goes in flames – funeral tower, sarcophagus, body, the lot. The eldest son does his duty by poking through the ashes to ensure that there are no bits of body left unburnt.

And where does your soul go after your cremation? Why, to a heaven which is just like Bali!

RELIGION

The Balinese are nominally Hindus but

Balinese Hinduism is a world away from that of India. At one time Hinduism was the predominant religion in Indonesia (witness the many great Hindu monuments in Java) but it died out with the spread of Islam through the archipelago. The final great Hindu kingdom, that of the Majapahits, virtually evacuated to Bali, taking not only their religion and its rituals but also their art, literature, music and culture. It's a mistake, however, to think that this was purely an exotic seed being implanted on virgin soil. The Balinese probably already had strong religious beliefs and an active cultural life. The new influences were simply overlaid on the existing practices – hence the peculiar Balinese interpretation of Hinduism. Of course there are small enclaves of other religions in Bali, particularly Muslims, whose mosques are often seen at ports and fishing villages around the coast.

Religion in Bali has two overwhelming features – it's absolutely everywhere and it's good fun! You can't get away from religion in Bali: there are temples in every village, shrines in every field, offerings being made at every corner. The fun element comes in because the Balinese seem to feel that religion should be an enjoyable thing – something the mortals can enjoy as well as the gods. It's summed up well in their attitude to offerings – you make up a lot of fancy food for the gods but once they've eaten the 'essence' you've got enough 'substance' left over for a fine feast.

Basically, the Balinese worship the same gods as the Hindus of India – the trinity of Brahma, Shiva and Vishnu – although the Balinese have a supreme god, Sanghyang Widi. This basic threesome is always alluded to, never seen, in Bali – a vacant shrine or empty throne tells all. Others of the secondary Hindu gods may occasionally appear, such as Ganesh, Shiva's elephant-headed son, but a great many other purely Balinese gods, spirits and entities have far more everyday reality. The rangda may bear a close relation to Durga, the terrible side of Shiva's wife Parvati, but it's certain that nobody in India has seen a barong!

To Balinese the spirits are everywhere, it's a reminder that animism is the basis of much of Balinese religion. The offerings put out every morning are there to pay homage to the good spirits and to placate the bad ones – the Balinese take no chances! And if the offerings thrown on the ground are immediately consumed by dogs? Well, so it goes, everybody is suspicious of dogs anyway.

Temples

The number of temples in Bali is simply astonishing – they're everywhere. In fact, since every village has several and every home has at least a simple house-temple there are actually more temples than homes. The word for temple in Bali is 'pura', which is a Sanskrit word literally meaning 'a space surrounded by a wall'. Like a traditional Balinese home a temple is walled in, so the shrines you see in rice fields or at magical spots such as by old trees are not real temples. You'll find simple shrines or thrones at all sorts of unusual places. They often overlook crossroads, intersections or even just dangerous curves in the road. They protect passers-by, or give the gods a ringside view of the accidents!

Like so much else of Balinese religion the temples, although nominally Hindu, actually owe much to the pre-Majapahit era. Throughout most of the year the temples are quiet and empty but at festival times they are colourful and active, with offerings being made, dances performed, gamelan music ringing out and all manner of activities from cockfights to gambling going on.

All temples are oriented not north-south but mountains-sea. *Kaja*, the direction towards the mountains, is the most important direction so at this end of the temple the holiest shrines are found. The direction towards the sea is *kelod*. The sunrise or *kangin* direction is the second most important direction so on this side you find the secondary shrines. Kaja may be towards a particular mountain – as Pura Besakih is pointed directly towards Gunung Agung – or it may just be the mountains in general, which run east-west along the length of Bali.

Temple Types There are three basic temple types which almost every village will have. The most important is the *pura puseh* (temple of origin) which is dedicated to the village founders and is located at the kaja end of the village. In the middle of the village is the *pura desa* for the spirits which protect the village community in its day-to-day life. At the kelod end of the village is the pura dalem (temple of the dead). The graveyard is also located here and the temple will often include representations of Durga, the terrible side of Shiva's wife Parvati. Both Shiva and Parvati have a creative and destructive side and it's their destructive powers which are honoured in the pura dalem.

Other temples include those dedicated to the spirits of irrigated agriculture. Rice growing is so important in Bali and the division of water for irrigation purposes is handled with such care that these *pura subak* or *pura ulun suwi* can be of considerable importance. Other temples may also honour dry-field agriculture as well as the flooded rice paddies.

In addition to these 'local' temples, Bali also has a lesser number of great temples. Each family worships its ancestors in the family temple, the clan in its clan temple and the village in the pura puseh. Above these come the temples of royalty or state temples and in many cases a kingdom would have three of these – a main state temple in the heartland of the state (like Pura Taman Ayun in Mengwi), then a mountain temple (like Pura Besakih or Pura Luhur at Batukau) and a sea temple (like Pura Luhur Ulu Watu or Pura Luhur Rambut Siwi).

Every house in Bali has its house temple which is at the *kaja-kangin* corner of the courtyard – where the mountain and sunrise sides meet. There will be shrines to the Hindu 'trinity' of Brahma, Shiva and Vishnu, to *taksu*, the divine intermediary, and to *tugu*, the lord of the ground.

Directional Temples & World Sanctuaries
Certain special temples in Bali are of such importance that they are deemed to be owned by the whole island rather than by individual villages or local community organisations. There are nine *kahyangan jagat* or 'directional temples' and six *sad-kahyangan* or 'world sanctuaries'. The directional temples are:

Temple	Place	Region
Pura Besakih	Besakih	centre
Pura Ulun Danu (Batur)	Kintamani	north
Sambu	Gunung Agung	north-east
Pura Lempuyang Luhur	near Tirtagangga	east
Pura Goa Lawah	near Padangbai	south-east
Pura Masceti	near Gianyar	south
Pura Ulu Watu	Ulu Watu	south-west
Pura Luhur	Batukau	west
Pura Ulu Danau (Candikuning)	Lake Bratan	north-west

Most of these temples are well known, easily accessible and familiar objectives for many tourist groups. Pura Besakih is, of course, the holiest of Balinese temples and encompasses separate shrines and temples for all the clans and former kingdoms. Pura Besakih is said to be a male temple; its female counterpart is Pura Ulun Danu. Overlooking the outer crater of Gunung Batur, Pura Ulun Danu was built in 1927 after its predecessor, actually within the crater, was destroyed by an eruption.

Goa Lawah is the famous bat cave temple, while Pura Ulu Watu is at the extreme southern end of Bali, at the end of the Bukit Peninsula. Pura Luhur on the slopes of Gunung Batukau is a rather remote temple with a reclusive feel while Pura Ulu Danau at Candikuning perches right on the edge of Lake Bratan.

Three of the temples are rarely seen by visitors to Bali. Pura Masceti, on the coast south of Gianyar, is easily reached but infrequently visited. It takes a stiff walk to reach remote Pura Lempuyang at the eastern end of the island.

It's not so easy to list the six 'world' sanctuaries' as there is considerable dispute as to which ones make the grade. Usually the six are drawn from the list of nine directional temples but other important temples like

Pura Pusering Jagat with its enormous bronze drum at Pejeng near Ubud or Pura Kehen in Bangli may also creep on to some lists.

Other Important Temples There are numerous other important temples around the island apart from the world sanctuaries and directional temples. They include:

Pura Maduwe Karang – an agricultural temple on the north coast famous for its spirited bas reliefs including one of a bicycle rider.

Pura Taman Ayun – the large and imposing state temple at Mengwi, north-west of Denpasar.

Pura Luhur Rambut Siwi – a beautiful coastal temple towards the western end of the island.

Pura Tirta Empul – the beautiful temple at Tampaksiring with springs and bathing pools at the source of the Pakerisan River, north of Ubud.

Tanah Lot – the enormously popular sunset temple perched on a rock just off the coast west of Denpasar.

Temple Festivals For much of the year Balinese temples are deserted, just an empty space. But every now and then they come alive with days of frenetic activity and nights of drama and dance. Temple festivals come at least once each Balinese year of 210 days. The annual 'temple birthday' is known as an *odalan*. Since most villages have at least three temples that means you're assured of at least five or six annual festivals in every village. But that's only the start – there can be special festival days common throughout the islands, festivals for certain temples, festivals for certain gods, and festivals because it just seemed like a good idea to have one.

Cockfights are a regular part of temple ceremonies – they're a convenient combination of excitement, sport, gambling and a blood sacrifice all rolled into one. Men keep fighting cocks as prized pets, carefully groomed and cared for, lovingly prepared for their brief moment of glory or defeat. On quiet afternoons the men will often meet in the banjars to compare their roosters, spar them against one another and line up the odds for the next big bout.

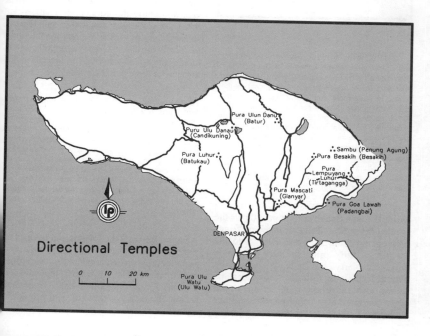

Directional Temples

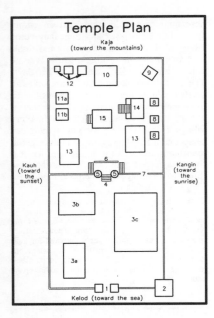

Temple Plan

Kaja
(toward the mountains)

Kauh
(toward
the
sunset)

Kangin
(toward
the
sunrise)

Kelod (toward the sea)

1	Candi Bentar
2	Kulkul Tower
3A	Bale Gong
3B	Paon
3C	Wantilan
4	Kori Agung or Paduraksa
5	Raksa or Dwarapala
6	Aling Aling
7	Side Gate
8	Small Shrines or Gedongs
9	Padmasana
10	Meru
11A	Eleven-Roofed Meru to Sanghyang Widhi
11B	Three-Roofed Meru to Gunung Agung
12	Small Shrines or Gedongs
13	Bale Piasan
14	Gedong Pesimpangan
15	Paruman or Pepelik

You'll often see the roosters by the roadside in their bell-shaped cane baskets – they're placed there to be entertained by passing activity. When the festivals take place the cocks are matched one against another, a lethally sharp metal spur tied to one leg and then, after being pushed against each other a few times to stir up the blood, they're released and the feathers fly. It's usually over in a flash – a slash of the spur and one rooster is down and dying. Occasionally a cowardly rooster runs and flees but in that case both roosters are put in a covered basket where they can't avoid fighting. After the bout the successful betters collect their pay-offs and the winning owner takes home the dead rooster for his cooking pot.

While the men slaughter their prized pets the women bring beautifully arranged offerings of prepared food, fruit and flowers to the temple, artfully piled in huge pyramids which they carry on their heads. Outside the temple, food stalls *(warungs)* and other stalls selling toys and trinkets are set up. In the outer courtyard a gamelan provides further amusement.

While all this activity is going on in and around the temple, the pemangkus suggest to the gods that they should come down for a visit and enjoy the goings-on. That's what those little thrones are for in the temple shrines, they're symbolic seats for the gods to occupy during festivals. Sometimes small images known as *pratimas* are placed on the thrones, to represent the gods.

Trances are an everyday feature of Balinese life, particularly at festivals. People seem to be able to go into a trance state in a flash and at that time they're supposed to be a medium of communication for the gods who temporarily possess their bodies. You may see a pemangku go into trance while offering his prayers, a young girl's eye's glaze over as she carries offerings into the temple, or the trance dancers, particularly in the Barong & Rangda dance. It's regarded as a holy state, so people in trance are carefully tended to and sprinkled with holy water to break the trance afterwards.

At some festivals the images and thrones of the deities are taken out of the temple and ceremonially carried down to the sea (or just to a suitable expanse of water if the sea is too distant) for a ceremonial bath. Gamelans follow the merry procession and provide a suitable musical accompaniment.

Back in the temple women dance the stately Pendet, an offering dance for the gods, and all night long there's activity, music and dancing. It's just like a country fair with food stands, amusements, games, stalls, gambling, noise, colour and confusion.

Finally, as dawn approaches, the entertainment fades away, the women perform the last Pendet, the pemangkus suggest to the gods that maybe it's time they made their weary way back to heaven, and the people wend their weary way back to their homes.

Typical Temple Design There is a great deal of variation in temple design but the small two-courtyard temple illustrated includes all the basic elements. Larger temples may have more courtyards and more shrines and even a similar small temple may have the less important buildings and shrines arranged in a different pattern.

1. Candi Bentar
   The *candi bentar* is the temple gateway, an intricately sculptured tower which looks as if it has been split down the centre and moved apart.
2. Kulkul Tower
   This is the warning drum tower from which a wooden split drum (kulkul) is sounded to announce events at the temple or warn of danger. At one time this included the sighting of an *amuk* or warning of a theft.
3. Bales
   These are pavilions, generally open-sided, for temporary use or for storage. They may include a bale gong (3A), where the gamelan orchestra plays during festivals, or a *paon* (3B), used as a temporary kitchen to prepare offerings for temple ceremonies. A particularly large bale used as a stage for dances or cockfights is known as a *wantilan* (3C).
4. Kori Agung or Paduraksa
   The gateway to the inner courtyard is an intricately sculptured stone tower (like the candi bentar) but entry is through a doorway reached by steps in the middle of the tower. The door is normally kept closed except during festivals.
5. Raksa or Dwarapala
   These are the statues of fierce guardian figures who protect the doorway and keep out evil spirits. Above the doorway there will be the equally fierce face of a *bhoma*, with hands outstretched to keep back unwanted spirits.

6. Aling Aling
   If Raksa and the bhoma slip up and an evil spirit does manage to slither through the entrance, the aling aling, a low wall directly behind the entrance, should keep them at bay since evil spirits find it notoriously difficult to make right-angle turns.
7. Side Gate
   For most of the year, when no ceremony is in process, entry to the inner courtyard is made through this side gate which is always open. Presumably, evil spirits don't think of getting in this way.
8. Small Shrines or Gedongs
   These usually include shrines to Ngrurah Alit and Ngrurah Gede who organise things and ensure that the correct offerings are made.
9. Padmasana
   This is the stone throne for the sun god Surya, and is situated at the most auspicious corner of the temple, the kaja-kangin corner (where the mountain and sunrise sides meet). The throne rests on the 'world turtle' or *badawang* which is held by two snake-like *nagas* (mythological serpents).
10. Meru
    These are multi-roofed Balinese shrines. Usually there will be an 11-roofed *meru* (11A) to Sanghyang Widhi, the supreme Balinese deity, and a three-roofed meru (11B) to the holy mountain Gunung Agung.
11. Small Shrines or Gedongs
    More small shrines will be found at the kaja (mountain) end of the courtyard. Typically these could include a shrine like a single-roofed meru to Gunung Batur, another of Bali's sacred mountains; a shrine known as the Maospait dedicated to the original Majapahit settlers who brought the Hindu religion to Bali; and a shrine to the taksu who acts as an interpreter for the gods. Trance dancers are said to be mouthpieces for the taksu or it may use a medium to convey the gods' wishes.
13. Bale Piasan
    These are open pavilions used for the display of temple offerings. There may be several of these bales.
14. Gedong Pesimpangan
    This is a stone building dedicated to the village founder or a local deity.
15. Paruman or Pepelik
    This open pavilion in the centre of the inner courtyard is where the gods are supposed to assemble to watch the ceremonies of a temple festival.

Temple Behaviour There are a number of ground rules for visiting Balinese temples.

Except on rare occasions, anybody can enter a temple any time they feel like it. The attitude is nothing like that found in parts of India where non-Hindus are firmly barred from temples. You don't have to go barefoot as in many Buddhist shrines, but you are expected to be appropriately dressed. You should always wear a temple scarf as a sash around your waist – see the What to Bring section in the Facts for the Visitor chapter. Priests should be shown respect, particularly at festivals. They are the most important people and should, therefore, be on the highest plane. Don't put yourself higher than them by, for example, climbing up on a wall to take photographs.

There will usually be a sign outside temple entrances warning you to be well dressed and respectful and also requesting that women not enter the temple during their periods. The pleasant little lakeside temple at Bedugul once had a 'no entry' sign announcing that 'It is forbidden to enter women during menstruation'. Unfortunately the sign was later changed to eliminate the double entendre.

LANGUAGE – BALINESE

Bahasa Indonesia, the national language of Indonesia you hear in Bali, is not Balinese. Balinese is another language entirely, with a completely different vocabulary and grammar and much more complex rules for its use. Balinese is also much more of a 'spoken' than a 'written' language since it is not taught in schools, although it is studied by a few scholars, particularly at the Gedong Kirtya library in Singaraja. Its written form is based on Sanskrit, and it does look like Hindi writing. It's the script used on the *lontar* books made from thin strips of palm leaf, and you sometimes see it on the signs that welcome you to, and farewell you from, every village in Bali. It's the language of day-to-day local contact but exclusively of the Balinese people. A Balinese person speaking to a Javanese or any other Indonesian from outside Bali speaks in Bahasa Indonesia.

Balinese is greatly complicated by its caste influences. There's high Balinese, low Balinese and even middle Balinese, plus a number of variations of the three. Basically, a low-caste person speaking to a high-caste person should use high Balinese. Conversely, a high-caste person speaking to a low-caste person uses low Balinese. When talking about yourself, however, you talk in low Balinese no matter who you are talking to! It sounds amazingly complicated: a choice of two different languages the use of which depends on knowing who you are talking to! Actually it's not quite that complex because the high Balinese words are principally restricted to words about people or their actions.

Middle Balinese has an even more restricted vocabulary. It's mainly used when one wishes to be very polite but doesn't want to emphasise caste differences. How does one Balinese know at which level to address another? Well, initially, a conversation between two strangers would commence in the high language. At some point the question of caste would be asked and then the level adjusted accordingly. But among friends a conversation is likely to be carried on in low Balinese no matter what the caste of the conversationalists. In today's world, caste differences, at least in the language, seem to be disappearing.

Don't worry about Balinese though. It's interesting to consider and fun to pick up a few words, but you're wiser to put any language-learning effort into Indonesian.

BAHASA INDONESIA

There are a vast number of local languages and dialects in Indonesia but Bahasa Indonesia (literally, 'Indonesia language') is all but identical to Malay, and is actively promoted as the one national language. Almost anywhere you go in Indonesia, including Bali, people will speak Bahasa Indonesia as well as their own local language. Many of them will also speak English as a third language.

Like any language Indonesian has its simplified colloquial form and its more developed literate language. For the visitor who wants to pick up enough to get by in the

the Tehuantepec region of his country and *The Eagle, the Gajuar and the Serpent* (1954) about the Indians of North America. He was also involved in theatre design and printmaking.

Walter Spies (1895-1942) Walter Spies was the father figure for the cast of '30s visitors and in many ways played the largest part in interpreting Bali to them and in establishing the image of Bali which still prevails today. The son of a wealthy diplomat, Spies was born in Moscow in 1895 and raised there during the final years of Czarist rule. At the age of 15 he was sent away to school in Dresden but returned to his family just as WW I broke out. Twice in his life Spies was imprisoned due to his nationality – on the first occasion he was interned as an enemy national, first near Moscow and then in a small town in the Ural mountains.

As the upheavals of the revolution swept Russia, Spies returned to his family in Moscow, then escaped from the country in disguise. In 1919 he was in Dresden, then moved to Berlin where he joined a circle of artists, musicians and film makers. In 1923 Spies abruptly left Europe for Java in what was then the Dutch East Indies. In Bandung (Java) he played the piano in a cinema and taught music to Dutch children in Yogyakarta. He then managed the Sultan of Yogyakarta's European orchestra, learning the gamelan along the way. He first visited Bali in 1925 and two years later moved there permanently.

Befriended by the important Sukawati family he built a house at the confluence of two rivers at Campuan, west of Ubud. Today the house is part of the Campuan Hotel, overlooking Murni'sWarung. His home soon became the prime gathering point for the most famous visitors of the '30s and Spies, who involved himself in every aspect of Balinese art and culture, was an important influence on its great renaissance. His visitors included Barbara Hutton, Charlie Chaplin, Noel Coward and Margaret Mead as well as many of the Western writers and artists whose names are now firmly linked with Bali in that era. Spies also attracted a talented and growing circle of Balinese artists.

In 1932 he became curator of the Bali Museum in Denpasar and with Rudolf Bonnet and Cokorda Gede Agung Sukawati, their Balinese patron, he founded the Pita Maha artists' co-operative in 1936. He co-authored *Dance & Drama in Bali*, which was published in 1938 and he created that most Balinese of dances, the Kechak, for a visiting German film crew. Despite his comfortable life in Ubud, he moved to the remote village of Iseh in eastern Bali in 1937.

In 1938 things suddenly went very wrong for poor Spies when a puritan clampdown in Holland spread to the Dutch colony and he was arrested for homosexuality. Spies was imprisoned in Denpasar, then moved to Java where he was held in jail in Surabaya for eight months. He was no sooner released than WW II commenced and, when the Germans invaded Holland in 1940, he was arrested again, this time as an enemy alien. Spies was held in Sumatra until the Pacific war began and on 18 January 1942 Spies, with other prisoners of war, was shipped out of Sumatra on the *Van Imhoff*, bound for Ceylon (Sri Lanka). The next day the ship was bombed by Japanese aircraft and sank near the island of Nias. Walter Spies was drowned.

Spies' paintings were a curious mixture of Rousseau and surrealism, the Rousseau influence mirrored in many Balinese paintings today. Attentive visitors will catch glimpses of what he saw all over the island. However, if Spies was only a talented artist his memory would be a much fainter one today. To his ability as a painter must be added his consuming interest in all aspects of Balinese art, culture and life, as well as his role as a window to Bali for other Western visitors and as a vital force in the encouragement and growth of Balinese art. Last, but far from least, he was also a colourful and fascinating character, clearly in love with life and in headlong pursuit of all it could offer.

Colin McPhee (1900-1965) A chance hearing of a record of gamelan music compelled American musician Colin McPhee to join the stream of talented '30s visitors. Artists, writers and anthropologists all recorded their impressions of the island but as a musician McPhee's outlook was unique. *A House in Bali* was not published until 1944, long after his departure from the island, but it remains one of the best written of the Bali accounts and his tales of music and house building are often highly amusing. The house in question was in Sayan, just west of Campuan and Ubud. More recent short-term residents in Sayan have included Mick Jagger and David Bowie. The beautiful Ayung River Gorge through Sayan and Kedewatan is now the site for some of Ubud's most luxurious small hotels.

After the war, McPhee taught music at UCLA and played an important role in introducing Balinese music to the West, encouraging gamelan orchestras to visit the USA.

Rudolf Bonnet (1895-1978) Rudolf Bonnet was a Dutch artist who, along with Walter Spies, played a major role in the development of Balinese art in the mid-30s. Bonnet arrived in Bali in 1929, two years after Spies, and immediately contacted him. In 1936 he was one of the principal forces behind the foundation of the Pita Maha artist's co-operative, and his influence on Balinese art to this day is very clear. Where Spies' work was often mystical, Bonnet's work concentrated on the human form and everyday Balinese life. To this day the numerous classical Balinese paintings with their themes of markets, cockfights and other aspects of day-to-day existence are all indebted to Bonnet.

Bonnet was imprisoned in Sulawesi by the Japanese during WW II and returned to Bali in the '50s to plan the Puri Lukisan Museum in Ubud. Foreigners, even one as in love with Bali as Bonnet, were not always welcome in Indonesia at this time and he left the island, but returned in 1973 to help establish the museum's permanent collection. He died in 1978, on a brief return visit to Holland. That same year brought the deaths of Cokorda Gede Agung Sukawati, the Ubud patron of both Bonnet and Spies, and Gusti Nyoman Lempad, the Balinese artist who had also played a prime role in the establishment of the Pita Maha. Bonnet's ashes were returned to his beloved Bali to be scattered at the 1979 cremation of Cokorda Gede Agung.

K'tut Tantri A woman of many aliases K'tut Tantri was still Vannine Walker, or perhaps it was Muriel Pearson, when she breezed in from Hollywood in 1932. She was born on the Isle of Man and grew up there and in Scotland before working as a journalist in Hollywood. The film *Bali, The Last Paradise* had served as the inspiration to send her to Bali, where she dyed her red hair black (only demons have red hair) and was befriended by the prince of the kingdom of Bangli.

She teamed up with Robert Koke to open the Kuta Beach Hotel in 1936, the first hotel at Kuta Beach. Later she fell out with the Kokes and established her own hotel, the Sound of the Sea. She stayed on when war swept into the archipelago, was imprisoned by the Japanese, survived long periods of solitary confinement during the war and then worked for the Indonesian Republicans in their postwar struggle against the Dutch. As Surabaya Sue she broadcast from Surabaya in support of their cause. Her book *Revolt in Paradise* (written as K'tut Tantri) was published in 1960 but those searching for more insights into Bali and its characters should note that the names not only of the people but also the villages have been changed. She was also known as Meng or Manx, from her childhood on the Isle of Man.

Robert & Louise Koke In 1936 Americans Robert Koke and Louise Garret arrived in Bali as part of a long trip through South-East Asia. They fell in love with the island and Kuta Beach and soon established the Kuta Beach Hotel, at first in partnership with K'tut Tantri although their accounts of the hotel differ widely!

Although the Dutch insisted that the hotel was nothing more than a few 'dirty native huts' it was an instant hit and Bali's '30s tourist boom ensured that it was always full. The rooms were a series of individual thatched-roof cottages, remarkably like the cottage-style hotels which are still popular in Bali today. Robert Koke, who learnt to surf in Hawaii, can also claim the honour of introducing surfing to Bali (the hotel logo includes a surfer). Boards were provided for use by hotel guests.

The Koke's success continued until the Japanese entry into the war. The pair made a last-minute escape from Bali, and when Robert Koke visited Bali just after the war, only traces of the hotel's foundations remained. In 1955 a new Kuta Beach Hotel was opened, the first postwar hotel at Kuta and close to the site of its original namesake. Robert Koke retired from a long career with the CIA in the '70s and in 1987 Louise Koke's long-forgotten story of their hotel was published as *Our Hotel in Bali*, illustrated with her incisive sketches and her husband's excellent photographs.

Other Western Visitors Numerous other Western personages made pilgrimages to Bali in the '30s. Charlie Chaplin and Noel Coward were the equivalents of today's rock star visitors, adding a touch of glamour to Bali as a destination.

Others played their part in chronicling the period – writers like Hickman Powell, whose book *The Last Paradise* was published in 1930 (the current paperback edition carries a publisher's note that the copyright owner is untraceable), and German author Vicki Baum, whose book *A Tale from Bali*, a fictionalised account of the puputan of 1906, is still in print.

Colin McPhee's wife Jane Belo does not even make a fleeting appearance in her husband's book *A House in Bali*, but in fact she was a talented anthropologist who also played a key role in interpreting Bali in the '30s. Margaret Mead also visited and wrote about Bali at this time. Another visitor from the '30s was the American dancer Katherine Mershon. ■

Arts & Crafts

Arts & Crafts

Craft shop in Bali (JL)

An offering to the gods (JL)

Paintings outside art gallery, Ubud (TW)

Every Balinese is an artist and craftsperson and until the tourist invasion, painting or carving was simply an everyday part of life. Bali had no art galleries or craft shops in those days – what was produced went into temples or was used for festivals. It's a whole different story now with hundreds, even thousands, of galleries and craft shops in every possible place a tourist might pass. The real problem with Balinese art and craft today is that there is simply too much of it. You can't turn around without tripping over more carved *garudas* (legendary gigantic birds), and in the galleries there are so many paintings that they're stacked up in piles on the floor.

Of course, much of this work is rubbish, churned out quickly for people who want a cheap souvenir. It's a shame because there is still much beautiful work produced, but you have to sort through a lot of junk to find it. Part of the problem is that Balinese art has always been something that is produced today, deteriorates tomorrow, is worn out the next day and thrown away the day after.

Indeed, it's the everyday, disposable crafts which are probably the most surprising in Bali. Even the simplest activities are carried out with care, precision and the Balinese artistic flair. Just glance at those little offering trays placed on the ground for the spirits every morning – each one a throwaway work of art. Look at the temple offerings, the artistically stacked pyramids of fruit or other beautifully decorated foods. Look for the *lamaks*, long woven palm leaf strips used as decorations in festivals and celebrations or the stylised female figures known as *cili*. See the intricately carved coconut-shell wall hangings or, at funerals, simply marvel at the care and energy that goes into constructing huge funeral towers and the exotic sarcophagus, all of which will soon go up in flames. The Balinese were always creators rather than preservers and this has never really been a problem because there is no shortage of time to be spent simply creating more works of art. The fertility of the earth and their own efficiency as farmers give the Balinese ample time for the pursuit of artistic activities.

The repetition that is so characteristic of Balinese arts & crafts is partly motivated by respect and admiration for traditional values and a need

Preparations for a cremation ceremony, Ubud (GE)

to feel a part of society, and partly by the economic benefits of mass-production. Yet, whatever the object – be it a frog with a leaf, a barong mask, or a cartoon figure – the end product will always be distinctly Balinese. Very little you see will be old, and even less antique.

To understand the crafts of Bali, it's important to know the crafts of Java, as the cultural and trading relationship between the two islands has always been strong. The ceremonial dagger (kris) so important in a Balinese family, has often been made in Java. Most of the sarongs that are worn for important ceremonies are made in central Java, except for the ikat sarongs from Gianyar. Similarly, Java is the main supplier of puppets and metalwork items including sacred images.

In many ways, Bali is a showroom for all the crafts of Indonesia. A typical tourist shop will sell puppets and batiks from Java, ikat garments from Sumba, Sawa and Flores, and textiles and woodcarvings from Bali, Lombok and Kalimantan. ■

Food for blessings (CK)

Palace entrance, Puri Ubud (TW)

Architecture & Sculpture

Of all the Balinese arts it's said that architecture and sculpture have been the least affected by Western influence and the tourist boom – nobody's taking temples home and your average stone statue doesn't roll up and stuff in your bag too easily. Architecture and sculpture are inextricably bound together – a temple gateway is not just put up, every sq cm of it is intricately carved and a diminishing series of demon faces is placed above it as protection. Even then it's not finished without a couple of stone statues to act as guardians. Thus architecture becomes sculpture and sculpture becomes architecture.

Architecture Although Balinese houses are often attractive places – due in large part to their beautiful gardens – they've never been lavished with the architectural attention reserved for *puras* (temples) and *puris* (palaces). Household layout is more or less standardised (see The Household section in the Facts about Bali chapter) and palaces are not exactly regular

Sidan Pura Dalem (JL)

constructions these days, although some of the flashy new hotels are making considerable use of traditional architectural and sculptural features – the Nusa Dua Beach Hotel at Nusa Dua is a good example. Basically, however, it's in the temples where you'll find traditional Balinese architecture and sculpture.

Temples are designed to set rules and formulae; for details see the Temples section in the Facts about Bali chapter. Sculpture serves as an adjunct, a finishing touch, to these design guidelines and in small or less important temples the sculpture may be limited or even nonexistent. In other temples, particularly some of the exuberantly detailed temples of northern Bali, the sculpture may be almost overwhelming in its intricacy and interest.

Sculpture Sculpture often appears in a number of set places in temples. Door guardians, of legendary figures like Arjuna or other protective personalities, flank the steps to the gateway. Similar figures are also often seen at both ends of bridges. Above the main entrance to a temple, Kala's monstrous face often peers out, sometimes a number of times – his hands reaching out beside his head to catch any evil spirits foolish enough to try to sneak in. Elsewhere other sculptures make regular appearances – the front of a *pura dalem* (temple of the dead) will often feature prominently placed images of the *rangda* (witch) while sculptured panels may show the horrors that await evildoers in the afterlife. Fine stone craftwork, often on a monumental scale, is also evident in the construction of new five-star hotels.

Batubulan, on the main highway from Denpasar to Gianyar, is a major stone-carving centre. Stone figures, varying in height from 25 cm to two metres, line both sides of the street. Stone craftsmen can be seen in action in the many workshops here as well as in an area north of the main road, around Karang.

Stone carving is the most durable art form. Most of the local work is made from a soft sandstone that, when newly worked, can be mistaken for cast cement. It can be scratched with a finger and is not particularly strong or dense. With age and exposure to the elements, the outer surface becomes tougher and darker.

Sculpture in Bali is still very much for local consumption rather than, as with painting or woodcarving, for visitors to take home. Yet,

Entrance to Blanco's house (TW)

Kala, Pura Luhur, Rambut Siwi (TW)

Stone carvings, Batubulan (TW)

Top Left: Stone-carved Singa (winged lion) (JL)
Top Right: Stone Ganesh (GB)
Bottom: Contemporary sculptures (GB)

although it's less affected by foreign influence than other art forms, many modern trends can still be seen and sculptors are happy to work on new and non-traditional themes. Japanese-style stone lanterns are currently popular.

Buying Sculpture Balinese stone is surprisingly light and it's not at all out of the realms of possibility to bring a friendly stone demon back with you in your airline baggage. A typical temple door guardian weighs around 10 kg. The stone, however, is very fragile so packing must be done carefully if you're going to get it home without damage. Some of the Batubulan workshops will pack figures quickly and expertly, usually with shredded paper. There are also many capable packing and forwarding agents, although bear in mind that shipping costs will almost certainly be more than the cost of the article. A typical Balinese stone door guardian, however, can be bought for around US$20 (including packaging), with a little negotiation. It'll scare the hell out of your neighbour's garden gnomes! ■

Young sculptors, Batubulan (TW)

Contemporary stone carving (JL)

Ceiling of the Kertha Gosa, Klungkung
(TW)

PAINTING

Of the various art forms popular in Bali, painting is probably the one most influenced both by Western ideas and Western demand. Prior to the arrival of Western artists after WW I painting was, like other Balinese art, primarily for temple and palace decoration. The influence of Western artists not only expanded it beyond these limited horizons, it also showed the way to whole new subject areas and, quite possibly most important of all, gave the artists new materials to work with.

Before the '30s Until the fateful arrival of the Western artists, Balinese painting was strictly limited to three basic kinds – *langse*, *iders-iders* and calendars. Langse are large rectangular decorative hangings used in palaces or temples. Iders-iders are scroll paintings hung along the eaves of temples. The calendars pictorially represent the days of the month, showing the auspicious days.

Paintings were almost always executed in *wayang* style – that is, they were imitative of *wayang kulit* (leather shadow puppets) with the figures almost always shown in either profile or three-quarters view.

'Wrongdoers get their just deserts', ceiling detail, Kertha Gosa, Klungkung (TW)

Figures in classical paintings were also like the wayang figures. The *alus* or 'refined' heroes were narrow and elongated and richly dressed while their *kasar* or 'rough' opponents were short, squat and ugly. The paintings were generally narrative style, rather like a cartoon comic strip, with a series of panels telling a story. Even the colours artists could use were strictly limited to a set list of shades.

At one time, classical paintings were all made on cotton cloth hand woven only on the island of Nusa Penida. Today, modern cloth is used although it is still coated with a rice-flour paste and burnished with a shell. The old natural colours (made from soot, clay, pig's bones and other such ingredients) are no longer employed either; today the paint is all modern oil and acrylic. Nevertheless, the final burnishing with a shell gives an aged look even to the new paints and these pictures are known as *lukisan antik* or 'antique paintings'.

Paintings are still done in these traditional styles – Klungkung is a centre for the wayang style of painting and you can see a fine original example of the style in the painted ceiling of the Hall of Justice (Kertha Gosa) in Klungkung. The village of Kamasan, a few km south of Klungkung, is the place where many of these paintings are actually produced. Kerambitan, near Tabanan to the west of Denpasar, is another centre for classical painting.

Classical paintings today may depict scenes from Balinese mythology or the Hindu epics and may still show action in serial comic-book style. Balinese calendars are still used to set dates and predict the future, although today most of them are painted for tourists. There are two types – the simpler yellow coloured calendars from Bedulu and the more complex classical calendars from Klungkung.

The Pita Maha Walter Spies and Rudolf Bonnet were the Western artists who turned Balinese artists around in the '30s. (See the earlier Western Visitors in the '30s section for more information about these two.) At that time painting was in a serious decline: painting styles had become stagnant and since few commissions were forthcoming from the palaces and temples, painting was virtually dying out as an art form.

Bonnet and Spies, with their patron Cokorda Gede Agung Sukawati, formed the Pita Maha (literally 'great vitality'), to encourage painting as

Cartoon-style painting with narrative panels (GB)

Young Artist painting by I Nyoman Dana (TW)

Rural scene by I Dab Alit, Taman, Ubud (GB)

Classical three-quarter view figure (GB)

Young Artist painting by M D Raju,
Penestanan (GB)

Rural scene by DW MD Dharmadi,
Batuan (GB)

an art form and to find a market for the best paintings. The group had more than 100 members at its peak in the 1930s.

The changes Bonnet and Spies inspired were revolutionary – suddenly Balinese artists started painting single scenes instead of narrative tales and using everyday life rather than romantic legends as their themes. Paintings influenced by the Pita Maha association are typically scenes of everyday life – harvesting rice, bartering in the market, watching a cockfight, presenting offerings at a temple or preparing a cremation.

Batuan is a noted painting centre which came under the influence of the Pita Maha at an early stage. Batuan painters produced dynamic black-ink drawings, good examples of which can be seen at Ubud's Puri Lukisan Museum. The style is noted for its inclusion of some very modern elements; sea scenes for example are likely to include the odd windsurfer.

Not only the themes changed, the actual way of painting also altered. More modern paint and materials were used and the stiff formal poses of old gave way to realistic three-dimensional representations. Even more important, pictures were painted for their own sake – not as something to cover a space in a palace or temple. The idea of a painting being something you could do by itself (and for which there might be a market!) was wholly new.

In one way, however, the style remained unchanged – Balinese paintings were packed full, every spare corner of the picture was filled in. A painted Balinese forest has branches and leaves reaching out to fill every tiny space and is inhabited by a whole zoo of creatures. For many of the new artists, idyllic rural scenes from some Balinese Arcadia or energetic festival scenes were the order of the day. Others painted engagingly stylised animals and fish. You can see fine examples of these new styles at the Puri Lukisan Museum in Ubud and, of course, find them in all the galleries and art shops.

The new artistic enthusiasm was short-lived, however, for WW II interrupted and then in the '50s and '60s Indonesia was wracked by internal turmoil and confusion. The new styles degenerated into stale copies of the few original spirits, with one exception: the development of the Young Artists style.

The Young Artists Dutch painter Arie Smit survived imprisonment by the Japanese during WW l and arrived in Bali in 1956. One day while painting in Penestanan, just outside Ubud, he noticed a young boy drawing in the dirt and wondered what he would produce if he had proper equipment to paint with. The story is regularly told of how the lad's father would not allow him to take up painting until Smit offered to und somebody else to watch the family's flock of ducks.

Other 'young artists' from Penestanan soon joined that first pupil, I Nyoman Cakra, but Arie Smit did not actively teach them. He simply provided the equipment and the encouragement and unleashed what was clearly a strong natural talent. An engaging new naive style quickly developed, as they painted typically Balinese rural scenes in brilliant technicolour.

The style quickly caught on and is today one of the staples of Balinese tourist art. Of course not all the artists are young boys any more, and the style is also known as work by 'peasant painters'. I Nyoman Cakra, the original Young Artist, still lives in Penestanan, still paints and cheerfully admits that he owes it all to Smit.

Modern Painting Balinese painting today is both strong and weak. It's strong in that there is so much of it going on but weak in that so much of it is exactly alike. Unfortunately, while there are a few truly creative people, there are also an enormous number of copyists – some of them excellent, some of them far from excellent.

One constant factor in Balinese painting is that it is almost always 'planned' – ie, drawn out and refined before any paint is applied. When the actual painting does take place it can often be done in an almost 'colour by number' manner. Indeed, some name artists will simply draw out the design, decide the colours and then employ apprentices to actually apply the paint. This once again leads to the mass production of remarkably similar themes which is so characteristic of Balinese art. A painting is esteemed not for being new and unusual but for taking a well-worn and popular idea and making a good reproduction of it.

Unfortunately, much of the painting today is churned out for the tourist market and much of that market is extremely undiscriminating about what it buys. Thus the shops are packed full of paintings in the various popular styles – some of them quite good, a few of them really excellent, most of them uniformly alike and uniformly poor

Painter in Ubud (TW)

Painter in Ubud (PW)

Festival scene by A A Rai, Ubud (TW)

Batuan painting by I Made Nyana (TW)

Gallery in Ubud (TW)

Barong dancer (GB)

in quality. Even worse, many artists have turned to producing paintings purely attuned to tourist tastes and with nothing Balinese about them. It's a sad thing to see 'instant Woolworths art' being turned out for the tourist trade although heroic surfing pictures painted to order are at least amusing. It's rare to see anything really new though – most painters aim for safety and that means painting what tourists will buy.

Buying Paintings If you want to buy wisely then try to learn a little about Balinese painting before making a purchase. Visit the galleries in Ubud and the Neka and Puri Lukisan museums to see some of the best of Balinese art as well as some of the European influences that have shaped it. Look at some of the books on Balinese art. An excellent short introduction to the subject is *Balinese Paintings* by A A M Djelantik (Images in Asia series, Oxford University Press, Singapore, 1986). *The Development of Painting in Bali* is a handy little booklet published by the Neka Museum which describes the various styles, and illustrates them with paintings from the Neka collection.

Finally, and most importantly, simply look at paintings. Once you've visited the two Ubud museums and seen some of the best work and examples of paintings that set the styles, visit other galleries. The Neka Gallery in Padangtegal near Ubud (not to be confused with the Neka Museum where the art is not for sale), the Agung Rai Gallery in Peliatan and the Sanggraha Kriya Asta Arts Centre in Tohpati, on the Ubud side of Denpasar, are excellent places to view high-quality work and get an idea of prices. There are many other galleries and you'll soon start to appreciate what's good and what isn't. If it looks good, and you like it, then buy it. You certainly won't make any mistakes – Balinese art is so reasonably priced that any buy is a good buy. If it's a good painting as well, then so much the...

Paintings can be transported in the cardboard tubes which have rolls of wrapped cloth around them, as supplied to drapers. Otherwise you can buy plastic tubes from hardware stores. If you do buy a painting, and can handle the additional weight, consider taking a frame back as well. These are often elaborately carved and works of art in themselves, and are very cheap, especially compared to framing costs in the West. ■

Movie posters – another form of painting (TW & JL)

Detail from carved temple doors, Sanur
(TS)

WOODCARVING

Like painting, woodcarving has undergone a major transformation over the past 50 years, from being a decorative craft to something done for its own sake. Prior to this change in attitude, woodcarving was chiefly architectural decoration – on carved doors or columns for example – or of figures such as garudas or demons with a protective or symbolic nature. There were also decorative carvings on minor functional objects, such as bottle stoppers, and the carved wooden masks used in Balinese dance and theatre. Yet, it was the same demand from outside which inspired new carving subjects and styles, just as it had done with painting. It was also some of the same Western artists who served as the inspiration.

As with the new painting styles, Ubud was a centre for the revolution in woodcarving. Some carvers started producing highly stylised and elongated figures, with the further change that the wood was sometimes left with its natural finish rather than being painted. Others carved delightful animal figures, some totally realistic, others complete caricatures. Other styles and trends developed: whole tree trunks carved into ghostly, intertwined 'totem poles'; and curiously exaggerated and distorted figures.

Any visitor to Bali is likely to be exposed to woodcarving in all its forms, whether it be the traditional ornate carved double doors seen in houses and losmen, the carved figures of gods carried in processions and seen in temples, or the myriad carved items in craft shops.

Almost all carving is of local woods, including *belalu*, a quick-growing light wood, and the stronger fruit timbers such as jackfruit wood. Ebony wood from Sulawesi has been used for the last 30 years or so.

Woodcarving is a craft practised throughout Bali. Tegalalang and Jati, on the road from Ubud to Batur, are noted woodcarving centres. Many workshops line the road east of Peliatan, Ubud, to Goa Gajah. The route from Mas, through Peliatan, Petulu and up the scenic slope to Pujaung, is also a centre for family-based workshops; listen for the tapping sound of the carvers' mallets. Carvers hold the timber steady with their feet while they work and groups of children are often given the task of painting the articles. Despite the gentle pace of this work, the volume and repetition can be daunting. You may pass a whole village producing nothing but fruit

1	4
2	
3	5

1: Woodcarver, Celuk (SG)
2: Woodcarving painter (TW)
3: Carved wooden naga (dragon); wheeled toys with an Indian influence(GB)
4: Wooden figure 'praying for prosperity', Celuk (TS)
5: Wooden statue, Celuk (TS)

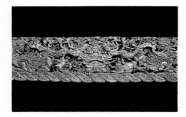

Wooden wall frieze (Tass)

Detail of wall frieze (Tass)

Wooden fruit (TW)

replicas, while another family may only carve garuda images.

An attempt to separate traditional and foreign influences is difficult. Like any craftspeople, the Balinese are keen observers of the outside world and have, as far as we know, always incorporated and adapted foreign themes in their work. Balinese carved religious figures may be based on Hindu mythology, but are very different from the same figures made in India. An Indian Ganesh is mostly a well-rounded, gentle elephant man, while the Balinese version bristles with intense emotion.

Carving, however, suffers from similar problems to painting in that there's an overwhelming emphasis on what sells, with the successful subjects mimicked by every carver on the block. 'Not another technicolour garuda' could easily be the tourist's lament. Still, there's always something interesting to see, the technical skill is high and the Balinese sense of humour often shines through – a frog clutches a large leaf as an umbrella, or a weird demon on the side of a wooden bell clasps his hands over his ears. You'll even find perfect replicas of every tropical fruit under the Balinese sun, including a complete, life-size banana tree!

Mask Carving Mask making is a specialised form of woodcarving, and only experts can carve the masks used in so many of Bali's theatre and dance performances. A particularly high level of skill is needed to create the masks used in the Topeng dance. The mask maker must know the movements that the performer of each topeng character makes so that his character can be shown by the mask. *Topeng* literally means 'pressed against the face', and a full collection of masks in the Topeng dance may number 30 or 40.

Other Balinese masks, such as the barong and rangda, are brightly painted and decorated with real hair, enormous teeth and bulging eyes.

Mas is recognised as the mask-carving centre of Bali, although there are also many craft shops along the Monkey Forest Rd in Ubud which have a large range of masks on display. The small village of Puaya, near Sukawati, also specialises in mask making. The Bali Museum in Denpasar has a good mask collection and is a good place to go to get an idea of styles before buying anything from the craft shops.

1	4	5
2		6
3		

1: Hindu-influenced carving (GB)
2: Singa (GB)
3: Garuda (GB)

4: Balinese god (GB)
6: Singa (GB)

5: Ganesh (GB)

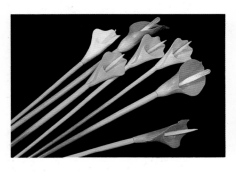

1	4
2	
3	5

1: Lambada, Lambretta, rooster etc (GB)
2: Traditional frog mask, fruit, duck & bike (GB)
3: Wooden lilies (GB)
4: Woodcarver's shop (TW)
5: Carved banana tree (GB)

1	5
2	6
3	7
4	

1: Topeng masks (GB)
2: Lombok masks (GB)
3: Topeng mask(GB)
4: Rangda mask (TW)

5: Topeng mask (GB)
6: Rangda mask (GB)
7: Barong mask (TW)

1: Flying dragon mobile (GB)
2: Bat mobile (Tass)
3: Flying frog mobiles (GB)
4: Balinese fisherman statue (GB)

Buying Woodcarvings There are few fixed prices for carved wooden items. Many factors determine costs, including the type of wood used, the novelty of the item and your powers of negotiation. If your idea is to send items home, packing and shipping costs can easily be more than the cost of the article. The simplest small carving can be found for 1000 rp or even less, while many good pieces can be bought for 30,000 rp, and there's no upper limit. If you're shopping around, you may see the same article vary in price by anything from 10% to 1000%!

Note that items made from harder woods may have an excess of moisture from Bali's tropical climate and in drier environments, the wood may shrink and crack. ■

Wooden dragon (JL)

Unpainted woodcarvings (GB)

Painted carvings (GB)

Rings, bracelets and a Bali suntan (GB)

JEWELLERY

Bali, along with Thailand and Mexico, is a major producer of world fashion jewellery and variations on the same designs are common to all three centres. The Balinese work is nearly always hand-constructed, rarely involving casting techniques, and uses imported silver. Balinese silver, mined near Singaraja, is also used for filigree and other traditional silverwork.

Celuk has always been the village associated with silversmithing. The large shops that line the road into Celuk have imposing, bus-sized driveways and slick credit-card facilities. If you want to see the 'real' Celuk, walk about a km east of the main road to visit the family workshops. Other silverwork centres include Kamasan, near Klungkung in eastern Bali and Beratan, south of Singaraja, in northern Bali.

Jewellery can be purchased made-up, or made-to-order – there's a wide range of earrings,

Balinese silver jewellery (GB)

bracelets and rings available, some using gemstones imported from all over the world. Different design influences can be detected from African patterning to the New Age preoccupation with dolphins and healing crystals. Patriot-missile pendants are also available! Prices start at around 1000 rp for silver stud earrings.

You'll find many jewellery workshops in other areas around Ubud. Tampaksiring, north-east of Ubud, has long been a centre for cheaper styles of fashion jewellery. Brightly painted, carved wooden earrings are popular and cheap, at around 800 rp. One of the more expensive jewellers producing modern European designs is Purpa, on Monkey Forest Rd, Ubud. Stop when you see the marble mansion and a prominent display of new cars. Many of the large exporters, including Mirah and Jonathon Jewellers, have outlets on the Legian and Kuta Beach roads. ∎

Balinese bracelet (Tass)

Wooden earrings – cheap and popular (GB)

Balinese ikat from Gianyar (GB)

WEAVING

Weaving is a popular craft and the standard woven Balinese sarong is not only very useful but also an attractive workaday item. You can use a sarong not only as a comfortable article of clothing but also as a bed top-sheet, a beach towel and a multitude of other uses.

Traditional batik sarongs are handmade in central Java, although the dyeing process has been adapted by the Balinese to produce brightly coloured and patterned fabrics for clothing, etc. Watch out for 'batik' fabric which has actually been screen-printed in factories. The colours in this are washed out compared to the rich colour of real batik cloth, and the pattern is often only on one side (in true batik cloth, the dye penetrates to colour both sides).

The Balinese also weave a variety of more complicated materials for ceremonial and other important uses. *Songket* cloth, for example, has gold or silver threads woven into the tapestry-like material and motifs include birds, butterflies, leaves and flowers. These sarongs are reserved exclusively for ceremonial occasions. Blayu, a small village in south-western Bali between

Batik sold in Bali (PW)

Left and right: Sarongs (GB)
       Bottom: Weaving stall in Tenganan, Bali (PW)

Balinese cloth bags (GB)

Bags made from cloth, leather and rattan (GB)

Mengwi and Marga, is a centre for songket weaving.

In various places in Indonesia you'll find material woven by the complex *ikat* process where the pattern is dyed into the threads *before* the material is woven. Ikat (known in Bali as *endek*) usually involves pre-dyeing either the warp or the weft thread. However, in the Bali Aga village of Tenganan, in eastern Bali, both the warp *and* weft are pre-dyed. This double-ikat process, called *gringsing* is practised nowhere else in Indonesia and is a complex and extremely time-consuming process.

Gianyar, in eastern Bali, is a major textile centre with a number of factories where you can watch sarongs being woven; a complete sarong takes about six hours to make. You can buy direct from the factories, although prices can be inflated in the tourist season due to large numbers of visitors from nearby Denpasar. The market is also a good place to buy textiles, if you know how to bargain. ∎

Ikat & batik cloth camera bags, passport wallets & cap (GB)

Top left: Batik patchwork pants (GB)
Top right: Screen-printed shirt (GB)
Bottom left: 'Antique' batik shirt (GB)
Bottom right: Batik shirt (GB)

Balinese kris & scabbard (Tass)

Ceramic lantern (GB)

KRIS

Often with an ornate, jewel-studded handle and sinister-looking wavy blade, the kris is the traditional and ceremonial dagger of Bali and Indonesia. Although a Balinese-made kris is slightly larger and more elaborate than one from Java, they are almost exactly the same shape. A kris can be the most important of family heirlooms, a symbol of prestige and honour. It is supposed to have great spiritual power and an important kris is thought to send out magical energy waves requiring great care in its handling and use. Even making a kris requires careful preparation, as does anything in Bali which involves working with the forces of magic. ■

WAYANG KULIT

Like krises, wayang kulit (leather puppet) figures are also magical items since the shadow plays are again part of the eternal battle between good and evil. The figures are cut from buffalo hide – wayang kulit means 'puppet of skin'. The intricate lace figures are carefully cut out with a sharp, chisel-like stylus and then painted. Although wayang kulit performances usually take place at night there are sometimes daytime temple performances, where the figures are manipulated without a screen. The figures are completely traditional: no variation is made from the standard list of characters and their standardised appearance. For more details, see the Wayang Kulit section in the Facts about Bali chapter.

Puppets are made in the village of Puaya, near Sukawati, south of Ubud, and in Peliatan, also near Ubud. ■

CERAMICS

Nearly all local pottery is made from low-fired terracotta. If you wish to see potters at work, visit the village of Pataen near Tanah Lot. Kapal and Ubung, north of Denpasar, are also pottery centres.

Most styles are very ornate, even for functional items such as vases, flasks, ash trays and lamp bases. Pejaten, near Tabanan, also has a number of pottery workshops producing small ceramic figures and glazed ornamental roof tiles. ■

Ceramic lanterns (GB & JL)

GAMELAN INSTRUMENTS

The Balinese and Javanese gamelan look similar but are tuned to different scales; (see the Gamelan section in the Facts about Bali chapter for more details about Balinese gamelan). If you are interested in seeing them being made, visit the village of Blahbatuh on the main road between Denpasar and Gianyar and ask for Gablar Gamelan. In northern Bali, Sawan, a small village east of Singaraja, is a centre for the manufacture of gamelan instruments. ■

LOMBOK ARTS & CRAFTS

Perhaps the best place to get an idea of Lombok's arts & crafts is the vast, covered market in Sweta. This is the largest market on Lombok, where you'll find a number of stalls specialising in local crafts like woodcarving, weaving and pottery.

Nearby Cakranegara is a centre for craftwork, particularly basket weaving, silverwork and cloth weaving.

Selamat Riady is a weaving factory close to Cakranegara in Mataram, where you can see ikat and songket cloth being made. It's a good

Lombok basket (GB)

Drummers at a cremation ceremony, Ubud (JP)

Left: Terracotta pots, Lombok (JL)
Top: Baskets, Lombok (JL)
Bottom: Weaver at work, Lombok (JL)

Wooden surveying tool (plumb line), Lombok (GB)

Cane-covered pottery, Lombok (GB)

Straw brush, Lombok (Tass)

place to get some idea of prices before you visit other smaller, weaving villages. There's such a range of quality and size that it's impossible to give a guide to prices, but the best pieces are magnificent and well worth paying for.

Sukarara and Pringgasela are villages which specialise in traditional ikat and songket weaving. In Sukarara, try the Taufik Weaving Company on Jalan Tenun which has sarongs, Sasak belts, tablecloths and many other pieces for sale.

Kotaraja is noted for its basketware and plaited mats, although much of the work appears to be sold directly for export.

Loyok, a tiny village a few km from Kotaraja, is also noted for its fine basketware, while Rungkang, a few km east of Loyok, is a centre for pottery. This pottery is made from a local black clay and the pots are often finished with woven cane for decoration and extra strength.

The small village of Penujak, six km south of Praya, is well known for its *gerabah* pottery, made from a local red clay. You can watch the pots being hand-built and fired in traditional kilns in the roadside workshops along the main street. Some of the larger pots would be difficult to carry, but there are also small animal-shaped figurines. ■

Artists in Postwar Bali

Bali's postwar visitors have never matched that brilliant period of the '30s when the island seemed to be packed with talented Western residents, all busy painting, composing or scribbling down their unique experiences. The war brought the artistic renaissance of the '30s to a juddering halt and it was not until the '50s that a new artistic impetus arrived, an impetus which has to some extent been waylaid by the spawning of 'mass-art' by mass tourism since the '70s.

While the visitors of the '30s ranged from artists and anthropologists to musicians and writers, more recent noted visitors have almost all been artists. Plenty of rock stars have been short-term visitors and *A House in Bali* has been recreated thousands of times with Australian or European vacation homes but there have been no writers to hold the faintest candle to the earlier chroniclers.

Arie Smit (1916-) Dutch painter Arie Smit was born in 1916 and was working as an artist in the colonial topographical service in Batavia, modern day Jakarta, when the Pacific war commenced. Captured by the Japanese he was taken first to Singapore and then to Thailand where he survived the infamous labour camps building the railway up to the Burmese border crossing – the 'Bridge on the River Kwai'.

Smit returned to Indonesia after the war and taught art in Bandung before moving to Bali to live as an artist from 1956. Smit's paintings have been exhibited in Bali and elsewhere in South-East Asia but his name will go down in the history books as the inspiration for the Young Artists movement. Arie Smit still lives in Ubud in Bali.

Theo Meier (1908-1982) A Swiss artist, Meier first visited Bali in 1936 and lived in Sanur before the war. Much of his prewar work was lost when the Japanese destroyed his Sanur studio but he returned to Bali after the war and lived for some time in Iseh in the house that Spies had established just before the war. In 1957 he moved to Chiang Mai in Thailand, where he lived until his death in 1982, although he was a frequent visitor to Bali.

Le Meyeur Belgian-born Le Mayeur moved to Bali in 1932 and lived there until his death in 1958. Le Mayeur succeeded in living the complete Balinese fantasy: marrying Ni Polok, a beautiful *legong* dancer. His fine house at Sanur is now preserved as a museum, in the shadow of the Hotel Bali Beach.

Donald Friend (1915-1990) Peripatetic Australian artist Donald Friend travelled to Bali in 1966 and, with occasional interruptions, spent most of his time there until he returned to Australia in 1977. He produced some of his finest work in Bali.

Antonio Blanco (1926-) Manila-born Spanish artist Antonio Blanco married a Balinese woman and moved to Bali in the late '50s. His house, near the river confluence in Campuan, is where he paints and where he lives the life of a colourful (and comfortable) artist. Visitors who pay the small admission price to enter his fine home often get a chance to hear his views on life, the universe and everything.

Han Snel (1925-) Dutch artist Han Snel was a conscript soldier sent to recapture the Dutch East Indies after the war. He deserted, took Indonesian citizenship and has lived in Bali since the 1950s, running one of Ubud's finest hotels with his Balinese wife. ■

Facts about Lombok

HISTORY

The earliest recorded society on Lombok was the relatively small kingdom of the Sasaks. The Sasaks were agriculturalists and animists who believed in the innate liveliness of 'inanimate' objects, as well as trees, plants and living creatures, and they practised ancestor and spirit worship. The original Sasaks are believed to have come overland from north-west India or Burma in waves of migration that predated most Indonesian ethnic groups. Few relics remain from the old animist kingdoms and the majority of Sasaks today are Muslim, although animism has left its mark on the culture. Not much is known about Lombok before the 17th century, at which time it was split into numerous, frequently squabbling states each presided over by a Sasak 'prince' – disunity which the neighbouring Balinese exploited.

Balinese Rule

In the early 1600s, the Balinese from the eastern state of Karangasem established colonies and took control of western Lombok. At the same time, the roving Makassarese crossed the strait from their colonies in western Sumbawa and established settlements in eastern Lombok. This conflict of interests ended with the war of 1677-78, which saw the Makassarese booted off the island, and eastern Lombok temporarily reverting to the rule of the Sasak princes. Balinese control soon extended east and by 1740 or 1750 the whole island was in their hands. Squabbles over royal succession soon had the Balinese fighting amongst themselves, and Lombok split into four separate kingdoms. It was not until 1838 that the Mataram kingdom subdued the other three, reconquered eastern Lombok (where Balinese rule had weakened during the years of disunity) and then crossed the Lombok Strait to Bali and overran Karangasem, thus reuniting the 18th-century state of Karangasem-Lombok.

While the Balinese were now the masters of Lombok, the basis of their control in western and eastern Lombok was quite different and this would eventually lead to a Dutch takeover. In western Lombok, where Balinese rule dated from the early 17th century, relations between the Balinese and the Sasaks were relatively harmonious. The Sasak peasants, who adhered to the mystical Wektu Telu version of Islam, easily assimilated Balinese Hinduism, participated in Balinese religious festivities and worshipped at the same shrines. Intermarriage between Balinese and Sasaks was common. The western Sasaks were organised in the same irrigation associations (the subak) that the Balinese used for wet-rice agriculture. The traditional Sasak village government, presided over by a chief who was also a member of the Sasak aristocracy, had been done away with and the peasants were ruled directly by the rajah or a land-owning Balinese aristocrat.

Things were very different in the east, where the recently defeated Sasak aristocracy hung in limbo. Here the Balinese had to maintain control from garrisoned forts and although the traditional village government remained intact, the village chief was reduced to little more than a tax collector for the local Balinese district head *(punggawa)*. The Balinese ruled like feudal kings, taking control of the land from the Sasak peasants and reducing them to the level of serfs. With their power and land-holdings slashed, the Sasak aristocracy of eastern Lombok were hostile to the Balinese. The peasants remained loyal to their former rulers and this enabled the aristocracy to lead rebellions in 1855, 1871 and 1891.

Dutch Involvement

The Balinese succeeded in suppressing the first two revolts, but the uprising of 1891 proved fatal. Towards the end of 1892 it too had almost been defeated, but the Sasak chiefs sent envoys to the Dutch resident in Buleleng (Singaraja) asking for help and inviting the Dutch to rule Lombok. This put the Dutch in the peculiar position of being invited to storm an island which they had barely taken so much as a sideways glance at. Although the Dutch planned to take advantage of the turmoil in Lombok they backed off from military action – partly because they were still fighting a war in Aceh (in Sumatra) and partly because of the apparent military strength of the Balinese on Lombok.

Dutch reluctance to use force began to dissipate when the ruthless Van der Wijck succeeded to the post of Governor General of the Dutch East Indies in 1892. He made a treaty with the rebels in eastern Lombok in 1894 and then, with the excuse that he was setting out to free the Sasaks from the tyrannical Balinese rule, sent a fleet carrying a large army to Lombok. Though the rajah quickly capitulated to Dutch demands, the younger Balinese princes of Lombok overruled him and attacked and routed the Dutch. It was a short-lived victory; the Dutch army dug its heels in at Ampenan and in September reinforcements began arriving from Java. The Dutch counterattack began, Mataram was overrun and the Balinese stronghold of Cakranegara was bombarded with artillery. The rajah eventually surrendered to the Dutch and the last resistance collapsed when a large group of Balinese, including members of the aristocracy and royal family, were killed in a traditional suicidal puputan, deliberately marching into the fire from Dutch guns.

Dutch Rule

The Dutch were now in control of Lombok and from here on the island becomes a case study in callous and inept colonial rule. A whole range of new taxes resulted in the impoverishment of the majority of peasants and the creation of a new strata of Chinese middlemen. The peasants were forced to sell more and more of their rice crop in order to pay the taxes, and as a result the amount of rice available for consumption declined by about a quarter from the beginning of the century to the 1930s. Famines took place from 1938 to 1940 and in 1949.

For nearly half a century, by maintaining the goodwill of the Balinese and Sasak aristocracy and using a police force that never numbered more than 250, the Dutch were able to maintain their hold on more than 500,000 people! The peasants wouldn't act against them for fear of being evicted from their land and losing what little security they had. There were several peasant uprisings against the Dutch but they were never more than localised rebellions, the aristocracy never supported them, and the peasants themselves were ill-equipped to lead a widespread revolt. Ironically, even after Indonesia attained its independence from the Dutch, Lombok continued to be dominated by its Balinese and Sasak aristocracy.

Post-Colonial Lombok

There are few physical reminders of Dutch rule on Lombok; the Dutch built little apart from the harbour at Ampenan (even then it was too small) and several aqueducts, some of which are still in use, including one at Narmada. The Balinese can still be found mostly in western Lombok, where they've retained their idiosyncratic Hindu customs. The relics of Balinese occupation and colonisation include their influence on the Sasak's unique Wektu Telu religion. Other leftovers of the Balinese presence include the temples they built at Cakranegara, Narmada, Lingsar and Suranadi, as well as the temple processions and ceremonies still seen on the island today.

Under Dutch rule the eastern islands of Indonesia, from Bali on, were grouped together as the Lesser Sunda Islands. When Sukarno proclaimed Indonesian independence on 17 August 1945, the Lesser Sunda Islands were formed into a single province called Nusa Tenggara, which means 'islands of the south-east'. This proved far too unwieldy to govern and it was subsequently divided into three separate regions – Bali,

West Nusa Tenggara and East Nusa Tenggara. Thus Lombok became part of West Nusa Tenggara in 1958.

GEOGRAPHY

Lombok is one of the 13,677 islands of Indonesia, all of which lie between continental Asia and Australia, forming a barrier between the Pacific and Indian Oceans. It is one of the two main islands of the province of West Nusa Tenggara, which is situated about halfway along the archipelago. Immediately to the west of Lombok is Bali, while to the east is Sumbawa, the other main island of West Nusa Tenggara. Lombok is 8° south of the equator and stretches some 80 km east to west and about the same distance north to south.

Lombok is dominated by one of the highest mountains in Indonesia. Soaring to 3726 metres, Gunung Rinjani can be seen, when not covered in cloud, from any point on the island. Situated in the north and well inland, Gunung Rinjani is an active volcano, which last erupted in 1901. It has a large caldera with a crater lake, Segara Anak, 400 metres below the rim and a new volcanic cone which has formed in the centre.

Central Lombok, south of Rinjani, is similar to Bali, with rich alluvial plains and fields irrigated by water flowing from the mountains. In the far south and east it is drier, with scrubby, barren hills resembling those in parts of Australia's outback. This area gets little rain, and often has droughts which can last for months. In recent years, a number of dams have been built, so the abundant rainfall of the wet season can be retained for year-round irrigation. The majority of the population is concentrated in the fertile but narrow east-west corridor sandwiched between the dry southern region and the slopes of Rinjani to the north.

Districts

Lombok is divided into three kabupaten (districts): West Lombok (capital Mataram); Central Lombok (capital Praya) and East Lombok (capital Selong). Mataram is also the administrative capital of the West Nusa Tenggara Province.

CLIMATE

In Lombok's dry season – from April to September – the heat can be so scorching that even in the mountains a sunshade or at least a broad-brimmed hat may be handy. At night the temperature can drop so much that a jumper (sweater) and light jacket are necessary, particularly inland and in the mountains. The wet season extends from October to March and January is often very stormy. Crossing from Bali by ferry during this period can be very unsettling with particularly rough seas, so if you've got a weak stomach, don't attempt it.

FLORA & FAUNA

Apart from banana and coconut palms, which grow in profusion over most of Lombok, the forests are confined largely to the mountain regions where they are extensive and dense, though logging is taking its toll. Teak and mahogany are among the forest timbers. Other native trees include bintangur, kesambi, bungur and fig, all of which are used widely for building houses and furniture. Much of the rest of the island is devoted to rice cultivation and the rice fields are every bit as picturesque as Bali's (though you don't see so many geese and ducks being taken out for their daily paddle in Lombok).

Several species of deer, including barking deer, as well as wild pigs, porcupines, snakes, numerous kinds of lizards – both large and small, frogs, turtles, long-tailed monkeys, civets and feral cattle are found here. Lombok is the furthest point west of Australia that the sulphur-crested cockatoo can be found.

The Wallace Line

In the 18th century, Sir Alfred Wallace postulated that, in terms of flora & fauna, Asia ended at Bali and Australasia began in Lombok. He observed that in Bali and to the west you find tropical vegetation, monkeys, tigers etc, while in the more arid country in

Lombok and further east there are thorny plants, cockatoos, parrots, lizards and marsupials. The so-called Wallace Line coincides with the narrow but exceptionally deep strait between Bali and Lombok, but it's now felt that the line is a fuzzy one. Though there are certainly differences in flora and fauna, these are believed to be due more to environmental differences than to the original distribution of species.

ECONOMY

Lombok's economy is based on agriculture and the rice grown here is noted for its excellent quality. However, the climate in Lombok is drier than Bali's and, in many areas, only one crop can be produced each year. In some years water shortages caused by poor rains can limit rice production, or even cause a complete crop failure, leading to rising prices and unstable markets. The last major crop failure was caused by drought in 1966, and as many as 50,000 people perished for want of food. In 1973 there was another bad crop, and though the outcome was not as disastrous, rice on Lombok rose to double the price it was on Bali.

Dam building and the improvement of agricultural techniques, partly a result of foreign-aid projects, will hopefully ensure better and more reliable crops in the future. Though rice is the staple crop there are small and large plantations of coconut palms, coffee, kapok, tobacco and cotton. In the fertile areas the land is intensively cultivated, often with a variety of crops planted together. Look for the vegetables and fodder trees planted on the levees between the padi fields. Crops such as cloves, vanilla, pepper and pineapples are gradually being introduced. Where possible, two rice crops are grown each year, with a third crop, perhaps of pineapples, grown for cash.

The people of Lombok do not share the same beliefs about the sea as the Balinese, and fishing is widespread along the coastline which, edged by coral, has many good spawning areas. Stock-breeding on Lombok is done only on a small scale.

Lombok is also keen to develop its tourist industry, perhaps inspired by Bali's obvious success. The first step in this direction was the development of Senggigi beach and particularly the up-market Senggigi Beach Hotel, owned by Garuda, the national airline. Both the Indonesian and the West Nusa Tenggara governments want to attract 'quality' tourists, and are promoting the establishment of high-class hotels, up to five stars. At Senggigi for example, apart from the existing mid-range to top-end hotels, there are two more nearing completion and construction is about to start on another two. On the beautiful and sparsely populated south coast, the government has acquired large tracts of beach-front land for 'co-developments', with foreign interests to provide the capital and perhaps some marketing connections. Roads are being improved and there's even talk of a new international airport somewhere east of Praya.

This is not good news for independent, low-budget travellers, or for the small local businesses which cater to them. Government policies are making it increasingly difficult to establish smaller places on the many beautiful but undeveloped beaches, and the type of development which the government would like is clearly beyond the capacity of local entrepreneurs to finance. There is also a concern that some of the budget places which already exist may be compulsorily acquired and/or closed down. The bright side of all this is that stringent environmental standards will be imposed on any new developments, hopefully preserving the ecology and natural beauty of Lombok, even if you won't be able to afford to enjoy it.

POPULATION & PEOPLE

Lombok has a population of just over two million, the majority living in and around the main centres of Ampenan, Cakranegara, Mataram, Praya and Selong. Almost 80% of the people are Sasak, about 20% are Balinese and there are minority populations of Chinese, Javanese and Arabs.

Sasaks

The Sasaks are assumed to have originally

come from north-western India or Burma, and the clothing they wear even today – particularly the women – is very similar to that worn in those areas. Sasak women traditionally dress in long black sarongs called *lambung* and short-sleeved blouses with a V-neck. The sarong is held in place by a four-metre long scarf known as a *sabuk*, trimmed with brightly coloured stripes. They wear very little jewellery and never any gold ornaments.

The Sasaks retain their own customs and culture and survive by cultivating rice, tobacco and various vegetables. They also keep small herds of cattle, water buffaloes and a few horses. Officially, most Sasaks are Muslims, but unofficially they retain many of their ancient animist beliefs and practices. Visitors would be very lucky to witness any traditional rituals, other than the extraordinary trial of strength known as *peresehan*. Unlike the Balinese they have not developed their dances or religious rituals as tourist attractions. Many of the traditional beliefs

have become interwoven with Muslim ideology.

There are a number of traditional Sasak villages scattered over the island; the most accessible are Sukarara and Sade in the south and Bayan and Senaru in the north.

Balinese

The Balinese originally settled in the west and the majority of Lombok's Balinese still live there today. They have retained their idiosyncratic Hindu customs, lifestyle and traditions intact. Historically, in their role as conquerors of Lombok, the Balinese ruled as feudal overlords and this, combined with their attitude of treating Lombok as a kind of penal colony for undesirable Balinese, caused friction and ill-will with the Sasaks. Even today, the Sasaks regard the Dutch as liberating them from an oppressive power. Occasionally you may still witness some animosity directed towards the Balinese, but it is rare to hear any criticism against the Dutch. The word Belanda (Hollander) is often called out as a welcome to Westerners passing through small villages.

By and large, however, the Balinese and Sasaks have co-existed amicably and the Balinese have made strong cultural contributions to the island. One of these contributions was the effect Balinese Hinduism had on the emergence of Lombok's Wektu Telu religion, a unique mix of animist, Islamic and Hindu philosophies. Other areas of influence include the spectacular temples they built at Cakranegara, Narmada, Lingsar and Suranadi which add greatly to the interest and beauty of Lombok's architecture and relics. The Balinese temple ceremonies and processions also contribute to the liveliness and attraction of the island.

The Balinese are also involved in commercial activities, particularly the tourist industry. Many of the cheap and mid-range hotels are run by Balinese, with the same friendliness and efficiency you find in Bali itself.

Chinese

The Chinese first came to Lombok with the

Dutch as a cheap labour force and worked as coolies in the rice paddies. Later they were given some privileges and allowed to set up and develop their own businesses, primarily restaurants and shops.

When the Dutch were ousted from Indonesia in 1949, the Chinese stayed and continued to expand their business interests. In the vicious reprisals following the abortive Communist coup of 1965, many Chinese were killed as suspected sympathisers. Even now their liberties and privileges are strictly curtailed by the government, which does not like the fact that the three million Chinese living in Indonesia control almost 70% of the economy. As a result they are prohibited from publishing their own newspapers, starting their own schools or forming political parties. Also they are not allowed dual citizenship and must adopt Indonesian surnames.

Most of the Chinese living in Lombok today are based in Ampenan and Cakranegara. Almost every shop and every second restaurant in Cakra is run or owned by the Chinese.

Arabs

In Ampenan there is a small Arab quarter known as Kampung Arab. The Arabs living here are devout Muslims who follow the Koran to the letter. They have no particular customs of their own but are inclined to hold themselves aloof from the other peoples of Lombok and marry amongst themselves. They are well educated and relatively affluent; many follow professions such as teaching and medicine, while others are insurance agents or office workers. Always friendly towards foreigners, they welcome the chance to practise their English and will often go out of their way to take you on sightseeing trips around the island.

ARTS
Weaving

Lombok is renowned for its traditional weaving. The techniques are handed down from mother to daughter. Each piece of cloth is woven on a handloom in established patterns and colours. Some fabrics are woven in as many as four directions and interwoven with gold thread. Many take at least a month to complete. Flower and animal motifs of buffaloes, dragons, lizards, crocodiles and snakes are widely used to decorate this exquisite cloth.

Several villages specialise in this craft and it is worth visiting one as a wider selection of cloth is often available. Sukarara, south of Cakranegara on the main road through Kediri and Puyung, and Pringgasela, in the mountains of East Lombok, are two villages that continue to produce fabrics using the *purbasari* technique.

Lombok also has a fine reputation for plaited basketware, bags and mats. Loyok and Kotaraja are two villages in East Lombok where this ancient Sasak craft is still practised.

Music & Dance

Lombok has some brilliant dances found nowhere else in Indonesia. But unlike Bali which encourages – in fact hustles – Westerners to go along to its dances, getting to see any on Lombok depends on word of mouth or pure luck. In West Lombok all the Balinese dances are performed, particular favourites being the Legong, Arja and Joget Bumbung. But there are also a wide variety of Sasak dances performed all over the island.

Cupak Gerantang This is a dance based on one of the Panji stories, an extensive cycle of written and oral stories originating in Java in the 15th century. Like Arjuna, Panji is a romantic hero and this dance is popular all over Lombok. It is usually performed at traditional celebrations, such as birth and marriage ceremonies, and at other festivities.

Kayak Sando This is another version of a Panji story but here the dancers wear masks. It is only found in Central and East Lombok.

Gandrung This dance is about love and courtship – *gandrung* means 'being in love' or 'longing'. It is a social dance, usually performed outdoors by the young men and women of the village. Everyone stands around in a circle and then, accompanied by a full gamelan orchestra, a young girl dances dreamily by herself for a time, before choosing a male partner from the audience to join her. The Gandrung is common to Narmada (West Lombok), Suangi and Lenek (East Lombok) and Praya (Central Lombok).

Oncer This is a war dance performed by men and young boys. It is a highly skilled and dramatic performance which involves the participants playing a variety of weird musical instruments in time to their movements. The severe black of the costumes is slashed with crimson and gold waist bands, shoulder sashes, socks and caps. It's performed with great vigour at adat festivals, both in central and eastern Lombok.

Rudat Also a traditional Sasak dance, the Rudat is performed by pairs of men dressed in black caps and jackets and black-and-white checked sarongs. The dancers are backed by singers, tambourines and cylindrical drums called *jidur*. The music, lyrics and costume used in this dance show a mixture of Islamic and Sasak cultures.

Tandak Gerok Traditionally a performance from eastern Lombok, the Tandak Gerok combines dance, theatre and singing to music played on bamboo flutes and the bowed lute called a *rebab*. Its unique and most attractive feature is that the vocalists imitate the sound of the gamelan instruments. It is usually performed after harvesting or other hard physical labour, but is also put on at adat ceremonies.

Genggong Seven musicians are involved in this particular performance. Using a simple set of instruments which includes a bamboo flute, a rebab and knockers, they accompany their music with dance movements and stylised hand gestures.

Barong Tengkok This is the name given to the procession of musicians who play at weddings or circumcision ceremonies.

Contemporary Music The Sasak enjoyment of music and dance extends to rock, and you're most likely to encounter it blaring from the cassette player in a taxi, bus or bemo. Indonesian performers, mostly from Java, do some pretty good cover versions of Western hits, as well as original rock songs, mostly in Indonesian and often with a strong reggae influence. Shops in Mataram have thousands of cassettes in stock, so if you hear something you like, note down the details and buy a copy to take home. Lombok bands can be heard at Senggigi, and young locals are enthusiastic on the dance floor.

Architecture
Traditional laws and practices govern Lombok's architecture, as they do any other aspect of daily life. Construction must commence on a propitious day, always with an odd-numbered date, and the frame of the building must be completed on that same day. It would be bad luck to leave any of the important structural work to the following day.

In a traditional Sasak village there are three types of buildings: the communal meeting hall or *beruga*, family houses or *bale tani*, and rice barns or *lumbung*. The beruga and the bale tani are both rectangular, with low walls and a steeply pitched thatched roof, though of course the beruga is larger. The arrangement of rooms in a family house is also very standardised – there is an open verandah or *serambi* in front, and two rooms on two different levels inside: one for cooking and entertaining guests, the other for sleeping and storage.

The lumbung, with its characteristic horseshoe shape, has become something of an architectural symbol on Lombok. You'll see rice barn shapes in the design of hotel foyers, entrances, gateways and even phone booths. On an island that has been regularly afflicted with famine, a rice barn must be a powerful image of prosperity.

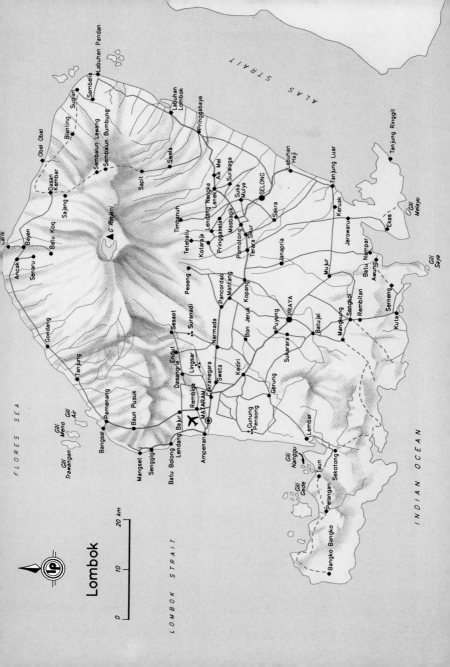

Top: Barong dance, Bali (TW)
Left: Two is enough, Bali (JL)
Right: Gunung Batur sunrise, Bali (JL)

CULTURE & CUSTOMS

Traditional law *(adat)* is still fundamental to the way of life on Lombok today, particularly customs relating to courting and marriage rituals, and circumcision ceremonies. Life is complex, rich and varied because both Balinese and Sasak adat systems are followed. In western Lombok you can see Balinese dances, temple ceremonies, and colourful processions with decorative offerings of flowers, fruit and food. However, these ceremonies are not nearly such an obvious part of daily life on Lombok as they are on Bali, and the idiosyncratic Sasak ceremonies are even less visible. Ask around and you can probably find when and where festivals are being held.

Birth

One of the Balinese rituals adopted by the Wektu Telu religion is a ceremony which takes place soon after birth and involves offerings to, and the burial of, the placenta. This ceremony is called *adi kaka* and is based on the belief that during the process of each birth, four siblings escape from the womb, symbolised by the blood, the fertilised egg, the placenta and the amniotic fluid that protects the foetus during pregnancy. If the afterbirth is treated with deference and respect, these four siblings will not cause harm to the newborn child or its mother. The placenta is buried close to the main entrance of the house, on the left-hand side if it's a girl child, on the right if it is a boy. Then follows a kind of 'christening' characterised by a ritualistic scattering of ashes known as *buang au* during which the priest names the newborn child. When the child is 105 days old it has its first haircut in another ceremony called the *ngurisang*.

Circumcision

The laws of Islam require that all boys be circumcised *(nyunatang)* and in Indonesia this is usually done somewhere between the ages of six and 11. Much pomp and circumstance mark this occasion on Lombok. The boys are carried through the village streets on painted wooden horses and lions with

tails of palm fronds. The circumcision is performed without anaesthetic as each boy must be prepared to suffer pain for Allah, and as soon as it is over they all have to enact a ritual known as the *makka* – a kind of obeisance involving a drawn kris dagger which is held unsheathed.

The makka ritual is upheld as a singular honour for the boys because it is regarded as a mystical rite, and apart from this occasion it is performed solely by adult men, and even then only rarely. After the ritual a party is held to celebrate the ceremony. If possible this is put on straight after a wedding, so that the same decorations – the marquee of bamboo supports and thatched palm, glasses, plates and chairs – can be used again.

Courting

Once again there's much pageantry in Sasak courting mores. Traditionally, teenage girls and boys are kept strictly apart except on certain festival occasions – weddings, circumcision feasts and the annual celebration of the first catch of the strange *nyale* fish at Kuta. On these occasions they are allowed to mingle with each other freely. However, if at one of these occasions a girl publicly accepts a gift from a boy – food for example – she is committed to marrying him.

Harvest time is another opportunity for courting. Traditionally the harvesting of rice was done with a razor-sharp bamboo cutter, and each head of grain was cut from the plant separately. This was the women's work; the men carried the sheaves away on shoulder-poles. Under the watchful eyes of the older men and women, a group of girls would approach the rice paddy from one side, a group of boys from the other. Each group would sing a song, each would applaud the other and each had a chance to circumspectly flirt with one another. This courtship ritual is still carried on in the more isolated, traditional villages.

Marriage Rituals

When the time comes to get married, young couples have a choice of three rituals: the first is an arranged marriage, the second a union between cousins and the third elopement. The first two are simple and uncomplicated: the parents of the prospective bridal couple meet to discuss the bride's dowry and sort out any religious differences. Having handled the business arrangements, the ceremony, *sorong serah*, is performed.

The third method is far more complicated and dramatic. Theoretically a young girl is forbidden to marry a man of lower caste, but this rule can be broken through kidnapping and eloping. As a result, eloping is still a widespread practice in Lombok, despite the fact that in most instances the parties involved – parents of both bride and groom and the couple intending to marry – are in the know. Originally it was used as a means of eluding other competitors for the girl's hand or in order to avoid family friction, but it also minimised the heavy expenses of a wedding ceremony!

The rules of this ritual are laid down and must be followed step by step. After the girl is spirited away by the boy, he is required to report to the kepala desa (head of the village) where he has taken refuge. He receives 44 lashes for such a 'disrespectful' action and has a piece of black cotton string wound around his right wrist to indicate to all that he has kidnapped his future bride. The kepala desa then notifies the girl's family through the head of their village. A delegation from the boy's family visits the girl's parents, and between them they settle on a price for the bride, which is distributed among members of the bride's family in recompense for losing her.

Traditional dowries are worked out according to caste differences; the lower his caste and the higher hers, the more he has to pay. There are four forms of payment: *bolongs* which are old Chinese coins with a square hole in the centre; *tumbaks*, ceremonial lances with gilt tips; *rombongs* which are rice bowls containing 225 bolongs and covered by a cloth half a metre square with a small knife or *pangat* placed across them; the fourth consists of coconut milk and red sugar. The rombongs are given to the mother of the bride and are symbolic of the milk she

fed her as a baby; the pangat is for the father of the bride. The bolongs must be kept within the family and handed down from generation to generation. The coconut milk and sugar, representing the bride and groom, are eaten and drunk together by the two families in celebration of the union.

Payment of 1000 bolongs, three tumbaks, one rombong and two coconuts is the going price when the boy and girl both come from the highest caste; 5000 bolongs, four tumbaks, one rombong and two coconuts is the price demanded when a boy from the second caste marries a girl from the highest; and 10,000 bolongs, seven tumbaks, one rombong and two coconuts is necessary when boys from the third and fourth castes marry 'above' themselves.

Once this has been settled the wedding begins. Generally the bride and groom, dressed in ceremonial clothes, are carried through the streets on a sedan chair on long bamboo poles. Boys carrying tumbaks lead the procession and the sounds of the gamelan (known as the *barong tengkok*) mingle with the shouts and laughter of the guests as the couple are swooped up and down and around on their way to the wedding place. Throughout the whole ceremony the bride, in an enormous gold and flowered headdress and dark sunglasses, must look downcast and unhappy at the prospect of leaving her family.

When the couple arrive they are seated with their backs to a wall, the man's headdress is removed and gold tincture is rubbed into his body and the faces of each. Finally the couple are given a ritual bathing, and then perform a series of symbolic acts, including feeding each other, to demonstrate their new status and duties to each other.

Death

The Balinese inhabitants of Lombok hold cremation ceremonies identical to those on Bali when one of their community dies, but members of the Wektu Telu religion and Muslims have their own rituals. The body of the dead person is washed and prepared for burial by relations in the presence of a holy man, and then wrapped in white sheets and sackcloth. The corpse is placed on a raised bamboo platform while certain sections of the Koran are read out and relations pray to Allah and call upon the spirits of their ancestors. The body is then taken to the cemetery and interred with the head facing towards Mecca. During the burial, passages of the Koran are read aloud in Sanskrit and afterwards more quotations from the Koran are recited in Arabic.

Relatives and friends of the dead place offerings on the grave – pieces of hand-carved wood if it's a man or decorative combs if it's a woman. Various offerings which include combs and cloth are also made in the village. Several ceremonies, involving readings from the Koran, are held on set days after the burial. These are performed on the third, seventh, 40th and 100th days after the death and a special ceremony, known as *nyiu*, is carried out after 1000 days have elapsed. During nyiu the grave is sprinkled with holy water and the woodcarvings or combs removed and stones put in their place.

A Muslim cemetery is typically a low hill covered with gnarled and twisted frangipani trees. Small 'headstones', about 40 cm high, stand under the trees. You'll see these cemetery mounds all over Lombok, and you might find them spooky places even if you're not superstitious.

There's also an interesting Chinese cemetery just north of Ampenan. Some of the graves are quite large and elaborately decorated. Wealthy Chinese are buried with many of the material possessions which they enjoyed during their life. Clothes, cooking equipment, radios, television sets and even motorbikes are said to be interred with their owners in this cemetery.

Contests

The Sasaks are fascinated by physical prowess and heroic trials of strength, fought on a one-to-one level. As a result they have developed a unique contest of their own and adapted others from nearby Sumbawa.

Peresehan This peculiar man-to-man combat is a great favourite all over Lombok. Usually held in the late afternoon in the open air, a huge crowd – all men apart from the occasional curious female traveller – gather together to watch two men battle it out with long rattan staves, protected only by small rectangular shields made from cow or buffalo hide. The staves are ceremoniously handed around the crowd lined up in a large roped-off area and then returned to the referee. With great drama the gamelan starts to play and two men, dressed in exquisite finery featuring turbans or head scarves and wide sashes at the waist, feign the movements of the contest about to be fought.

Having shown everyone how it is supposed to be done, the men look around the crowd for contestants, who are carefully chosen to match each other as closely as possible in height and strength. Skill is another matter altogether. Anyone can be chosen; some perform several times during the afternoon, others refuse to take part at all. While it is quite permissible to refuse, it is clearly of great status to win. Those who agree to participate must quickly find scarves to wrap around their heads and waists if they haven't already got them (the head gear and waist sash are supposed to have magical protective powers) then they take off their shirts and shoes, roll up their trousers, pick up their staves and shields and begin laying into each other.

The performance is umpired or refereed by the *pekembar*, usually one of the two men who select the contestants. If either of the fighters loses his headscarf or waistband the contest is stopped immediately until he puts it back on. It goes for three rounds – often five with more experienced fighters – or until one of the two is bleeding or surrenders. The pekembar can also declare the contest over if he thinks things are getting too rough. This often happens, for though the movements are very stylised, there is absolutely nothing carefully choreographed or rigged about the Peresehan – unlike Western wrestling matches. Both contestants generally finish with great welts all over them, the crowd gets wildly excited and each fighter has his own groupies cheering him on. At the end of each contest the winner is given a T-shirt or sarong, and the loser also gets some small token.

Before the event, as part of the spectacle and atmosphere, they often hold a greasy pole contest. Two tall poles are erected, topped by a gaily decorated, large wooden wheel with a number of goodies dangling from it, like cloth, bags and shorts. Amid much mirth and merriment two small boys attempt to clamber up the slippery pole and untie the loot. Strictly speaking they are supposed to untie one article at a time, slide down to the bottom and then climb up again for the next one. But a lot of 'cheating' goes on, particularly when the crowd's attention is trained on the more violent spectacle of the *peresehan*, which generally starts before this is over.

Lanca This particular trial of strength originated in Sumbawa, but the Sasaks have also adopted the *lanca* and perform it on numerous occasions, particularly when the first rice seedlings are planted. Like peresehan it is a contest between two well-matched men, who use their knees to strike each other. It involves a fair amount of skill and a lot of strength.

Sport

It's something of a generalisation, but it seems that the Sasaks are much keener on competitive sports than the Balinese. There's quite a large football (soccer) stadium near Cakranegara, and every town has a football field. Just north of Mataram is a substantial horse racing track, and there is a golf course nearby as well as a few tennis courts. Volleyball also seems to be popular.

RELIGION
Wektu Telu

Lombok has a unique religion, Wektu Telu, which originated in northern Lombok in a village called Bayan. Approximately 30% of the population of Lombok belongs to this faith, although the numbers are slowly diminishing as more and more young people turn to Islam.

The word *wektu* means 'result' in the Sasak language, while *telu* means 'three' and signifies the complex mixture of the three religions which comprise Wektu Telu: Balinese Hinduism, Islam and animism. Members of the Wektu Telu religion regard themselves as Muslims, although they are not officially accepted by the Muslims as such.

The fundamental tenet of Wektu Telu is that all important aspects of life are underpinned by a trinity. One example of this principle is the trinity of Allah, Mohammed and Adam. Allah symbolises the one true God, Mohammed is the link between God and human beings and Adam represents a being in search of a soul. The sun, the moon and the stars are believed to represent heaven, earth and water. The head, body and limbs represent creativity, sensitivity and control. Another trinity involves the three methods of reproduction – through seeds, eggs or sexual reproduction.

On a communal basis the Wektu Telus hold that there are three main duties which they must fulfil: belief in Allah, avoiding the temptations of the devil and co-operating with, helping and loving other people. The faithful must also pray to Allah every Friday, meditate and undertake to carry out good deeds.

The Wektu Telus do not observe Ramadan, the month-long period of abstinence so important in the Islamic faith. Their concession to it is a mere three days of fasting and prayer. They also do not follow the pattern of praying five times a day in a holy place, one of the basic laws of the Islamic religion. While prayer and meditation are of supreme importance in their daily rituals, the Wektu Telus believe in praying from the heart when and where they feel the need, not at appointed times in places specifically built for worship. According to them, all public buildings serve this purpose and all are designed with a prayer corner or a small room which faces Mecca. Wektu Telus do not make a pilgrimage to Mecca, but their dead are buried with their heads facing in that direction.

As for not eating pork, the Wektu Telus consider everything which comes from Allah to be good.

Castes Unlike the Muslims, the Wektu Telus have a caste system. There are four castes, the highest being Datoe, the second Raden, the third Buling and the fourth Jajar Karang.

Islam

More than half the population of Lombok are Muslims, the majority living in the central and eastern parts of the island. There are a few closed Muslim settlements on Lombok, Labuhan Lombok being one.

Islam reached Indonesia in the 13th century through peaceful Gujarati merchants arriving on the eastern coast of Lombok via Sulawesi (the Celebes), and on the west coast via Java. Today it is the professed religion of 90% of the Indonesian people and its traditions and rituals affect all aspects of their daily life. Friday afternoon is the officially decreed time for believers to worship and all government offices and many businesses are closed as a result. Arabic is taught in all Indonesian schools so the Koran can continue to be read and studied by successive generations. Scrupulous attention is given to cleanliness, including ritualistic washing of hands and face. The pig is considered to be unclean and is not kept or eaten in strict Muslim regions. Indonesian Muslims may have more than one wife though this is not common on Lombok, partly because few men can afford to keep a second wife. There are also many who scrimp and save throughout their lives to make the pilgrimage to Mecca to circle the black stone Ka'aba seven times. Those who have done this, *haji* if they are men, *haja* if they're women, are deeply respected.

Islam not only influences routine daily living and personal politics but also affects the politics of government. Orthodox Muslims demand that the whole population observe religious holidays and that the government protects and encourages Islam.

Since independence was declared, Indonesia has had two serious uprisings, both instigated by reactionary Muslim extremists. Following the 1972 elections four Muslim political parties were forced to amalgamate to become the United Development Party (PPP) and they lost political clout in the process. Power brokers around Suharto view the idea of a strong Islamic bloc in the People's Representative Council, the country's most influential policy-making body, as a security risk and a situation to be avoided at all costs.

The founder of Islam, Mohammed, was born in 571 AD and began his teachings in 612. He forged together an early Hebraic kind of monotheism and a latent Arab nationalism, and by 622 was beginning to gain adherents. Mohammed did not evince supernatural powers, but he did claim he was God's only teacher and prophet, charged with the divine mission of interpreting the word of God. Mohammed's teachings are collated and collected in the scripture of Islam, the Koran, which was compiled from his oral and written records shortly after his death. It is divided into 14 chapters and every word in it is said to have emanated from Mohammed and been inspired by God himself, in the will of Allah.

Much of the Koran is devoted to codes of behaviour, and much emphasis is placed on God's mercy to mankind. Mohammed's teachings are heavily influenced by two other religions – Judaism and Christianity – and there are some surprising similarities, including a belief in heaven, hell and one true God. The Koran has an account of creation almost identical to the biblical Garden of Eden, and other myths which are very similar to those in the old testament, such as Noah's Ark and Aaron's Rod.

The fundamental tenet of Islam is 'there is no god but Allah and Mohammed is his prophet'. The word 'Islam' means submission, and the faith demands unconditional surrender to the wisdom of Allah, not just adherence to a set of beliefs and rules. It involves total commitment to a way of life, philosophy and law. Theoretically it is a democratic faith in which devotion is the responsibility of the individual, unrestricted by hierarchy and petty social prerequisites, and concerned with encouraging initiative and independence in the believer. Nor, in theory, is it bound to a particular locale: the faithful can worship in a rice field, home, mosque or mountain. In practice it is a moralistic religion, and its followers are duty-bound to fulfil many restrictive rituals and laws such as the washing of hands and face, worshipping five times a day, reciting the Koran, almsgiving, fasting during the month of Ramadan, and saving to make the pilgrimage to Mecca. It is also fatalistic in that everything is rationalised as the will of Allah.

In Indonesia the dogma of Islam has become interwoven with aspects of animist, Hindu and Buddhist precepts, so developing a peculiar twist of its own. These precepts affect the Muslim way of life from peripheral details like architecture to fundamental attitudes like the treatment of women. Many Indonesian mosques do not have minarets and instead feature onion-shaped cupolas. The muezzin of Indonesia today are a dying breed; often, prerecorded tapes are played over a loudspeaker. Indonesian Muslims also pray in a distinctive manner with their hands pressed together, fingers extended, touching the chest, lips or forehead.

Muslim women in Indonesia are allowed more freedom and shown more respect than women in some other Third World countries. They do not have to wear facial veils, nor are they segregated or considered to be second-class citizens. There are a number of matrilineal and matriarchal societies and sometimes special mosques are built for women. Muslim men in Indonesia are only allowed to marry two women and must have the consent of their first wife to do so. This contrasts with Muslims in other parts of the world, who can have as many as four wives. Throughout Indonesia it is the women who initiate divorce proceedings where necessary, under the terms of their marriage agreement.

LANGUAGE

Most people on Lombok are bilingual, speaking their own ethnic dialect, Sasak, as well as the national language, Bahasa Indonesia, which they are taught at school and use as their formal and official mode of communication. Sasak is not derived from Malay, and has no relationship to Malay's modern successor, Bahasa Indonesia. So don't expect to be able to understand Sasak if you can speak Indonesian.

Apart from those working in the tourist industry, few people on Lombok speak English, and this includes police and other officials. Nevertheless, it seems that English is becoming more widely spoken, in Lombok as in the rest of the world. Travellers without a grasp of Bahasa Indonesia can get by, but some knowledge of it enhances an understanding of the island and could also be invaluable in an emergency, such as a lost passport or accident. Outside the main centres, finding anyone who can say more than a few phrases like 'hello', 'where do you come from' or 'good evening Mister', is extremely rare. If you can't speak Indonesian, arm yourself with a phrasebook and dictionary.

Greetings & Civilities

Sasak does not have greetings such as 'Good morning'. A Sasak approaching a friend working in the rice field might ask, in the local language, 'What are you doing?', even if it's perfectly obvious. Similarly, someone obviously going to the market might be asked 'Where are you going?', simply as a form of greeting. Local people will frequently ask foreigners questions like this in English (it may be their only English!) as a greeting. Don't get annoyed – they are just trying to be polite. A smile and a 'hello', or a greeting in Indonesian, is a polite and adequate response.

Facts for the Visitor

VISAS & EMBASSIES

Visitors from Australia, New Zealand, the UK, Canada, the USA and most of Western Europe don't need a visa to enter Indonesia. Provided you have a ticket out of the country and your passport has at least six months' validity at the time of your arrival, you'll be issued with a tourist card which is valid for a 60-day stay. Keep the card with your passport as you'll have to hand it back when you leave the country. Remember it's good for 60 days, not two months – some travellers have been fined for overstaying by only a day or so. It's not possible to get an extension on a tourist visa, unless there's a medical emergency or you have to answer legal charges. If you want to stay longer in Indonesia you have to leave the country and re-enter. Some long-term foreign residents have been doing this for years.

The only other catch is that you must enter and leave Indonesia through certain approved 'gateways'. In actual fact 99% of arrivals and departures are through these ports or airports anyway, but if Bali is just part of a larger Indonesian trip and you plan to enter or leave through a very strange place (which basically means Jayapura in Irian Jaya) then you'd better check the visa situation before you depart.

There are visas, particularly a business visitor's visa, which may be valid for a longer period. If you have one of these visas, you must register with an immigration office after being in Indonesia for three months.

In Denpasar the immigration office (*kantor imigrasi*) is in the south of Denpasar, just around the corner from the main post office at Jalan Panjaitan 4. If you have to visit this office, make sure you wear your most respectable clothes.

Indonesian Embassies & Consulates

Embassies and consulates outside Indonesia include:

Australia
Embassy, 8 Darwin Ave, Yarralumla, Canberra ACT 2600 (☎ 273 3222)
Consular offices in Sydney, Darwin, Melbourne and Perth
Canada
Embassy, 287 Maclaren St, Ottawa, Ontario K2P OL9 (☎ 236 7403/4/5)
Consular offices in Toronto and Vancouver
Denmark
Embassy, Orejoj Alle I 2900, Hellerup, Copenhagen (☎ 624422, 625439)
Germany
Embassy, Bernkasteler Strasse 2, 5300 Bonn 2 (☎ 310091)
Consular offices in Berlin, Bremen, Dusseldorf, Frankfurt, Hamburg, Hannover, Kiel, Munich and Stuttgart
Hong Kong
Consulate General, 127-129 Leighton Rd, Causeway Bay, Hong Kong (☎ 5 7904421/2/3/4)
Malaysia
Embassy, Jalan Tun Razak 233, Kuala Lumpur (☎ 421011, 421141, 421228, 421354, 421460)
Consular offices in Kota Kinabalu and Penang
Netherlands
Embassy, 8 Tobias Asserlaan, 2517 KC Den Haag (☎ 070 469796)
New Zealand
Embassy, 70 Glen Rd, Kelburn, Wellington (☎ 758695/6/7/8/9)
Norway
Embassy, Inkonitogata 8, 0258 Oslo 2 (☎ 441121)
Papua New Guinea
Embassy, Sir John Guisa Drive, Sel 410, Lot 182, Waigani, Port Moresby (☎ 253544, 253116/7/8)
Philippines
Embassy, 185/187 Salcedo St, Legaspi Village, Makati, Manila (☎ 855061/2/3/4)
Consular office in Davao
Singapore
Embassy, 7 Chatsworth Rd, Singapore 1024 (☎ 7377422)
Sweden
Embassy, Strandvagen 47/V, 11456 Stockholm (☎ 635470/1/2/3/4)
Switzerland
Embassy, 51 Elfenauweg, 3006 Bern (☎ 440983/4/5)
UK
Embassy, 157 Edgeware Rd, London W2 2HR (☎ 499 7661)

USA
Embassy, 2020 Massachusetts Ave NW, Washington DC 20036 (☎ 7755200/1/2/3/4)
Consular offices in Chicago, Honolulu, Houston, Los Angeles, New York and San Francisco

Foreign Embassies & Consulates

Despite Bali's great number of foreign tourists there is little diplomatic representation there. The embassies are all in Jakarta, the national capital, and most of the foreign representatives in Bali are consular agents (or honorary consuls) who can't offer the same services as a full consulate. For most nationalities this means a long trek to Jakarta if your passport is stolen. For emergency passports, US citizens have to go to the US Consulate General in Surabaya.

In Bali Fortunately for the great number of Australian visitors there is an Australian consulate on the Sanur side of Denpasar. The Australian consul will also help citizens of other Commonwealth countries while they're in Bali, including those from Canada, New Zealand, Papua New Guinea and the UK. (Commonwealth citizens, including Aussies, make up about 52% of visitors to Bali, so the office can be overworked at times.) Japan also has a full consulate in Denpasar, but all the others listed below are consular agents. Both the Australian consulate and the US consular agent emphasise the importance of visitors to Bali taking out adequate travel insurance, preferably with a cover for emergency medical evacuation.

Australia
Jalan Raya Sanur 146, Denpasar; PO Box 243 (☎ 35092/3, fax 31990)
France
Jalan Sekar Waru 3, Blanjong, Sanur Kauh (☎ 87152, 88090, fax 89054)
Germany
Jalan Pantai Karang 17, Sanur (☎ 88535, fax 88826)
Italy
Jalan Padanggalak, Sanur (☎ 88372, 88777)
Japan
Jalan Mochammad Yamin 9, Renon (☎ 34808, fax 31308)

Netherlands
Jalan Iman Bonjol 599, Denpasar (☎ 51094, 51497, fax 52777)
Norway & Denmark
Jalan Serma Gede 5, Sanglah, Denpasar (☎ 35098)
Sweden & Finland
Jalan Segara Ayu, Sanur (☎ 80228, 88407)
Switzerland
Jalan Legian Kelod, Legian (☎ & fax 51735)
USA
Jalan Segara Ayu 5, Sanur (☎ 80228, 88478, fax 87760)

In Jakarta

Australia
Jalan M H Thamrin 15, Jakarta (☎ 323109)
Canada
5th floor, Wisma Metropolitan, Jalan Jen Sudirman, Kav 29, Jakarta (☎ 510709)
Denmark
4th floor, Bina Mulia Building, Jalan H R Rasuna Said, Kav 10, Jakarta (☎ 518350)
Germany
Jalan M H Thamrin 1, Jakarta (☎ 323908, 324292, 324357)
India
Jalan Rasuna Said 51, Jakarta (☎ 518150)
Japan
Jalan M H Thamrin 24, Jakarta (☎ 324308, 324948, 325396, 325140, 325268)
Malaysia
Jalan Imam Bonjol 17, Jakarta (☎ 3321709, 336438, 332864)
Netherlands
Jalan H R Rasuna Said, Kav S3, Kuningan, Jakarta (☎ 511515)
New Zealand
Jalan Diponegoro 41, Jakarta (☎ 330552, 330620, 330680, 333696)
Norway
4th floor, Bina Mulia Building, Jalan H R Rasuna Said, Kav 10, Jakarta (☎ 517140, 511990)
Papua New Guinea
6th floor, Panin Bank Centre, Jalan Jen Sudirman, Jakarta (☎ 711218, 711225/6)
Philippines
Jalan Imam Bonjol 6-9, Jakarta (☎ 348917)
Singapore
Jalan Proklamasi 23, Jakarta (☎ 348761, 347783)
Sri Lanka
Jalan Diponegoro 70, Jakarta (☎ 321018, 321896)
Sweden
Jalan Taman Cut Mutiah 12, Jakarta (☎ 333061)

Thailand
    Jalan Imam Bonjol 74, Jakarta (☎ 343762, 349180)
UK
    Jalan M H Thamrin 75, Jakarta (☎ 330904)
USA
    Jalan Medan Merdeka Selatan 5, Jakarta (☎ 360360)

DOCUMENTS

Apart from your passport and visa, there is no particular documentation required to visit Bali and Lombok. Although a health certificate isn't necessary, you should get any vaccinations you need (see the Health section in this chapter). If you plan to drive yourself, or ride a motorbike, you should bring an International Driving Permit, endorsed for motorbikes if necessary. If you have a driving licence at home, an international permit is easy to obtain from your national motoring organisation. You should take out travel insurance, and it's a good idea to bring a copy of the policy and/or evidence that you're covered.

CUSTOMS

Indonesia has the usual list of prohibited imports including drugs, weapons and anything remotely pornographic. In addition, any printed matter in Indonesian, any books containing Chinese characters, Chinese medicines, cassette players, and Indonesian currency in excess of 50,000 rp are prohibited. You can bring in two litres of alcohol, 200 cigarettes, and cameras and film without restriction. If you have nothing to declare, customs clearance is quick and painless.

Indonesia is a signatory to the Convention on International Trade in Endangered Species (CITES) and as such bans the import and export of products made from endangered species. In particular, it is forbidden to export any product made from green sea turtles or turtle shells (see the Sea Turtles aside in the Facts about Bali chapter). In the interests of conservation, as well as conformity to customs laws, please don't buy turtle shell products.

It's also forbidden to export antiquities, ancient artefacts or other cultural treasures, so if someone tries to sell you an 'ancient' bronze statue, remind them of this law and they may decide it's not so old after all!

MONEY
Currency

The unit of currency in Indonesia is the rupiah (rp) – there is no smaller unit. You get coins of 5, 10, 25, 50 and 100 rp, but 5s and 10s are really only found in banks – nothing costs less than 25 rp. Notes come in 100, 500, 1000, 5000 and 10,000 rp denominations.

Exchange Rates

The exchange rate is not artificially set – it's a more-or-less free market rate which is reasonably stable as the rate of inflation is quite low. There's no black market.

A$1	= 1543 rp
US$1	= 1973 rp
£1	= 3485 rp
NZ$1	= 1106 rp
S$1	= 1179 rp
HK$1	= 254 rp

1000 rp	=	A$0.65
1000 rp	=	US$0.51
1000 rp	=	£0.29
1000 rp	=	NZ$0.90
1000 rp	=	S$0.85
1000 rp	=	HK$3.94

Carrying Money

It is illegal to bring more than 50,000 rp of Indonesian currency into or out of Indonesia. Bring your money in travellers' cheques, for security and convenience. US$, UK£ and A$ are the most negotiable, particularly in more remote areas. NZ$ can be difficult to exchange at a fair rate.

The major credit cards (Visa, MasterCard, American Express) are accepted by most of the bigger businesses that cater to tourists. You sign for the amount in local currency (rupiah) and the bill is converted into your domestic currency – the rate of exchange is usually quite good. You can also get cash advances on some credit cards.

Changing Money

Changing money is quite easy in Bali. The exchange rate for travellers' cheques may be slightly better than for cash, but is generally about the same. In the main tourist centres of Kuta, Sanur and Ubud there are lots of moneychangers, as well as the banks. The exchange rates offered by moneychangers are very similar to the banks, often better, and their service is quicker. The exchange counter at the airport sometimes gives lower rates than places in town.

Banking hours are from 8 am to noon, Monday to Friday and from 8 to 11 am on Saturday with some banks closing an hour earlier. Moneychangers have longer opening hours but usually open later in the morning.

Away from the main centres, the story is a little more complicated, though it's by no means difficult. Smaller towns may not have banks, and even if they do, you might not be able to exchange foreign currency. Even Ubud, the major tourist centre after the Kuta-Sanur area, doesn't have a bank, but the moneychangers there offer rates almost as good as in Kuta.

If you're out in the sticks, beware of the two standard Asian money problems. First of all it's difficult to change big notes – breaking a 10,000 rp note in an out-of-the-way location can be a major hassle. Secondly, away from the major centres notes tend to stay in circulation much longer and can get very tatty – when they get too dog-eared and worn looking they're difficult to spend. This isn't the major problem it can be in remote parts of Indonesia but it's instructive to compare the age of the notes you get in Kuta with those you get in areas with fewer tourists.

In Lombok, US$ are the most readily exchanged, though other currencies are negotiable in the banks. Exchange rates on Lombok are a couple of points lower than on Bali. Travellers' cheques can be changed in the main towns and tourist areas, but US$ cash may be more negotiable in remote areas. In Mataram there are a number of big banks and a few moneychangers. You can also change travellers' cheques at Senggigi and at the bank in Praya, but don't go further afield without making sure you have enough currency. Travellers often seem to find they spend longer on the Gili Islands than they had planned, and then have to make a money run back to Mataram when funds dwindle. When you get money changed in Lombok make sure they give you plenty of smaller denomination notes. In the villages it's often very difficult to get change for big notes.

Receiving Money

Having money sent to you in Bali is not easy, so don't wait until you're desperate. The Bank Ekspor-Impor is supposedly the best for inward money transfers from abroad. American Express also have a money transfer service called MoneyGram, which is expensive but quick and reliable. A cash advance on your credit card might be easier and cheaper than having money sent.

Costs

Bali and Lombok are great travel bargains. Of course you can spend as much as you want to – there are hotels where a double can be US$100 or more a night, where lunch can cost more than US$25 per person and a helicopter can be arranged for you if you're desperate to see Bali *fast*. At the other extreme you can find rooms for US$2 and get a filling meal from a warung (food stall) for a few hundred rupiah – say 50c.

In general, travellers who don't need air-con and 24-hour service will discover they can get good rooms almost anywhere on Bali for under US$10; sometimes as little as US$3 will get you a fine room. On Lombok, cheap rooms are not as numerous or as nice, but are still under US$10. Steering clear of the international air-con places once again, US$8 will get you an excellent meal for two, with a big cold bottle of beer at most tourist restaurants, while even at relatively flashy places like Poppies in Kuta it's hard to spend more than US$15 for two. A good meal for two for US$5 is no problem and you don't

even have to get into the really rock-bottom warungs to eat for under US$2.

Transport is equally affordable – remember that Bali and Lombok are small islands. *Bemos* (usually minibuses) are the local form of public transport and they're pretty cheap – a 40-km trip will cost you about 2000 rp, say US$1. If you want your own wheels you can hire a motorbike for around US$6 a day, a Suzuki jeep for US$22 a day, or charter your own bemo, complete with driver, from about US$20 a day.

Entry Charges Nearly every temple or site of touristic interest will levy an entry charge or ask for a donation from foreigners – which means a Javanese just as much as a German, as any non-Balinese is a foreigner. Usually the charge will be 250 rp, occasionally less, very occasionally more. If there is no fixed charge, and a donation is requested, 250 rp is also a good figure – ignore the donation book figures indicating that somebody has just paid over 2500 rp. Zeros are easy to add. Entry charges, a few places like Narmada apart, are not so common on Lombok, but they'll usually want a donation on some pretext, and it's good manners to make one.

At some temples you may be asked to rent a temple scarf though this may be included in the entry charge or donation. Buy your own at any market or general store – they only cost a few hundred rupiah and if you do much temple visiting they soon pay for themselves as well as allowing you to feel 'well dressed' at temples where scarves are not available.

Many government-run tourist attractions, such as the Bali Museum in Denpasar and the Bali Barat National Park, also charge an insurance premium of 50 rp or so on top of the admission price. This supposedly covers you against accident or injury while you're there, or maybe it just covers the management against you suing them. It won't add greatly to your peace of mind, but it's only a few cents and you have to pay it anyway.

Tipping

Tipping is not a normal practice in Bali or

Lombok so please don't try to make it one. The expensive hotels slap a 21% service and government tax on top of their bills but there are no additional charges at lower-priced establishments.

Begging

You may be approached by the occasional beggar on the streets of Kuta and Legian – typically a woman with a young child. Begging has no place in traditional Balinese society, so it's likely that at least some of these beggars come from elsewhere. Begging is virtually unknown on Lombok, but if children think you're going to give something away, you'll see nothing but out-stretched palms.

Bargaining

Many everyday purchases in Bali require bargaining. This particularly applies to clothing and arts and crafts, but can also apply to almost anything you buy in a shop. Meals in restaurants, accommodation and transport are generally fixed price although when supply exceeds demand you may often find hotels willing to bend their prices a little, rather than see you go next door. This particularly applies in places like Kuta, Lovina and Candidasa where there are lots of 'next doors' to go to! On the other hand, bemo drivers have a well-earned reputation for taking foolish Westerners for whatever they're willing to pay. In that case your bargaining has to be a matter of finding the right price and thus beating down their excessive demands to a proper level. The easiest way is simply to ask another passenger what the *harga biasa* (regular price) is. Then you offer the correct fare and don't accept any arguments.

In an everyday bargaining situation the first step is to establish a starting price. It's usually easiest to simply ask the sellers their price rather than make an initial offer, unless you know very clearly what you're willing to pay. You then have to make a counter offer, but you can start the psychological game moving your way immediately if you can get the seller to cut the price before you even start. Ask if that is the 'best price' and chances are you'll find it's cheaper straight off. Your counter offer should be a worth-while notch below what you're willing to pay, but not so low as to be ludicrous. If your offer is simply too low then either the seller is going to decide you're just uninterested or you're going to have to start moving in his direction immediately. Making a silly offer is, incidentally, a good way of getting rid of a persistent salesperson. But be careful, lots of people have ended up buying things they didn't want because their silly offer was accepted!

Just what your initial offer should be depends to a large extent on the item for sale and who is selling it. As a rule of thumb your starting price could be anything from one-third to two-thirds of the asking price – assuming that the asking price is not com-pletely crazy. Then, with offer and counter offer, you move closer to an acceptable price – the seller asks 25,000 rp for the painting, you offer 15,000 rp and so on until eventu-ally you compromise at 20,000 rp – 22,000 rp if they're a better bargainer, 18,000 rp if you are! Along the way you can plead your end-of-trip poverty or claim that Ketut down the road is likely to be even cheaper. The seller is likely to point out the exceptional quality and plead poverty too. An aura of only mild interest helps – if you don't get to an acceptable price you're quite entitled to walk away. Actually walking away often does help!

A few rules apply to good bargaining. First of all it's not a question of life or death where every rupiah you chisel away makes a differ-ence. Bargaining should be an enjoyable part of shopping in Bali so treat it as such; main-tain your sense of humour and keep things in perspective – remember, 1000 rp is about half a US$1. Secondly, when you reach a price, you're committed. When your offer is accepted you have to buy it, don't decide then that you don't want it after all. Finally, the best buy is said to be at the 'morning price'. The seller feels that making a sale to the first potential customer of the day will ensure good sales for the rest of the day. So the trader is more likely to settle for a lower bid from the early-morning customer.

Bargaining is nowhere near such an obvious aspect of everyday life on Lombok, nor is it so much fun. Nevertheless you are expected to bargain, particularly for items like antiques, cloth or basketware. If you manage to get the price down to half, you can consider yourself a skilful bargainer on Lombok, whereas on Bali this is about the norm. Usually you will end up paying about two-thirds of the starting price on Lombok and sometimes you may only be able to get a nominal amount knocked off the starting figure.

If you have any difficulty knowing when and where to bargain in Lombok, don't be embarrassed to ask. While they are more reserved than the Balinese and may not volunteer this information, they will soon let you know whether it's on or not. In fact they will probably give you a line about special Lombok prices and advise you without so much as a blink of the eye that you will pay twice as much on Bali for a similar item. A very dubious statement! However, there is no doubt that you can get some very good bargains on Lombok if you're prepared to take your time.

As with Bali, restaurant prices on Lombok are invariably fixed and, because Lombok has a smaller range of budget accommodation, the competition is not so keen and hotels are less likely to drop their prices. Unlike Bali, many shops on Lombok have fixed prices but, once again, if you have any doubts ask whether it's permissible to bargain. Nearly every village on Lombok has a market at least once a week where there are numerous stalls selling food, clothes, handicrafts and many other items. Markets are great places for bargaining.

Don't get hassled by bargaining. Remember that no matter how good you are at it there's always going to be someone who is better, or will boast about how they got something cheaper than you did. Don't go around feeling that you're being ripped off all the time. There are obviously times when you will be, but both Bali and Lombok are very cheap places to travel around and you should remember that in most instances the locals will pay less than foreigners. Both the Balinese and the Sasaks consider this to be eminently fair, as in their eyes, all Westerners are wealthy, as are Javanese wealthy enough to travel; and as for Japanese visitors ... With handicrafts and clothes, remember that quality is more important than price – when you get that treasure home, you won't be worried that you might have got it for a few thousand rupiah less.

If you are accompanied by a local on a shopping spree you will find it harder to get down to bargaining basics. Whether guides get some commission for taking visitors to certain stalls or not, they will tend to feel very uncomfortable seeing one of their fellows being 'beaten down' by a foreigner, particularly one who is a shrewd bargainer. It reflects on both the guide and the shopkeeper, and each loses face. The advantages of finding things more easily and quickly is often outweighed by this local loyalty.

WHEN TO GO

The cooler dry season, from April to October, is the best time to visit Bali or Lombok, but there are also distinct tourist seasons which alter the picture. Remember that Bali is Australia's favourite Asian getaway, so from Christmas till the end of January Bali can be packed out with Australians, and at that time of year the air fares from Australia are also higher. The Australian school holidays, in early April, late June-early July, and late September, also see Australians flocking in. The European summer holidays also bring crowds – July for the Germans, August for the French.

The Muslim fast of Ramadan applies to Lombok but it is unlikely to pose any major problems. During the month of Ramadan Muslims are not allowed to eat, drink or smoke between sunrise and sunset, so some restaurants are closed during the day. The end of Ramadan is a major celebration and holiday, so transport and accommodation may be more crowded, but it's an interesting time to be there.

WHAT TO BRING

'Bring as little as possible' is the golden rule of good travelling. It's usually better to leave something behind and have to get a replacement when you're there than to bring too much and have to lug unwanted items around.

You need little more than lightweight clothes – the temperature is uniformly tropical year-round so short-sleeved shirts or blouses and T-shirts are the order of the day. A light sweater is, however, a good idea for cool evenings and particularly if you're going up into the mountains. Kintamani, Penelokan and the other towns in the central mountains can actually get bloody cold, so a light jacket may also be necessary. You'll also need more protective gear if you're going to be travelling by motorbike. Bare skin is never a good idea and up in the hills travelling by motorbike can get very chilly indeed.

Even down near the coast a little protection can be a good idea to avoid sunburn. A hat and sunglasses are also useful to ward off that tropical sun. On the beach almost anything – as long as it's something – goes. Bikini tops are a rare sight on Bali's tourist beaches, but bring one for more remote beaches, and definitely if you're going to Lombok.

Remember that in much of Asia, including Bali and particularly Lombok, shorts are not considered polite attire for men or women. Similarly, sleeveless singlet tops are not considered respectable – you're supposed to cover your shoulders and armpits. At Kuta and the other beach resorts shorts and singlets have become a part of everyday life, and in any case tourists are considered a little strange and their clothing habits are expected to be somewhat eccentric. However in temples and government offices, you're expected to be 'properly' dressed, and shorts, singlets and thongs don't fulfil that expectation.

To be properly dressed in a temple you should also wear a temple scarf – a simple sash loosely tied around your waist. Many of the larger temples rent them out for about 200 rp, but you can buy one yourself for 1000 rp or less. You'll soon recoup the cost if you visit many temples, and you're certain of being politely dressed even at temples where there are no scarves for rent.

The Indonesian authorities have become somewhat fed up with Western slobs turning up at public offices dressed in cast-offs. The 'how to dress' posters you see in Bali and Lombok may be amusing but there's a message behind them. If you want to renew a visa, or even get a local driving licence, ask yourself how you'd dress in a similar situation back home.

TOURIST OFFICES

Unlike many other Asian countries, Indonesia does not have a national tourist office pumping out useful brochures nor a network of branches with all the facts at their fingertips. What it does have tends to be piecemeal, and variable from place to place. Garuda, the

Indonesian airline, has better information brochures than you're likely to find from the government offices. In Denpasar there is both the Badung District tourist office (for southern Bali) and a Bali government tourist office. In Kuta, the tourist office on the corner of the airport road and Jalan Bakungsari is pretty good. The local office in Ubud is also good.

In Lombok the West Nusa Tenggara regional tourist office is at Jalan Langko 70, Ampenan, diagonally opposite the telephone office. It has a couple of coloured brochures with information on places of interest, accommodation, restaurants and so on, plus a map of Ampenan, Mataram, Cakranegara and Sweta.

BUSINESS HOURS
Most government offices are open from 8 am daily except Sunday and close at 3 pm Monday to Thursday, 11.30 am on Friday and 2 pm on Saturday. Usual business office hours are from 8 am to 4 pm, Monday to Friday. Some also open on Saturday morning. Banks are open from 8 am to noon, Monday to Friday and from 8 to 11 am on Saturday.

HOLIDAYS & FESTIVALS – BALI
Balinese calendars, with illustrations for each day indicating what activities that day is auspicious for, are popular souvenirs. Apart from the everyday Western calendar, the Balinese also use two local calendars, the *saka* and the *wuku* calendar. The wuku calendar is used to determine festival dates. The calendar uses 10 different weeks, each from one to 10 days and all running simultaneously! The intersection of the various weeks determines auspicious days. The seven-day and five-day weeks are of particular importance. A full year is made up of 30 individually named seven-day weeks.

The Galungan festival, Bali's major feast, is held throughout the island and is an annual event in the wuku year. During this 10-day period all the gods, including the supreme deity Sanghyang Widi, come down to earth for the festivities. Barongs prance from temple to temple and village to village.

The last and most important day of the 10-day festival is called Kuningan. Forthcoming dates include:

	Galungan	Kuningan
1992	16 July	26 July
1993	11 February	21 February
	9 September	19 September
1994	7 April	17 April
	3 November	13 November

There are numerous festivals around the time of Galungan and Kuningan. These include:

Place	Festival	Date
Batukau	Pura Luhur	Galungan + 1 day
Serangan	Pura Sakenan	Kuningan & Kuningan + 1 day
Tanah Lot	Pura Tanah Lot	Kuningan + 4 days
Ulu Watu	Pura Luhur	Kuningan + 10 days
Goa Lawah	Pura Goa Lawah	Kuningan + 10 days
Mengwi	Pura Taman Ayun	Kuningan + 10 days

The Hindu saka calendar is a lunar cycle that more closely follows our own year in terms of the length of the year. Nyepi is the major festival of the saka year – it's the last day of the year, the day after the new moon on the ninth month. Nyepi also marks the end of the rainy season and the day before is set aside as a day of purification across the island; absolutely nothing goes on – like a sort of super-Sabbath. That night evil spirits are noisily chased away with cymbals, gongs, drums and flaming torches and on Nyepi everyone stays quietly at home. Nyepi generally falls towards the end of March or the beginning of April.

Certain major temples celebrate their festivals by the saka rather than the wuku calendar. This makes the actual date difficult to determine from our calendar since the lunar saka does not follow a fixed number of days like the wuku calendar. The full moons around the end of September to the beginning of October or from early to mid-April are often the times for important temple festivals.

The Balinese also have a major annual festival by the Western calendar – Indonesian Independence Day falls on 17 August, celebrating Sukarno's proclamation of independence on that day in 1945. Final freedom from the Dutch did not come until several years later.

HOLIDAYS & FESTIVALS – LOMBOK

Lombok is mainly Muslim, but also has Bali Hindus and Wektu Telus, and all three religions have their own holidays and festivals.

Most of Lombok's religious festivals take place at the beginning of the rainy season around October to December, or at harvest time around April to May. During these periods there are celebrations in villages all over the island, and people dress in their most resplendent clothes and flaunt status symbols such as sunglasses and watches. Wooden effigies of horses and lions are carried in processions through the streets and the sound of the gamelan reaches fever pitch.

While most of these ceremonies and rituals are annual events, most of them do not fall on specific days in the Western calendar. This means you have to keep your eyes open and listen carefully in order to find out when they are being held. The Muslim year is shorter than the Western one so their festivals and events fall at a different time each year:

Festival	1992	1993
Ramadan	6 March	24 February
Idul Fitri	1 April	22 March
Maulid Nabi	9 September	30 August
Mi'raj Nabi	31 January	21 January

The Muslim Idul Fitri festival, at the end of Ramadan, can be a particularly difficult time for travellers to get around. All public transport is booked out and bemos double in price; accommodation can also be difficult to find. If you're in Lombok at this time,

don't plan on travelling anywhere. Stay put, preferably in a Balinese-run hotel, but don't miss the celebrations on the streets. Other festivals and ceremonies include:

Ramadan Ramadan is the ninth month of the Muslim calendar, the month of fasting or *puasa*. During Ramadan people rise early for a big breakfast, then abstain from eating, drinking and smoking until sunset. Many visit family graves and royal cemeteries, recite extracts from the Koran, sprinkle the graves with holy water and strew them with flowers. Special prayers are said at mosques and at home. During this time many restaurants are closed, and foreigners eating or smoking in public are regarded with contempt that can border on aggression. By the end of the month, many Muslims' tempers are frayed to snapping point. It is more difficult to travel on Lombok during Ramadan, as tourist and transport services may be curtailed, often in a way that is unexpected and unpredictable for a visitor.

Puasa This Wektu Telu festival is held in deference to the Muslim period of abstinence. The three days of fasting and prayer begin at the same time as Ramadan.

Idul Fitri Also called Hari Raya, this is the first day of the 10th month of the Muslim calendar and the end of Ramadan. This climax to a month of austerity and tension is characterised by wild beating of drums all night, fireworks and no sleep. At 7 am everyone turns out for an open-air service. Women dress in white and mass prayers are held followed by two days of feasting. Extracts from the Koran are read and religious processions take place. Gifts are exchanged in this time of joy and mutual forgiveness. Pardon is asked for past wrongdoings. Everyone dresses in their finest and newest clothes and neighbours and relatives are visited with gifts of specially prepared food. It is traditional to return to one's home village, so many Indonesians are travelling at this time. At each house visited, tea and sweet cakes are served and visiting continues until all the relatives have been seen.

Hari Raya Ketupat This is a Wektu Telu celebration held at Batulayar, near Senggigi, seven days after the end of Ramadan.

Idul Adha This day of sacrifice is held on the 10th day of the 11th month of the Muslim calendar. People visit the mosque and recite passages from the Koran.

Maulid Nabi Mohammed Also called Hari Nata, Mohammed's birthday is held on the 12th day of the 12th month of the Arabic calendar.

Mi'raj Nabi Mohammed This festival celebrates the ascension of Mohammed.

Pujawali This is a Bali Hindu celebration held every year at the Kalasa Temple at Narmada in honour of the god Batara, who dwells on Lombok's most sacred mountain, Gunung Rinjani. At the same time the faithful who have made the trek up the mountain and down to Lake Segara Anak hold a ceremony called *pekelan*, where they throw gold trinkets and objects into the lake.

Perang Ketupat The annual rain festival at Lingsar, between October and December, when the Wektu Telus and the Balinese Hindus give offerings and pray at the temple complex, then come out and pelt each other with *ketupat*, sticky rice wrapped in banana leaves (see the Lingsar section in the West Lombok chapter).

Harvest Ceremony Held at Gunung Pengsong some time around March or April as a thanksgiving for a good harvest, this Bali Hindu ceremony involves a buffalo being dragged up a steep hill and then sacrificed.

Pura Meru A special Bali Hindu ceremony held every June at full moon in this splendid Balinese temple in Cakranegara.

Bersih Desa This festival occurs at harvest time. Houses and gardens are cleaned, fences whitewashed, roads and paths repaired. Once part of a ritual to rid villages of evil spirits, it is now held in honour of Dewi Sri, the rice goddess.

Independence Day This marks the anniversary of Indonesian independence from Holland in 1945. It's celebrated all over Indonesia on 17 August and is the biggest Indonesian national holiday. Dances, public entertainment, performances, processions, sporting events – you name it, it all happens. School children and young girls and boys spend months preparing for it.

POST & TELECOMMUNICATIONS
Postal Rates
Airmail charges for postcards are: Australia 600 rp, Europe 800 rp and the USA 1000 rp. Sending large parcels (maximum size, 10 kg) is quite expensive, but at least you can get them properly wrapped and sealed at low cost from nearly every post office or postal agency. Mail charges from Lombok are slightly higher, as all mail is sent via Bali.

Receiving Mail
There are poste restante services at the various post offices around Bali and since the Denpasar post office is so inconveniently situated, you're better off having mail sent to you at Kuta, Ubud, Singaraja or other more convenient locations. Mail should be addressed to you with your surname underlined or in capital letters, then Kantor Pos (which, of course, means post office), the town name, then Bali, Indonesia.

If you're having mail sent to you on Lombok you may come across a few hassles collecting it. There is only one post office on Lombok with a poste restante service. It's on the edge of Mataram, as inconveniently situated as the one in Denpasar, and though there's another post office in Ampenan all poste restante mail is automatically redirected to the Mataram office. Other post offices on Lombok are at Cakranegara, Lembar, Narmada, Praya, Tanung and Selong.

Telephone
The telecommunications service in Indonesia is provided by Permuntel, a government monopoly. It's usually possible to get onto the international operator or get an international connection within half an hour or so, but it can take longer.

Many phone numbers changed during 1991, especially in southern Bali. (For example, all numbers in Sanur had an extra 8 added before the first digit.) If a phone number in this book is wrong, that's probably the reason. Unfortunately, phone books are hard to come by, but the directory assistance operators (☎ 108) are very helpful and

some of them do speak English. If you call directory assistance, and have to spell out the name of the establishment whose number you want, try to use the Alpha, Bravo, Charlie system of saying the letters. It's widely understood, whereas the usual English letter pronunciation (ay, bee, see etc) can get hopelessly confused with the way letters are pronounced in Indonesian. If you don't know the Alpha Bravo Charlie system, just use simple, common words to help the operators identify the letters.

Permuntel has a number of *kantor telekomunikasi* (telecommunications offices) from which you can make international and long-distance calls. Sample costs for a three-minute call from Denpasar are 16,650 rp to Australia, New Zealand and the USA, 15,600 rp to Canada, and 18,540 rp to Western Europe and the UK. On Lombok, from the telephone office in Mataram, sample costs for a three-minute call include 25,025 rp to Australia, New Zealand and the USA, and 28,600 rp to Western Europe and the UK.

There are also private telephone offices called *wartels* (warung telekomunikasi) in various places, including Kuta, Sanur and Lovina. These provide a pretty good service at similar prices to the Permuntel offices. Public phones are only for local calls. You cannot make direct-dial international calls yourself, but there are some Home Country Direct phones, where one button gets you through to your home country operator and you pay with a credit card or reverse the charges. One of these can be found at the airport, outside the international terminal, and another in the Hotel Bali Beach. There are card phones in several locations including the airport's domestic departure lounge.

Reverse-charge calls from a telephone office can be very time-consuming, but some travellers believe it is cheaper to call reverse charge than to pay on the spot. This isn't true in my case – a three-minute reverse-charge call from Sanur to Melbourne appeared on my phone bill at A\$15.80, but paying in Sanur would have cost about 17,000 rp, or A\$11.33. It probably depends on your home telephone company, and whether you pay the phone bill yourself at the number you call.
James Lyon

Fax, Telex & Telegraph
Fax and telegraph services are available in the main Permuntel offices, and many hotels and other businesses now have a fax number.

TIME
There are three time zones in Indonesia. Bali and Lombok and the islands of Nusa Tenggara to the east are on Central Standard Time, which is eight hours ahead of GMT or two hours behind Australian Eastern Standard Time.

Thus, not allowing for variations due to daylight-saving time, when it's noon in London it's 8 pm in Bali and Lombok, 8 pm in Perth, 10 pm in Sydney and Melbourne, 7 am in New York and 4 am in San Francisco and Los Angeles.

As Bali is close to the equator, days and nights are approximately equal in length. The sun pops up over the horizon at 6 am and drops down the other way at 6 pm. And what spectacular orange-fire sunsets Bali can provide!

ELECTRICITY
Electricity is usually 220-240 volts AC in Bali and Lombok. In some smaller villages in Bali, and many in Lombok, it's 110 volts, so check first. It's usually fairly reliable, and blackouts are not an everyday occurrence, though the electricity grid, like the telecommunications network, is running at its maximum capacity. In many small towns, and even in parts of larger towns, electricity is a recent innovation – if you travel around very much you're likely to stay in the odd *losmen* where lighting is provided with oil lamps. Even where there is electricity you're likely to find that the lighting can be very dim. Lots of losmen seem to have light bulbs of such low wattage that you can almost see the electricity crawling laboriously around the filaments. If 25 watts isn't enough to light your room it might be worth carrying a more powerful light bulb with you.

Street lighting can also be a problem – there often isn't any. If stumbling back to your losmen down dark alleys in Kuta or through the rice paddies in Ubud doesn't appeal, a torch (flashlight) can be very useful.

LAUNDRY

All the fancier hotels advertise laundry services, and charge quite steeply for them. The cheaper places don't advertise the fact, but generally will wash clothes for you at a pretty reasonable price. Allow 24 hours, or a bit longer if it's been raining and the clothes won't dry. Laundry charges are directly proportional to the cost of staying at the hotel.

WEIGHTS & MEASURES

All of Indonesia, including Bali and Lombok, uses the metric system. For those accustomed to the imperial system, there is a conversion table at the back of this book.

BOOKS & MAPS
Early Accounts

Credit for launching today's image of Bali as an island paradise can be given to Gregor Krause, a German doctor who worked for the Dutch government in the southern Bali town of Bangli in 1912. Krause was a talented photographer as well as a doctor and his images of Bali, published in Germany in 1920 in two volumes under the title *Bali*, was an instant success. It was later republished in a single volume and in many other languages.

Krause's images of Bali as an exotic jungle paradise with colourful ceremonies and handsome people played a large part in the Western fascination with Bali in the late '20s and '30s. Krause can also claim credit for bringing the bare Balinese breast to Western attention, an aspect of Bali to which he paid great attention in both photographs and prose. A selection of his pioneering photographs and text have recently been published as *Bali 1912* (January Books, Wellington, 1988), a book of great interest but such stunningly bad design that it's almost painful to look at.

Art, Culture & History There are many interesting books on Bali's art and culture but the best is still *Island of Bali* by the Mexican artist Miguel Covarrubias. First published in 1937 by Alfred A Knopf and widely available today as an Oxford University Press Paperback, this book is a very worthwhile investment for anybody with a real interest in Bali; few people since have come to grips with Bali as well as Covarrubias. It's readable yet learned, incredibly detailed yet always interesting. Every subsequent guide to Bali owes this book a great debt. The closing speculation (remember, this was written in the 1930s) that tourism may spoil Bali is thought-provoking but it's also a real pleasure to discover, through reading the book, how much of Bali is still exactly the way Covarrubias describes it.

The Oxford Paperback series also includes *Dance & Drama In Bali* by Beryl de Zoete & Walter Spies. Originally published in 1938 this excellent book draws from Walter Spies' deep appreciation and understanding of Bali's arts and culture. He was yet another of the long-term Western visitors to Bali in the 1930s.

The '30s Visitors Western visitors to Bali in the '30s were a cultured and varied lot, many of whom had an irresistible urge to put their experiences down on paper. Fortunately many of those classic early accounts have been republished. Oxford University Press's Asian-based Oxford Paperback series is doing great work in this area. Hickman Powell's very readable *The Last Paradise* (Oxford Paperback) was first published in 1930 and was one of the first signs of the explosion of Western accounts which followed. At times, however, it gets quite cloyingly over-romantic – everything is just too beautiful and too noble.

Colin McPhee's *A House In Bali* (Oxford Paperback again) is a wonderful account of a musician's lengthy stays in Bali to study gamelan music. He's an amazingly incisive and delightfully humorous author and the book itself is superbly written. Like so many other Western 'discoverers' of Bali his stay was in the 1930s but the book was first published in 1944.

Vicki Baum's *A Tale from Bali* (Oxford

Paperback) is again from that magical time in the 1930s. She was another visitor who came under the spell of Walter Spies and her historical novel is based around the events of the 1906 puputan which brought the island under Dutch control.

K'tut Tantri's *Revolt in Paradise* (Harper & Row, New York, 1960) tells, through the eyes of a Western woman, of life on the island during the 1930s and in the midst of the post WW II Indonesian revolution. Besides her Balinese name she has also been known as Vannine Walker, Muriel Pearson or a number of other pseudonyms. She lived for some time at Kuta Beach in the 1930s, stayed in Indonesia when the war broke out and suffered at the hands of the Japanese, then worked on the Indonesian side during its struggle for independence from the Netherlands.

Our Hotel in Bali by Louise G Koke (January Books, New Zealand, 1987) is interesting because K'tut Tantri may have been in partnership with the Kokes in their hotel at some point, though perhaps not; it's very hard to tell from either book! Louise and Robert Koke established the original Kuta Beach Hotel in the mid-30s and ran it until WW II spread to the Pacific. Louise Koke's fascinating account of running their hotel was written during the war but not published until 1987. It's a long way from the prewar Kuta to the Kuta of today.

Walter Spies was the keystone of the prewar Bali set and his colourful, multidimensional and ultimately tragic life make him a fascinating character, quite apart from his undeniable role in the development of Balinese art. *Walter Spies & Balinese Art* by Hans Rhodius & John Darling (Terra, Zutphen, 1980) is an intriguing account of his life, his art and his influence on Balinese art.

For more about the fascinating cast of Western characters in Bali in the 1930s, see the Western Visitors in the '30s section in the Facts about Bali chapter.

Modern Guides & Descriptions

Hugh Mabbett's *The Balinese* (January Books, New Zealand, 1985) is a readable collection of anecdotes, observations and impressions of Bali and its people. Although it doesn't pretend to be a new version of Covarrubias' classic account it does, in many respects, bring that book up to date. See the Kuta section in the South Bali chapter for information on *In Praise of Kuta*, a fascinating book from the same author.

Bali, The Ultimate Island by Leonard Leuras and R Ian Lloyd (Times Editions, Singapore, 1987) is indeed the ultimate coffee-table book on Bali. It's a heavyweight volume with superb photographs both old and new together with an interesting text which manages to take some new angles on this heavily written about and photographed island.

Leonard Leuras, this time in partnership with Rio Helmi, takes another look at the island in *Bali High – Paradise from the Air* (Times Editions, Singapore, 1990). It's a collection of photographs of Bali taken from a helicopter and provides some surprising new perspectives and angles. Some of the most interesting shots are actually not of Bali at all, but of neighbouring Lombok.

Insight Bali (APA Productions, Singapore) is a guidebook-cum-photographic souvenir with some excellent photographs, and some maps filched from earlier editions of this guide! For travel further afield in Indonesia look for Lonely Planet's *Indonesia – a travel survival kit* or to continue beyond Indonesia there's *South-East Asia on a shoestring*.

Over the years there have been a number of interesting *National Geographic* features on Bali including an article in the September 1963 issue on the disastrous eruption of Gunung Agung earlier that year.

Art, Culture & History For information on Bali's complex and colourful arts and culture look for the huge, and expensive, *The Art & Culture of Bali* (Oxford University Press) by Urs Ramseyer .

Balinese Paintings by A A M Djelantik (Oxford University Press, 1986) is a concise and handy overview of the field. An economical and useful introduction to Balinese painting can also be found in *The Development of Painting in Bali* published by the Neka Museum in Ubud. It covers the various schools of painting and also has short biographies of well-known artists, including many of the Western artists who have worked in Bali.

Adrian Vickers' *Bali – A Paradise Created* (Penguin Books, Ringwood, 1989 in Australia; Periplus Books in the USA and Indonesia) traces Balinese history and development by concentrating on the island's image in the West. Vickers' thesis is that the impression is a manufactured one, the result of a conscious decision to create an image of an ideal island paradise. There's some fascinating material on the Western visitors of the '30s, energetic image creators every one of them, but the book is at times disappointingly dry, especially considering its rich source material.

Phrasebooks

You only need to see the Language section in the Facts about Bali chapter to be convinced of what a wise investment a phrasebook is for Bali. *Indonesia Phrasebook* is a concise and handy introduction to Bahasa Indonesia from the Lonely Planet Language Survival Kit series. There's little opportunity to use Balinese (rather than Bahasa Indonesia) in Bali and it's a far too complicated language to pick up without serious study, but a few words can be interesting and fun. In Denpasar, look for a handy little booklet entitled *Balinese Vocabulary – 1000 Basic Words* (Yayasan Swastiastu Pusat, Bali) compiled by N Shadeg.

Bookshops

There are bookshops in Kuta, Sanur and Ubud, with limited selections of new books. Elsewhere, the bookshops have mostly second-hand books. The Krishna Bookshop on Jalan Legian in Kuta and the Family Bookshop on Jalan Tanjung Sari in Sanur have a wide selection of English-language books, particularly on Indonesia. The Ubud Bookshop, on the main road in the centre of Ubud, also has a good selection.

Good small selections can also be found at the Bali Foto Centre at Kuta, at Murni's Warung in Ubud, and at the Neka Gallery in Ubud. None of them has a lot of books but they all have interesting selections, including some books you won't find elsewhere. You will often find Asian-based Oxford Paperback books at these places. Prices of the same book will vary widely so it may be worth shopping around. In some (but not all) of the big hotels the mark-up on books is particularly severe.

If you just want something easy to read on the beach then your best bet will be the numerous second-hand bookshops around Kuta, Legian and Sanur. You might also find the odd interesting book on Bali in these shops.

In Lombok there are a couple of bookshops on Jalan Pabean in Ampenan and others in Cakranegara but it's hard to pick up any new books in English. There's a place selling second-hand books on Gili Trawangan, and if you're in Senggigi and desperate for a read, you could go and see Pearl, at Santai Cottages in Mangset, a few km to the north. It's not possible to get a Sasak/English dictionary, or even a Sasak/Indonesian one.

Maps

Nelles Verlag's 1:180,000 full-colour sheet map of Bali is excellent, and easily obtained in Bali. Lombok maps are much harder to come by – the West Nusa Tenggara tourist office publishes a colour map, with the main towns on one side and Lombok and Sumbawa on the other. It's not very detailed or accurate, but it seems to be the only one around. Every other map given out by anyone else appears to be a copy of the tourist office one! Because Bali is so humid, paper gets damp and soggy and maps start coming to pieces after a few days' use – if you find a solution, let us know.

MEDIA
Newspapers
The English-language *Bali Post* comes out twice a month, and has quite good information on what's happening in Bali. There are Indonesian-language papers too, both national and local, but apparently nothing in the Balinese language. There are other English-language papers published in Indonesia and available on Bali. The *Jakarta Post*, the *Indonesian Observer* and the *Indonesian Times* are probably the most popular and readily available. These carry international and national news and are worth reading, but don't expect serious political debate or a trenchant critique of Indonesian government policy.

Radio & TV
The government radio station, Radio Republic Indonesia (RRI) has information and entertainment, and an English-language news service twice a day. There's also a commercial radio station in Denpasar which broadcasts contemporary Indonesian music, amongst other things.

Short-wave broadcasts, including Radio Australia, Voice of America and the BBC World Service, can be picked up, though the Indonesian government might not like what is said at times. This may even be why it's illegal to bring in a radio/cassette player.

The government operates a national TV network, Televisi Republik Indonesia (TVRI), which reaches the whole country via satellite and microwave links. Every village is supposed to have at least one TV set, as part of the government's information and education policies. As well as educational programs, pro-government news and information services in Indonesian, there are also Indonesian music, dance and drama programmes, subtitled reruns of imported entertainment programmes (usually from the USA) and pro-government news programmes in English.

Television may pose a much greater threat to Balinese culture than mass tourism. It's not so much that the content of the TV programming threatens to undermine traditional beliefs – Balinese culture is amazingly resilient. But when you see a whole warung-full of people watching a sit-com (even a Balinese sit-com; there is such a thing) with obvious enjoyment, you wonder if there will ever be enough time for practising traditional dances, playing the gamelan or attending to the business of the banjar (Balinese village council). Let's hope so!

FILM & PHOTOGRAPHY
Film is widely available at reasonable prices. For print film, 100 ASA Fujicolor or Kodacolor Gold costs about 5000 rp for a 24-exposure roll, 7500 rp for a 36-exposure roll. A 36-exposure roll of 100 ASA Fujichrome slide film costs around 10,000 rp, processing not included. Developing and printing is widely available, very cheap and of quite good quality. You can get colour print film done in a few hours in the innumerable photographic shops in Kuta, Sanur, Ubud and elsewhere, while slide film takes two or three days. The processing cost for a roll of 24 colour prints is about 6600 rp and for a roll of 36, about 9300.

In Lombok colour print film is readily available at numerous outlets in Ampenan, Mataram and Cakranegara, including general stores and chemists (drugstores) as well as specialist film and camera shops. There is some colour transparency film around, but it's not easy to find. The price of film in Lombok is similar to Bali, but Lombok does not have as many facilities for developing and printing.

Bali is very photogenic – you can go through lots of film. There are a number of basic rules for photography in Bali. First of all, shoot early or late in the day – from 9 am until 3 pm the sun is intense and straight overhead, so you're likely to get a bluish washed-out look to your pictures. If you have to shoot at that time of day, a skylight filter will cut the haze. A lens hood will reduce any problems with reflection or direct sunlight on the lens.

Those lush, green, rice fields come up best if backlit by the sun. For those oh-so-popular sunset shots at Kuta or Lovina, set your meter exposures on the sky without the sun making an appearance – then shoot at the sun. Beware of the sharp differences between sun and shade – if you can't get reasonably balanced overall light you may have to opt for exposing only the light area or the dark area correctly. Or use a fill-in flash. It's surprisingly dark in the shade of the trees, particularly in the understorey of a forest, so you will find it difficult to take photos of monkeys or flowers without a flash.

Finally, and most important of all, photograph with discretion and manners. Unsurprisingly, many people don't like having a camera lens shoved down their throats – it's always polite to ask first, and if they say no then don't. A gesture, a smile and a nod are all that is usually necessary. There's one place not to take photographs at all – public bathing places. Just because the Balinese bathe in streams, rivers, lakes or other open places doesn't mean they don't think of them as private places. Balinese simply do not 'see' one another when they're bathing and intruding with your camera is no different to sneaking up to someone's bathroom window and pointing your camera through.

HEALTH

Travel health depends on your predeparture preparations, your day-to-day health care while travelling and how you handle any medical problem or emergency that does develop. While the list of potential dangers can seem quite frightening, with a little luck, some basic precautions and adequate information, few travellers experience more than upset stomachs.

Travel Health Guides

There are a number of books on travel health:

Staying Healthy in Asia, Africa & Latin America, Volunteers in Asia. Probably the best all-round guide to carry, as it's compact but very detailed and well organised.

Travellers' Health, Dr Richard Dawood, Oxford University Press. Comprehensive, easy to read, authoritative and also highly recommended, although it's rather large to lug around.

Where There is No Doctor, David Werner, Hesperian Foundation. A very detailed guide intended for someone, like a Peace Corps worker, going to work in an undeveloped country, rather than for the average traveller.

Travel with Children, Maureen Wheeler, Lonely Planet Publications. Includes basic advice on travel health for younger children.

Predeparture Preparations

Travel & Health Insurance A travel insurance policy is a very good idea – to protect you against cancellation penalties on advance purchase flights, against medical costs through illness or injury and against theft or other loss of your possessions. The policies handled by STA Travel and other student travel organisations are usually good value. Personal liability cover is also a good idea, particularly if you plan to rent a car or motorbike ('third party' insurance is not usually included in the rental deal), though some policies specifically exclude liability arising from use of a motor vehicle.

Some travel insurance policies include access to a medical evacuation service if there's an emergency in a place where appropriate, first-class medical care is unavailable. Medical evacuation firms serving Bali include Asian Emergency Assistance (AEA), World Access International (WAI), and International SOS Assistance. A policy which includes access to the services of one of these firms, or an equivalent, is recommended, even if you think you're most unlikely to need it. Medical costs, and therefore medical insurance, are not very expensive in this area, so you can afford not to skimp on your cover.

Read the small print carefully as it's easy to be caught out by exclusions. As an example, some travel insurance policies widely available in Australia specifically exclude motorbike injuries if you don't hold a current Australian motorbike licence. It's obviously designed to cut out all the inexperienced riders who obtain a Balinese licence, but could also catch people travelling through Australia who hold, say, a British or US motorbike licence.

Medical Kit A small, straightforward medical kit is a wise thing to carry. A possible kit list includes:

- Aspirin or Panadol – for pain or fever.
- Antihistamine (such as Benadryl) – useful as a decongestant for colds, allergies, to ease the itch from insect bites or stings or to help prevent motion sickness.
- Antibiotics – useful if you're travelling well off the beaten track, but they must be prescribed and you should carry the prescription with you.
- Kaolin preparation (Pepto-Bismol), Imodium or Lomotil – for stomach upsets.
- Rehydration mixture – for treatment of severe diarrhoea, this is particularly important if travelling with children.
- Antiseptic, mercurochrome and antibiotic powder or similar 'dry' spray – for cuts and grazes.
- Calamine lotion – to ease irritation from bites or stings.
- Bandages and Band-aids – for minor injuries.
- Scissors, tweezers and a thermometer (note that mercury thermometers are prohibited by airlines).
- Insect repellent, sunscreen, suntan lotion, Chapstick and water purification tablets.

Health Preparations Make sure you're healthy before you start travelling. If you are embarking on a long trip make sure your teeth are OK; there are lots of places where a visit to the dentist would be the last thing you'd want to do.

If you wear glasses take a spare pair and your prescription. Losing your glasses can be a real problem, although in many places you can get new spectacles made up quickly, cheaply and competently.

Pharmaceuticals are somewhat up and down in Indonesia. If it's available at all it's likely to be available without prescription, but don't count on finding just what you want or, if you do find it, that it will be exactly the same as you're used to. If you have to take some particular medicine it's wise to bring it with you.

Immunisation There are no health entry requirements for most visitors to Indonesia but it's wise to be vaccinated against cholera, typhoid and tetanus and have them recorded in a yellow International Health Certificate booklet. You can arrange these vaccinations through your doctor or at your local health centre.

Plan ahead for getting your vaccinations as some of them require an initial shot followed by a booster, while others should not be given together. Most travellers from Western countries will have been immunised against various diseases during childhood but your doctor may still recommend booster shots against measles or polio, diseases still prevalent in many developing countries. The period of protection offered by vaccinations differs widely and some are contraindicated if you are pregnant.

Cholera Some countries may require cholera vaccination if you are coming from an infected area, but protection is not very effective, lasts only six months and is contraindicated for pregnancy.
Tetanus & Diptheria Boosters are necessary every 10 years and protection is highly recommended.
Typhoid Protection lasts for three years and is useful if you are travelling for long in rural, tropical areas. You may get some side effects such as pain at the injection site, fever, headache and a general unwell feeling.

Medical Problems & Treatment
Stomach Upsets The chief health risk to most visitors to Bali or Lombok seems to be the infamous 'Bali Belly'. A lot of visitors get travellers' diarrhoea but it's usually not a serious health risk and with a little care you can generally avoid it completely. Most cases of Bali Belly probably happen to inexperienced travellers whose stomachs are simply rebelling against something new and different, or to people who have just taken foolish risks.

How to avoid Bali Belly? Well, be a little careful in what and where you eat – avoid small local warungs if you're not sure your digestive system has built up a little resistance. Water, ice drinks and cooked food that has been left to cool for too long are all big risks. If you're worried about stomach problems then well-cooked food is always safest. Never drink unboiled water – tea or coffee and bottled soft drinks are safe. Mineral water, in sealed plastic bottles, is available almost everywhere. Major brands of packaged ice cream are usually OK, but don't touch the locally made ice cream sold on the street.

Don't go overboard on being careful – you'll miss out on a lot if you view every meal with suspicion. Bali is not an inherently unhygienic place and most of the time you can eat and drink pretty much anything you please with little risk.

If worst comes to worst and you do come down with something don't rush straight to the medicine chest. If you can fight it off without the aid of modern medical science you'll have built up some resistance against a repeat performance. Dehydration is the main danger with any diarrhoea, particularly for children, so fluid replenishment is the number one treatment. Weak black tea with a little sugar, soda water, or soft drinks allowed to go flat and diluted 50% with water are all good. With severe diarrhoea a rehydrating solution is necessary to replace minerals and salts. You should stick to a bland diet as you recover. Fruit and fruit juice can aggravate diarrhoea so avoid these altogether.

If you have to resort to outside assistance, Lomotil or Imodium can be used to bring relief from the symptoms, although they do not actually cure the problem. Only use these drugs if absolutely necessary, eg, if you *must* travel. For children Imodium is preferable, but do not use these drugs if the patient has a high fever or is severely dehydrated.

Antibiotics can be very useful in treating severe diarrhoea especially if it is accompanied by nausea, vomiting, stomach cramps or mild fever. Three days of treatment should be sufficient and an improvement should occur within 24 hours.

Dysentery Although it's unlikely that you would get dysentery on Bali or Lombok, it's worth pointing out the symptoms to avoid confusion with Bali Belly. Dysentery is a serious illness caused by contaminated food or water and is characterised by severe diarrhoea, often with blood or mucus in the stool. While you will recover from a simple case of the runs in a couple of days, dysentery will continue for a week or more depending on the type.

There are two kinds of dysentery. Bacillary dysentery is characterised by a high fever and rapid development; headache, vomiting and stomach pains are also symptoms. It generally does not last longer than a week, but it is highly contagious. Amoebic dysentery is more gradual in developing, has no fever or vomiting but is a more serious illness. It is not a self-limiting disease: it will persist until treated and can recur and cause long-term damage. A stool test is necessary to diagnose which kind of dysentery you have, so you should seek medical help urgently.

Giardia This intestinal parasite is present in contaminated water. The symptoms are stomach cramps, nausea, a bloated stomach, watery, foul-smelling diarrhoea and frequent gas. Giardia can appear several weeks after you have been exposed to the parasite. The symptoms may disappear for a few days and then return; this can go on for several weeks. Metronidazole (known as Flagyl) is the recommended drug, but it should only be taken under medical supervision. Antibiotics are of no use.

Viral Gastroenteritis This is caused not by bacteria but, as the name suggests, by a virus. It is characterised by stomach cramps, diarrhoea, and sometimes by vomiting and/or a slight fever. All you can do is rest and drink lots of fluids.

Hepatitis Hepatitis A is the more common form of this disease and is spread by contaminated food or water. The first symptoms are fever, chills, headache, fatigue, weakness, aches and pains. This is followed by loss of appetite, nausea, vomiting, abdominal pain, dark urine, light-coloured faeces and jaundiced skin; the whites of the eyes may also turn yellow. In some cases there may just be a feeling of being unwell or tired, accompanied by loss of appetite, aches and pains and the jaundiced effect. You should seek medical advice, but in general there is not much you can do apart from resting, drinking lots of fluids, eating lightly and avoiding fatty foods. People who have had hepatitis must forego alcohol for six months after the illness, as hepatitis attacks the liver and it needs that amount of time to recover.

Hepatitis B, which used to be called serum hepatitis, is spread through sexual contact or through skin penetration – for instance, it could be transmitted via dirty needles or via blood transfusions. Avoid having your ears pierced, tattoos done or injections where you have doubts about the sanitary conditions. The symptoms and treatment of type B are much the same as for type A, but gamma globulin as a prophylactic is effective against type A only.

Worms In a place like Bali or Lombok, where there are many animals around, the likelihood of getting worms increases. Some of the symptoms to watch out for include loss of appetite, distended stomach and an itchy anus.

These parasites are most common in rural, tropical areas. They can be present on unwashed vegetables or in undercooked meat and you can pick them up through your skin by walking in bare feet. Infestations may not show up for some time, and although they are generally not serious, if left untreated they can cause severe health problems. A stool test is necessary to pinpoint the problem and medication is often available over the counter.

Malaria Bali and Lombok are officially within the malarial zones but actually the risk of malaria in Bali is very low, particularly in the southern Bali tourist enclave. Despite some success in controlling mosquito numbers on Lombok, however, there is still a risk of Malaria there. The risk is greatest in the wet months and in remote areas. The strain may also be Chloroquine resistant, (see below).

Whether you intend to visit only Bali or both Lombok and Bali, it's wise to take precautions against malaria by taking either a weekly or daily antimalarial tablet. Your doctor will probably have a personal recommendation for one form or the other.

Malaria is spread by mosquito bites and symptoms include headaches, fever, chills and sweating which may subside and recur. Without treatment malaria can develop more serious, potentially fatal effects.

Antimalarial drugs do not actually prevent the disease but suppress its symptoms. Chloroquine is the usual malarial prophylactic; a tablet is taken once a week for two weeks prior to arrival in the infected area and six weeks after you leave it. (Unfortunately there is now a strain of malaria which is resistant to Chloroquine and if you are travelling in an area infected with this strain an alternative drug is necessary. East and central Africa, Papua New Guinea, Irian Jaya, the Solomons and Vanuatu are the most dangerous areas, but note that other places are not necessarily 100% safe: only in Central America, the Middle East and West Africa is Chloroquine completely effective. Where resistance is reported you should continue to take Chloroquine but supplement it with a weekly dose of Maloprim or a daily dose of Proguanil.)

Chloroquine is quite safe for general use, side effects are minimal and it can be taken by pregnant women. Maloprim can have rare but serious side effects if the weekly dose is exceeded and some doctors recommend a check-up after six months of continuous use. Fansidar, once used as a Chloroquine alternative, is no longer recommended as a prophylactic, as it can have dangerous side effects, but it may still be recommended as a treatment for malaria. Chloroquine is also used for malaria treatment but in larger doses than for prophylaxis. Doxycycline is another antimalarial for use where chloroquine resistance is reported; it causes hypersensitivity to sunlight, so sunburn can be a problem.

You can easily take further precautions by avoiding mosquito bites. In the evening, when mosquitoes are most active, cover bare skin, particularly your ankles. Use an insect repellent and/or burn mosquito coils to repel them and at night sleep under a cover. Actually, mosquitoes are not a real nuisance in Bali – at certain times of the year you don't even see them. The risk of infection is higher in rural areas and during the wet season.

Dengue Fever There is no prophylactic available for this mosquito-spread disease; the main preventative measure is to avoid mosquito bites. A sudden onset of fever, headaches and severe joint and muscle pains are the first signs before a rash starts on the trunk of the body and spreads to the limbs and face. After a further few days, the fever will subside and recovery will begin. Serious complications are not common.

Tetanus This potentially fatal disease is found in undeveloped tropical areas. It is difficult to treat but is preventable with immunisation. Tetanus occurs when a wound becomes infected by a germ which lives in the faeces of animals or people, so clean all cuts, punctures or animal bites. Tetanus is known as lockjaw, and the first symptom may be discomfort in swallowing, or stiffening of the jaw and neck; this is followed by painful convulsions of the jaw and whole body.

Rabies Rabies is found in many countries and is caused by a bite or scratch from an infected animal. Dogs are a noted carrier. Any bite, scratch or even lick from a mammal should be cleaned immediately and thoroughly. Scrub with soap and running water, and then clean with an alcohol solution. If there is any possibility that the animal is infected, medical help should be sought immediately. Even if the animal is not rabid, all bites should be treated seriously as they can become infected or can result in tetanus. A rabies vaccination is now available and

should be considered if you are in a high-risk category – eg, if you intend to explore caves (bat bites could be dangerous) or work with animals.

Sunburn In the tropics, the desert or at high altitude you can get sunburnt surprisingly quickly, even through cloud. Use a sun block and take extra care to cover areas which don't normally see sun – eg, your feet. A hat provides added protection, and you should also use zinc cream or some other barrier cream for your nose and lips. Calamine lotion is good for mild sunburn.

Prickly Heat Prickly heat is an itchy rash caused by excessive perspiration trapped under the skin. It usually strikes people who have just arrived in a hot climate and whose pores have not yet opened sufficiently to cope with greater sweating. Keeping cool but bathing often, using a mild talcum powder or even resorting to air-conditioning may help until you acclimatise.

Heat Exhaustion Dehydration or salt deficiency can cause heat exhaustion. Take time to acclimatise to high temperatures and make sure you get sufficient liquids. Salt deficiency is characterised by fatigue, lethargy, headaches, giddiness and muscle cramps and in this case salt tablets may help. Vomiting or diarrhoea can deplete your liquid and salt levels. Anhydrotic heat exhaustion, caused by an inability to sweat, is quite rare. Unlike the other forms of heat exhaustion it is likely to strike people who have been in a hot climate for some time, rather than newcomers.

Stroke This serious, sometimes fatal, condition can occur if the body's heat-regulating mechanism breaks down and the body temperature rises to dangerous levels. Long, continuous periods of exposure to high temperatures can leave you vulnerable to heat stroke. You should avoid excessive alcohol or strenuous activity when you first arrive in a hot climate.

The symptoms are feeling unwell, not

sweating very much or at all and a high body temperature (39°C to 41°C). Where sweating has ceased the skin becomes flushed and red. Severe, throbbing headaches and lack of co-ordination will also occur, and the sufferer may be confused or aggressive. Eventually the victim will become delirious or convulse. Hospitalisation is essential, but meanwhile get the patient out of the sun, remove their clothing, cover them with a wet sheet or towel and fan them continually.

Infections Hot weather fungal infections are most likely to occur on the scalp, between the toes or fingers (athlete's foot), in the groin (jock itch or crotch rot) and on the body (ringworm). You get ringworm (which is a fungal infection, not a worm) from infected animals or by walking on damp areas, like shower floors.

To prevent fungal infections wear loose, comfortable clothes, avoid artificial fibres, wash frequently and dry carefully. If you do get an infection, wash the infected area daily with a disinfectant or medicated soap and water, and rinse and dry well. Apply an anti-fungal powder like the widely available Tinaderm. Try to expose the infected area to air or sunlight as much as possible and wash all towels and underwear in hot water as well as changing them often.

Motion Sickness Eating lightly before and during a trip will reduce the chances of motion sickness. If you are prone to motion sickness try to find a place that minimises disturbance – near the wing on aircraft, close to midships on boats, near the centre on buses. Fresh air usually helps; reading or cigarette smoke doesn't. Commercial anti-motion-sickness preparations, which can cause drowsiness, have to be taken before the trip commences; when you're feeling sick it's too late. Ginger is a natural preventative and is available in capsule form.

Sexually Transmitted Diseases Sexual contact with an infected sexual partner spreads these diseases. While abstinence is the only 100% preventative, using condoms

is also effective. *(Kondoms* are available from supermarkets and drugstores *(apotik)* for about 500 rp each.) Gonorrhoea and syphilis are the most common of these diseases; sores, blisters or rashes around the genitals, and discharges or pain when urinating are common symptoms. Symptoms may be less marked or not observed at all in women. Syphilis symptoms eventually disappear completely but the disease continues and can cause severe problems in later years. The treatment of gonorrhoea and syphilis is by antibiotics.

There are numerous other sexually transmitted diseases, for most of which effective treatment is available. However, there is no cure for herpes and there is also currently no cure for AIDS. The latter is common in parts of Africa and is becoming more widespread in Thailand and the Philippines. Using condoms is the most effective preventative.

AIDS can also be spread through infected blood transfusions; most developing countries cannot afford to screen blood for transfusions. It can also be spread by dirty needles – vaccinations, acupuncture and tattooing can potentially be as dangerous as intravenous drug use if the equipment is not clean. If you do need an injection it may be a good idea to buy a new syringe from a pharmacy and ask the doctor to use it.

Cuts, Bites & Stings Skin punctures can easily become infected in hot climates and may be difficult to heal. Treat any cut with an antiseptic solution and mercurochrome. Where possible avoid bandages and Band-aids, which can keep wounds wet. Cuts on your feet and ankles are particularly troublesome – a new pair of sandals can quickly give you a nasty abrasion that can be difficult to heal.

Coral cuts are notoriously slow to heal, as the coral injects a weak venom into the wound. Avoid coral cuts by wearing shoes when walking on reefs, and clean any cut thoroughly.

Local advice is the best way of avoiding contact with jellyfish. The box jellyfish, found in inshore waters around northern

Australia during the summer months, is potentially fatal, but stings from most jellyfish are simply rather painful. Dousing in vinegar will de-activate any stingers which have not 'fired'. Calamine lotion, antihistamines and analgesics may reduce the reaction and relieve the pain.

Women's Health
Gynaecological Problems Poor diet, lowered resistance due to the use of antibiotics for stomach upsets and even contraceptive pills can lead to vaginal infections when travelling in hot climates. Keeping the genital area clean, and wearing skirts or loose-fitting trousers and cotton underwear will help to prevent infections.

Yeast infections, characterised by a rash, itch and discharge, can be treated with a vinegar or even lemon-juice douche or with yoghurt. Nystatin suppositories are the usual medical prescription. Trichomonas is a more serious infection; symptoms are a discharge and a burning sensation when urinating. Male sexual partners must also be treated, and if a vinegar-water douche is not effective, medical attention should be sought. Flagyl is the prescribed drug.

Pregnancy Most miscarriages occur during the first three months of pregnancy, so this is the most risky time to travel. The last three months should also be spent within reasonable distance of good medical care, as quite serious problems can develop at this time. Pregnant women should avoid all unnecessary medication, but vaccinations and malarial prophylactics should still be taken where possible. Additional care should be taken to prevent illness and particular attention should be paid to diet and nutrition.

WOMEN TRAVELLERS
Single women travelling solo in Bali will get a lot of attention from Balinese guys, which could be a hassle, but generally the guys are unlikely to get aggressive or violent. There is a gigolo scene at Kuta, Sanur and Lovina. It's usually pretty harmless, though some guys, particularly at Lovina, are con-artists who practise elaborate deceits, or downright theft, to get a girl's money.

On Lombok, people are pretty reserved, and women are generally treated with respect. The sort of harassment which Western women often experience in Muslim countries is very unusual, though not totally unheard of. Respectful dressing is probably a good idea – beachwear should be reserved for the beach, and basically the less skin you expose the better. Attitude can be as important as what you wear. Never respond to come-ons or rude comments. Completely ignoring them is always best. A haughty attitude can work wonders. In India you might call it a hint of the *memsahib*!

Of course, a husband (which equals any male partner) or children also confer respectability, but the husband doesn't have to be present. Some women travellers wear a wedding ring simply for the aura it confers. The imaginary husband doesn't even have to be left at home – who is to say you're not meeting him that very day?

Some precautions are simply the same for any traveller, male or female, but women should take extra care not to find themselves alone on empty beaches, down dark streets or in other situations where help might not be available.

On the whole, Bali and Lombok are safer for women than most areas of the world and, with the usual care and caution, women can feel secure travelling alone there.

DANGERS & ANNOYANCES
Theft
There has been a substantial increase in the number of thefts from tourists in the last year or so. Violent crime is relatively uncommon, but there is a lot of bag snatching, pickpocketing and thieving from losmen rooms.

Snatchers often work in pairs from a motorbike – they pull up next to someone in a busy area, the guy on the back grabs the bag and slashes the strap, the guy on the front hits the throttle, and they're gone within half a second. The bulky money belts which many travellers now wear *outside* their clothes are particularly vulnerable.

Pickpockets on bemos are also prevalent. The usual routine is for somebody to start a conversation to distract you while an accomplice steals your wallet, purse or whatever. Bemos tend to be pretty tightly packed, and a painting, large parcel, basket or the like can serve as a cover.

Losmen rooms are often not at all secure, particularly at Kuta and other tourist areas. Don't leave valuables in your room and beware of people who wander in and out of losmen; keep your room locked if you're not actually in it. Thefts from cars are also becoming more common. Many foolish people lose things by simply leaving them on the beach while they go swimming. You can leave airline tickets or other valuables in the safe deposit boxes which are found at many moneychangers.

Some years ago there were mugging incidents down some of Kuta's less frequented *gangs* (alleys) at night, but that activity rapidly diminished when Kuta banjars organised vigilante groups to patrol at night.

Rip-Offs & Cons

Bali has such a relaxed atmosphere that most visitors tend not to be on the lookout for rip-offs and cons. Although there's no doubt that these do occur, they're not all that common and are usually restricted to the tourist areas.

It's hard to say when an 'accepted' practice like overcharging becomes an unacceptable rip-off, but be warned that there are some people in Bali (not always Balinese) who will engage in a practised deceit in order to get money from a visitor.

One such con involves a friendly local discovering a serious problem with your car or motorbike – it's blowing smoke, leaking oil, or a wheel is wobbling badly. Fortunately, he has a brother/cousin/friend nearby who can help, and before you know it they've put some oil in the sump, or changed the wheel, and are demanding an outrageous sum for their trouble. At that stage you have to pay – you can't return the oil, or the work that has been done. The con relies on creating a sense of urgency, so beware of anyone who

tries to rush you into something without mentioning a price.

Another con involves exploiting the sympathy which a relatively affluent visitor might have for a poorer Balinese. The routine often involves a Balinese guy taking a foreign friend to see 'his' village – usually it's not the guy's own village but the friend doesn't know that. The visitor may be shocked by the poor circumstances of the Balinese friend, who might also concoct a hard-luck story about a sick mother who can't pay for an operation, a brother who needs money for his education or an important religious ceremony that they can't afford. Visitors have often been persuaded to hand over quite large sums of money on such a pretext. A healthy scepticism is your best defence.

Most Balinese would never perpetrate a rip-off, but it seems that very few would warn a Westerner when one is happening. Not many people would pick your pocket on a bemo, but neither would they expose a pickpocket if they saw his fingers in your bag. Bystanders will watch someone put oil in your car unnecessarily for a rip-off price, and they may look uncomfortable and embarrassed about it, but they won't tell you what the right price is. Maybe it's because they'll get a share of the money later, or maybe they find it entertaining, but it's probably more a matter of loyalty to one's own. Be suspicious if you notice that bystanders are uncommunicative and perhaps uneasy, and one guy is doing all the talking.

Drugs

The old image of floating sky-high over Bali has faded considerably. There are some government posters around, suggesting that 'you don't need drugs to experience the magic of Bali', and even the posters have faded. The marijuana and mushrooms of the Bali drug scene were imported tastes, and were never a part of traditional Balinese culture. You may well be offered dope on the street, particularly in Kuta, but you're unlikely to get a good deal, and you may even be turned in to the police by the dealers themselves. The authorities take a dim view of recreational drug use, as always, and losmen owners can be quick to turn you in.

Those who want to go in search of Bali's famed magic mushrooms *(oong)* should remember that their effect is very variable. Some people have stratospheric highs but a lot more suffer deep-down lows.

When you come back home remember that, though drugs are scarcely available in Bali, your local customs department may still think that it's a hippie dope scene.

One drug has, however, become very popular in Bali – alcohol. There are lots of bars and pubs around, and an awful lot of empty beer bottles. The local firewater, *arak*, is distilled from rice wine and can be very strong. Overdosing on this stuff has probably caused more foreigners to freak out than all the other drugs in Bali combined.

Fortunately, the number of Westerners in jail for drug offences in Bali is now quite small. It's not that the authorities are becoming lenient – they're not. It's just that the whole scene is way out of fashion.

Western visitors in Bali who fall foul of the drug laws end up in jail, sometimes for uncomfortably long periods. If you take Jalan Legian from Kuta through Legian and on beyond you'll soon see the Kerobokan Jail off to the right of the road. Under Indonesian law you can be convicted for not turning somebody else in for a drug offence. There have been cases of wives going to prison because they did not inform on their husbands. Information on visiting Westerners in jail was posted on the notice board in Poppies Restaurant in Kuta. Inmates are very happy to have visitors, and gifts of books, fruit, yoghurt and other hard-to-obtain items are much appreciated. Female prisoners get a particularly hard deal as there are fewer of them and their area is much smaller.

Drugs are absolutely unheard of on Lombok. The closest you would get there would be betel nut. Many of the locals – particularly villagers in the more isolated areas – chew this mild drug constantly. Alcohol is scarce on Lombok, largely because the island is predominantly Muslim. Beer, *brem* (rice wine) and tuak (palm beer) are available at *rumah makans* (restaurants) in the main centres and tourist areas, but in the isolated villages, or stricter Muslim towns like Labuhan Lombok, forget it.

TAKING THE CHILDREN

Bali is a great place to travel with children – there can hardly be a place in the world where children are loved as much as they are in Bali. There will always be somebody ready to help you out and always other children ready to play with them. The Wheelers' children, Tashi and Kieran, have been to Bali several times during the research and updating of the various editions of this book. Maureen Wheeler's notes follow:

Travelling with children anywhere requires energy and organisation, however, in Bali the problems are somewhat lessened by the Balinese affection for children – all children. To the Balinese, children seem to be considered communal property – everyone has a responsibility towards them, and everyone displays great interest in any Western child they meet. You will have to learn to give their ages in Bahasa Indonesia (bulan means month, tahun means year), say what sex they are *(laki* is a boy, *perempuan* is a girl) and whether you are breast-feeding your baby *(susu mama)*. Actually the women are most surprised if you do feed the child yourself and they will gather around and make comments and approving noises as they are convinced that 'susu mama' is the best.

Health & Food

Health and food are the main concerns of most parents travelling in Asia as there seem to be so many dangers for an adult, yet alone a young child. On our first visit to Bali with the children Kieran, our younger child, was four months old, and on the most recent trip Tashi, the elder one, was seven. With this experience I can say that, with a only a little extra care, travel in Asia need be no more dangerous than anywhere else.

For travelling babies I think it is essential that they are breast-fed until they are 12 months old. Below the age of eight months the problems involved in carrying bottles, sterilising them, keeping them sterile, getting them to the right temperature, preparing formula hygienically, etc, are too mind-boggling to consider. With breast-feeding it is always there and it is always just right.

For babies from eight months, who are still getting their main nourishment from milk but are also eating, Bali is no problem. Mashed bananas, eggs, peelable fruit, bubur (which is also known as chicken porridge – rice cooked to a mush in chicken stock), and chicken with the skin peeled off, are all generally available. In Kuta, Sanur and probably Ubud you will find jars of baby food if you want something to fall back on. In the travellers' places (Kuta, Sanur, Ubud, Lovina Beach) yoghurt, pancakes, sometimes wholemeal bread, health foods, fruit juices and milk shakes are all available and all suitable as 'tastes' for this age group.

Older children, say one and over, who are really eating will have no problems. If you get away from the tourist areas the local food can be modified. Some children will really enjoy fried rice, others can become *mee* (noodle) addicts. Even if these don't appeal, eggs and fruit are a good standby and can be served up in recognisable forms.

Cartons of milk, flavoured and plain, are available from stores all over the island. This is long-life milk that comes in the same sealed boxes as fruit juice, complete with straw. (Ask for 'ultra', for ultra high temperature (UHT) pasteurisation.) The milk is a real lifesaver as it doesn't go off too quickly after opening, although don't keep it opened for more than 24 hours. If your baby uses a bottle, carry bottle-sterilising tablets and ask your losmen or restaurant for some boiling water to soak the bottle and teat overnight whenever you think it might be a good idea. I found that the plastic cylindrical container that baby wipes come in was an ideal size for a small bottle and teat. If you clean one of these and take it with you it makes a very compact 'steriliser unit' complete with lid.

The main concern, of course, is that since you have to eat out all the time you have no control over how hygienically the food is prepared. In Bali, my experience has been that most of the places that travellers eat in are fairly safe. If you are eating in 'untried' areas then the cardinal rules are don't eat uncooked food and don't drink fruit juices, or any other drinks which use water or ice. Teach your children to always wash their hands after going to the toilet and before meals. Carry baby wipes for the occasions when soap and water aren't available.

I always carried a water container which was used only for boiled water. I also dropped a steriliser tab in to make doubly sure. I used this mainly for teeth cleaning but also for drinking when nothing else was available.

In Bali, bottled water is available in most places. Ensure that the brand of water is a reputable one and that the seal is intact.

If your child does develop stomach trouble, it may be no more than 'tourist trots'. This is generally characterised by very loose to liquid stools, frequently passed. If your child does not appear to be suffering pain from stomach cramps, if the stools do not contain blood or mucus, if there is no fever and if your child does not appear to be ill, then don't worry but do take care.

If, however, any of the other mentioned symptoms are present, find a doctor quickly. The major danger is dehydration and it is a good idea to carry an electrolyte mixture with you for such cases. This usually comes in powder form, in individual sachets, and has to be mixed with water so make sure the water is clean. This solution should be given to your child at the recommended intervals. Your child may be tired and not interested in eating, but don't worry, they will soon regain any lost weight once they are well. The main concern is to keep up fluid intake and let the child rest. Ask your doctor to recommend a kaolin mixture for your child before you go, Pepto Bismal is very good for mild runs and can be given to quite young children.

Apart from stomach upsets (although during our trips to Bali our children have had absolutely no stomach troubles) there are few other health problems.

It is a good idea to treat any cut or scratch with respect, no matter how slight it is. Mer-

Top: Ulu Watu, Bali's prime surfing break (LP)
Bottom: Poppies, Kuta, Bali (TW)

Top: Street vendor, Kuta Beach, Bali (GE)
Left: Sanur Beach, Bali (CK)
Right: Offerings to the gods, Kuta Beach, Bali (TW)

curochrome should be put on immediately. In a tropical climate any scratch can quickly become infected and be very slow to heal. A good antibiotic cream (nongreasy) or powder would be a useful addition to the medical kit. Something like Stingose is good for treating mosquito bites and there is an Aerogard lotion which is good and can also be used as a repellent. An antihistamine may also be useful if your child has several bites and is having trouble getting to sleep. Antihistamines are also useful as a preventative for travel sickness.

Still on the subject of mosquitoes, Bali is officially in the malarial zone and although the risk is slight, your children should take malarial prophylactics, particularly if you're going to be travelling around. If you're going to Lombok then malarials are definitely required. Some doctors recommend the daily tablets while others the weekly one but I strongly recommend that with children you opt for the weekly one. Then you're only going to face a major battle getting the tablet down a protesting toddler's throat once a week instead of every single morning. You can also get antimalarials for children in syrup form.

You should provide additional protection against malaria by keeping mosquitoes away. Malaria-carrying mosquitoes really only appear after dark, so, at night-time use a good insect repellent (lotions and creams last longer than sprays). Loose cotton pyjamas which cover most of the body are a good idea. A mosquito net is good if you can work out a way of stringing it up. Burning mosquito coils may not appeal but they do help to keep the little devils away and a good insecticide which you can spray around your room before you go out for an evening meal helps to keep the mozzie population down.

A child running a temperature should be kept cool: bathe him or her frequently, remove clothes, and administer infant panadol or a similar analgesic every three to four hours. If the temperature does not come down, call a doctor. An infant analgesic, medicine measure or dropper, a thermometer, a bandage and some Band-aids are probably all you need to carry. Just about everything is available in Sanur or Kuta and the big hotels will be able to recommend a doctor, whether you are staying there or not.

Never let your child run around in bare feet – remember, there are many animals leaving their calling cards all over the walkways, and various worms and other parasites can enter through the feet. While on the subject of animals it is a good idea to instil in your children a healthy respect for the animals that they will encounter. Balinese dogs do not arouse a desire in many adults to pat them, but children are often oblivious to appearances. Rabies is still widespread in Indonesia and monkeys, squirrels and bats can also transmit it.

The sun is another potential hazard. I covered both my children with a total sun block for the first few days, then graduated to a regular protective lotion which for babies should be used just about every time you go out. Even if your children seem to tan easily I would suggest that protection against the sun be taken at all times. A light kaftan is useful, and hats are a must for very small children. Remember, a child can burn in a few minutes, even walking to the restaurant just around the corner at lunch time. There is also a gel which is an insect repellent and sun block in one. It would be useful in keeping the flies away at the beach but check to make sure that the sun block is strong enough.

If your child gets sunburnt use something like Caladryl which is a calamine lotion, mild antiseptic, antihistamine and skin soother all rolled into one.

On the whole, my children have been remarkably healthy during their trips to Bali. When Tashi disappeared with the local children to play at their home at first I worried that she might be offered a drink of well water and become ill, but it never seemed to happen. I think it is important to try and maintain a balance between being overanxious for their safety (which means that your child will miss out on many social experiences) and being too relaxed.

Nappies/Diapers

I carted 80 or so disposable nappies with me on our first 'with the children' Bali trip. They are very light, so it is no problem with your weight allowance, but they are bulky. Disposables are available at Kuta's European market, at Sanur and in many other places as well. They're expensive but not astronomically so. I carried a plastic mat, baby wipes, vaseline and a good cream for sore bottoms (all available in Kuta). A number of medium-sized plastic bin bags is a good idea to put the dirty nappies in before disposing of them. I have met travelling families who took cloth nappies and washed them each day. I, however, didn't fancy that idea much as having to carry a dirty, soggy nappy with me on a day's trip really did not appeal.

What do the Balinese do about this problem? Basically, like most people in the Third World, they don't do anything. Babies often go around bare-bottomed and where it happens, it happens. You just hope they aren't sitting on your knee at the time! On the second trip I only carried half a dozen disposables and Kieran was toilet trained by the time we left Bali.

Baby-Sitting & Child Care

On our first 'with the children' Bali trip, romantic dinners at Poppies seemed to be few and far between. On subsequent trips, however, we were able to organise baby-sitters regularly. It's easy and cheap. Upmarket hotels and losmen will organise baby-sitters for you, usually from the workers at the hotel. They will set a rate which is generally not excessive – 4000 rp for two children for one day seems to be about the going rate at the moment. I have no qualms about leaving children with Balinese child minders. The only problem is they will be very disappointed if the children are asleep when they arrive, and may even want to wake them up to play with them!

If you are staying at more modest losmen you will find little sisters of the losmen owner will haunt your room in order to see and play with your children. Generally speaking any child over nine will be a per-

fectly responsible child minder and can be trusted. However, if the child cries the Balinese get most upset and insist on finding mother and handing the child over with a reproachful look. I remember pushing Kieran, screaming, in his stroller along one of Kuta's busiest roads. I wasn't allowed to progress very far before several Balinese stopped me and told me the child was crying, and I was expected to do something immediately. No good trying to explain that he would very shortly go to sleep and that I wouldn't let him scream for too long, I had to pick him up there and then.

Your child's social life can be quite hectic. Tashi had a lovely time playing with the Balinese children. It didn't seem to matter that they didn't speak the same language, they communicated beautifully. She learnt to make offerings to the gods, go to the market and help keep losmen clean. She learnt a little Indonesian and, on our subsequent trips to Bali, was thrilled to resume a friendship with Ketut whom she remembered well.

You will meet lots of locals who will want to photograph your child. That can be very nice but your toddler may be a bit fed up with all the attention. Tashi learnt to yell 'go away' when they went too far, and I thought that was fair enough. It can become very upsetting for children if they are the centre of too much adult interest.

One thing to be aware of on the beach is that many Balinese children are not good swimmers although they may splash around quite happily in the shallows. If your children can swim well they can easily attract local children to depths beyond their abilities. You have a responsibility to keep an eye out for them as well!

Equipment

Apart from what I have already mentioned, I think a stroller or, if your child is old enough, a backpack carrier, is essential. It may seem a nuisance to carry on and off planes, buses, bemos, etc, but unless you carry something that your child can sit in, you are condemned to having your child on your knee constantly, at meals and everywhere else. We had a stroller for Kieran on the first trip as he was too young for the back carrier and it was most useful in restaurants when I wanted to eat a meal in peace. It caused a great deal of amusement amongst the Balinese who obviously thought it was more evidence of our ingenuity, although utterly useless in a Balinese context where a never-ending stream of sisters, brothers, aunts and so on are available to help get Ketut or Nyoman from A to B.

Actually the stroller came in very useful on the plane going to Bali: the Garuda crew were nonplussed to find that the bassinet they produced so proudly did not work. I put the stroller up in front of our seats so that we didn't have to hold Kieran the entire trip to Bali. A few books for older children, their familiar teddy, a bag full of Lego pieces, little people, or various little vehicles, are all the toys they will need. The Balinese children do not have such things and will gather around to watch. You can use these occasions to encourage your children to invite the children to play with them. While your child may not be at an age where sharing appeals, it is worthwhile because the local children are so thrilled with the toys and so pleased to get a chance to play with them. Towards the end of the trip they also make nice presents for any child who has been a particular friend.

Older Children

Problems diminish as your children get older. The more they understand about Bali the more they'll enjoy it, so encourage them to learn about Balinese customs, art, dancing and religion. On our second and third 'with the children' trips we seemed to run into many more Western children in Bali and each trip seemed to be better and easier than the one before.

SURFING

Bali has long had a reputation as something of a surfing Mecca, an image helped on its way by a number of superb surf-travel films. Kirk Willcox, who was editor of the Australian surfing magazine *Tracks* during the publication of the first edition, compiled the following 'Surfer's Guide to Bali' for Australian readers. Since then, the island of Nusa Lembongan has become widely known as a great surfing location, and surfers have been finding great waves on some of Lombok's less accessible reefs. There are now also charter yachts which take groups of surfers around various breaks, for a day trip or a two-week surfari to great breaks on Lembongan, Lombok and Sumbawa which just can't be reached by land. You'll see them advertised in the surfing press. One hundred-dollar-a-day package tours for surfers – what's the world coming to!

Going to Bali and not surfing is akin to going to the snowfields for two weeks and not leaving the bar. Besides all its culture and charm, Bali is surfing. A month here with good swell can provide the surfing holiday of your lifetime. The best way to approach a surfing trip to this lush, tropical isle is to ease yourself into it, familiarise yourself with the numerous breaks, and then cut loose. You will find that you will be able to test, and even stretch, a few of your own limits, especially during bigger swells.

Equipment & Getting it There

To surf the place properly you need the right equipment. For a small board, the one you usually ride in Australia will be adequate. A few inches on your usual length won't go astray. As your knowledge of the island's breaks grows, and the surf increases accordingly, you will find an urge to surf the bigger waves, eight foot and upwards, even if you have never surfed this size before. In Bali, surfing this size on your small board is ridiculous. The main problem is getting into the wave early enough to avoid disaster. It is here that you will need a gun. For a surfer of average height and build a board around the seven foot mark is perfect.

Bali's waves aren't as heavy as Hawaii's but they can still pack a punch, especially the reef breaks. But before you start worrying about the live coral reefs you will need to think about your boards and how to get them there in one piece. You will have no opportunity to make a mess of yourself if you don't get your boards there in reasonable condition in the first place.

There are a number of good travel covers on the market. The best are made in the USA and are quite expensive. Most surfers don't have a lot of money so your best bet is to improvise. Go to your local surf shop and ask them for some bubble plastic which they receive many of their new boards in. Wrap your equipment in this, taking particular care to protect the nose and tail, and then use a normal cloth board cover on top of this. If you have removable fins, all the better. Take them out and pack them with your luggage, making sure you have the screws in a safe place. And while you're at it, buy an extra fin or two.

When packing your bag, pay attention to some other necessary items which will help you have a good surfing trip. The obvious one is wax. What is not so obvious is the choice of wax and basically it comes down to personal preference. Remember, you will be surfing in tepid water and the sun is extremely hot. (Like what you would surf in your bathtub, or think of a typical hot summer day.) Sticky wax can be very good. The best idea is to take a mix and to take a lot, say 10 blocks. What you don't use you can give to the local surfers or board carriers, or to other surfers travelling further on.

In case your board suffers damage, you should pack some resin, hardener, glass and sandpaper. Surfboard materials are quite hard to come by in Bali and it is always advisable to have your own. Even if you don't know what to do with this ding repair equipment, you can always find someone who does. Unrepaired dings mean injuries to yourself and others and one of the prime objectives you must keep in mind when surfing in Bali is to avoid injuries. A serious injury can mean the end of a holiday and weeks spent recuperating at home.

To protect your feet take a pair of wetsuit booties. These are extremely useful when you have to walk across the coral reefs at low tide. They also provide some protection in mean wipeouts, especially if you land feet

first. If you land head first, that's a different matter. If you don't like the feel on your board, have a large pocket sewn on your boardshorts and put them on only when you have to traverse the reefs.

A wetsuit vest is also very handy. Not only does it protect you from chills on windy, overcast days (yes, it does occasionally get overcast in Bali) but it also provides some protection to your back and chest during a fall on the sharp, coral reefs. If you are a real tube maniac and will drive into anything no matter what the consequences, you are advised to take a short-sleeved springsuit. If you are an exceedingly poor surfer with a penchant for coral reefs, you are well advised to take a full-length steamer or, better still, think about going somewhere else for your surfing holiday, like Balmoral Beach in Sydney Harbour.

Surviving Surfing

The first thing you will notice about Bali, after the humidity, is the strength of the sun. Unless you have a good tan when you leave home, wear a T-shirt when surfing and take ample supplies of a good sun block. If you don't you will find yourself missing out on a good surf simply because you can't move.

This takes us on to medical matters and your well-equipped medical kit could become your best friend. Not only are the coral reefs a danger but the Balinese have quaint cactus fences along bike trails. Spin out here and you'll end up looking like a pin cushion and feeling much worse. A bottle of surgical spirit is excellent. Splash it liberally on your cuts each night and also take a needle to remove sea urchin spines. You can even get these little gremlins in your fingers while paddling across the shallow reefs, though they usually inflict themselves upon your feet. Decent Band-aids that won't come off in the water are also necessary. Elastoplast is excellent. There are fairly well-stocked chemists in Bali but it is easier to take your own. Don't forget cotton buds for cleaning wounds.

Take a good pair of joggers for the walk into Ulu Watu – it's three km and very rocky.

Joggers are also vital equipment on your bike, if you decide to hire one. Transporting your board is difficult unless you have a boardstrap. Just buy a normal one and add some foam padding to the shoulder, the more padding the better. While on the bike with your board any animal which comes within 20 metres should be treated as a traffic hazard. Give the same respect to any car and, more so, any truck.

If you manage to write yourself off severely while surfing, or on the way to surfing, which is just as dangerous, head to the top hotels where there are good doctors. There are also private Balinese doctors' surgeries where you'll be stitched up with what resembles thick string. Don't go to the general hospital. It's where people go when they want to die. If you don't feel quite like dying, go to the expensive private annexe. If you nearly feel that bad, however, get on the next plane home. You might regret trying to be a hero. On the same sort of line, brush up on basic mouth-to-mouth resuscitation. You will be surprised how often you might be called upon to use it, especially around the beach breaks in the late afternoon when the swell is a solid six foot. It is a popular sport among the Europeans and other foreigners to go to Bali to drown. You can at least help keep their thrill-seeking to a minimum.

Where to Surf

After arriving in Bali, finding accommodation, getting transport and basically settling in, you are ready for your first surf in Bali. Taking an educated guess, you are now probably sitting outside your losmen somewhere in southern Bali, taking your board out of its cover. Slowly, but deliberately, prepare it and yourself for your first surf. *Don't* rush into this. Take your time and take stock of the situation around you. It's all foreign and different and you should treat the surf the same way.

Kuta & Legian For your first plunge into the warm Indian Ocean, try the beach breaks around Halfway Kuta, or up at Legian, or at Kuta Reef. If you are a bit rusty, start at the beach breaks. The sand here is finer than in Australia and consequently is packed harder so it is harder when you hit it. Treat even these breaks with respect. They provide zippering left and right barrels over shallow banks and can be quite a lot of fun. Some days you will not feel like travelling anywhere on the island looking for surf and you will be content with little sessions out here.

It is also here that you will encounter most of the local Balinese surfers. Over the years their surfing standard has improved enormously and because of this, and also because it is their island, treat them with respect. By and large they're usually quite amenable in the water, although some surfers have found their holidays cut short by a falling out with the locals. Avoid getting into fights and give them the benefit of the doubt on a wave.

To the south of the beach breaks, about a km out to sea, lies Kuta Reef, a vast stretch of coral reef which provides a variety of waves. The main break is a left-hander. The easiest way out there is by outrigger. You will be dropped out there and brought back in for a fee. Kuta Reef can be a very fine left, especially around the five to six foot mark, its optimum size. Over this it tends to double up and section. At five to six feet it peels across the reef and has a beautiful inside tube section; the first part is a good workable wave. The reef is well-suited for backhand surfing. It's not surfable at dead low tide but you can get out there not long after the tide turns. The boys on the boats can advise you if necessary.

When the swell is at its optimum size here, looking further south along the reef (remember facing out to the ocean is west) you will notice another left, usually with fewer surfers out. This wave is more of a peak and provides a short, intense ride. There are even more breaks out there, but that's for you to explore as you get the urge.

Ulu Watu OK, say Kuta Reef is five to six feet today, then Ulu Watu, that most famed surfing break on Bali, will be six to eight feet with bigger sets. Kuta and Legian sit on a huge bay. Ulu is way out on the southern extremity of the bay, and it consequently picks up more swell than Kuta. It's about a half-hour journey. If you go by bemo you will have to walk the last part in, about three km. A cap is useful to shade you from the sun. A young Balinese will carry your board and gear (a small backpack is very useful) into Ulu for a fee. He will also wax your board, get drinks for you and carry the board down into the cave, one of the only ways out to the waves.

Ulu Watu is a phenomenal spot and you will easily see why it has earned its reputation. After the walk through cow paddocks and fields you will get your first glimpse of the ocean. If you go by bike you can ride most of the way in. Walkers use the same track, with a few short cuts. A concrete stairway leads into the Ulu Gorge and in front of you is a sight you will never forget, especially if a decent swell is running. The thatched warungs (food stalls) are set on one side of the gorge, above the cave; one warung is right on the edge of the cliff. The Ulu Watu bay stretches out in front of you. In the shade you can eat, drink, rest, even stay overnight. It is one of the best set ups for surfers in the world and everything is carried in by the Balinese.

Ulu Watu has about seven different breaks. The most commonly surfed are the Inside Corner and the Peak. If it is your first trip here, sit for a while in the shade and survey the situation. See where other surfers are sitting in the line up and watch where they flick off. The Corner is straight in front of you to the right. It's a fast-breaking, hollow left that holds about six foot. The reef shelf under this break is extremely shallow so try to avoid falling head first. As the tide comes up, the Peak starts to work. This is good from five to eight feet with bigger waves occasionally right on the Peak itself. You can take off from this inside part or further down the line. A great wave.

When the swell is bigger, Outside Corner starts operating. This is a tremendous wave break and on a good day you can surf one wave for hundreds of metres. The wall here on a 10-foot wave jacks up with a big drop and bottom turn then the bowl section. After this it becomes a big workable face. You can usually only get tubed in the first section. When surfing this break you need a board with length, otherwise you won't be getting down the face of any of the amazing waves.

Out behind the Peak, when it's big, is a bombora appropriately called the Bommie. This is another big left-hander and it doesn't start operating till the swell is about 10 foot. On a normal five to eight foot day there are also breaks south of the Peak. One is a very fast left, and also very hollow, usually only ridden by goofy-footers because of its speed. There is another left running off the cliff which forms the southern flank of the bay. It breaks outside this in bigger swells and once it's seven foot a left-hander pitches right out in front of a temple on the southern extremity. Know your limits.

Observe where other surfers paddle out and follow them. If you are in doubt, ask someone. It is better having some knowledge than none at all. Climb down into the cave and paddle out from there. When it's bigger you will be swept to your right. Don't panic, it is an easy matter to paddle around the whitewater from down along the cliff. Coming back in you have to aim for the cave. When it's bigger, come from the south side of the cave as the current runs to the north. If you miss the cave, paddle out again and repeat the procedure. If you get into trouble ask for help from a fellow surfer and remember not to panic – that's the worst thing you can do.

Padang Padang So, you've survived your first surf at Ulu and now realise, if you've done everything right, that there is no need to be afraid of the place. Feel like something that's more of an adrenalin rush? Yes? Well then, you're ready for Padang Padang. This is a super-shallow reef break, again a left, north of Ulu towards Kuta. There are a number of ways to get there. If you are at Ulu you can simply walk along a narrow cliff track and climb down to the beach. Again, check this place carefully before venturing out.

If you can't surf tubes, backhand or forehand, don't go out. Padang is a tube. After a ledgey take-off, you power along the bottom before pulling up into the barrel. So far so good, now for the tricky part. The last section turns inside out like a washing machine on fast forward. You have to drive high through this section, all the time while in the tube. Don't worry if you fail to negotiate this trap, plenty of other surfers have been caught too. After this the wave fills up and you flick off. Not a wave for the faint-hearted and definitely not a wave to surf when there's a crowd.

Canggu After all this you might like a nice, gentle right-hander, with perhaps the choice of a left. The place for you is Canggu. This beach, with a softer reef bottom, is to the north of Kuta, on the northern extremity of the bay. Five to six foot is an optimum size for Canggu. It's a good right-hander that you can really hook into, plus there's the left. There's also a warung or two here. Motorbike is the best way to get to Canggu. You have to walk along the beach if you come by bemo because the track between the rice paddies has eroded away.

Medewi Further up the island is a softer left called Medewi. This wave has a big drop, which fills up then runs into a workable inside section. It's worth surfing if you feel like something different, but to catch it you need to get up early in the morning.

These are the waves you usually surf in the dry season. The swells thunder in from the south-south-west and the wind is often offshore.

Sanur During the wet season, roughly November to March, you surf on the Sanur side of the island. There are some very fine reef breaks over there. Sanur itself is a hollow, right-hand reef which has excellent barrels. From there you can see a number of reefs further offshore and most of them are surfable. The problem with the wet season is getting around safely. Bali's dirt tracks become very muddy and slippery. The main

road to Sanur is now very good so the back roads of Kuta are the ones to worry about.

If this is your first trip to Bali, this is probably enough grounding. There are many semi-secret spots on the island. Ulu is a definite favourite and is an excellent wave both backhand and forehand. As a surfer you can still do a lot of adventuring in Bali exploring new spots. On days when it seems too flat, or you don't think there is any decent surf around, talk to the locals. They'll be able to point you in the right direction.

If you snap your board in half, there are several surf shops selling second-hand boards.

Don't approach the surf lacking in confidence, but equally important don't paddle out at new reefs overly confident. Feel the place out. Here your sixth sense is as good as your other five.

Nusa Lembongan
This is one of the smaller islands of the Nusa Penida group, which is separated from the south-east coast of Bali by the Selat Badung (Badung Strait). The strait is very deep, and generates huge swells which break over the reefs off the north coast of Lembongan. There are three main breaks, plus one off the coast of the smaller Nusa Ceningan. Two of the breaks are right-handers, which are hard to find on Bali. Lembongan is pretty well known to surfers now, and there are quite a few places to stay and eat, though there are still those who like to think it's a secret spot. You get there by boat from Sanur – see the Nusa Penida chapter for details.

Lombok
The southern coasts of Lombok get the same swells that generate Bali's big south coast breaks, and there are certainly some great waves. The main problem is getting to them. Lombok's Kuta Beach is the most accessible, and even that's difficult to get to by public transport. There are places to stay and eat there, and boat owners who will take you out to the reef breaks. Other places which you can get to by land, with difficulty, include

Silung Blanak, Mawun, and Serewei Beach on the south coast, and Bangko Bangko, or Desert Point, at the south-western tip of Lombok. None of these places have any tourist facilities at all. The easiest way to surf these areas is with a surf tour on a chartered yacht (see earlier in this section) which will enable you to access some other breaks as well.

DIVING

With its warm water, extensive coral reefs and abundant marine life, Bali offers some superb diving possibilities. If you just want to do a little snorkelling, there's pretty good coral reef Nusa Dua, Sanur and along the Lovina beach strip on the north coast. There's also good snorkelling at Padangbai, off the beach or from boats which can take you out to the fine reefs offshore. Lombok's Gili Islands are also good for snorkelling. Most places that have coral will have a place that rents masks, snorkels and fins for a few thousand rupiah per day, but check the quality of the equipment before you take it away.

Scuba diving offers more demanding possibilities, though obviously it is more expensive and often requires transport, by land or water, to get to the best sites. There are a number of operations conducting diving trips for visitors, and there are also package tours specifically for scuba divers. If you want to do a package tour, find a reputable operator through a Garuda office, your local dive club, or one of the scuba diving magazines. Diving may not be so good during the wet season, from about October to April, as storms may reduce visibility.

If you're travelling independently, and you just want the occasional dive, make sure you bring your scuba certification. The international safety code does not enable operators to let you dive without a recognised certification, and only a few of them have qualified instructors who could train you to a minimum certification level. Most of the main qualifications are recognised, including those of PADI, NAUI, BSAC, FAUI and SSI. Keen divers might also bring their own mask and regulator, though all the equipment is available.

When you get to Bali, contact one of the dive operators in the southern tourist area, particularly Sanur – they can arrange trips to the main dive sites around the island. The cost depends on the number of people in the group and the distance to the dive site. For a group of six divers on a local trip, count on about US$45 for two dives. A trip to Pulau Menjangan from Sanur will cost about US$70 or US$80.

Alternatively, try contacting a local dive operator in a resort or tourist development near the dive site you're interested in. This might be a bit cheaper as you're not paying the dive operator to arrange transport for you or your equipment. There are at least 10 dive operators on Bali and one on Lombok, so the following is only a partial list:

Bali Marine Sports
  Jalan Bypass Ngurah Rai, Blanjong, Sanur (☎ 88776, fax 87872)
Balina Beach Bungalows
  Balina, Klungkung
Spice Dive
  Lovina Beach, Buleling
Albatross Diving Adventures
  Gili Trawangan, Lombok, PO Box 67 Mataram, (☎ 0364 22353)

In addition, a number of hotels seem to have diving equipment and a compressor for filling tanks, but don't advertise locally as dive-trip operators. These probably have the facilities to cater for package-tour diving groups. However, if you've got your certification, and your money, they may take you out if they can include you in a suitably sized group. You'll find operators like this (you can't miss their noisy compressors) at Padangbai, Tulamben, and Permai Beach Cottages near Lovina.

Dive Sites

Some of Bali's main dive sites are listed below, roughly in order of their accessibility from southern Bali. For more details on accommodation, food and getting to these places, see the entry on each one in the chapters on Bali.

Nusa Dua The beach is nice, white and gently sloping, but for the best diving, take a boat trip to the reef. Colourful corals are seen between three and 20 metres.

Sanur Very accessible by boat from the main tourist beach, Sanur's reef is colourful and has lots of tropical fish which can be seen at depths less than 12 metres.

Padangbai This beautiful bay is not overrun with tourists, but has diving facilities, food and accommodation. You can dive from the beach or take a boat to many offshore reefs and islands. Note, however, that the currents are strong and unpredictable and that there are also sharks – it's recommended for experienced divers only.

Tulamben A trip to Tulamben takes you through some of the lushest and most attractive countryside in Bali, though when you get to the east coast it's dry and barren by contrast. There's an amazing reef with an 800-metre drop off into Lombok Strait. The other main diving attraction is the wreck of the USS *Liberty*, which is spectacular but eerie, encrusted with marine flora and inhabited by thousands of tropical fish. It's close to the shore and can easily be appreciated by snorkellers, but divers will find it even more interesting – depths are less than 25 metres.

Amed Also on the east coast, not far south of Tulamben, Amed has a very isolated black-sand beach. You dive from the beach, which slopes gently then drops off to about 35 metres. There are many fish here, both small and large, and spearfishing is permitted. Note, however, that spearfishing with scuba gear is generally regarded as unethical.

Lovina Beach Area The strip of beaches west of Singaraja has an extensive coral reef, with pools of very calm water. You can dive or snorkel from a boat, but you don't have to

go deep to enjoy the area – it's a good spot for beginners.

Pulau Menjangan 'Deer Island' is in the Bali Barat (West Bali) National Park, accessible by boat from Teluk Terima. It has superb, unspoilt coral (partly because of the absence of human development in the area), lots of sponges and fish, and a spectacular drop-off. It's regarded as the best diving on Bali. The remote location and the park entrance fees make this a more expensive dive, but it's worth it. There is limited accommodation available at Teluk Terima, but Spice Dive, in Lovina, is the nearest diving operation.

Nusa Lembongan You enter from the white-sand beach which slopes gently out to the reef, where diving is from five to 20 metres down. There are some impressive underwater grottos in the area. There are no dive operators on Lembongan, so you'll need to organise the trip from mainland Bali, an hour or so away by boat.

LANGUAGE COURSES

Bahasa Indonesia is one of the easiest languages to learn, and it is almost indispensable for travel to the more remote parts of the country. Even in Bali, a little knowledge of the national language enables you to meet and communicate with more people, learn more about the culture and cope better with everyday travel problems.

There are private tutors, whom you might contact through newspaper ads or notice boards in places like Ubud.

The Indonesia Australia Language Foundation (IALF) runs courses in Bahasa Indonesia suitable for adults at various levels of competence in the language. For more information contact Tony Crooks (☎ 36559), IALF, Universitas Udayana, Jalan Sudirman, Denpasar.

OTHER ACTIVITIES
Windsurfing

Most windsurfing is done in the tourist areas of southern Bali, though there are certainly lots of other possible locations. It doesn't seem to have taken off as surfing has, perhaps because it's harder to travel with windsurfing equipment, or perhaps because you can windsurf on virtually any stretch of water closer to home. Equipment can be hired on the beach at Sanur, and near Benoa Point where the Nusa Dua water-sports enthusiasts are catered for. You'll also find windsurfers at Kuta, Candidasa and Lovina, and at Senggigi Beach on Lombok. Often you'll have to wait for high tide, when the lagoons inside the coral reefs are deep enough. Windsurfing has caused damage to coral formations in some areas, so be aware of where you're going.

White-Water Rafting
Rafting is a newcomer to Bali's range of outdoor activities, and is easy to enjoy as a day trip from Kuta, Sanur, Nusa Dua or Ubud. Operators will pick you up from your hotel, take you to the put-in point (usually on the Ayung River), provide all the equipment and guides, and return you to your hotel afterwards. Lunch is also included.

There are at least two operators. Sobek Expeditions (☎ 88796) run rafting trips all over the world and are associated with Bali Maharani Tours & Travel in Sanur. Their trips cost US$57 all-inclusive. Bali Adventure Rafting (☎ 51292) is a local operation which runs slightly shorter trips for US$45. You book with them at Yanies Restaurant in Legian.

Trekking/Hiking
Bali is not usually thought of as a trekking destination, but a surprising number of visitors climb Gunung Batur to see the sunrise. In fact there are numerous other possibilities for treks in the Batur area, around the volcanoes near Bedugul and in the Bali Barat National Park. Perhaps the biggest challenge is a climb of Gunung Agung (3142 metres).

Bali does not offer remote wilderness treks – it's too densely populated. For the most part, you make day trips from the closest village, often leaving before dawn to avoid the clouds which usually blanket the peaks by mid-morning. So you won't need a tent, sleeping bag or stove.

Walking should also be considered as a means of getting around, particularly by those who can travel light and want to explore the backblocks. Away from the main roads you can walk from village to village on small tracks and between the rice paddies, eating where you like and staying in losmen in the larger villages – there's usually somewhere, or someone to put you up. Stop early though, so you can flag down a bemo if you do find yourself stuck. Walking around the beaches is another possibility. Despite the enormous number of tourists in Bali, it's relatively easy to find places where tourists are a rarity. Of course you have to be content with a pretty basic standard of food and accommodation. If you're considering a walking trip, look carefully at a map, note the places near your planned route and look them up in this book.

On Lombok, a climb up Gunung Rinjani (3726 metres) is the big challenge for trekkers. This involves at least two nights camping out, but the necessary equipment can be hired in town. There are several routes up, and a world of possibilities for those who want to spend some days hiking in a relatively remote area. If you just want to explore the countryside on foot, visiting a number of villages, the area of central Lombok, between the main east-west road and the southern slopes of Rinjani, is recommended.

Cycling
For information on cycling, see both the Bali and Lombok sections of the Getting Around chapter.

ACCOMMODATION
Around Bali
Finding a place to stay in Bali is no problem. In fact, at the bottom end of the market, accommodation in Bali is probably the best in the world for the price. Two or three dollars can get you a fine room in many places, and US$10 can get you something terrific. In this book, we don't try to 'recommend' the 'best' place to stay in each

area, or even the 'best value' place. It's too subjective and too changeable. If we did 'recommend' a place, it would probably be full when you got there, it would be likely to increase its prices as its business boomed, and it would hardly be fair to places down the street which you might find just as good. Instead, we try to give *you* a feel for the various types of accommodation available, and the going price for a room of a certain standard, then you can make your own informed choices.

Bottom End If you're going to travel around Bali rather than stay in one place and make day trips (or stay in one place and never move from the beach), then it's the bottom-end places which will be of interest. Cheap hotels in Bali are usually known as losmen, and many of them are terrific. A losmen is a small hotel, often family run, which rarely has more than 10 or 12 rooms; names usually include the word 'losmen', 'homestay' or 'inn'.

Losmen are often built in the style of a Balinese home – that is, a compound with an outer wall and separate buildings around an inner garden. In Bali you usually live outside – the 'living room' is an open verandah and enclosed rooms are only used for sleeping or specific activities like cooking. Similarly, in a losmen your room is generally just that; four walls and a couple of beds. Outside the room there will be a verandah area with chairs and a table.

Apart from the fact that it's pleasant to be sitting out in the garden, this plan has a second very important benefit. You're out there with all the other travellers, not locked away inside a room. So you can talk, meet people and learn more about Bali.

There are losmen all over Bali and they vary widely in standards but not so widely in price. In a few places you'll find a room for as low as 3000 rp, but generally they're in the 8000 to 12,000 rp range. Some of the cheap rooms are definitely on the dull and dismal side, but others are attractive, well kept and excellent value for money.

Some interesting losmen to try include the

places at Penelokan (for the terrific view over the volcano), the water palace losmen at Tirtagganga, a number of the losmen along the Lovina beaches (for attractive rooms at wonderfully low prices), the Artha Sastra Inn at Bangli and some of the pleasant losmen in Ubud.

Middle Range In Kuta, Legian, Denpasar, Lovina, Ubud and Sanur you can also find a good selection of middle-range hotels. At the beaches they're often constructed in Balinese bungalow style. They're often called something or someone's bungalows or cottages – *Made's Beach Bungalows* or *Sunset Cottages*. Mid-range for this book will generally be taken as something between US$7 and US$20 per night for a double – about 13,000 to 40,000 rp. Above that is 'top end', below that is 'bottom end'. A typical mid-range place might charge 15,000/20,0000 rp for single/double occupancy, and perhaps 5000 rp more for an extra bed or two to accommodate a family. This price should include a light breakfast (pineapple, banana and mango fruit salad, toast and tea/coffee), tea or coffee on request throughout the day, and your own bathroom with shower and toilet.

Top End The top of the top end is at Nusa Dua, and it is world class. Some of the luxury places at Sanur, Legian and even Ubud are not far behind. Our research budget doesn't run to an in-depth comparison of their merits, so we can't say which are the best! Whether you regard these super-luxury places with contempt or envy, there are two points worth making.

Firstly, the best of them feature contemporary architecture in a genuine Balinese style which is both distinctive and attractive. A luxury resort hotel on Bali does not look like a clone of one on Majorca or Maui or Mazatlán. Typically the rooms face inwards, to a lush landscaped garden, in a layout that has its origins in a traditional family compound *(pekarangan)*. The hotel lobby is often styled on a bale banjar, the meeting hall of a community or village. The rooms and public areas are decorated with Balinese paintings, woodcarvings and stonework of the highest quality, and commissions for these works can keep a whole village gainfully employed for months.

Secondly, many of the three- and four-star standard hotels are very cheap. Cheap that is, for the people on package holidays who have got a week's accommodation in one these palaces for not much more than the cost of their air fare. Of course they get stung savagely for drinks, tours and extra meals. But those who eat only their prepaid breakfast in the hotel, then sneak out for a day's independent sightseeing with lunch at a street stall and dinner in the night market, can have a bit of the real Bali, and a dab of decadence, at a budget price.

Around Lombok

The accommodation picture in Lombok is somewhat different. Although there are no big 'international' hotels in the main town, there is no shortage of accommodation. In the Senggigi Beach area there are some major luxury hotel developments and the government is keen to develop other beaches with four-star hotels. There are some basic beach bungalows in the Senggigi area, a few at Lombok's Kuta beach, lots of them on the Gili Islands and some more likely to appear in the villages around Tetebatu and on the east coast. Typically, a Lombok beach bungalow is a hut on stilts, with a small verandah out the front. Almost all of them are at the bottom of the price range, about 8000/12,000 rp for singles/doubles, including a light breakfast. This boom in budget accommodation may be forestalled by government restrictions aimed at preserving the best beach areas for more up-market developments.

Outside the areas mentioned above, accommodation can be scarce. This is not a major problem as you can make day trips to most parts of the island quite easily. If this doesn't appeal, and you want to get out and see more of Lombok, you can usually stay with the *kepala desa* or *kepala kampung* (village headman). They are generally very

hospitable and friendly, not only offering you a roof over your head but also a minimum of two meals a day – obviously you don't get a room of your own, just a bed. What you pay for this depends on the deal you reach with the kepala desa. Sometimes he may offer it to you for nothing but more often some payment will be expected, although it could be as little as 2000 rp.

If you intend to visit remote areas and stay with a kepala desa it is a good idea to have one or two small gifts to offer – cigarettes go down well, as do instant photographs, balloons for the children, soap or foreign coins. Then if he won't allow you to pay for accommodation and food, you will feel happier in being able to reciprocate his kindness in a small way, and promote good will for future travellers at the same time.

Basic accommodation on Lombok is not quite as good value as on Bali. Prices start at around 7500/10,000 rp for singles/doubles. As in Bali the quality varies, with some places being depressing and dirty while others are attractive and bright. Many are close to mosques, which can be deafeningly noisy – if you don't like being woken up at 5 am, avoid these like the plague. Still others are more or less permanently full with students from out of town or people from villages who have found work in the main centres. They're all interesting and all cheap.

The Mandi

Successfully coping with the *mandi* is an important factor in coming to grips with life in a losmen. Running water is not part of everyday life in Indonesia, and to get around this many losmen will have a mandi-style bathroom, though more and more places do have a Western-style bath now, usually with a hand-held shower head. The word 'mandi' simply means to bath or to wash. Instead of taps and a sink or bath the mandi is a large water tank beside which you'll find what looks like a plastic saucepan. You *do not* climb in the tank. That's the worst error to make! What you do is scoop water out of the mandi tank and pour it over yourself, then soap yourself down and repeat the scooping and showering procedure.

A warning: mandi water is often icy cold, it usually comes from wells way down deep. You will have to get used to cold water because losmen have nothing else. Even in most middle-price hotels hot water is a rarity. Anyway you're in the tropics and you will soon forget what hot water feels like.

Bathing is a regular and social practice in Bali – every pool, lake, stream or even water channel seems to be in almost constant use as an outside bathhouse. If you're at the *air panas* (hot springs) by Lake Batur try joining the evening bath time, half the village seems to be there for a social soak and chatter and you're quite welcome to shed your inhibitions and join in. Note, however, that just because the Balinese bathe in public doesn't mean that they don't consider their bathing places to be private. See the important note in the Film & Photography section of this chapter.

The Toilet

Just as mandis are disappearing in favour of Western-style showers, the old Asian-style toilets are also being replaced by Western-style, sit-down toilets. You'll still encounter the Asian toilets though, and they're like those you find everywhere east of Europe – two footrests and a hole in the ground. You squat down and aim. They're basic but you soon get used to them, and they have one considerable advantage over Western-style toilets – keeping them clean doesn't take much effort.

Most losmen on Lombok are still designed with mandis and squat-down toilets. Only at the more expensive hotels will you find Western-style showers and toilet facilities.

As with mandis there is often no running water to flush toilets whether they be Asian- or Western-style. In that case you just reach for that plastic saucepan again, scoop water from the mandi tank and flush it away.

Apart from places which definitely cater to the tourist trade, you won't find toilet paper in restaurant toilets – so bring your own, or learn to wash yourself with water

(left hand only, if you're a purist). To locate a toilet ask for the *kamah mandi* or the WC (pronounced 'way-say').

FOOD

There's no question that you'll eat well in Bali, the dining possibilities are endless, the prices often pleasantly low and the taste treats terrific. What you're less likely to do is eat Balinese – the places that prepare real Balinese food are few and far between although they're becoming a little more common, particularly in Ubud. *Babi guling* (spit-roasted suckling pig) and *betutu bebek* (duck roasted in banana leaves) are probably the only truly Balinese dishes you'll see with any regularity and both of them usually require advance warning to prepare.

A good restaurant with some interesting Balinese dishes is the Ubud Restaurant down the Monkey Forest Rd in Ubud. Also see the information in the Ubud section about Ketu Suartana's Balinese feasts.

In many of Bali's tourist areas you'll be lucky to find even Indonesian food – apart from a token nasi goreng – let alone Balinese food. Some Western dishes have been so well assimilated on to the Balinese menu you'd be forgiven for thinking they originated there. Take jaffles for example! Of course in places not so squarely aimed at the tourist mainstream you'll find a more normal range of Indonesian dishes.

This leads to the great paradox of eating in Bali – the cheaper the place, the tastier the food. The really cheap places are for the locals, and they serve the genuine article. At the most makeshift street stall, for 500 rp you can get a nasi goreng that's out of this world – hot and spicy, with fresh ingredients that are cooked while you wait. Of course you might have to sit on the curb to eat it, and the plate may not be as carefully washed as you would like. At the tourist restaurant around the corner, a nasi goreng could cost 2000 rp, but it mightn't be freshly cooked (these restaurants offer lots of dishes to lots of customers and need to prepare ingredients beforehand), and it won't have the same spicy taste (dishes tend to be wimped down for what the Balinese see as 'tourist tastes'). Fried noodles *(mee goreng)*, satay and soup *(soto)* are other street-stall staples.

Food in Indonesia is Chinese influenced, although there are a number of purely Indonesian dishes. The following is a list of some of the dishes you're most likely to find:

apam – delicious pancake filled with nuts and sprinkled with sugar

bakmi goreng – fried noodles

cap cai – usually pronounced 'chop chai' this is a mix of fried vegetables sometimes with meat as well

fu yung hai – a sort of sweet and sour omelette

gado gado – another very popular Indonesian dish, steamed bean sprouts, various vegetables and a spicy peanut sauce

lontong – rice steamed in a banana leaf

mee goreng – fried noodles, sometimes with vegetables, sometimes with meat; much the same story as nasi goreng

mee kuah – noodle soup

nasi campur – steamed rice topped with a little bit of everything (some vegetables, some meat, a bit of fish, a krupuk or two). It's a good, simple, usually tasty and filling meal.

nasi goreng – this is the most everyday of Indonesian dishes, almost like hamburgers are to Americans, meat pies to Australians, fish & chips to the British. Nasi goreng simply means fried *(goreng)* rice *(nasi)* and a basic nasi goreng may be little more than fried rice with a few scraps of vegetable to spice it up a little. Fancier nasi gorengs may include meat, while a 'special' or *istemiwa* nasi goreng usually means with a fried egg on top. Nasi goreng can range from the blandly dull to the very good.

nasi Padang – Padang food, from the Padang region of Sumatra, is popular all over Indonesia. It's usually served cold and consists of rice (once again) with a whole variety of side dishes. A whole selection of dishes are laid out before you and your final bill is calculated by the number of empty dishes. Nasi Padang is traditionally

eaten with your fingers and it's also traditionally very hot *(pedas* not *panas)*. It's hot enough to burn your fingers, let alone your tongue.

nasi putih – white rice, usually plain, and either boiled or steamed

opor ayam – chicken cooked in coconut milk

pisang goreng – fried banana fritters, a popular streetside snack

rijstaffel – Dutch for 'rice table', Indonesian food with a Dutch interpretation, it consists of lots of individual dishes with rice. Rather like a glorified nasi campur or a less heated nasi Padang. Bring a big appetite.

sambal – a hot spicy chilli sauce served as an accompaniment with most meals

satay – one of the best known Indonesian dishes, satay are tiny kebabs of various types of meat served with a spicy peanut sauce. Street satay sellers carry their charcoal grills around with them and cook the satay on the spot.

The following is a list of food words which may be useful:

asam manis – sweet and sour; for example, ikan asam manis (sweet and sour fish)

ayam – chicken; for example, ayam goreng (fried chicken)

babi – pork; since most Indonesians are Muslim, pork is rarely found elsewhere in the archipelago but in Bali it's a popular delicacy

daging – beef

dingin – cold

dragonflies – a popular Balinese snack, caught with sticky sticks and then roasted!

enak – delicious

garam – salt

gula – sugar

ikan – fish, there's a wide variety available in Bali

ikan belut – eels; another Balinese delicacy, kids catch them in the rice paddies at night

kare – curry, as in kare udang (curried prawns)

kentang – potatoes

kepiting – crab

kodok – frog; frogs' legs are very popular in Bali and frogs are caught in the rice paddies at night

krupuk – prawn crackers; they often accompany meals

mentega – butter

udang karang – lobster; very popular in Bali and comparatively economical

makan – the verb 'to eat' or food in general, *makan pagi* is breakfast, *makan siang* is the midday meal

manis – sweet

pahat – no sugar

panas – hot (temperature)

pasar malam – night market, often a great source of interesting and economical food stalls

pedas – hot (spicy)

rumah makan – restaurant, literally 'house to eat' or 'house for food'

sayur – vegetables

soto – soup, usually fairly spicy

telor – egg

udang – prawns

warung – food stall combined with a sort of Indonesian small general store.

The only real difference in food between Lombok and Bali is that there are fewer tourist restaurants on Lombok – which means you'll be eating local Indonesian dishes in most places. In Bahasa Indonesia the word *lombok* means chilli pepper and they're used liberally in Indonesian cooking so unless you like having your mouth on fire beware of adding even more. Particularly as you can't always drink litres of water to cool yourself down!

By and large the Chinese restaurants on Lombok are cleaner and have more variety and tastier food than the Indonesian rumah makan, but as with Bali there is no question that you will eat well and cheaply.

The locally produced brands of ice cream available in Kuta and other well-touristed places are safe to eat. Peters (the locally licensed version of the well-known Australian brand) is quite good though Campina is generally the best. The Indonesians are keen snackers so you'll find lots of street-stall snacks such as peanuts in palm sugar, shredded coconut cookies or *pisang goreng*.

Fruit

It's almost worth making a trip to Bali or Lombok just to sample the tropical fruit. If you've never gone beyond apples, oranges and bananas you've got some rare treats in store when you discover rambutans, mangosteens, salaks or zurzat. Some of the favourites include:

avocado – avocado enthusiasts can suffer overkill in Bali, they're plentiful and cheap

blimbing – the 'starfruit' is a cool, crispy, watery tasting fruit – if you cut a slice you'll immediately see where the name comes from.

durian – the most infamous tropical fruit, the durian is a large green fruit with a hard, spiky exterior. Cracking it open reveals a truly horrific stench. Hotels and airlines in Asia often ban durians so it's not surprising that becoming a durian aficionado takes some time! One description of the durian compared it to eating a superb raspberry blancmange inside a revolting public toilet but true believers even learn to savour the smell.

jambu – guava; the crispy, pink, pear-shaped ones are particularly popular

jeruk – jeruk is the all-purpose term for citrus fruit and there is a wide variety available in Bali. Jeruk are chiefly grown in the central mountains. The main varieties include the huge *jeruk muntis* or *jerunga*, known in the west as the pomelo. It's larger than a grapefruit but with a very thick skin, a sweeter, more orange-like taste and segments that break apart very easily. Regular oranges are known as *jeruk manis*, sweet jeruk. The small tangerine-like oranges which are often quite green are *jeruk baras*. Lemons are *jeruk nipis*.

mangosteen – one of the most famous tropical fruits the mangosteen is a small purple-brown fruit. The outer covering cracks open to reveal tasty pure-white segments with an indescribably fine flavour. Queen

Custard Apple

Pineapple

Durian

Victoria once offered a reward to anyone able to transport a mangosteen back to England while still edible.

nanas pineapples

nangcur – also known as jackfruit, this is an enormous yellow-green fruit that can weigh over 20 kg. Inside there are hundreds of individual bright-yellow segments with a distinctive taste and a slightly rubbery texture. As they ripen on the tree each nangcur may be separately protected in a bag.

papaya or *paw paw* – these fruits are not that unusual in the west

pisang – these are bananas and the variety of pisang found in Bali is quite surprising

rambutan – a bright red fruit covered in soft, hairy spines; the name means hairy. Break it open to reveal a delicious white fruit closely related to the lychee.

salak – found chiefly in Indonesia the salak is immediately recognisable by its perfect brown 'snakeskin' covering. Peel it off to reveal segments that in texture are like a cross between an apple and a walnut but in taste are quite unique. Bali salaks are much nicer than any others.

sawo – they look like a potato and taste like a pear

zurzat – also spelt sirsat and sometimes called white mango, the zurzat is known in the west as custard apple or soursop. The warty green skin of the zurzat covers a thirst-quenching interior with a slightly lemonish, tart taste. You can peel it off or slice it into segments. Zurzats are ripe when the skin has begun to lose its fresh green colouring and become darker and spotty. It should then feel slightly squishy rather than firm.

DRINKS

A variety of the popular Western soft drink brands are available in Bali and Lombok – usually in small bottles rather than cans. Coca-Cola, 7-Up, Sprite and Fanta are all there. Prices are typically from around 700 rp in warungs and can be more than 1000 rp in the expensive restaurants. Bottled drinking water has become quite the thing in Bali, a 1.5 litre bottle costs around 1200 rp.

Beer is expensive compared to other things in Bali – in some places you can actually get a losmen room for less than the price of a bottle of beer – but it's still cheaper than in most Western countries. The three popular brands are San Miguel, Anchor and Bintang. Bintang is often the most expensive. The usual prices are around 2000 to 2500 rp for a large bottle (620 ml) or 1500 rp for a small (320 ml), but you can pay much more in pricier restaurants. In a five-star hotel at Nusa Dua a large beer will set you back 10,000 rp or more.

Some other popular Indonesian and Balinese drinks, both alcoholic and non-alcoholic, include:

Coconuts

air jeruk – lemon juice or orange juice
air minum – drinking water (*air* is water)
arak – distilled rice brandy, one stage on from brem; it can have a real kick. It's usually homemade although even the locally bottled brands look home produced. It makes quite a good mixed drink with 7-Up or Sprite. Mixed with orange juice it's called an *arak attack*.
brem – rice wine, either home produced or the commercially bottled brand Bali Brem. It tastes a bit like sherry – an acquired taste but not bad after a few bottles!
es buah – more a dessert than a drink, es buah is a curious combination of crushed ice, condensed milk, shaved coconut, syrup, jelly and fruit. It can be surprisingly delicious.

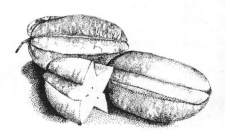

Starfruit

es juice – although you should be a little careful about ice and water the Balinese make delicious fruit drinks which are generally safe to try. In particular the ice-juice drinks are a real taste treat – just take one or two varieties of tropical fruit, add crushed ice and pass through a blender. You can make mind-blowing combinations of orange, banana, pineapple, mango, jackfruit, zurzat or whatever else is available.
kopi – fresh coffee, grown in Bali. *Kopi Bali*

Jackfruit

is strong, black and thick – the bottom third is textured, like Turkish coffee in a big cup. *Kopi susu* is milk coffee. Instant coffee is also available in places.

lassi – a refreshing yoghurt-based drink

stroop – cordial

susu – milk, not a very common drink in Indonesia although you can get long-life milk in cartons; ask for 'ultra'

teh – tea, some people are not enthusiastic about Indonesian tea but if you don't need a strong, bend-the-teaspoon-style brew you'll probably find it's quite OK

tuak – palm beer, usually home-made

ENTERTAINMENT
Cinemas
You'll find a *bioskop* (cinema) in every large town on Bali, and quite a few on Lombok as well. Lurid posters advertising the latest offering are highly visible – often they'll be mounted on a truck which cruises through town with a loudspeaker blasting out rave reviews and bites from the sound track. Balinese tastes in movies are varied in that they like blood-and-guts epics from anywhere in the world – Hong Kong or Hollywood, India or Java. They don't mind a bit of romance or some humour either, but mainly it's action, excitement, suspense and passion.

They usually play films with the original soundtrack, subtitled in Indonesian, so if it's something from the USA, in theory you'll be able to understand it. In practice, there can be a high level of audience participation as they don't need to hear the words, and you probably don't either in most of the films.

But you should check out a bioskop, it's a big social scene for young Balinese and there's usually a good atmosphere.

In the tourist areas you can see a fair selection of recent popular films, but they're most commonly shown on a video in a bar or restaurant. Bali's not a great place for film buffs to indulge their hobby.

Other Entertainment
Balinese dance performances and shadow puppet plays are popular entertainments for tourists, but of course they're much more than that. For more information see the section on Music & Dance in the Facts about Bali chapter.

Cockfights are the most popular entertainment for Balinese men, although technically they're illegal except as part of a temple festival. For more details, see the section on Temples in the Facts about Bali chapter.

Bull racing is an annual event in Negara, and is also held occasionally in the Buleling District on the north coast.

THINGS TO BUY
The most popular purchases are Balinese and Indonesian arts and crafts, which are discussed in the colour Arts & Crafts section, and also clothes.

All sorts of clothing is made locally, and sold in hundreds of small shops in all the main tourist areas, but especially Kuta. It's mostly pretty casual, but it's not just beachwear – you can get a tailor-made red leather jumpsuit, or just about anything else you want. If you're into shopping, you won't need any more advice. They take plastic!

Getting There & Away

Most international visitors will fly to Bali, either directly or via Jakarta. Lombok is usually visited as a side trip from Bali, by plane, ferry or hydrofoil. For island hoppers, there are frequent ferries and local flights between eastern Java and Bali, and from Lombok to Sumbawa and east through Nusa Tenggara.

Bali

AIR

Until recently, flying to Denpasar, the main town and airport of Bali, was complicated by flight restrictions: the Indonesians wanted to ensure that Jakarta, the Indonesian capital, remained the gateway to the country and therefore restricted the availability of flights into Bali. So to get to Denpasar from many countries you had to fly to Jakarta and transfer to a domestic flight from there.

There are indications, however, that this policy is being relaxed and quite a number of national airlines including Air New Zealand, Garuda, Qantas, Singapore Airlines and Thai International are now flying directly to Denpasar.

Arriving in Bali

The airport arrival procedures are fairly typical. The hotel booking counter in the luggage arrival hall has only the more expensive places on its list, with nothing much under US$20. Once through customs you're out with the touts and taxi drivers. There's a tourist information counter inside the arrival area while outside there is a quick and efficient money change office which is usually open for international arrivals, though it sometimes gives a pretty low rate of exchange compared to moneychangers in the main towns. The touts will be working hard to convince you to come and stay at their place in Kuta and if you're not sure where

you intend to stay they may be worth considering – see the Kuta section for more details.

Transport from the airport is quite simple. To stop tourists being fleeced by taxi drivers there's an official taxi counter where you pay for a taxi in advance. Prices from the airport are:

Kuta Beach (to Jalan Bakung Sari)	4500 rp
Kuta-Legian (to Jalan Padma)	6000 rp
Legian (beyond Jalan Padma)	9000 rp
Denpasar	9000 rp
Sanur	12,000 rp
Nusa Dua	12,000 rp
Oberoi Hotel (beyond Legian)	10,000 rp
Ubud	34,000 rp

You can, however, start walking towards the gate in which case the taxi drivers will descend upon you independently and they can be negotiated down to slightly lower rates! The truly impecunious should keep walking all the way to the airport gate, a couple of hundred metres from the international terminal, where they'll find the bemo stop. The even more impecunious (and lightly laden) can walk straight up the road into Kuta, although it's a more pleasant stroll along the beach.

To/From Australia

There are direct flights from Sydney, Melbourne, Brisbane, Perth, Darwin and, believe it or not, Port Hedland. Only Garuda operates the Darwin service and only Qantas flies from Brisbane. Both Garuda and Qantas operate flights on the other sectors.

Both airlines operate direct Melbourne to Denpasar flights some days of the week, and via Sydney on the other days. Some Garuda flights go from Melbourne to Denpasar via Sydney while others go from Sydney via Melbourne. Flight time from Melbourne to Denpasar is about 5½ to 6½ hours; Sydney to Denpasar is slightly shorter. For West Australians Bali is almost a local resort. Perth to Denpasar flying time is just 3½ hours, less time than it takes to go from Perth to the east coast of Australia.

Via Timor & Nusa Tenggara There's one very interesting alternative to the Garuda or Qantas flights and that is to take Merpati from Darwin to Kupang on the island of Timor. From Kupang there are regular flights to Bali or you can island-hop through the Nusa Tenggara archipelago to Bali. The Merpati agent in Darwin is Natrabu (☎ 81 3695) at 10 Westlane Arcade off Smith St Mall. The Darwin to Kupang fare is A$200 one-way or A$330 return. From there the Kupang to Bali fare is about A$170, making the total cost from Darwin to Bali around A$370 one-way or A$670 return. It's a roundabout route but quite a bit cheaper than the direct Garuda flight.

There are two discount fares available between Australia and Bali. Excursion fares are available to anyone, but the other category, tour-inclusive fares, are only available in connection with a holiday package. Both fares have a high and a low season. The high season means the Christmas holiday period. For an excursion fare this is from 22 November to 15 January, and for a tour-inclusive fare it's 10 December to 19 January. At certain times during the peak season, flights to or from Australia are very heavily booked and you must plan well ahead if you want to visit Bali then. In particular getting back to Australia at the end of January, just before Australian schools start after the summer break, can be difficult.

Fares to Denpasar in A$ are:

From	Season	One-Way	Return	Tour-inclusive
Melbourne, Sydney or Brisbane	high	750	1070	960
	low	630	900	830
Perth or Darwin	high	430	760	690
	low	370	670	580
Port Hedland	high	460	790	720
	low	390	705	630

To get the tour-inclusive package fare you have to combine the fare with an accommodation package. Some tour operators and travel agencies can arrange tour-inclusive fares and minimal accommodation packages that cost about the same as the cheapest advance purchase fare. Packages are particularly good bargains on short trips as they include accommodation. Cheap children's tour-inclusive fares are also available. Tour-inclusive fares for low-season departures allow a maximum stay of 45 days; for high-season departures the maximum stay is 90 days.

Tour-inclusive fares can be offered with 'voucher' tours. You buy a package in Australia which includes air fares and hotel accommodation. You're given vouchers which can be used to pay for accommodation at a number of hotels around the island. Sometimes the vouchers can also be used for motorbike or bicycle rental, even for meals. Usually the vouchers are good for the cheaper losmen and hotels – don't expect three-star accommodation. The real bargain with this set up is that the total cost on a short trip can actually be lower than the straight return excursion fare. The vouchers are just a useful bonus – you don't even have to use them.

Package Tours Complete package tours from Australia can also be a real bargain. There are a variety of tour types available. Straightforward tours include your air fare, airport transfers, hotel accommodation and perhaps some meals and the odd sightseeing tour. The price varies depending on when you go, how long you stay and what class of hotel you stay in. The hotels will generally be in Kuta, Sanur or Nusa Dua. Some typical costs from Sydney or Melbourne on a twin-share basis are from around A$800 for seven days (five nights) and from A$850 for 14 days. Extra nights can cost from as little as A$20 per person.

Travel agencies and airline offices will have plenty of colourful brochures to whet your appetite. Check a few brochures because costs vary quite a bit from one operator to another – even on packages using the same hotels. Sightseeing tours and extensions can be made, but a lot of the tours offered can be obtained far more cheaply in Bali. You can rent a whole minibus in Bali for US$21 a day – including driver and fuel. Some packages offer a supplementary visit to Lombok, usually stopping at Senggigi.

To/From New Zealand

Both Garuda and Air New Zealand operate direct flights from Auckland to Denpasar. The full economy fare is NZ$1860 one-way and NZ$3720 return. Return excursion fares are around NZ$1450 in the low season and NZ$1600 in the high season. Low season is from 16 January to 14 December; high season from 15 December to 15 January. Generally, an advance purchase excursion fare allowing a maximum stay of 35 days will be cheaper than a 90-day excursion fare. The cheapest one-way ticket from Auckland to Denpasar costs around NZ$1400 in both the high and low seasons.

To/From Europe

Ticket discounting is a long established business in the UK and it's wide open – the various agencies advertise their fares and there's nothing under the counter about it at all. To find out what is available and where to get it, pick up a copy of the giveaway newspapers *TNT, Southern Cross,* or *Trailfinder* or the weekly 'what's on' guide *Time Out*. These days discounted tickets are available all over the UK, they're not just a London exclusive. The magazine *Business Traveller* also covers cheap fare possibilities.

A couple of excellent places to look are Trailfinders at 194 Kensington High St, London W8 (☎ 938 3939) and at 46 Earl's Court Rd (☎ 938 3366), and STA Travel at 74 Old Brompton Rd, London W7 (☎ 581 1022) and at Clifton House, 117 Euston Rd (☎ 388 2261).

Garuda is one of the enthusiastic fare discounters in London so it's relatively easy to find cheap fares to Australia with stopovers in Indonesia. It's not, however, such a bargain to travel one-way or return to Bali.

A London to Australia ticket with a stopover in Jakarta (or Singapore or Bangkok for that matter) costs around £700, plus another £100 to include Bali. London to Denpasar costs around £300 one-way and £600 return.

Another alternative is to fly London to Singapore for around £280 one-way or £470 return and then make your own way down to Bali by air or sea and land.

To/From North America

You can pick up interesting tickets from the USA to South-East Asia, particularly from the US west coast or from Vancouver. In fact the intense competition between Asian airlines has resulted in ticket-discounting operations very similar to the London bucket shops. To find cheap tickets simply scan the travel sections of the Sunday papers for agencies – the *New York Times, San Francisco Chronicle-Examiner* and the *Los Angeles Times* are particularly good. The network of student travel offices known as Council Travel are particularly good and there are also Student Travel Network offices which are associated with STA Travel.

From the US west coast you can get to Hong Kong, Bangkok or Singapore for about US$800 to US$1000 return and get a flight from there to Bali. Discount tickets for a Hong Kong to Denpasar flight can be bought for around HK$3000 (roughly US$400) and return tickets for around HK$4500 (about US$600). You can also find interesting fares from Hong Kong via Bali to Australia. Singapore to Denpasar costs around S$400 one-way and S$550 return.

These days there are plenty of competitive fares offered to Indonesia from the USA. Fares from Los Angeles to Denpasar cost around US$800 one-way and US$1400 return in the high season (June, July, August and December) and around US$700 and US$1300 in the low season.

Alternatively, Garuda has a Los Angeles, Honolulu, Biak, Denpasar route which is an extremely interesting back-door route into Indonesia and good value at US$472 one-way or about US$800 return. Biak is a no-visa entry point for most nationalities.

Air Travel Glossary

Apex Apex, or 'advance purchase excursion' is a discounted ticket which must be paid for in advance. There are penalties if you wish to change it.

Bucket Shop An unbonded travel agency specialising in discounted airline tickets.

Bumped Just because you have a confirmed seat doesn't mean you're going to get on the plane – see Overbooking.

Cancellation Penalties If you have to cancel or change an Apex ticket there are often heavy penalties involved, insurance can sometimes be taken out against these penalties. Some airlines impose penalties on regular tickets as well, particularly against 'no show' passengers.

Check In Airlines ask you to check in a certain time ahead of the flight departure (usually 1½ hours on international flights). If you fail to check in on time and the flight is overbooked the airline can cancel your booking and give your seat to somebody else.

Confirmation Having a ticket written out with the flight and date you want doesn't mean you have a seat until the agent has checked with the airline that your status is 'OK' or confirmed. Meanwhile you could just be 'on request'.

Cross-Border Tickets Sometimes it is cheaper to fly to countries A, B, C rather than just B to C, usually because country A's airline is desperate to sell tickets or because the currency in A is very weak. Authorities in B can get very unhappy if you turn up for the flight from B to C without having first flown from A to B. Be cautious about discounted tickets which have been issued in another city, particularly in Eastern European cities.

Discounted Tickets There are two types of discounted fares – officially discounted (see Promotional Fares) and unofficially discounted. With unofficially discounted tickets you usually get what you pay for and the lowest prices often impose drawbacks like flying with unpopular airlines (Eastern European or Middle Eastern airlines for example), inconvenient schedules (only one flight a week and it leaves at 1 am) or unpleasant routes and connections (you get from A to B by a roundabout route and have to change airlines half way with a long wait at the airport). A discounted ticket doesn't necessarily have to save you money – an agent may be able to sell you a ticket at Apex prices without the associated Apex advance booking and other requirements. Discounted tickets only exist where there is fierce competition, they are rarely available on domestic routes if the country only has one or two domestic airlines or in similarly tightly controlled regions.

Freedoms An airline's right to take passengers between various cities is defined by six 'freedoms'. Unofficially discounted tickets are often associated with fifth freedom flights – where an airline from country A has the right to fly passengers between country B and country C – or sixth freedom flights – where the airline in country B can fly passengers from A to C as long as the flight goes through B.

Full Fares Airlines traditionally offer first class (coded F), business class (coded J) and economy class (coded Y) tickets. These days there are so many promotional and discounted fares available from the regular economy class that few passengers pay full economy fare.

Lost Tickets If you lose your airline ticket an airline will usually treat it like a travellers' cheque and, after inquiries, issue you with another one. Legally, however, an airline is entitled to treat it like cash and if you lose it then it's gone forever. Take good care of your tickets.

Maximum Permitted Mileage (MPM) Between city A and city Z there is an officially defined MPM and so long as you do not exceed that distance you can fly via B, C, X, Y and points in between if you have a full fare, unlimited stopover ticket. These days, however, full-fare tickets are rather rare.

No Shows No shows are passengers who fail to show up for their flight, sometimes due to unexpected delays or disasters, sometimes due to simply forgetting, sometimes because they made more than one booking and didn't bother to cancel the one they didn't want.

On Request An unconfirmed booking for a flight, see Confirmation.

Open Jaws A return ticket where you fly out to one place but return from another. If available this can save you backtracking to your arrival point.

Overbooking Airlines hate to fly empty seats and since every flight has some passengers who fail to show up (see No Shows) airlines often book more passengers than they have seats. Usually the excess passengers balance those who fail to show up but occasionally somebody gets bumped. If this happens guess who it is most likely to be? The passengers who check in late of course.

Promotional Fares Officially discounted fares like Apex fares which are available from any travel agent or direct from the airline.

Reconfirmation At least 72 hours prior to departure time of an onward or return flight you must contact the airline and 'reconfirm' that you intend to be on the flight. If you don't do this the airline can delete your name from the passenger list and you could lose your seat. You don't have to reconfirm the first flight on your itinerary or if your stopover is less than 72 hours. It doesn't hurt to reconfirm more than once.

Restrictions Discounted tickets often have various restrictions on them – advance purchase is the most usual one (see Apex). Others are restrictions on the minimum and maximum period you must be away, such as a minimum of 14 days or a maximum of one year. See Cancellation Penalties.

Standby A discounted ticket where you only fly if there is a seat free at the last moment. Standby fares are usually only available on domestic routes.

Tickets Out An entry requirement for many countries is that you have an onward or return ticket, in other words, a ticket out of the country. If you're not sure what you intend to do next, the easiest solution is to buy the cheapest onward ticket to a neighbouring country or a ticket from a reliable airline which can later be refunded if you do not use it.

Transferred Tickets Airline tickets cannot be transferred from one person to another. Travellers sometimes try to sell the return half of their ticket, but officials can ask you to prove that you are the person named on the ticket. This is unlikely to happen on domestic flights but can easily happen on an international flight where tickets may be compared with passports.

Travel Agencies Travel agencies vary widely and you should ensure you use one that suits your needs. Some simply handle tours while full-service agencies handle everything from tours and tickets to car rental and hotel bookings. A good one will do all these things and can save you a lot of money but if all you want is a ticket at the lowest possible price, then you really need an agency specialising in discounted tickets. A discounted ticket agency, however, may not be useful for other things, like hotel bookings.

Travel Periods Some officially discounted fares, Apex fares in particular, vary with the time of year. There is often a low (off-peak) season and a high (peak) season. Sometimes there's an intermediate or shoulder season as well. At peak times, when everyone wants to fly, not only will the officially discounted fares be higher but so will unofficially discounted fares or there may simply be no discounted tickets available. Usually the fare depends on your outward flight – if you depart in the high season and return in the low season, you pay the high-season fare. ■

To/From Asia

You are certain to find cheap fares to Bali from Asia (Bangkok, Singapore and Hong Kong for example) and an increasing number of these will be direct flights to Denpasar. For some flights, however, you will have to enter Indonesia at Jakarta and then fly to Bali.

To/From Java

Garuda fares from Denpasar include Surabaya for 72,000 rp, Yogyakarta for 93,000 rp and Jakarta for 170,000 rp. Merpati and Bouraq also fly from Denpasar to various centres in Java and their fares will always be lower than Garudas'. Note that if you want to change your ticket with Garuda there's a

10,000 rp cancellation and reissuance charge.

To/From Other Parts of Indonesia

In some instances it is cheaper to fly to other parts of Indonesia from Bali than from Java. For example, from Denpasar to Ujung Pandang (Sulawesi) the fare is cheaper (120,000 rp) than from Surabaya (Java) to Ujung Pandang (160,000 rp). There are flights from Denpasar to other parts of Nusa Tenggara including Kupang and Dili in Timor.

SEA

To/From Java

The standard travellers' route from Java to Bali is by bus from Surabaya to Denpasar, crossing the Bali Strait by ferry. There are numerous bus companies operating on this route, and many of them travel overnight. The fare includes the ferry crossing and often a meal at a rest stop along the way. There are also direct bus services between Yogyakarta and Denpasar.

In Bali you can get tickets from numerous agencies in and around Kuta, Ubud and other tourist areas. You'll also find a collection of bus company offices, and other agencies, at the Suci bus station in Denpasar. Fares depend on the bus and cost more with air-con. Buses to Surabaya range in price from 16,000 to 19,000 rp and to Yogyakarta they vary from 25,000 to 32,000 rp. Air-con buses to Jakarta cost around 48,000 rp.

When you book you're assigned a seat number; check the seating chart and try to avoid the front rows – the night-bus drivers rush along like maniacs and who wants to be first to find out about the accident? In fact the night buses make the Denpasar to Surabaya trip so rapidly that early evening departures are liable to arrive at an uncomfortably early hour in the morning.

The ferry that shuttles back and forth across the narrow strait between Bali and Java takes only 15 minutes to cross one-way. Costs are 2000 rp for an adult (less for a child). You can take a a car across for about 25,000 rp (the cost depends on the size of the car) and a motorbike for around 3000 rp. On the Java side the terminus is not actually in the Java ferry port of Banyuwangi. It's right out of the town at Ketapang but there is regular transport into Banyuwangi. Buses to other parts of Java depart straight from the ferry terminal.

To/From Other Islands

The Pelni ship *Kelimutu* makes a loop through the islands every two weeks, travelling from Padangbai to Lembar, Ujung Pandang (Sulawesi), Bima (Sumbawa), Waingapu (Sumba), Ende (Flores), and Kupang (Timor). It returns via the same ports in reverse order.

LEAVING BALI

Don't forget to reconfirm your flight at least 72 hours before departure. There are Garuda offices in Denpasar and at the Kuta Beach Hotel in Kuta. Garuda and Qantas both have offices in the Hotel Bali Beach at Sanur. Reconfirming is very important in the peak holiday periods when there always seem to be people waiting at the airport hoping for a spare seat. Travel agencies will offer to reconfirm for you, for a fee, but some have been notoriously lax about actually making reconfirmations. You should receive a small computer printout with all the details on it, in cryptic airline-speak.

Come departure time Denpasar airport holds no surprises. Alcohol drinkers can try the airport snack bar or wait until they've passed through immigration and try the cafeteria bar. The duty-free shop and souvenir shops here only accept foreign currency. The departure lounge cafeteria takes rupiah. You can change excess rupiah back into hard currency at a bank counter by the check-in desks.

Departure Tax There's a departure tax on domestic flights (3,500 rp) and international (11,000 rp) flights. Only children under two years of age are exempt from this.

Lombok

There is no international airport on Lombok, but it's quite accessible by air and sea from the neighbouring islands. The vast majority of travellers arrive from Bali, less than 100 km away, while those island-hopping from the east will reach Lombok from Sumbawa. It's also possible to fly directly from Java to Lombok.

AIR

There are about seven flights per day with Merpati from Denpasar to Mataram, at about 42,000 rp. Strangely, it's about 1000 rp cheaper to fly in the other direction. It's a very short flight, about 25 minutes, with fine views of Nusa Penida, the south-eastern coast of Bali and the Gili Islands. Though the ferry is much cheaper, many low-budget travellers still fly to save the time and expense of getting to and from the ports of Padangbai and Lembar.

There is one Merpati flight a day between Mataram and Sumbawa Besar (47,000 rp) and on some days these continue on to Bima. Merpati has regular flights between Mataram and Surabaya (81,900 rp), Yogyakarta (134,450 rp) and Jakarta (192,400 rp). There should be at least one flight per day, but schedules are variable.

SEA
To/From Bali

Perama has services running to/from Kuta, Sanur, Ubud, Lovina, Candidasa and Padangbai on Bali and Lembar, Mataram, Senggigi, Bangsal and the Gili Islands on Lombok. For example, a ticket from Ubud in Bali through to one of the Gili Islands off the Lombok coast costs 17,500 rp, including the ferry to Lombok and a boat to the island, with all the connections in between. On public transport you could probably do this trip for about 10,000 rp (if you weren't overcharged) but it would involve four bemo connections, the ferry and a boat. It would probably take longer and, if you missed a connection, you might have to spend a night somewhere in between. Perama has an office or agency in most of the places mentioned earlier – you usually have to book the day before.

Ferry There are at least two ferries a day between Padangbai (Bali) and Lembar (Lombok) and up to four services at busy times such as Ramadan. Scheduled departure times from Padangbai are 8 and 11 am, 2 and 5 pm, and from Lembar at 8 and 10 am, 2 and 5 pm. The schedules vary, so check first. *Ekonomi* costs around 4000 rp, 1st class 5700 rp. You can take a bicycle (600 rp), motorbike (4300 rp) or car (49,000 rp for a Suzuki Jimny).

For 1st-class passengers there's an air-conditioned cabin with aircraft-type seats, a snack bar and video entertainment. Ekonomi passengers sit on bench seats or wherever they can find a spot. It can be a long and uncomfortable trip in either class, and very hot outside the 1st-class cabin. Food and drinks are available on board or from the numerous hawkers who hang around the wharf until the ferry leaves. The trip takes at least four hours, sometimes up to seven; the afternoon ferries seem to be slower than the morning ones.

Hydrofoil A hydrofoil service now operates between Bali's Benoa Port and Lembar Harbour on Lombok. Scheduled departure times from Benoa are 8.45 am and 3.30 pm, and from Lembar 10.45 am and 3.30 pm. The trip takes about two hours and costs 35,000 rp to Lombok, 32,000 rp the other way. The service is run by the Nawala company which has offices in Denpasar (☎ 31339) at Jalan Iman Bonjol 234 and Mataram (☎ 21655) at Jalan Langko 11A. Tickets can also be bought at Manu Madi Tours (☎ 88901) in Sanur and at Benoa Port and Lembar Harbour. Perama also sell hydrofoil tickets with bus connections to/from Benoa and Lembar.

Perhaps to compete with the air service, the operators like to pretend the hydrofoil is an aircraft, with a check-in time, boarding passes and a uniformed steward. Although not much cheaper than flying, the hydrofoil is a fun trip and is certainly much quicker, more comfortable and more convenient than the ferry.

Incidentally, though the service may be new, the two hydrofoils certainly are not – they were on the Hong Kong to Macau run for a few years before being brought to Indonesia. If the service is successful, it may be extended to provide a Lombok to Sumbawa connection.

To/From Sumbawa

Passenger ferries leave Labuhan Lombok (in eastern Lombok) for Poto Tano (Sumbawa) at 8 and 9.30 am, noon, 3 and 5 pm. In the other direction, boats depart Poto Tano at 7 and 9 am, noon, 2.30 and 5 pm. Departure times may change, depending on demand and goodness knows what other local considerations. The trip takes about 1½ hours and costs around 2500 rp in ekonomi A, 1500 rp in ekonomi B, 500 rp for a bicycle, 3000 rp for a motorbike and 27,000 rp for a car.

Perama has bus-ferry-bus connections between Lombok and Sumbawa Besar, Dompu and Bima on Sumbawa.

Getting Around

Public transport and rental options are similar on Bali and Lombok: there are cheap bemos and buses that run on more or less set routes within or between towns and, if you want your own transport, you can charter a whole bemo or rent a car, motorbike or bicycle. Both islands also have tourist shuttle buses operating between the major tourist centres. These are more expensive than public transport but are more comfortable and convenient.

Bali

BEMO

Bemos are *the* Balinese form of public transport. These days most bemos are minibuses, although the old basic version, a small pick-up truck with a row of seats down each side, is still around. You might even see some of the old, three-wheeled types in Denpasar. Most bemos operate on a standard route for a set fare, picking up and dropping off people and goods anywhere along the way. Unless you get on at a regular starting point, and get off at a regular finishing point, the fares are likely to be fuzzy. The cost per km is pretty variable, but it's cheaper on longer trips. The minimum fare is about 200 rp.

The best way of finding out what the fare should be is to ask your fellow passengers what the harga biasa (standard price) should be. Bemo drivers are always ready to overcharge the unwary but are usually good-humoured about it. If they ask 500 rp, and you know damn well it should only be 200 rp, they'll take the correct fare with a grin. Equally, if they put up a big protest about the correct fare being 500 rp when you're only offering 200 rp, they're probably right. Beware of *harga turis* (tourist price) for bemos, which are increasingly prevalent in Bali. Sometimes they'll charge extra if you have a big bag, which seems pretty fair

as two Balinese might fit in the space taken up by some travellers' backpacks.

Around Kuta and Sanur, beware of getting on an empty bemo. There are some unscrupulous drivers who will inform you, at the end of the ride, that they weren't really plying the route, and you've just chartered the whole bemo!

A minibus may be called a 'colt', from the Mitsubishi Colt minibuses made under licence in Indonesia, though the term is no longer widespread. On short trips, all bemos operate the same way and charge the same fares, regardless of whether they are old-style bemos, colts, or any other type of minibus. On many longer routes, minibuses have replaced, or supplemented, full-sized buses. Minibuses are generally more expensive than buses over the same route, but are more comfortable and depart more frequently, ie as soon as they're full.

Every town and village has a bemo station, or just a place where bemos and buses stop. Larger towns may have several bus/bemo stations. Denpasar is the hub of Bali's transport system, and it has five stations. To go from one part of Bali to another it is often necessary to go via one or more of the Denpasar stations.

Chartering a Bemo

An excellent way for a group to get around is to charter a bemo; for many trips, it's so much more convenient than using public bemos . For example, to go by public bemo from Sanur to Ubud, you would go first to the Kereneng bus station in Denpasar (500 rp), then transfer to the Batubulan bus station (500 rp), then take a third bemo to Ubud (700 rp). Alternatively you can, with a little bargaining, charter a whole bemo to take you straight there for around 18,000 to 20,000 rp. Between eight people that works out about the same as the roundabout route through Denpasar, but it's much faster, and you can be dropped at the door of your final destination.

Warning
Beware of pickpockets – on certain bemo routes they've become notorious. You'll find them mainly on the Denpasar to Kuta and Denpasar to Ubud routes where they tend to prey on unwary travellers. Their mode of operation seems to be for one operator to engage you in friendly conversation, while his accomplice cleans you out, often using a painting, parcel or similar cover to hide the activity. Sometimes half the people on the bemo will be in on the game, and the odds will really be stacked against you.

If you want to make stops on the way this will add a little to the cost. Regular bemos carry around 12 people so multiplying the usual fare by 12 should give you a rough idea of what you'd expect to pay on a particular route.

It's easy to arrange a charter – just listen for one of the frequent offers of 'transport, transport' in the street, or approach a driver yourself. Try to deal directly with the driver because any intermediaries or touts will expect a cut somewhere.

To charter a bemo for a day, work on about 40,000 to 50,000 rp, although the cost depends on where you want to go. If you're planning to start early, finish late, and cover an awful lot of territory, then you will have to pay more. Make sure you agree in advance whether petrol is included or extra. The cost is comparable to hiring a car for a single day, so you get the driver virtually for nothing. You don't have to worry about a licence or insurance, and a driver who knows the way round can be a real asset, particularly if you're in Denpasar or one of the larger towns. A good driver will act as a personal guide, interpreter, and source of information for just about everything. Of course you can stop when you like, to take photos, shop or whatever. However, one problem, particularly if you're shopping, is that you might finish up going where your driver wants you to go and not where you thought you wanted to go.

TOURIST SHUTTLE BUS

In the main tourist areas you'll see signs advertising tourist shuttle buses direct to other destinations on Bali, and they are usually comfortable and reliable. Although considerably more expensive than public transport, these minibuses are much cheaper and more convenient than chartering a bemo.

Tourist shuttle buses have been organised into a virtual network by the Perama company. Perama operates regular, scheduled minibuses, and full-sized buses, to and from all the main tourist areas on Bali, with connections to Java, Lombok and Sumbawa. There may be other tourist bus companies, and these may also provide a good service, but Perama seems to be the most established and is widely recommended. Perama's head office in Kuta is at Jalan Legian 20 (☎ 0361-51551, 51875, fax 51170), and there are also offices in Candidasa, Lovina and Ubud. In Sanur, Perama buses stop outside the Si Pino Restaurant, near the Hotel Bali Beach, and you can phone the Kuta office to book. Always try to book the day before with Perama; a bigger bus will be put on if needed.

Perama's prices are fixed, and you can get a schedule and a list of fares at any of its offices. Fares from Kuta to Ubud via Sanur are 4000 rp; to Lovina 10,000 rp; to Padangbai and Candidasa 7500 rp; and to the airport 3500 rp. The fare from Kuta to Mataram and Senggigi on Lombok costs 13,000 rp with the ferry and 25,000 rp on the hydrofoil.

MOTORBIKE

Motorbikes are a popular way of getting around Bali but also a controversial one; they very definitely have their pluses and minuses. The minus points are the danger and the distance that riding keeps you from certain everyday interactions with the Balinese.

There is no denying the dangers of motorbike riding in Bali: combined with all the normal terrors of riding are narrow roads, unexpected potholes, crazy drivers, buses and trucks which tend to behave as though they own the road, children darting out in front of you, bullocks lumbering across your path, dogs and chickens running around in circles, unmarked road works, unlit traffic at night, and 1001 other opportunities for you to do serious harm to yourself. Every year a number of visitors to Bali come home in a box. Bali is no place to learn to ride a motorbike.

The distance drawback is that on a motorbike you forsake many opportunities to come to grips with Bali. You don't meet people the way you do on a bemo, and many things can be missed because you are concentrating on the road. Furthermore, motorbikes are an unpleasant intrusion in many places in Bali because they can be noisy, distracting, annoying and unwanted.

On the other hand, motorbikes have some important plus points. The major one is the enormous flexibility they give you. Bali may have various not-to-be-missed sights but the best things it has to offer are completely unplanned. You come round a corner and there it is – a procession, a mouthwateringly beautiful piece of scenery, or a temple decked out for a festival. Travelling around on a bike you can stop if you want to, and not continue until 10 minutes or 10 hours later. If you're travelling in a bemo you may just shoot straight by or even miss it altogether. Robert Pirsig in *Zen & the Art of Motorcycle Maintenance* relates driving a car to watching television and compares riding a bike as being *in* the picture. Unhappily, riding a bemo can be television with a dozen people between you and the screen.

I have to admit that although I've covered many km around Bali by bus and bemo, I've probably covered more by motorcycle. I think I've always ridden carefully and I've never had anything resembling a hairy moment in Bali. I have had some truly beautiful moments biking round Bali: those days when every corner seems to bring another breathtaking chunk of landscape into view; rolling lazily down sweeping, traffic-free roads where the artistry of the terraced rice paddies is pure magic.

Tony Wheeler

Finding a Motorbike

Motorbikes for hire in Bali are almost all between 90 and 125 cc with 100 cc as the usual size. You really don't need anything bigger as the distances are short and the roads are rarely suitable for travelling fast. Anyway what's the hurry?

Rental charges vary with the bike and the period of hire. The longer the hire period the lower the rate, the bigger or newer the bike the higher the rate. Typically you can expect to pay around 8000 to 12,000 rp a day. A newish 125 cc in good condition might cost 12,000 rp a day. If you want a bike for only one day you might have to pay more.

Renting a motorbike in Bali is not like zipping around to your friendly Avis or Hertz agency with its current rates brochure in hand. The majority of the bikes are rented out by individual owners, probably to raise a little extra money towards paying for it. There are a few places around Kuta which seem to specialise in motorbike hire but generally it's travel agencies, restaurants, losmen or shops with a sign out saying 'motorcycle for hire'. You can ask around or, if you've got an 'I need a motorbike' look about you somebody is certain to approach you. Kuta is the main bike hire place but you'll have no trouble finding a motorbike to rent in Ubud, Sanur or Lovina. Check the bike over before riding off – there are some poorly maintained pieces of junk around.

Licence

If you have an International Driving Permit endorsed for motorbikes you have no problems. If not, you have to obtain a local licence and this is straightforward and easy, but time-consuming. The bike owner will take you into Denpasar where you'll probably find 50 or so other would-be bike renters lined up for their licence. You're fingerprinted, photographed, given a written test (to which you are told the answers in advance) and then comes the hard part. After a friendly sendoff from the police riding tester, who wishes you luck and gives you the cheerful news that if you fail you can always try again, off you go. You ride once around a circle clockwise, once around anti-clockwise, then ride slalom through a row of tin cans – without putting your feet down or falling off. Don't run into the police officer's car either. Eventually everyone passes and is judged fit to be unleashed onto Bali's roads. It costs 25,000 rp and the whole process takes about four hours.

Apart from your licence you must also carry the bike's registration paper with you. Make sure the bike's owner gives it to you before you ride off.

Insurance

These days insurance seems to be a fixed requirement in Bali. It's quite expensive – it can cost nearly as much as the bike rental itself – and whether it actually does you much good if worst comes to worst is not entirely clear. Make sure, however, that your personal travel insurance covers you while you're biking. Some travel insurance policies have some nasty small print that may exclude coverage for motorbike riding.

The best advice is: don't have an accident, but remember if you do that it was your fault. The logic behind this is Asian and impeccable: 'I was involved in an accident with you. I belong here, you don't. If you hadn't been here there wouldn't have been an accident. Therefore it was your fault.' So make sure your travel insurance policy also covers you for personal liability, in case you have to pay for damage to other vehicles, people or property.

On the Road

Once you've cleared the southern Bali traffic tangle the roads are remarkably uncrowded.

The traffic is heavy from Denpasar south to Kuta and Sanur; to the east about as far as Klungkung; and to the west about as far as Tabanan. Over the rest of the island the traffic is no problem at all, and in most places it's very light.

Finding your way around is no problem. Roads are well signposted and maps are easily available. Off the main routes, roads often become very potholed, but are usually surfaced – there are few dirt roads in Bali. Petrol is sold by the government-owned Pertamina company and is still reasonably cheap – around 500 rp a litre.

Bali has quite a few petrol (gas) stations but they often seem to be out of petrol, out of electricity or simply on holiday. In that case look for the little roadside fuel shops where they fill your tank with a plastic jug and a funnel. They usually have a hand-written sign that reads 'premium'. I was once told to avoid these places because the petrol they sold was 'second hand'! In fact, it does sit round in open containers and is quite likely to be contaminated with water or dirt, though I've never had any trouble with it.

James Lyon

Although Bali is in the tropics it's still wise to dress properly for biking. Remember that if you fall off, your skin and the pavement don't go well together. Thongs, shorts and a T-shirt are not going to protect you. As well as protection against a spill, be prepared for the weather. Down on the plains it may be warm all year round but it can get amazingly cold on a cloudy day in the mountains. Coming over the top of Batur you might wish you were wearing gloves. And when it rains in Bali, it really rains so be ready for that as well. Don't ignore the sun either. If you're riding on a hot day you're just offering your uncovered arms and face up for burning, so cover up and use a sun block.

Around the Island

Don't plan on any island tour in Bali going to schedule – festivals, ceremonies, cremations, processions or almost anything could be there to distract you from your intended itinerary. Given a minimum of a week a possible round-trip route could be:

Day 1	Kuta to Candidasa	110 km
Day 2	Candidasa to Penelokan via Amlapura	140 km
Day 3	around Lake Batur	
Day 4	Penelokan to Lovina	90 km
Day 5	at the beach	
Day 6	Lovina to Kuta via Bedugul	140 km

Of course that's a fairly high-speed trip and your starting and finishing point doesn't have to be Kuta, it could just as easily be Ubud, Singaraja or anywhere else you choose.

CAR RENTAL

Car rental in Bali has become very easy in recent years. The big international rental operators have a token presence there but they're very expensive and you'll do far better with the local operators. The most popular vehicles for rent are the small Suzuki Jimnys, but you can also find open VW safari vehicles, regular cars, minibuses and virtually anything else. The Suzukis, with their compact size, good ground clearance and low gear ratio are well suited to exploring Bali's back roads, though some people find them a bit small and cramped. Really, almost anything is fine over Bali's limited distances, although the VWs cannot be locked up so you cannot leave things safely inside them. Typical costs are around 35,000 to 40,000 rp a day including insurance and unlimited km. If you rent for a week you can expect to get one day free, which makes the cost as little as 30,000 rp per day. Agencies at Kuta, Sanur, Lovina etc will have signs out advertising cars for rent.

As with motorbikes, it's a good idea to check rental cars carefully before you drive off. Don't wait until you really need the horn, wipers, lights, spare tyre, or registration papers before you find they're not there. It's unusual to find a car with a speedometer/odometer that works.

Renting a minibus-style bemo is also possible. Some bemo drivers are more than happy to take a few days off while you drive their bemo around. We met an American family who rented one for a month! These days tourists driving bemos are a sufficiently 'normal' sight that people don't even bother to flag you down!

There are some drawbacks to renting cars though. A rental car may cost more than chartering a bemo for the day. Being in your own car makes you even more remote from the people and the countryside, and you may not want to stop too long in one place if you're paying 30,000 rp a day. Rental cars have to be returned to the place from which they were hired – you can't do a one-way rental. Also, you may be asked higher prices at hotels and shops if you arrive by car – they know you can afford it. Then there is the impact on Bali's road system, parking facilities and environment generally – what would happen if every tourist wanted to drive around Bali in their own car? For a group or a family wanting to have a quick trip around the whole island, a rental car is a good option. If you want to travel more slowly, stopping for a day or so in a number of places, then you'd be better off on tourist shuttle buses (for convenience) or public bemos and buses (for value and lots of local contact).

Road Rules & Risks

It's very common to hear visitors complaining about crazy Balinese drivers, but often it's because they don't understand the local conventions of road use. Most of the drivers on Bali's roads are professionals, and usually they're pretty good. The main thing to remember is the 'watch your front' rule – it's your responsibility to avoid anything that gets in front of your vehicle. A car or motorbike pulling out in front of you, in effect, has the right of way. Often they won't even look up the road to see what's coming, though they usually listen for the horn. So that's the second rule – use your horn to warn anything in front that you're there, especially if you're about to overtake. Thirdly, driving is on the left side of the road in Bali, more or less, and you should try to follow this rule (though it's probably not as important as the first two rules).

Avoid driving at night, or even at dusk. Many bicycles, carts and other horse-drawn vehicles don't have proper lights, and street lighting is limited to the main towns. It's terrifying to discover that you're about to run up the back of a mobile satay stand when there are at least three invisible bicycles which you'll hit if you try to avoid it, and the bemo behind you is blaring its horn and about to overtake.

HITCHING

Yes, you can even hitchhike around Bali. Two Dutch travellers have reported that while hitching you meet a lot of nice people, enjoy the scenery and 'it's a good experience to ride around Bali, standing in the back of a truck!'

BICYCLE

Seeing Bali by pushbike has become much more popular in recent years. Nowadays more people are giving it a try and more places are renting bikes – some people are even bringing their bikes with them. You can usually bring your pushbike with you in your baggage – some airlines (Qantas for example) may carry it free. Most of the information on renting and using bicycles which follows is based (with necessary updating) on *Bali by Bicycle* by Hunt Kooiker. Originally published by the author in 1977, this handy little booklet is now, unfortunately, out of print.

Cycling in Bali

At first glance Bali, with its high mountains, narrow bumpy roads, tropical heat and frequent rain showers does not seem like a place for a bicycle tour. However, far from being obstacles, the mountains can be turned into allies. With the judicious help of two short bemo trips to scale the central mountains you can accomplish a beautiful, mostly level or downhill, 200 km circle trip of Bali.

It is true Bali has narrow roads but once you're out of the congested southern region the traffic is relatively light, and the bumpy roads are not a great problem if you invest in a good, padded seat. Since a large part of the 200 km trip is level or downhill the tropical heat problem literally turns into a breeze. Frequent roadside food stalls also make it remarkably easy to duck out of a passing rain shower.

The main advantage of seeing Bali by bicycle is the quality of the experience. You can cover many more km by bemo, bus or motorbike but will you really see more? By bicycle you can be totally accessible to the environment. Without the noise of a motorbike you can hear the wind rustling in the rice paddies and the sound of a gamelan orchestra practising as you pass by.

The slower speed of cycling helps to bridge the time warp between the rush of the West and the calm of Bali. You will have time to greet people by the roadside and feel their warm response.

Renting a Bicycle

There are plenty of bicycles for rent in Bali. If you wanted to buy a bicycle, 10-speed bicycles are becoming quite common and Denpasar has a number of bicycle shops selling spare parts and complete bicycles. There are numerous bike rental shops in Kuta, Legian, Sanur and Ubud. The challenge though is finding a bike that works! Rental choices run from one-speed clunkers with terrible seats to one-speed clunkers with terrible seats, no reflectors, bell, lights or brakes. Fortunately, some of the rental shops are open to making special arrangements – Hunt Kooiker gives an example where he arranged to buy a used bike from a shop, then spent a little money and rather more time refurbishing it before selling it back to the shop 2½ months later. His 'rental cost' worked out to less than 100 rp per day!

Alternatively, if your trip is shorter, you can take a bicycle for the usual rental rates – start bargaining down from around 3000 rp per day if the bike is any good. Rates by the week or longer periods are, of course, much cheaper. Instead of agreeing to pay the full amount in cash it's worth bargaining to improve the bike and deduct the cost. Buy a new padded seat in Denpasar, take it to the rental shop and offer to replace their old,

Top: Chinese Temple, Benoa, Bali (JL)
Bottom: Hotel bungalow, Campuan, near Ubud, Bali (TW)

Top: Early morning in Ubud, Bali (JL)
Left: A gamelan in procession, Ubud, Bali (TW)
Right: Drive-through Banyan tree, Cupuan, Bali (JL)

distorted, hard-as-tacks seat with the new seat if they'll discount the first part of your rental. Besides making your touring infinitely more enjoyable you will also gain good karma from all the people who rent the same bicycle after you!

What to Look For For touring it is absolutely essential that your bike is in good repair. A checklist of things to look for when picking out your bike includes:

Brakes Both the front and rear brakes must be able to stop your bike individually in case one should malfunction on a steep downhill. Check the brake blocks (the rectangular hard rubber pads which press against the rims) to see that they are symmetrically positioned and show even wear with plenty of rubber left. They should be about 25 mm away from the wheel so that they do not rub any part of the rim when you spin the wheel. The real test is whether or not they can hold the bike still when clamped while you push forward with all your strength. If in doubt, buy yourself some new brake blocks, they're very cheap. Do not go into the central mountains without good brakes.

Wheels & Tyres Before agreeing to rent the bike, turn it upside down and spin the wheels. Check the rims carefully for deep rust spots which could cause the wheel to buckle under stress. Look at the rim as it moves by the brake blocks. If the wheel wobbles you will have shimmering problems. Also squeeze the spokes to check for loose or broken ones.

Avoid bikes with bald or soft tyres. Sure the shop will offer to pump them up but you're the one who will have to do it every day after that.

Bell, Light & Back Reflector A bell and light are both very useful things to have in working order. The bell should be positioned out on the handlebar so it can be used with your hand still gripping the brake. Be sure to spin the front wheel with the generator engaged to make sure the light works. A new back reflector is a good investment if there isn't one on the bike.

Seat The condition of *your* seat on a long ride depends on the condition of your bicycle seat. Consider buying a new, soft, padded one or at least a tie-on foam seat cover. You can purchase either of these at a Denpasar bike shop. Invariably the seats will be pushed down to rest on the frame with the correct legroom for a midget. Ask to have the seat raised so that when you are sitting on it you can straighten your leg fully to touch the lower pedal with your heel. If you are very tall it is worth buying an extra long pipe to raise the seat.

Other Accessories A carrier rack over the rear mudguard is ideal for carrying a small bag of belongings. One or two elastic shock cords with hooks at each end will help to secure the baggage. Many bikes are equipped with a claw-like key lock which guards against petty theft. A much sturdier steel cable lock may be a worthwhile purchase.

Final Checks Most bikes are never oiled by the rental shops and because people ride them on salty beaches they get badly corroded and don't pedal smoothly. Find a can of oil and lightly oil all moving parts including the crankshaft and chain. Check to see if all the nuts are securely tightened, especially those to the seat, the brake linkage cables and the brake rims, which tend to vibrate loose.

Bicycles are used extensively by the Balinese themselves and even the smallest village has some semblance of a bike shop. Some shops will allow you to borrow tools to work on your own bike. A small gift of peanuts or an offer of an ice juice is greatly appreciated by the lender. If you're not used to working on bicycles ask someone from the shop to repair it for you. Labour charges are very low – a flat tyre might cost less than a dollar. The best shops for any extensive repairs are in Denpasar.

Packing for Touring

It is quite possible to tour Bali by bicycle with nothing but the clothes on your back – and this book! The distance between losmen is always within a day's ride. Food stalls are numerous and there is no need for camping equipment. All losmen provide a sheet which can double as a sarong while you wash your clothes.

However, it's more convenient to carry at least a minimum of gear with you. This would include riding shorts and T-shirt, and a pair of long trousers for temple festivals or cool mountain evenings. Women can consider a skirt and T-shirt, and a nicer shirt or blouse for festivals. Sandals and an optional pair of running shoes are useful if you want to climb Gunung Batur. A sash is essential for visiting many temples. You'll also need a swimsuit as skinny-dipping is not appreciated.

Other useful things include a torch, mosquito coils, matches, soap, towel, toothbrush, sun hat, sun block and some zinc oxide to protect your nose from the sun.

Bring as little as possible. Besides having to carry the baggage on your bicycle, if you want to park your bike to explore an area on foot you'll have to carry your bag or find some place to stash it.

The 200 km Circle Tour

This route is designed to take in the greatest number of points of interest with the minimum use of motorised transport and the maximum amount of level or downhill roads. The tour is divided into six days of riding in a clockwise direction. Evening stops have been planned where there are convenient losmen. The minimum daily distance is about 20 km, the maximum is 53 km but 20 to 30 km of the latter distance will probably be covered by bemo.

Of course there are losmen in other villages along the route and it is also possible to stay in most villages which do not have losmen. Just ask to speak with the headman (kepala desa) of the village. The trip can also be done in reverse. Interposed within the basic six-day tour are suggestions for side trips. These trips, plus extra days spent exploring each area, can easily evolve into a two-week trip. An estimated riding time has been given for each day.

Day 1 – Kuta to Bedugul 53 km (37 km by bicycle), riding time seven hours.

The first day is a long one so it's best to get an early start. Leave the tourists and Westernised Balinese of Kuta and ride north along Jalan Legian. Soon the traffic will disappear and you'll be riding along exquisitely terraced rice fields interspersed with small villages. Continue north to Sempidi where numerous roadside food stalls offer tea, bananas and peanuts to boost your energy reserves.

If you begin your trip at low tide you can do the first seven km north along the beach's firm, moist sand. Turn inland around the Bali Oberoi Hotel as further on the sand becomes soft and you'll get bogged down. The hotel's long driveway connects with the main road and you can continue north to Sempidi, the junction with the Denpasar to Gilimanuk road.

Ride west towards Gilimanuk from Sempidi until you reach the turn-off north to Mengwi. The quiet, almost cloistered, Pura Taman Ayun with its surrounding moat is only half a km east of the main road in Mengwi. Continuing north from Mengwi 15 km to Desa Perean you will notice by your breathing that the gentle 1% to 5% gradient is gradually increasing. From Perean to Bedugul is a 700-metre vertical rise spread over 16 km so this is the place to throw your bicycle into the back of a bemo. Bemos come along every 10 to 30 minutes until about 4 pm. The fare for one bicycle usually equals the fare for one person.

Bedugul has several places to stay. Note the change in vegetation and the sturdier housing construction compared to the lowlands. Small outrigger canoes can be rented by the hour on Lake Bratan. The lake is large enough for some safe skinny-dipping out in the middle. It's a pleasant paddle across from the losmen to Pura Ulu Danau.

Day 2 – Bedugul to Singaraja 21 km, riding time three hours.

The first km is uphill, followed by a breezy downhill sprint past the Bukit Mungsu market which sells vegetables and wild orchids. For several km the road goes up and downhill. Then there is a three km steep ascent to the unnamed 1400-metre pass – cyclists can usually think of several obscene names for it! From the pass there is a steep 15-km descent to the coastal town of Singaraja. This is where good brakes are most needed. You may want to stop periodically to cool the brake rims and unmould your hands from the brake levers.

Singaraja is a rather hot and dusty town. There are some bicycle repair shops there and a wide choice of losmen. You can continue west along the coast to the beach strip around Lovina (seven to 13 km from Singaraja) or turn east to Yeh Sanih.

Day 3 – Singaraja to Penelokan 56 km (36 km up to Penulisan by bemo then the final 10 km by bike).

Ride 10 km east of Singaraja to Kubutambahan where you find the turn-off heading south to Kintamani and Gunung Batur. Visit the temple of Pura Maduwe Karang at Kubutambahan before turning inland. It's 36 steep km uphill from there to Penulisan so once again it's wise to load your bicycle aboard a bemo, although there aren't many going this way. Penulisan is the highest point on the ride and it's an easy descent from there to Kintamani (four km) or Penelokan (10 km). At 1745 metres, Penulisan's Pura Tegeh Koripan is Bali's highest temple and on a clear day, which is rare, it offers a superb panorama of half the island.

Kintamani (1504 metres) has several losmen with fireplaces, and a large and colourful market every three days. Penelokan (1371 metres) has a couple of losmen perched on the rim of the volcano looking down to Lake Batur and Gunung Batur. Frequent stops by tour buses encourage swarms of vendors.

You can take the windy road from Penelokan down to the village of Kedisan on Lake Batur, and around the lake's north shore to the hot springs. You can also climb to the top of the volcano, or hike around the southern shore to the Bali Aga village of Trunyan.

From Penelokan there are at least five routes down the slopes of Gunung Batur back to Denpasar. Listed is the route via Klungkung with a side trip to the temple at Besakih. Two alternate routes are listed in the following section – they lead either to the Ubud area or Bangli.

Day 4 – Penelokan to Klungkung 31 km (excluding Besakih), riding time four hours.

Turn left half a km south of the fruit stands which are at the intersection of the road down to Lake Batur. A small sign reads 'Bandjar Abang' and the narrow road leads uphill. If you reach a fork in the main road with a sign for Denpasar and Bangli you've gone too far – retreat. The narrow road goes up and down small hills as it heads east along the southern rim of the crater with lovely views of Gunung Batur and the lake. Approximately four km along the road is a dip with a sign 'Menanga'. Turn right and continue downhill to Rendang with fine views of Gunung Agung all the way. Rendang is the turn-off for Besakih.

From Rendang to Besakih is six km, mostly uphill. There's a 500-metre rise in eight km. Consider leaving your bike at the crossroads and taking a bemo both ways or putting the bike in a bemo going up and having a nice ride down. Pura Besakih, at 1000 metres, rests on the misty slopes of Gunung Agung, the 'navel of the world'. Beautiful and eerie, Besakih is considered the 'mother temple' of Bali.

From Rendang to Klungkung, a gradual downhill ride of 12 km, is considered one of the most pleasant bike trips in Bali. The road passes through some of Bali's richest rice land. Linger at the expensive restaurant at Bukit Jambul – the view is free and magnificent.

Klungkung has several restaurants and places to stay. The main attraction is the Kertha Gosa at the town's main intersection, with excellent examples of the Klungkung style of painting and architecture. Two km south is the village of Kamasan, known for the wayang style of painting and for its gold- and silverwork.

Day 5 – Klungkung to Denpasar 31 km, riding time six hours.

The entire road is well surfaced but traffic is quite heavy. Although there is a total descent of 70 metres, the road crosses several lush river gorges, causing some uphill walking and downhill gliding. Main places of interest along the way are Gianyar (local weaving industry), Batuan (painting and weaving), Celuk (woodcarving and silver- smithing), and Batubulan (stone sculpture).

Day 6 – Denpasar to Kuta (via Sanur & Benoa) 24 km, riding time five hours.

Take your life in your hands and head east on Jalan Gajah Mada, the main street of Denpasar, and continue the six km to Sanur. If you feel enterprising you can even rent your bike to an 'international' hotel guest – they pay about the same per hour as you pay per day. Check out the hotel swimming pools with their swim-up bars and underwater bar stools.

From Sanur the 'superhighway' runs about eight km to the turn-off south to Benoa Harbour. The sideroad turns into a causeway leading to Benoa Port, where the Lombok hydrofoil docks.

After leaving Benoa, backtrack along the causeway and turn west. You can divert off the new highway to the old and now virtually deserted Sanur to Kuta road which runs par- allel to the new highway, just north of it. You eventually emerge on the main Kuta to Den- pasar road next to a petrol station. You have completed the 200 km round trip and are back at the start. Congratulations!

Alternative Routes from Penelokan to Denpasar On the fourth day of the 200 km circle tour, you have a choice of routes from Penelokan back to Denpasar.

Penelokan to Ubud The route from Pene- lokan to Ubud via Tampaksiring is 35 km long and riding time is about five hours.

This route used to be pretty rough-and- ready from Kayuambua down to Tampaksiring, but after improvements it's now a fine road. About half a km south of Penelokan the road forks. Take the right fork marked 'Denpasar' and nine km later you're in the small junction town of Kayuambua. The left fork leads to Bangli, the right fork takes you to Tampaksiring eight km further on. The road runs down verdant volcano slopes past fields of banana, sweet potato and corn, all partially obscured by roadside groves of bamboo.

At the main intersection in Tampaksiring a road east leads to Tirta Empul with its holy spring. There are lots of warungs and hand- icraft shops here. Carved chess sets with characters from the *Ramayana* are a local speciality. Another km down from Tirta Empul is the turn-off to the 11th-century rock-face memorials at Gunung Kawi, about a km off the main road. Back on the road it's an easy 10 km downhill to Bedulu. About a km before Bedulu is the small village of Pejeng with its 'Moon of Pejeng' bronze drum in the Pura Penataran Sasih. You turn right at the Bedulu junction and half a km along the road is the Goa Gajah (Elephant Cave). Then it's on to Peliatan and Ubud.

Ubud to Denpasar The route from Ubud to Denpasar is 26 km and riding time is about four hours.

There are several ways down to Kuta from the Ubud area. Heading straight south for four km the road passes through the wood- carving village of Mas, another six km is the weaving village of Batuan and then through Celuk, known for its woodcarvings as well as fine gold and silversmiths. From Batuan to Denpasar (16 km) there are many trucks, bemos and cars competing for road space, which makes that part of the trip mentally exhausting.

An interesting alternative is the quiter backroad via Sibang. Except for the first few km, which require some uphill walking, it's an easy descent with little traffic until you are in Denpasar proper. From Denpasar to Kuta is the same as the previous Klungkung route.

Penelokan to Bangli The 20-km route from Penelokan to Bangli takes about three hours. At the fork in the road half a km south of Penelokan take the left fork marked 'Bangli' and head south. Bangli has an important temple, Pura Kehen, and a couple of places to stay. Continue south from Bangli and you join the Klungkung to Denpasar route about 26 km from Denpasar.

Day Trips from Kuta

Kuta to Benoa & Sanur This is an 18-km one-way trip. See the round-trip details for this route. From Sanur you can either backtrack to Kuta, or take the Sanur to Denpasar and Denpasar to Kuta roads although they have very heavy traffic. Or take a bemo back.

Kuta to Ulu Watu This 19-km one-way trip is strenuous and not recommended for beginners or for anyone not used to tropical heat .

Head south to the airport turn-off and continue on the asphalt road to the junction of the Ulu Watu and Nusa Dua roads. The road to Ulu Watu winds up and down, inexorably climbing to the dusty village of Pecatu at 250 metres. This is one-third of the round-trip distance and the most arduous part of the route but it is possible to put the bike on a bemo this far.

From Pecatu it's a further five km up and downhill to Pura Luhur Ulu Watu, the temple perched on a cliff high above the sea. Return by the same route which will require considerable walking uphill to Pecatu and then mostly downhill and level pedalling back to Kuta.

Kuta Beach Rides At low tide short rides along the firm, moist sand can be beautiful. Heading north from Kuta you can ride for up to seven km before the sand changes and will no longer support a bicycle. At that point you can either retrace your tracks or head inland to the road and return via Legian. After tripping along the salty beaches it's wise to throw a few buckets of freshwater on your bike to keep it from rusting.

Distances around Bali in km

Bangli																	
42	Besakih																
88	109	Bedugul															
40	61	48	Denpasar														
13	34	75	27	Gianyar													
168	89	148	128	155	Gilimanuk												
56	40	128	78	51	206	Amlapura											
49	55	57	9	36	137	87	Kuta										
28	70	116	68	41	196	86	70	Kintamani									
18	21	88	40	13	168	38	49	48	Klungkung								
135	156	115	95	122	33	173	104	163	135	Negara							
36	37	104	56	29	184	24	65	56	16	151	Padangbai						
20	62	112	64	33	192	78	73	8	40	159	48	Penelokan					
80	122	30	78	93	85	100	87	52	100	112	108	60	Singaraja				
43	64	55	7	30	135	81	8	72	43	102	56	71	85	Sanur			
61	82	43	21	48	107	99	30	89	61	74	77	85	73	28	Tabanan		
23	67	73	25	10	153	61	34	48	23	120	39	40	100	28	46	Ubud	
53	74	61	13	40	141	91	4	81	53	108	69	77	91	12	34	38	Airport

Several people have written to us about cycling in Bali. Nigel Daniel gave us his thoughts:

I had no problems in transporting my bike on Garuda, on both international and domestic flights. All I did was remove the pedals from each arm. I did not even have to play around with the handle bars.

I followed the around Bali itinerary which was in the book and did not resort to bemos on the climb to Bedugul and Kintamani. The Bedugul climb is not too steep and I feel that anyone who has an OK bike (10 speed) can make this climb without a bemo. The Penulisan climb is a completely different story. It's very, very tough going, especially in the tropical heat. Also you cannot get any drinking water until you reach Penelokan so if you intend to ride that stretch carry lots of water – at least four cyclist bottles. I had about 15 warm Sprites that day because I ran out of water!

The ride from Rendang to Amlapura has great scenery and no traffic. Except for a few easy hills between Muncan and Selat it's pretty well downhill all the way. From Amlapura it's not far to Candidasa and dead flat on to Klungkung.

Nigel Daniel, Australia

Lombok

Lombok has an extensive network of roads, although there are many outlying villages that are difficult to get to by public transport. There is a good main road across the middle of the island between Mataram and Labuhan Lombok, and quite good roads to the south of this route on the plain between Rinjani and the southern highlands. It's more difficult to travel north and east of Rinjani or down to the south coast, where there are either bad roads or no roads at all, or good roads with little or no public transport. The situation may be improving as the government has instituted an ambitious road improvement scheme as part of a long-term plan to put Lombok on the tourist map. A new coastal road has been mooted and other roads are being built. You can get around the whole island and to many of the more remote locations if you have your own transport.

One problem with getting around Lombok is that public buses and bemos are generally restricted to main routes. Away from these, you have to hire a horse-drawn cart, get a lift on a motorbike, or walk. In the north-east and the south there is usually some public transport between the bigger towns, but it might mean waiting a long time and riding in the back of a truck. A rented car, particularly one with good ground clearance, will get you to most places where there's a road, but if you charter a vehicle, the driver might want to stay on sealed roads. If you are exploring these regions under your own steam, bear in mind two things: firstly, food and drinking water are often scarce so it's a good idea to carry your own; secondly, so few Westerners have been in these parts that you may be regarded as a sensation by villagers you come across.

During the wet season many roads are flooded or washed away, and others are impassable because of fallen rocks and rubble, making it impossible to get to many out-of-the-way places. The damage may not be repaired until the dry season.

Like Bali, Lombok has the usual Indonesian methods of transport: bemos, buses, minibuses, horse-drawn carts (*dokars*) and outrigger canoes (prahus) for short sea voyages. Taxis are also available on Lombok and charge either by the hour, or a fixed sum for a particular distance such as from the airport to Senggigi.

Warning

Like many Indonesians, people on Lombok don't travel well, and often suffer from travel sickness on buses and boats. This might be a problem for you as well as them!

Most public transport stops at 10.30 or 11 pm, often earlier in more isolated areas. If you find yourself out in the sticks without your own wheels you can try to charter a bemo or just make yourself as comfortable as you can until sunrise.

BEMO & BUS

The cheapest and most common way of getting around is by bemo or minibus (sometimes called a 'colt') for shorter distances or bus for longer stretches. On rough roads in remote areas trucks may be used as public transport vehicles. There are several bemo terminals on Lombok. The main one is at Sweta, a couple of km out of Cakranegara. Here buses, minibuses and bemos depart for various points all over the island. Other terminals are at Praya and Kopang, and you may have to go via one or more of these transport hubs to get from one part of Lombok to another.

Public transport fares are fixed by the provincial government and at Sweta there is a prominently displayed list of fares to most places on the island. This does not stop the bus and bemo boys from trying to take you for a ride, so check the notice board before setting off. Otherwise watch what the locals are paying or ask someone on the bemo what the going rate is. Children on a parent's knee are free, up to about 11 they cost around half price. You may have to pay more if you have a big bag.

As with all public transport in Indonesia, drivers wait until their vehicles are crammed to capacity before they contemplate moving. Often there are people, produce, caged birds, stacks of sarongs, laden baskets, even bicycles hanging out the windows and doors and at times it seems you're in danger of being crushed to death or at least asphyxiated. More often than not you won't be able to organise yourself to get a good vantage spot to see much of the countryside. However, most people are very friendly, many offer to share their food with you, most ask where you come from (be prepared for lots of *dari manas*) and generally want to find out all they can.

Chartering a Bemo

While you can get to most of the accessible places on Lombok by bemo, bus, horse-drawn cart, or a combination of all three, many trips involve several changes and a lot of waiting around. If you're pressed for time, and you can get a few people together, hiring a bemo by the day, or even from one village to the next, can be cheap and convenient. One limitation of chartering a bemo to explore more remote parts of Lombok is that

the driver may be reluctant to venture off the sealed roads. They don't want to damage their vehicle and, if the truth be known, some of them are not very skilled drivers.

These days hiring bemos is becoming almost as common on Lombok as on Bali so it's quite feasible and easy to arrange. Work out where you want to go and be prepared for some hard bargaining. Try to stick to your original plan but if you don't, and you stop off somewhere else on the way, be prepared to pay extra. As on Bali, prices for chartering bemos are worked out roughly by the number of passengers a regular bemo carries (ie 12) multiplied by the normal fare, or about 25 rp per person per km for a full load. A reasonable price to pay for chartering a bemo for the day would be 35,000 to 40,000 rp, depending a bit on how far you want to go.

You can probably arrange to charter a bemo through your losmen or hotel, or alternatively you can simply go to a bemo stop and ask the drivers. Check that the vehicle is roadworthy. Does it have good tyres? Do the lights and wipers work? A straightforward trip can quickly turn into a nightmare when you find yourself out after dark, in the rain, with a wiperless and lightless bemo!

MOTORBIKE

There are motorbike rental places in the main centres of Lombok but not as many as there are in Bali. They are also not as easy to find: you won't see the 'motorbike for hire' signs stuck up all over the place that you see in Bali. You have to ask around, but there are individual owners who rent out their bikes, and a couple of specialist places in Ampenan and Mataram. The bikes and the rental charges are very similar to Bali: the longer you hire one for, the cheaper it becomes.

A great advantage of having a motorbike is that you can get to the more inaccessible places with relative ease and you can make side trips and stops when you feel like it. Once you get out of the main centres there's not much traffic on the roads, apart from people, dogs and water buffaloes, but you do have to contend with numerous potholes and people at work upgrading the roads. This can be particularly hazardous at night when you round a corner and come slap up against a grader, rocks piled into the middle of the road and 44-gallon drums of tar. Warning signs are rarely, if ever, put up when roadworks are in progress, and up in the mountains there are perilous and unprotected drops down sheer cliff faces to the valley below. Once off the main roads you will find yourself on dirt tracks and in for a rough ride.

Petrol can also be a problem. There are petrol stations around the larger towns, but out in the villages petrol can be difficult to find. If you intend going to out-of-the-way places it may be advisable to take some with you, so long as you can carry it safely. If not, it's available from small wayside shops – look out for signs that read *premium*, or *press ban* (literally 'tyre repair').

Try to get a motorbike which is in good condition. This is a real problem in Lombok, firstly because there aren't as many well-kept motorbikes available as there are in Bali and secondly, getting 'off the beaten' track (and away from spare parts and mechanical help) happens very quickly. It's a bad combination, potentially unreliable motorbikes and limited help when they go wrong. So if you've got a choice between a better more expensive bike and a worse but cheaper one, in Lombok the better one is the best bet.

CAR RENTAL

Car hire on Lombok is usually a less formal arrangement than on Bali – basically you arrange to borrow a car from a private owner. The owners rarely insist on a licence and sometimes want you to leave a passport for security. There is usually an insurance cover for damage to other people or property, but the car itself is usually uninsured and you drive it at your own risk. It costs about 35,000 to 50,000 rp per day for a small vehicle such as a Suzuki Jimny, depending on where you get it and how you bargain. If you take it for a few days or a week you should get a discount. Between four people it can be quite a cheap way to get around.

Hotels in Ampenan, Mataram or Senggigi can often arrange car or motorbike hire as can some of the tourist-type shops. There are some 'official' car rental companies in Mataram which have a wider range of vehicles, but these tend to be more expensive.

Town	Distance from Sweta (km)
Narmada	6
Kopang	25
Selong (East Lombok)	47
Pringgabaya	60
Labuhan Lombok	69
Sambelia	89
Airport	7
Pemenang	31
Bayan	79
Lembar	22
Ampenan	7
Suranadi	13
Sesaot	15
Praya	27
Tetebatu	46
Lingsar	10
Gunung Pengsong	8
Kuta	52
Batu Bolong	10

BICYCLE

The story on bicycle hire is much the same as that for motorbikes. Bicycles are for rent in and around the main centres of Lombok, but are not generally a popular form of transport around the island, either among the locals or with travellers. This is probably because many of the local inhabitants cannot afford a bicycle, and those who have the money for such luxuries would save up for a motorbike. If you want to explore Lombok by bicycle you'll probably have to bring your

Dokar/Cidomo

own or be prepared to do some maintenance work on one of the old rust buckets you will find there.

DOKAR/CIDOMO

Dokars are the jingling, horse-drawn carts found all over Indonesia. The type most used on Lombok is more correctly known as a *cidomo*, but the word dokar is understood. The two-wheeled carts are usually brightly coloured with decorative motifs, and are fitted out with bells that chime when they're in motion. The small ponies that pull them often have long colourful tassels attached to their gear. A typical dokar has bench seating on either side which can comfortably fit three people, four if they're all slim. It's not unusual, however, to see a dozen or more passengers, plus several bags of rice and other paraphernalia piled up in a cart.

The dokar is a picturesque way of getting around if you don't get upset by the harsh treatment of animals – however, as the horses are the owner's means of survival, they're looked after reasonably well. Dokars are a very popular form of transport in many parts of Lombok, and often go to places that bemos don't, won't or can't.

The minimum price is 100 rp but it's unlikely that you'll be taken anywhere for less than 150 rp. Count on paying around 250 rp per person per km.

PRAHU & SAMPAN

These elegant, brilliantly painted, outrigger fishing boats, looking rather like exotic dragonflies, are used for short inter-island hops and for travelling from Bangsal Harbour to the Gili Islands.

BALI

Denpasar

The capital of Bali, with a population of around 250,000, Denpasar has been the focus of a lot of the growth and wealth in Bali over the last 15 or 20 years. It now has all the bustle, noise and confusion which one associates with the fast-growing cities of Asia. It also has an interesting museum, an arts centre and lots of shops. Denpasar means 'next to the market', and the main market (called Pasar Badung) is said to be the biggest and busiest in Bali. The city, sometimes referred to as Badung, is the capital of the Badung District which incorporates most of the tourist areas of southern Bali and the Bukit Peninsula.

Those who have visited Bali over a number of years will tell you that Denpasar was a pleasant, quiet little town 15 years ago. It still has the tree-lined streets and some pleasant gardens, but today the traffic, noise and pollution make it a difficult place to enjoy. Most tourists and travellers find it more comfortable and convenient to stay at Kuta, Legian or Sanur, and only venture into Denpasar for the few bits of bureaucratic business which cannot be done elsewhere. If you're one of those who feel that Bali is overcrowded with tourists, you'll find that tourists are vastly outnumbered in Denpasar – it mightn't be a tropical paradise, but it's as much a part of 'the real Bali' as the rice paddies and temples.

Orientation & Information

The main street of Denpasar, Jalan Gajah Mada, becomes Jalan Surapati in the centre, Jalan Hayam Wuruk in the east, and finally Jalan Sanur before turning south then east and heading towards Sanur. This name-changing is common for Denpasar streets, and is one source of confusion. Another problem is the proliferation of one-way traffic restrictions, sometimes for only part of a street's length, which often change and are rarely marked on any maps. For example, sections of Gajah Mada and Surapati are one-way only, from west to east, but there's a short section near the Jalan Veteran intersection where it's two-way. Despite, or perhaps because of, these control measures, the traffic jams can still be intense. Parking can also be difficult, so avoid driving – take taxis, bemos or walk.

In contrast to the rest of Denpasar, the Renon area, south-east of the town centre, is laid out on a grand scale with wide streets, large car parks and big landscaped blocks of land. This is the area of government offices, many of which are impressive structures, built with lavish budgets in modern Balinese style. If you come here to collect mail or visit the immigration office you can have a look around. It's reminiscent of Canberra or Brasilia or the embassy district of New Delhi – a place to visit in a chauffeured limousine.

Tourist Office The Badung District tourist office is on Jalan Surapati 7, just past the roundabout and across the road from the Bali Museum. A useful calendar of festivals and events in Bali, and a pretty good map, are available. The office is open Monday to Thursday from 7 am to 2 pm, Friday from 7 to 11 am and Saturday from 7 am to 12.30 pm. The Bali government tourist office is in the Renon area, but doesn't provide much information.

Money All the major Indonesian banks have their main Bali offices in Denpasar, principally along Jalan Gajah Mada. The Bank Ekspor-Impor Indonesia, which is a block to the south, is probably the best for transfers from overseas.

Post The main Denpasar post office, with a poste restante service, is in the Renon area. It's a long way from the nearest bemo station, and a real nuisance if you have only come into town to pick up your mail. Avoid getting mail sent to you here – the offices in Kuta or Ubud are much more convenient.

Telecommunications Permuntel, the telecommunications authority, has an office at Jalan Teuku Umar 6, near the intersection with Diponegoro. You can make international phone calls and send telegrams and faxes. A three-minute call costs about 16,000 rp to Canada, 17,000 rp to Australia, New Zealand or the USA, and 19,000 rp to Western Europe.

Foreign Consulates See the Facts for the Visitor chapter for information about foreign diplomatic representation on Bali, including addresses of the consulates and consular agents in Denpasar.

Immigration The immigration office or kantor imigrasi (☎ 27828) is at Jalan Panjaitan 4, in the Renon area, just around the corner from the main post office. It's open Monday to Thursday from 7 am to 2 pm, Fridays from 7 to 11 am and Saturdays from 7 am to 12.30 pm. If you have to apply for changes to your visa, get there on a Sanglah-bound bemo and make sure you're neatly dressed.

National Parks Office The Direktorat Perlindungan dan Pengawetan Alam (Directorate of Nature Conservation & Wildlife Management, or PPA) is responsible for managing Indonesia's nature reserves and national parks. It has an office south of Denpasar but doesn't have much information of value to tourists. (If you're planning to visit the Bali Barat National Park you can get better information and pay your entry fees at Labuhan Lalang, the northern entrance to the park.) To get to the PPA office, you take a Benoa-bound bemo from Denpasar and get off at the Kampung Suwang turn-off. Then you walk east for 400 metres – the PPA office is on the left-hand side.

Medical Services Denpasar's main hospital, Rumah Sakit Umum Propinsi (RSUP) is in the southern part of town in Sanglah, a couple of blocks west of Jalan Diponegoro. The hospital has a new casualty department and intensive care unit, supported by a Japanese aid project. It's probably the best place to go in Bali if you have a serious injury or urgent medical problem.

Walking Tour
If you wander down Jalan Gajah Mada, past all the shops and restaurants, you come to the towering statue of Batara Guru at the intersection of Gajah Mada and Veteran. The four-faced, eight-armed statue is of the god Guru, Lord of the Four Directions. He keeps a close eye on the traffic swirling around him.

Beside the intersection is the large Puputan Square, commemorating the heroic but suicidal stand the rajahs of Badung made against the invading Dutch in 1906.

At the junction of Jalan Hasannudin and Jalan Imam Bonjol (the road to Kuta) is the Puri Pemecutan, a palace destroyed during the 1906 invasion, now rebuilt and operating as a hotel.

Bali Museum
The museum consists of an attractive series of separate buildings and pavilions, including examples of the architecture of both the palace (puri) and temple (pura). There is a split gateway *(candi bentar)*, a warning drum (kulkul) tower, and an elevated lookout. The large building in the second courtyard, with its wide verandah, is like the palace pavilions of the Karangasem kingdom where rajahs would hold audiences. Various other palace building styles from Tabanan and Singaraja can also be seen in this courtyard.

Exhibits include both modern and older paintings, arts and crafts, tools and various items of everyday use. Note the fine wood and cane carrying cases for transporting fighting cocks. There are superb stone sculptures, krises, wayang kulit figures and an excellent exhibit of dance costumes and masks, including a sinister rangda, a healthy looking barong and a towering barong landung figure. It's a good place to see authentic, traditional paintings, masks, woodcarving and weaving before you consider buying something from the craft and antique shops.

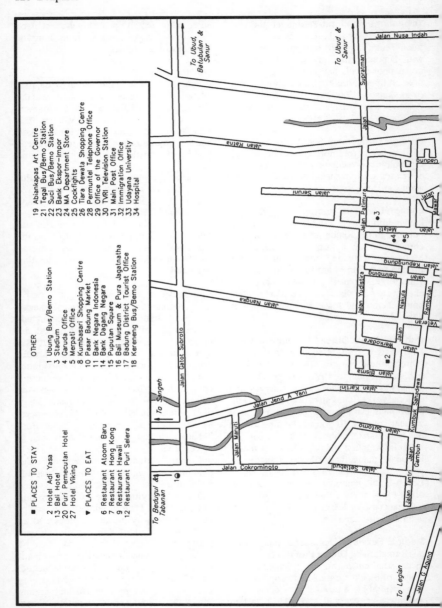

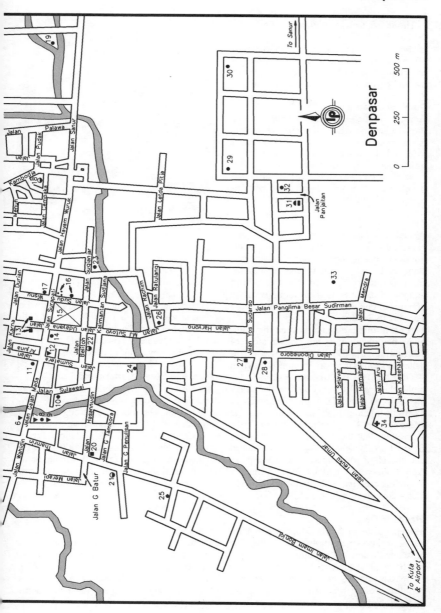

The museum was originally founded by the Dutch in 1932. Admission to the museum is 200 rp for adults, 100 rp for children, plus 50 rp a head for insurance. The museum is open daily (except Monday) from 8 am to 5 pm and closes 1½ hours earlier on Friday.

Pura Jagatnatha
Adjacent to the museum is the state temple Pura Jagatnatha. This relatively new temple is dedicated to the supreme god, Sanghyang Widi and his shrine, the *padmasana*, is made of white coral. The padmasana (throne, symbolic of heaven) tops the cosmic turtle and the *naga* (mythological serpent) which symbolise the foundation of the world.

Arts Centres
Abiankapas, the large arts centre on Jalan Nusa Indah, has an exhibit of modern painting and woodcarving together with a dancing stage, craft shop, restaurant and other facilities. Dances are held regularly and temporary exhibits are held along with the permanent one. It's open from 8 am to 5 pm Tuesday to Sunday.

A bit further out again, beyond the Batubulan bemo station, is the Conservatory of Performing Arts (SMKI) which was established in 1960 as the Konservatori Kerawitan (KOKAR). This is a training institution for high-school age students, and in the mornings you can watch dance practices and hear a variety of gamelan orchestras. On the same site is Sekolah Tinggi Seni Indonesia (STSI), formerly called the Academy of Indonesian Dance (ASTI), which runs more advanced courses. Here you may also see dance practices. Both groups hold public performances at Abiankapas, particularly during the summer arts festival in June and July.

Places to Stay
Most people who stay in Denpasar are Indonesian visitors, principally on business. The noise, confusion and pollution is simply too much for most tourists. Once upon a time Denpasar was the *only* place to stay, and people made day trips to the beaches at Sanur or Kuta. Now Sanur and Kuta are far more

Topeng mask, Bali Museum

comfortable environments, and people who want to visit more than just beaches in Bali head up to Ubud. There are plenty of places to stay in Denpasar, however, and you won't be bothered by a surfeit of tourists.

Places to Stay – bottom end
Adi Yasa (☎ 22679), at Jalan Nakula 11, was once one of the most popular travellers' hotels in Bali. The rooms are arranged around a garden, and it's a pleasant, well-kept and friendly place, even if it's no longer a travellers' mecca. Rooms are 8000 rp with shared mandi, 12,000 rp with private bathroom, breakfast included. There are several other cheap losmen around, but most travellers on a tight budget head for Kuta, a short bemo ride away.

Places to Stay – middle
There are a number of mid-range places on or near Jalan Diponegoro, the main road on the south side of town. The *Hotel Viking* (☎ 26460), at No 120, has economy rooms from 12,500 rp for singles and air-con rooms up to 50,000 rp. (Even quite small hotels

catering to Indonesians often have a wide range of rooms, facilities and prices. If the first room you're offered is too expensive, or too grotty, it's always worth asking for something else.)

Further south on the eastern side of Diponegoro is the *Hotel Rai*, a middling to expensive place catering mainly to business travellers. There are some similar places in the small streets behind the Rai, and these may be a bit quieter. Other hotels in the southern part of Diponegoro include the *Queen* and the *Oka*. The popular Hotel Denpasar at Diponegoro 103 has been demolished, but may rise again.

The *Puri Pemecutan Hotel* is in the rebuilt palace at the junction of Jalan Hasannudin and Jalan Imam Bonjol (the road to Kuta), handy to the Tegal bemo station. Singles/doubles in A-class rooms, with air-con, phone, TV and private bathroom, cost 40,000/50,000 rp; B-class rooms cost 25,000/30,000 rp; and C-class rooms, 12,500/15,000 rp, so you should find something to suit your budget.

Places to Stay – top end

There are no luxury hotels of Sanur standard in Denpasar, but the three-star *Bali Hotel* (☎ 25681/5), at Jalan Veteran 3, is only a notch down from that level. It's a pleasantly old-fashioned place dating from the Dutch days. You wouldn't call it a masterpiece of colonial architecture, but there are some nice Art-Deco details (look at the light fittings in the dining room and the leadlight windows in the lobby) and the place has a sense of history. Singles/doubles start at about US$43/48 including breakfast; rooms with air-con cost an extra US$5. A suite costs US$72. Some of the rooms are actually on the other side of Jalan Veteran, so you'll have to walk across the road to use the dining room, bar and swimming pool. If you want to sample the atmosphere without paying for a room, just come for the rijstaffel dinner.

Places to Eat

The eating places in Denpasar cater for local people and Indonesian visitors rather than for Western tourists. A number of restaurants along and near Jalan Gajah Mada are operated by and for the Chinese community, and many of them serve very good Chinese food.

The *Restaurant Atoom Baru*, at Gajah Mada 98, is a typical Asian (as opposed to Western) Chinese restaurant. It's big, spartan and has an interesting menu with lots of seafood, and dishes such as beef balls soup (1500 rp) and pig's bladder with mushrooms (5500 rp). Other main courses are from 3000 to 7000 rp. Across the road is the *Restaurant Hong Kong* with Chinese and Indonesian food and cafeteria-style self-service or a menu. It's a bit classier, with tablecloths and air-conditioning, and a bit pricier. The *Restaurant Hawaii*, around the corner in the Kumbasari shopping centre, has an oriental set menu for 5000 rp and a European set menu for 6500 rp. Further down Gajah Mada is the relatively expensive *Restaurant Puri Selera* which does excellent Chinese food.

At Jalan Kartini 34, just off Gajah Mada, the *Depot Mie Nusa Indah* is a reasonably priced and friendly Indonesian restaurant. There are also several Padang food restaurants along Gajah Mada.

You'll find excellent and cheap food at the market stalls by the Suci bus station and at the other markets, especially in the evenings. A number of rumah makans down Jalan Teuku Umar serve real Balinese food, as well as the standard Indonesian fare.

The *Bali Hotel* on Jalan Veteran dates from the Dutch era, and is decorated in true Dutch East Indies colonial style. You can get a rijstaffel in the old-fashioned dining room for 7000 rp and the service is friendly and efficient.

Entertainment

Dances in and around Denpasar are mainly for tourists – there are regular performances at the Abiankapas arts centre, and a Barong & Rangda dance every morning at the SMKI or STSI schools in nearby Batubulan. Wayang kulit performances can be seen a couple of times a week at the Puri Pemecutan. Cockfights used to be held regularly near the Kuta bemo station; officially they're banned, but in practice they probably continue as before.

There are a number of cinemas (bioskop) in Denpasar. US movies are popular, particularly 'action movies', along with kung fu titles from Hong Kong, the occasional Indian epic and some Indonesian productions. Movies are usually in the original language, subtitled in Bahasa Indonesia. They are advertised in the papers, and also with garish posters on which your favourite actor may be unrecognisable.

For Western-style bars, discos and nightclubs you'll have to go to Kuta or Sanur. You'll find the younger, more affluent denizens of Denpasar congregating around the shopping centres in the evening, and later around their local bioskop. There are always students keen to practise their English, and you might meet some around the Udayana University campus near the southern end of Jalan Panglima Besar Sudirman.

Things to Buy

Denpasar has no particular crafts of its own, but there are numerous 'factories' around town churning out mass-produced handicrafts. There are also many shops selling crafts from Bali and from other Indonesian islands.

Countless craft shops line Jalan Gajah Mada, the main shopping street of Denpasar. The main market, the three-storeyed building of Pasar Badung, is a bit to the south, near the east bank of the river. Kumbasari is another market/shopping centre, on the opposite side of the river from Pasar Badung.

There are now two Western-style shopping centres in Denpasar – quite a recent innovation for Bali. The MA department store in Jalan Diponegoro, and the Tiara Dewata shopping centre on Jalan MJ Sutoyo are both very popular with affluent Balinese, and are good places to pick up clothing, fashion goods and toys.

At Tohpati, about six km north-east of town just beyond the Sanur to Batubulan road intersection, is the government handicraft and arts centre, Sanggraha Kriya Asta (☎ 22942). This large shop has an excellent collection of most types of Balinese arts and crafts. Prices are fixed, and most of the items are of good quality so it's a good place to look around to get an idea of what's available, what sort of quality to expect and at what prices. The best of the work here is really superb, and worth a trip just to see. Prices for these pieces can be well over 1,000,000 rp. Don't be too alarmed – that's about US$520, and not unreasonable for something that may have taken a trained and talented person several months to make. It's open Monday to Friday from 8.30 am to 5 pm, and on Saturday from 8.30 am to 4.30 pm, closed Sunday. If you telephone they'll send a minibus to collect you from Denpasar, Kuta, Legian or Sanur.

Getting There & Away

Denpasar is the focus of road transport in Bali – here you'll find buses, colts and minibuses bound for all corners of the island. There are also buses for Java, boat tickets, train tickets and the Garuda, Merpati and Bouraq airline offices.

See the Getting There & Away chapter for details of transport between Bali, Lombok, Java and the other Indonesian islands.

Air It's not necessary to come into Denpasar to arrange booking, ticketing or reconfirmation of flights. Most of the travel agencies in Kuta, Sanur, Ubud or other tourist areas can provide these services.

The Garuda office, at Jalan Melati 61, was closed for major renovations in 1991. Merpati (☎ 35556/7), next door at Jalan Melati 57, may be able to help with Garuda arrangements as it's now a subsidiary of Garuda, though it would probably be better to find a Garuda agency in one of the tourist areas. Merpati's hours are Monday to Friday from 7 am to 4 pm, Saturday from 7 am to 1 pm and Sunday from 9 am to 1 pm. Merpati has flights to Lombok and the other islands of Nusa Tenggara.

Bouraq (☎ 23564, 22252) at Jalan Kamboja 45D, has similar fares to Merpati and flies to destinations in Java and Nusa Tenggara.

Bus The usual route for land travel between Bali and Java is the Denpasar to Surabaya day or night bus. There are a number of bus companies for this run, found mainly around the Suci bus station or along Jalan Hasannudin. If you're staying in Kuta, however, there's no need to trek into Denpasar for tickets as there are numerous agencies at Kuta. Tickets through to Lombok are also available, combining bus and either the ferry from Padangbai or the hydrofoil from Benoa.

Bemo For travel within Bali, Denpasar has five stations for bemos and/or buses, so in many cases you'll have to transfer from one station to another if you're making a trip through Denpasar. Kereneng used to be the station for northern and eastern Bali, but it became so congested that bemos and buses for these destinations now operate from the new station at Batubulan, about six km north-east of town. If, for example, you were travelling from Kuta to Ubud you'd get a bemo from Kuta to the Tegal bemo station in Denpasar (400 rp), transfer to the Kereneng station (500 rp), transfer again to Batubulan (500 rp), then take a bemo from there to Ubud (500 rp). (You might be able to get directly from Tegal to Batubulan, but this doesn't seem to be a regular service yet.) Squadrons of three-wheeled mini-bemos shuttle back and forth between the various stations and also to various points in town, though they are progressively being replaced with more conventional, four-wheeled mini-buses. The Jalan Thamrin end of Jalan Gajah Mada, for example, is a stop for the transfer bemos. You'll find transfer bemos lined up for various destinations at each of the stations.

Fares vary from around 300 to 500 rp between the stations. You can also charter bemos or little three-wheelers (cheaper of course) from the various stations. You could, for example, arrive from Surabaya at Ubung or Suci stations and charter a mini-bemo straight to Kuta rather than bothering with transferring to Tegal station and then taking

a bemo to Kuta. Between a few people it might even be cheaper.

Further afield, fares vary with the type of bus you take. The smaller minibuses are more expensive than the larger old buses. The stations and some of their destinations and fares are:

Tegal – south of the centre on the road to Kuta, this is the station for the southern peninsula.

Kuta	400 rp
Legian	500 rp
Airport	500 rp
Nusa Dua	1000 rp
Sanur (blue bemo)	500 rp
Ulu Watu (before 10 am)	1500 rp
Ubung	300 rp
Suci station	300 rp
Kereneng station	500 rp
Batubulan station	500 rp

Ubung – north of the centre on the Gilimanuk road, this is the station for the north and west of Bali. To get to Tanah Lot take a bemo to Kediri, and another one from there. To get to the Lovina beaches, take a bemo to Singaraja, and another one from there.

Kediri	800 rp
Mengwi	900 rp
Negara	3000 rp
Gilimanuk	3500 rp
Bedugul	1700 rp
Singaraja	2500 rp
Tegal station	500 rp
Kereneng station	500 rp
Batubulan station	500 rp

Ubung is also the main station for buses to Surabaya, Yogyakarta and other destinations in Java.

Surabaya	19,000 rp
Yogyakarta	25,000 rp
air-con	32,000 rp
Jakarta	48,000 rp

Kereneng – east of the centre, off the Ubud road, this is now just an urban transfer station.

Tegal station	500 rp
Ubung station	500 rp
Suci station	500 rp
Batubulan station	500 rp

Batubulan – this is the new station for the east and central area of Bali.

Ubud	700 rp
Gianyar	700 rp
Tampaksiring	900 rp
Klungkung	1000 rp
Bangli	1000 rp
Padangbai	1500 rp
Candidasa	1500 rp
Amlapura	2500 rp
Kintamani	1700 rp
Tegal station	500 rp

Suci – south of the centre, this station is mainly just the bemo stop for Benoa (700 rp) but the offices of many of the Surabaya bus lines and shipping line agencies are also here. Benoa bemos also leave from the Sanglah market.

Train There are no railways in Bali but there is a railway office where you can get tickets to Surabaya or other centres in Java. This includes a bus ride to Gilimanuk and the ferry across to Banyuwangi in Java from where you take the train.

Boat The usual boat route out of Bali (not counting the short Bali to Java ferry which is included in bus-ticket prices) is the ferry from Padangbai to Lombok. Usually you get tickets for one of the daily ferries at Padangbai, but some agencies now sell inclusive bus-ferry-bus tickets through to destinations in Lombok. Tickets for the Benoa to Lombok hydrofoil are sold by agencies on a similar basis. Pelni and other shipping agencies are at the Suci bus station if you wish to inquire about boat transport further afield.

Getting Around
Three-wheeled mini-bemos shuttle back and forth between the various Denpasar bus stations and Jalan Gajah Mada. The set fares vary from 200 to 400 rp: Tegal to Ubung 400 rp, Ubung to Kereneng 400 rp, Kereneng to Suci 200 rp, Kereneng to Tegal 400 rp. You can also charter these tiny bemos (they'll even buzz you out to Kuta Beach) or you can find taxis. Agree about all prices before getting on board because there are no meters.

Despite the traffic, dokars (horse-drawn carts) are still very popular around Denpasar; again, agree on prices before departing. Note that dokars are not permitted on Jalan Gajah Mada and may also be barred from some other streets with heavy vehicle traffic.

South Bali

The southern part of Bali, south of the capital Denpasar, is the tourist end of the island. The overwhelming mass of visitors to Bali is concentrated down here. All the higher priced package tour hotels are found in this area and many visitors only get out on day trips. Some never leave it at all.

The Balinese have always looked towards the mountains and away from the sea – even their temples are aligned in the kaja direction (towards the mountains) and away from the inauspicious kelod direction (towards the sea). So Sanur and Kuta, being fishing villages, were not notable places prior to the arrival of mass tourism. Today they're Bali's major international resorts, but they're artificial enclaves, not really part of Bali at all. Of course the residents have made the most of their new found opportunities, particularly in Kuta where an enormous number of small, locally run losmen and restaurants have sprung up, though many of the Balinese who work at Kuta and Sanur are from other parts of the island. The Indonesian government is determined that the rest of Bali should remain as unspoilt as possible, so all future large-scale development will be confined to this southern region, particularly the newer tourist enclave at Nusa Dua.

The southern region and Singaraja in the north are areas which have been most influenced by the world outside Bali. Even some of Bali's earliest legends relate to this area. The first European to make his mark in the south was Mads Lange, a Danish copra trader who set up at Kuta about 1830. Lange had some success in persuading local rajahs to unite against the Dutch encroachments from the north but he also made enemies and was later poisoned and buried at Kuta. The Dutch takeover of the south finally took place at Sanur in 1906. The Balinese fell back all the way from Sanur to Denpasar and there the three princes of the kingdom of Badung made a suicidal last stand, a puputan which wiped out the old kingdoms of the

south. When the Japanese left Indonesia after WW II the Dutch again returned to Bali at Sanur.

Sanur was an early home for visiting Western artists and is still an artistic centre, famed for its gamelan orchestras. The courtly Arja opera and wayang kulit (shadow puppets) are also popular at Sanur and a positive mania for flying gigantic kites has swept the region.

An unfortunate side effect of the building explosion in the south has been massive destruction of the coral reefs. Coral makes an excellent building material, both ground down to make lime and cut as whole building blocks. The blocks are very attractive and, since the coral grows a little after it has been removed from the water, it actually locks itself together. But as more and more coral is removed there will be fewer and fewer fish and the unprotected beaches can quickly disappear. Some prime offenders, where you can see literally whole stretches of coral reef turned into walls, include the Bali Hyatt at Sanur, the Bali Oberoi at Legian and Poppies Cottages at Kuta.

KUTA & LEGIAN

Kuta is the budget beach in Bali. It's only a couple of km from the airport and for many people it's their first and only taste of the island. Kuta may be good fun and quite a scene but Bali it most certainly is not. If you want to get any taste of the real Bali then you have to abandon the beaches and get up into the hills, where the tourist impact is not so great and where Bali's 'soul' has always been.

Still, most visitors will hit Kuta to start with so it might as well be enjoyed. Basically Kuta Beach is a strip of pleasant palm-backed beach with some fine surf (and tricky undercurrents that take away a few swimmers every year) plus the most spectacular sunsets you could ask for.

Behind the beach, a network of narrow roads and alleys (known as gangs) run back to the most amazing hodgepodge of big hotels, little hotels (losmen), restaurants, bars, food stalls (warungs) and shops. There are

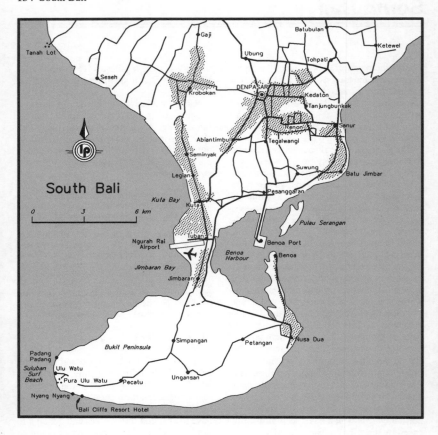

hundreds of different places to stay at Kuta and Legian and still more are being opened. Kuta is a totally self-contained scene and, with so many places to work your way through, it's hardly surprising that so many people get stuck there semi-permanently.

Although the original Kuta Beach Hotel was operating in the 1930s (its modern namesake opened in 1959) Kuta only really began to develop as a resort in the late '60s. At first, most people made day trips there from Denpasar but gradually more hotels opened and, in the early '70s, Kuta was an extremely pleasant place to stay with its relaxed losmen, pretty gardens, friendly places to eat and delightfully laid-back atmosphere. Then travellers began to abandon Denpasar as the traffic there became intolerable and Kuta started to grow faster and faster. Legian, the next beach village north, sprang up as an alternative to Kuta in the mid-70s. At first it was a totally separate development but Kuta sprawled north towards Legian and Legian spread back towards Kuta until today you can't tell where one ends and the other begins.

Unhappily, all this rampant development, almost all of it totally unplanned, has taken its toll. Old hands who first visited Bali in the late '60s or early '70s will find Kuta a rather sad and seedy place. Fortunately, new arrivals, and even old hands who avoid making too many comparisons, may still find it just fine – for a short stay.

Orientation & Information

An important Kuta landmark is 'Bemo Corner', the intersection of Jalan Pantai Kuta (Kuta Beach Rd) and Jalan Legian (Legian Rd). Other important roads are Jalan Bakung Sari, running parallel to Jalan Pantai Kuta and, in Legian, Jalan Melasti and Jalan Padma. Smaller lanes or alleys, really too small for cars although they do squeeze down some of them, are known as gangs. The best known is Poppies Gang.

You can visit Bali and never have to leave Kuta. There are hotels, restaurants, travel agencies, banks, moneychangers, a post office, doctors, markets, motorbike and car rental places; in fact, you name it and Kuta has it. Kuta and Legian, once separate little villages, have merged and are now just the names for different sections of one long, continuous beach.

Tourist Office The large building on the corner of Jalan Bakung Sari and the airport road has tourist information counters for Bali and several other regions in Indonesia. The Bali counter has some brochures and copies of a Bali tourist newspaper.

Money There are now several banks around Kuta but for most people the numerous moneychangers are faster, more efficient, open longer hours and offer equally good rates of exchange. The only reason to use a real bank is for some complicated money transfer or other bank-like activity.

A number of the moneychangers have safety deposit boxes where you can leave airline tickets or other valuables and not have to worry about them during your stay in Bali.

Post There's a post office near the cinema and night market, off the airport road. It's small, efficient and has a sort-it-yourself poste restante service. The post office is open Monday to Saturday from 8 am and closes at 11 am on Friday and at 2 pm on the other days of the week. There's also a postal agency on Jalan Legian, about half a km along from Bemo Corner. If you want mail sent there have it addressed to 'Kuta Postal Agent, Jalan Legian, Kuta'. These Kuta post

---

What's Wrong with Kuta?

What's gone wrong with Kuta? There are many good restaurants, the beach and surf can be terrific, the quiet losmen down remote gangs can be relaxed and pleasant but at some time or other you have to venture back on to Jalan Legian and the traffic down this main street is horrific. The constant stream of sellers importuning you to buy, buy, buy can be a little wearing too but the main problem is planning and people. There's too little of one and too many of the other.

Too little isn't the word for Kuta's planning – there's none at all. Anybody seems to have been able to build almost anything anywhere. The result is that many hotels are only accessible down narrow gangs – which is no problem except that people insist on using these footpaths for motorbike races and even try to squeeze cars and trucks down them. Jalan Legian is a typical narrow island road, wide enough for one vehicle or perhaps one and a half at a squeeze yet it carries a near continuous flow of buses, bemos, taxis, cars, trucks and motorbikes. Even a complicated one-way traffic system has not saved the road; it remains a noisy, confused, evil-smelling, frustrating cacophony.

As for the people – well, 15 years ago Kuta was one of the great overland travel stops, one of 'the three Ks' – Kabul in Afghanistan, Kathmandu in Nepal and Kuta. But travellers don't come to Kuta anymore. It's strictly a beach resort for people who want surf and sand, cheap food and cold beer. Where you used to get peacefully stoned freaks gazing at the sunset you now have numerous bars where loud-mouthed drunks get plastered every afternoon, clamber clumsily on to their motorbikes and, mercifully, fall off at the first corner. Even the beach isn't what it once was and many Balinese have voiced concern that they're in danger of ruining the already badly damaged local environment. ■

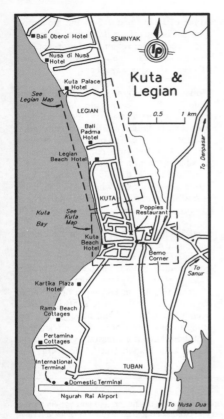

Kuta & Legian

however, make international calls quite quickly if you pay in cash. Reverse-charge calls are much more time-consuming. A Home Country Direct phone where one button gets you through to your home country operator can be found outside the airport's international terminal. There are card phones in several locations including the domestic departure lounge. There's also a Permuntel phone office across the car park from the terminals.

Bookshops If you develop a real interest in Kuta read Hugh Mabbett's *In Praise of Kuta* (January Books, Wellington, New Zealand, 1987). It's widely available in Bali and recounts Kuta's early history and its frenetic modern development. There are fascinating accounts of Kuta's local entrepreneurs, the development of surfing and what happens to visitors who get caught with drugs.

Kuta and Legian have lots of little bookshops selling new and second-hand books. The best place to look for English-language books (new ones) is the Krishna Bookshop on Jalan Legian.

Dangers & Annoyances If you have something stolen in Kuta you can almost certainly put it down to your own carelessness. Theft, though increasing, is still not an enormous problem and when visitors do lose things it is usually from unlocked hotel rooms or from the beach. Always lock your room, even at night. Valuable items should be checked with reception or, if not needed, left in a security box. Going into the water and leaving valuables unwatched on the beach is simply asking for trouble.

Some years ago Kuta had a number of muggings but the problem was handled with quite amazing efficiency and in a very traditional fashion. The local banjars organised vigilante patrols and anybody they came across who wasn't a tourist or a local Balinese had to have a damn good reason for being there. Thefts in the dark gangs stopped dead and there has been no repeat performance.

The efficient Kuta Lifesaving Club is modelled on the Australian system and

offices and the one in Ubud are much more convenient than the main Denpasar post office. The tourist office on the corner of the airport road and Jalan Bakung Sari also has a small post office counter, which is open longer than the main post office and is more convenient.

Telephone There are wartels (private telephone offices) on Jalan Legian and on Jalan Bakung Sari in Kuta (see map). You cannot yet dial international calls yourself nor are there the card phones which are becoming increasingly common in Indonesia. You can, guards patrol areas at Kuta and Legian. The surf at Kuta can be tricky and there are drownings every year, many of them visitors from other Asian countries who are not good swimmers. In 1980, before the lifesaving club got under way, there were 18 deaths; since then, the number has varied from five to 13 a year.

Kuta Beach is much more likely to cost you money than your life, however. The whole beach is now fenced off and you're charged admission. Also, there are usually more sellers on the beach than swimmers – you're constantly importuned to buy anything from a cold drink to a massage or a hair-beading job. What can cost you a whole lot more money is to leave things on the sand while you're in the water. Believe it or not this is how a lot of people lose their passports each year!

Places to Stay

Kuta and Legian have hundreds of places to stay with more still being built. Apart from central Kuta and around Jalan Padma and Jalan Melasti in Legian, the area is, surprisingly, far from crowded. Even in the central area you only have to walk a couple of steps back from the main street to find palm trees and open fields.

Kuta has numerous mid-range and top-end hotels, many of them catering to international package-tour visitors, but there are also a great many cheap and attractive places to stay. Standards have risen over the years and although you can still find a few of the old rock-bottom places, even cheaper losmen have bathrooms these days.

Beware of throwaway words like 'beach', 'seaview', 'cottage' and 'inn' when it comes to Kuta hotel names. Places with 'beach' in their name may not be anywhere near the beach and a featureless three-storeyed hotel block may rejoice in the name 'cottage'. The honourable line about building nothing taller than a palm tree also seems to be going out the window, unless there are plans to grow some awfully tall palm trees. Note that any hotel north of Jalan Pantai Kuta in Kuta and south of Jalan Melasti in Legian is going to

be separated from the beach by the coast road, even if the hotel is described as being on the beach front.

Places to Stay – bottom end

Once upon a time even the cheapest Kuta losmen was an attractive and relaxed place built around a lush and well-kept garden. Today there are lots of places which have obviously been thrown together as quickly and cheaply as possible to try and turn over maximum rupiah with minimum effort.

What to look for in a losmen? You can start with that well-known advice from real estate agents – location, location, location. Many places are close to busy roads where the traffic noise and exhaust fumes can make you think you're in the centre of some busy Western city. There are also places so isolated that getting to a restaurant is a major trek. Where do you want to be – close to the action or away in the peace and quiet? It's often possible to find a good combination of both factors – a place far enough off the main roads to be quiet but close enough so that getting to the shops and restaurants is no problem.

Then you can look at what the rooms are like and how pleasant and generally well kept the losmen is. For those interested in experiencing Balinese culture, look for a losmen which is fairly small and as much like a traditional Balinese home as possible. That is, enclosed by an outer wall and built around a central courtyard and garden. The courtyard should be an attractive and peaceful place to sit around and read or talk. It should also be clean and well kept. Many cheaper losmen still offer breakfast, even if it's only a couple of bananas and a cup of tea. It's a pleasant little extra that disappears as you move up the price scale.

With so many places to choose from it's quite easy to wander from place to place until you find one that suits. If it's late, you're not in a wandering mood or you've hit one of those rare occasions when everything seems to be full, you can be certain someone will ask 'Do you want a room?' – you'll have no trouble finding a place. The main secret to

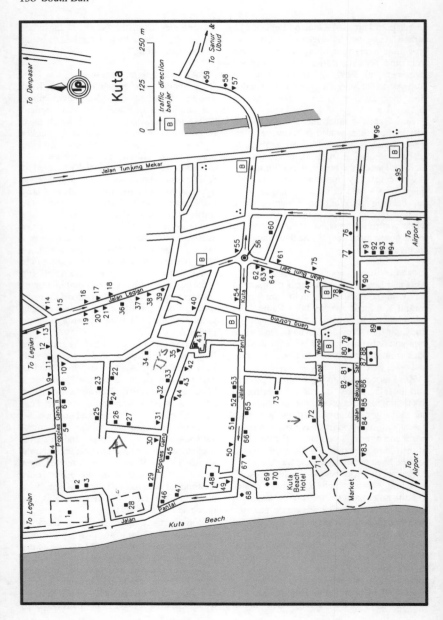

■ PLACES TO STAY

1	Sahid Bali Seaside Hotel
2	Puri Beach Inn
3	Indah Beach Hotel
4	The Bounty Hotel
5	Poppies Cottages II
6	Palm Garden Homestay
8	Barong Cottages
11	Taman Sari Cottages
22	Puri Ayodia Inn
23	Sari Bali Bungalows
24	Suji Bungalows
25	Sorga Cottages
26	Mimpi Bungalows
27	Berlian Inn
28	Kuta Seaview Cottages
29	Kuta Puri Bungalows
33	Mutiara Bungalows
34	Kempu Taman Ayu
36	Viking Beach Inn
41	Poppies Cottages I
43	La Walon Bungalows
45	Cempeka
46	Sari Yasa Samudra Bungalows
47	Aneka Beach Bungalows
48	Yasa Samudra Bungalows
51	Kodja Beach Inn
52	Bali Summer Hotel
53	Budi Beach Inn
60	Anom Dewi Youth Hostel
65	Suci Bungalows
66	Yulia Beach Inn
70	Kuta Beach Hotel
71	Kuta Cottages
72	Asana Santhi (Willy) Homestay
73	Ida Beach Inn
84	Ramayana Seaside Cottages
85	Kuta Beach Club
86	Agung Beach Bungalows
89	Flora Beach Hotel
92	Bamboo Inn
93	Zet Inn
94	Jesen's Inn II

▼ PLACES TO EAT

7	Bali Corner Restaurant
9	Twice Pub Restaurant
10	Tubes Bar
12	Batu Bulong Restaurant
13	SC (Sari Club)
14	George & Dragon
16	Burger King
17	Peanuts Disco, Koala Blu Pub & Other Bars
18	Indah Sari Seafood
19	SC Restaurant
20	Twice Bar
21	Mini Restaurant
30	Tree House Restaurant
31	Warung Transformer
32	Nusa Indah Bar
35	TJs
37	Prawita Garden Restaurant
38	Aleang's
40	Poppies
42	Fat Yogi's Restaurant
44	Kempu Cafe
49	Made's Juice Shop
50	Melasti Restaurant
54	Made's Warung
55	Quick Snack Bar
57	Kentucky Fried Chicken
61	Casablanca Bar
62	Dayu II
63	Wayan's Tavern
64	Bali Indah
67	Green House Restaurant
74	Bagus Pub
75	Serrina Japanese Restaurant
77	Gantino Baru Padang Restaurant
78	The Pub
79	Bali Blessing Restaurant
80	Bali Bagus Restaurant
81	Nagasari Restaurant
82	Dayu I
83	Rama Bridge Restaurant
90	Gemini Chinese Restaurant
91	Kuta Plaza Restaurant
96	Night Market

OTHER

15	Kuta Postal Agency
39	Perama
56	Bemo Corner
58	Supermarket
59	Petrol Station
68	Kuta Lifesaving Club
69	Garuda Office
76	Tourist Information Office
87	Supermarket
88	Wartel Telephone Office
95	Post Office

losmen hunting is to remember that there are lots more of them – if you don't like your first choice it's very easy to move somewhere else.

You can still find basic losmen for around 10,000 rp a double although Kuta is not as good value as other parts of Bali. The bottom end extends up to about 30,000 rp (US$15); above that is middle range. As you move up the price scale you get private bathrooms, Western-style toilets, better furnishings and a generally less spartan atmosphere. The prices are likely to be higher closer to central Kuta than they would be further out.

With so many places to choose from and so many of them so similar in what they offer it's almost redundant to make specific recommendations. The 17 places that follow offer a wide variety of standards at an equally wide variety of locations, from the centre of busy Kuta to the outer reaches of Legian. The location key number on the Kuta or Legian map is indicated after the name:

Anom Dewi Youth Hostel (Kuta No 60) Right in the thick of things in central Kuta, this YHA associated losmen offers standard rooms at 10,000 and 12,000 rp.

Baleka Beach Inn (Legian No 12) At the northern end of Legian this place has rooms from 12,000 to 25,000 rp and a swimming pool.

Bamboo Inn (Kuta No 92) This traditional little losmen in central Kuta is some distance from the beach but close to the restaurants and bars. Good rooms cost 10,000 to 15,000 rp including breakfast.

Berlian Inn (Kuta No 27) A good central location just off Poppies Gang and rooms at 15,000 to 25,000 rp make this place good value.

Budi Beach Inn (Kuta No 53) This old-style losmen is in a busy location on Jalan Pantai Kuta and has rooms from 10,000 to 20,000 rp for singles and from 12,000 to 25,000 rp for doubles.

Jesen's Inn II (Kuta No 94; ☎ 52647) This inn, a pleasant little two-storeyed block with a garden, is close to the centre of Kuta yet in a reasonably quiet location. It's some distance from the beach but good value at 10,000 to 15,000 rp.

Kempu Taman Ayu (Kuta No 34) Just around the corner from TJ's and Poppies, this long-running and friendly little place has fairly standard rooms at 9000 to 12,000 rp.

La Walon Bungalows (Kuta No 43) On Poppies Gang, handy for the beach and the Kuta 'scene', La Walon has pleasant little rooms with verandah and open-air bathrooms. It's good value at 20,000 rp for a double including breakfast.

Legian Beach Bungalows (Legian No 34) Right in the centre of Legian on busy Jalan Padma these bungalows cost US$10 to US$15 for singles and US$12 to US$18 for doubles.

Palm Garden Homestay (Kuta No 6) This is a neat and clean place in a quiet location and the rooms are good value at 15,000 to 20,000 rp.

Puri Ayodia Inn (Kuta No 22) This small and very standard losmen is in a quiet but convenient location and has rooms for just 10,000 rp.

Sari Yasai Beach Inn (Legian No 7) On Jalan Purana Bagus Taruna, at the northern end of Legian, this small losmen has rooms at 12,000 rp.

Sinar Beach Cottages (Legian No 16) Towards the northern end of Legian, this pleasant little place has a garden and rooms at 15,000/17,000 rp for singles/doubles.

Sinar Indah (Legian No 22) Also at the midpoint between Jalan Padma in central Legian and Jalan Purana Bagus Taruna at the northern end of Legian, this standard-style losmen has rooms at 8000 to 20,000 rp plus bigger rooms with kitchen facilities.

Sorga Cottages (Kuta No 25) There's a pool, the location is quiet and the rooms are 12,500 to 21,000 rp with fan and 21,000 to 31,500 rp with air-con.

Three Sisters (Legian No 37) One of Legian's original losmen still offers straightforward rooms at low prices and a very central location. Rooms are 12,000 rp.

Yulia Beach Inn (Kuta No 66) This standard small hotel on Kuta Beach Rd has been going for years. Rooms are US$10 to US$22 for singles, US$12 to US$25 for doubles.

Places to Stay – middle

There are a great many mid-range hotels, which at Kuta means something like US$15 to US$60. A 15.5% tax and service charge is usually tacked on as well. The majority of these places cater to visitors on one or two-week package tours and many of them are utterly featureless and dull. They seem to have a checklist of amenities which must be supplied and so long as these 'essentials' (like air-conditioning and a swimming pool) are in place, nothing else matters. Balinese style is unlikely to make an appearance and monotonous rectangular blocks or places with the maximum number of rooms crammed into the minimum space are all too familiar.

As usual, there are exceptions. The following list includes 12 mid-range places, all with swimming pools unless otherwise noted, which are either good value or offer some style:

Asana Santhi (Willy) Homestay (Kuta No 72) Right in the heart of Kuta and not far from the beach, this attractive small hotel is surprisingly relaxed for its central location. The well-kept rooms have interesting furnishings and art and there's a good central swimming pool. Air-con rooms are US$30 to US$45.

Bali Niksoma Inn (Legian No 13) Right on the beach towards the northern end of Legian this smaller hotel has two-storeyed units in relatively spacious grounds with rooms from US$20 to US$60.

Bali Sari Homestay (Legian No 23) On the northern side of Legian this smaller hotel is a short walk from the beach and has attractively designed rooms, some of them with a touch of eccentricity. Rooms are US$40/45 for singles/doubles.

Bruna Beach Inn (Legian No 53) This simple and straightforward place has a good central location near the beach. The rooms are nothing special but they're cheap with prices from US$12 to US$25 for singles and US$17 to US$30 for doubles.

Kuta Cottages (Kuta No 71; ☎ 51101) Close to the beach, near the end of Jalan Bakung Sari, this older hotel is reasonably priced at US$18 to US$25 for singles and US$22 to US$30 for doubles.

Kuta Seaview Cottages (Kuta No 28; ☎ 51961) By the beach, but separated from it by the road, the rooms are definitely not cottages and most of them don't have any view of the sea. Yet despite the cramped site and three-storeyed block, prices are good value at US$25/30 for singles/doubles.

Legian Beach Hotel (Legian No 44; ☎ 51711) PO Box 308, Denpasar. On the beach at Jalan Melasti in the heart of Legian this large hotel has a wide variety of rooms, most of them in three-storeyed blocks, with singles from US$35 to US$75, doubles at US$40 to US$80.

Mimpi Bungalows (Kuta No 26) This small hotel is good value in a pleasant location with a nice little pool. Rooms cost US$15 to US$35.

Mutiara Bungalows (Kuta No 33) Conveniently located on Poppies Gang, the Mutiara is also excellent value with a spacious, lush garden and straightforward if slightly tatty fan-cooled rooms with verandah at US$17.

Nusa di Nusa (Kuta & Legian; ☎ 51414) PO Box 191, Denpasar. Well north of Legian in Seminyak and right on the beach you get isolation and a better stretch of beach in exchange for the distance from restaurants, entertainment and shopping. Very pleasant rooms cost US$25 to US$30 for singles, US$30 to US$35 for doubles and there are also family 'bungalows' for US$75, and houses with two or three bedrooms and a kitchen for US$150.

Poppies Cottages I (Kuta No 41) Still setting the standard for what a good Bali hotel should be, Poppies has an exotically lush garden with cleverly designed and beautifully built rooms. It's right in the centre of things on Poppies Gang and has a swimming pool every bit as stunning as the overall design. At US$51/56 for singles/doubles it's right at the top of the mid-range category.

Poppies Cottages II (Kuta No 5) The earlier Poppies is not quite so stunning in its design or setting nor is it quite as central. There is no pool but it's cheaper at US$23/28.

Places to Stay – top end

Although Kuta isn't like Nusa Dua or Sanur where most (if not all) the hotels are strictly at the top end of the price range, there are still some places in this category. These include some of Kuta's larger hotels, one of which, the Bali Oberoi, is a contender for the top of the 'best hotels in Bali' ranking.

All of the hotels in this bracket will have air-conditioning, swimming pools and other mod cons. There will be a 15.5% tax and service charge on top of the quoted prices. Eight of the more popular or more interesting places in this category include:

Bali Intan Cottages (Legian No 46; ☎ 51770) PO 1002, Denpasar. On Jalan Melasti, close to the beach in Legian, this very standard large hotel has rooms in two-storeyed blocks plus cottages with singles at US$65 to US$75, doubles at US$70 to US$80.

Bali Oberoi Hotel (Kuta & Legian; ☎ 51061) PO Box 351, Denpasar. Situated right on the beach at Seminyak, way up beyond Legian, the Bali Oberoi is isolated and decidedly deluxe with beautiful individual bungalows and even some villa rooms with their own private swimming pools. The regular rooms are US$150 to US$240 while the villa rooms start at around US$300.

Bali Padma Hotel (Legian No 26; ☎ 52111) PO Box 1107 TBB, Legian. This big 400-room hotel is on the beach on Jalan Padma in the middle of Legian. Rooms are in two- or three-storeyed blocks or in six-room units and cost from US$100 to US$120 for singles, US$110 to US$130 for doubles.

Kartika Plaza Hotel (Kuta & Legian; ☎ 51067) PO Box 84, Denpasar. Right on the beach, just south of central Kuta, this larger hotel has rooms at US$80/85.

Kul Kul Hotel (Legian No 52; ☎ 52520) PO Box 97, Denpasar. Separated from the beach by the road just south of Jalan Melasti in Legian, this big hotel has two- and three-storeyed blocks plus bungalows in relatively spacious grounds. Rooms cost from US$83.

Kuta Beach Hotel (Kuta No 70; ☎ 51361) PO Box 393, Denpasar. The original Kuta hotel is close to the site of its prewar predecessor of the same name. Unfortunately there's no sense of history here and the rooms are somewhat dull and tired. The location is very central at the beach end of Jalan Pantai Kuta and you can walk right out on to the beach but, with singles/doubles from US$71/80 up to US$90/112, it's not great value.

Kuta Palace Hotel (Kuta & Legian; ☎ 51433) PO Box 244, Denpasar. At the northern end of Legian, this big hotel is right on the beach and has a pleasant pool and garden. Singles cost from US$65 to US$75, doubles from US$75 to US$85.

Pertamina Cottages (Kuta & Legian; ☎ 23061) PO Box 121, Denpasar. On the beach at the airport end of Kuta this large deluxe hotel has rooms at US$107 to US$112.

Places to Eat

There are countless places to eat around Kuta and Legian, ranging from tiny hawker's carts to fancy restaurants, cheap warungs to bars and pubs, steakhouses to juice bars. Like so much else about Kuta there's not much which is truly Indonesian or Balinese – you could stay in Kuta for a month, eat in a different place for every meal and never have to confront so much as a humble nasi goreng. In Kuta the cuisine is pseudo-Western from top to bottom and always seems to be going through some transient craze whether it's a spate of Mexican restaurants or the discovery of pizzas.

Prices in Kuta's fancier restaurants are no longer rock bottom either. If you want to eat cheaply try places like *Depot Viva* on Jalan Legian, the food carts which cater to local workers or the night market near the post office. Many of the fancier places have Australian wine for around 3500 rp a glass.

Around Kuta Places may come and go but

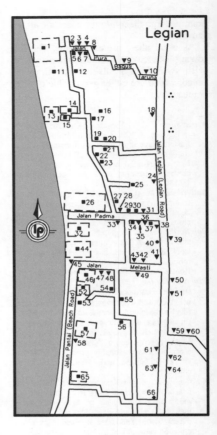

Poppies has been one of the most popular restaurants ever since it opened in the early '70s. The food is very basic – you're not going to get any culinary surprises but nor are you going to get any awful shocks. It's on Poppies Gang, close to the heart of things, with a beautiful garden, attentive service and most main courses cost from around 6000 to 9000 rp.

A few steps beyond Poppies is *TJ's*, the place in Kuta for Mexican food. Again the ambience is cranked up high and while Mexico may be a long way from Bali the food is surprisingly good. In this deservedly

Bounty Hotel

■ PLACES TO STAY

1	Kuta Palace Hotel
5	Orchid Garden Cottages
7	Sari Yasai Beach Inn
11	Mabisa Beach Inn
12	Baleka Beach Inn
13	Bali Niksoma Inn
14	Bali Coconut Hotel
15	Maharta Beach Inn
16	Sinar Beach Cottages
17	Adika Sari Bungalows
19	Bhvana Beach Cottages
20	Abdi Beach Inn
21	Surya Dewata Beach Cottages
22	Sinar Indah
23	Bali Sari Homestay
25	Sri Ratu Cottages
26	Bali Padma Hotel
27	Garden View Cottages
29	Legian Village Hotel
30	Puspasari Hotel
32	Bali Mandira Cottages
34	Legian Beach Bungalows
37	Three Sisters
44	Legian Beach Hotel
46	Bali Intan Cottages
52	Kul Kul Hotel
53	Bruna Beach Inn
54	Camplung Mas
55	Legian Mas Beach Inn
56	Sayang Beach Lodging
57	Kuta Jaya Cottage
65	Bali Anggrek Hotel

▼ PLACES TO EAT

2	Topi Koki Restaurant
3	Swiss Restaurant
4	Arak Bar
6	Sawasdee Thai Restaurant
8	Rum Jungle Road
9	Bamboo Palace Restaurant
10	Benny's Cafe
18	Restaurant Glory
24	Warung Kopi
28	Legian Snacks
31	Restaurant Happy
33	Padma Club Restaurant
35	Rama Garden Restaurant
36	Norman Garden Restaurant
38	MS Restaurant
39	Ned's Place
41	Do Drop Inn
42	Gosha Restaurant
43	Bali Waltzing Matilda Too
45	Karang Mas Restaurant
47	Restaurant Puri Bali Indah
48	Legian Garden Restaurant
49	Orchid Garden Restaurant
50	Manhattan Restaurant & Bar
51	Made's Restaurant
58	Southern Cross Restaurant
59	Yanies
60	Il Pirata
61	The Bounty
62	Depot Viva
63	Za's Bakery & Restaurant
64	Mama's German Restaurant

OTHER

40	Wartel Telephone Office
66	Krishna Bookshop

popular restaurant main courses are 5000 to 8000 rp.

Further down Poppies Gang towards the beach there are several popular places for light meals. *Fat Yogi's* turns out pretty good pizzas from a genuine wood-fired pizza oven and their croissants aren't bad at breakfast time either. Further down the gang there's *Warung Transformer* and the pleasant *Tree House Restaurant*, a good place for an excellent and economical breakfast.

On Jalan Pantai Kuta (Kuta Beach Rd), quite close to Poppies, is *Made's Warung*. Like Poppies, this simple open-fronted place has been going since the early '70s and it's probably the best place in Kuta for people watching, both visitors and the local glitterati. The food is getting a touch expensive these days but there's always somebody unusual to watch from first thing in the morning until late at night. Bali has lots of Made's so *Made's Juice Shop*, at the beach end of the road, is no relation although it's also popular.

Jalan Buni Sari, which connects Jalan Pantai Kuta with Jalan Bakung Sari, has some more long-term survivors including the *Bali Indah, Wayan's Tavern* and *Dayu II*. These three turn out standard dishes at reasonable prices. Further along this short street there are some popular pubs including *The Pub* itself – the original Kuta pub, though not in its original location. See the Entertainment section for more details.

On Jalan Bakung Sari the *Gemini Restaurant* is a popular choice for Chinese dishes. Across the road is the *Gantino Baru*, a nasi Padang specialist. Down Jalan Bakung Sari towards the beach there are several restaurants including *Dayu I* and the supermarket which has many Western-style goods.

Along Jalan Legian There are lots of possibilities down Jalan Legian. Most of the time the road is an almost continuous traffic jam and a table near the road can mean you have to shout to be heard. Right on Bemo Corner is the *Quick Snack Bar*, a good place for a snack or breakfast (the yoghurt is particularly good). A little further along is *Aleangs*, another popular snack bar with good yoghurt, cakes and ice cream, plus lots of traffic noise.

Continue north towards Legian and you reach the *Mini Restaurant*, which is not very 'mini' at all. It's a big, open, busy place serving simple food at low prices. Across the road is Kuta's disco and bar centre, with the extremely popular Koala Blu pub and Peanuts disco. In the same vicinity there are several Western fast-food outlets. Slightly hidden off the eastern side of Jalan Legian is *George & Dragon*, reputed to have the best Indian curries in Bali. On the other side of the road is the *LG Club*, a big, bright restaurant where you choose your seafood at the front and it's cooked in the frenetic open kitchen area to one side.

Continue north along Jalan Legian to *Depot Viva* (see the Legian map). It's an open-roofed place with surprisingly good Indonesian and Chinese food despite the restaurant's bare and grubby appearance. The prices are pleasantly low too, which accounts for its steady popularity. Across the road is the *The Bounty*, notable for its amazing shipstern architecture, and then *Za's Bakery &* *Restaurant* which is not only a good spot for breakfast but also has a menu featuring everything from pasta to curries.

Just off Jalan Legian is *Yanies* with excellent burgers from 3500 to 6000 rp. A little further along this same road is *Il Pirata*, noted both for its very good pizzas at 5000 to 7000 rp and for its late opening hours.

Return to Jalan Legian and you'll soon be in the heart of Legian, with numerous restaurants on Jalan Melasti, Jalan Padma and the other Legian streets. Further along Jalan Legian itself you'll come to the ever popular *Do Drop Inn* and *Restaurant Glory*.

Around Legian Jalan Melasti has several good restaurants including the big *Orchid Garden Restaurant*, the *Legian Garden Restaurant* and the *Restaurant Puri Bali Indah* with excellent Chinese food. Jalan Padma also has restaurants but some of the most interesting places in Legian are further north on Jalan Purana Bagus Taruna, the somewhat twisting road leading to the big Kuta Palace Hotel. Right by the hotel entrance is the *Topi Koki Restaurant* which has a pretty good go at la cuisine Française. The menu features main courses at 7000 to 10,000 rp, wine by the glass at 4500 rp; a meal complete with pre-dinner drinks, starter, main course, dessert and coffee could reach 50,000 rp for two. Not bad for pretty authentic French food.

A little further back from the beach is the *Swiss Restaurant* which is popular with homesick Deutschlanders; main courses cost from 5000 to 10,000 rp and Indonesian dishes a bit less. Other restaurants along this street include the *Sawasdee Thai Restaurant*, *Yudi Pizza* and, closer to Jalan Legian, the big and very popular *Bamboo Palace Restaurant* and the small, but also popular, *Benny's Cafe*.

Entertainment

Nightspots are scattered around Kuta and Legian, many along Jalan Legian. Discos go through strange fads – five nights a week you need a crowbar to clear a space on the dance floor but come back three months later and there's not a body in sight. One year you

Top: Goa Lawah (Bat Cave), Bali (TW)
Left: Rice terraces near Tirtagangga, Bali (TW)
Right: Pura Besakih, on the slopes of Gunung Agung, Bali (TW)

Top: Sunrise, Padangbai, Bali (GE)
Bottom: Candidasa, Bali (TW)

can't even find enough space to park your motorbike outside – come back next year and there's enough room to dump an elephant. So if the places listed here turn out to be ever so dull and dreary – don't blame us.

Some of the wilder drunken excesses of Kuta have been cleaned up. The pub crawls, where bus loads of increasingly noisy and drunken revellers were hauled from one venue to another, have been cut back considerably. Plus many pubs and discos have been closed down and others concentrated into a sort of 'combat zone' on Jalan Legian. There everybody can get as drunk as they like without bothering other people.

The centrepiece of the Jalan Legian entertainment complex is the large *Peanuts* disco – it's rather like an Australian barnyard-pub venue, which might explain its popularity. Admission is usually around 5000 rp and this includes a couple of drinks. There's a series of open bars flanking the entrance road into Peanuts. These places kick off earlier than the main disco, and continue even after it's in full swing. For some reason *Koala Blu* has been the firm favourite for some time and Koala Blu T-shirts seem to pop up all over Asia. After midnight it's quite a scene with music blasting out from every bar, hordes of people, mostly upright but some decidedly horizontal, and out in the parking lot lines of bemos and dokars waiting to haul the semiconscious back to their hotels.

There are other places. If you're in pursuit of this sort of activity you'll soon hear about them.

Bars & Pubs You can make a fairly clean division between the bars you go to for a drink and the ones you go to for entertainment, music and pick-ups. It's generally immediately clear which category they fall into. The *Casablanca* on Jalan Buni Sari is definitely in the noise and activity category; ideal if you can handle beer drinking contests, cheese and vegemite sandwich eating contests, ladies' arm wrestling contests and other scenes of Australian depravity. Also on Jalan Buni Sari is the *Pub Bagus* and *The Pub,* one of Kuta's original bars. The Pub is still a popular place for a beer without the associated noise and confusion.

Down Poppies Gang the *Nusa Indah Bar* is a straightforward and pleasant little open-air place with about the cheapest beer prices around. Head further north to Poppies Gang II and just off Jalan Legian is *Tubes Bar* with video movies every night and a giant concrete wave complete with an embedded surfboard where you can stand for heroic surfing snapshots! Continue a little further up Jalan Legian to the *Sari Club* (SC for short), a big, noisy, crowded, open-air bar. There are numerous other bars of all sorts along Jalan Legian.

Things to Buy
Parts of Kuta are now almost door-to-door shops and over the years these have become steadily more sophisticated. Of course there are still many simple stalls as well as many of these cheaper shops are now crowded together in 'art markets' like the one at the beach end of Jalan Bakung Sari. With so many things to buy around Kuta it's very easy to be stampeded into buying things you don't really want during the first few days of your stay. In fact you need real endurance not to succumb to something, there are so many people trying to sell to you. Unless you want to end up with lots of things you can definitely do without, get an overall impression before you consider buying anything and shop around before you do buy. Some items of interest follow.

Crafts If it's made anywhere in Bali then 10 to one you can find it on sale at Kuta. Of course, Kuta isn't really the centre for any of Bali's notable crafts but the Kuta shops will have arts and crafts from almost every part of the island, from woodcarvings to paintings to textiles and just about everything else in between.

Clothing Clothes, on the other hand, are a Kuta speciality and Kuta has become the centre for Bali's energetic rag trade. Countless boutiques for men and women display the sort of Balinese interpretations of the latest styles which now find their way all over the world. You may never need to wear a sports coat or leather boots in Bali but you can certainly find plenty of them on sale and at competitive prices. You'll probably see the same items later on in shops from Berkeley to Double Bay at 10 times the cost.

Other Items The pirate cassette business was run out of town a few years ago but it's bounced back with 100% legal tapes which still considerably undercut anything you'd buy in the West. There are lots of tape shops around Kuta with a wide range of all the latest hits.

One thing there is no harm in paying for as soon as you arrive is a massage. Kuta has countless masseurs operating along the beach or coming around to the hotels – for just a few thousand rp, they'll quickly prove you have dozens of muscles you never knew existed.

Getting There & Away
Air See the Getting There & Away chapter for details of flying to or from Bali. Kuta has lots of travel agencies but if you're looking for onward tickets, Bali is no place for cheap bargains. If you're looking for a discounted deal to a faraway place wait until you get to Singapore.

If you already have tickets and need to reconfirm, there's a small Garuda office (☎ 24764) in the Kuta Beach Hotel at the beach end of Jalan Pantai Kuta. The office sometimes gets hopelessly crowded so it's a good idea to arrive before opening time or during the lunch break and be at the head of the queue. It's open Monday to Friday from 7.30 am to 4 pm, Saturday and Sunday from 9 am to 1 pm.

There's a Qantas office and another Garuda office at the Hotel Bali Beach in Sanur. The myriad Kuta travel agencies will offer to make reconfirmations for you but there's a charge and some agencies are said to be less than scrupulous about actually reconfirming.

Bus From Kuta there are buses to other

places in Bali and direct to Java although the cheaper public buses generally depart from the Denpasar bus stations. Fares from Kuta include Surabaya from 19,000 rp, Yogyakarta from around 29,000 rp and Jakarta for 48,000 rp.

Perama, on Jalan Legian, operates regular tourist shuttle buses direct from Kuta to the other main tourist centres in Bali. These services save you having to get to the appropriate bus station and find the bus you want and, since they don't make frequent intermediate stops they're much faster. Services include Sanur and Ubud for 4000 rp, Padangbai and Candidasa for 7500 rp, Kintamani for 7000 rp and Lovina for 10,000 rp. Perama also operates bus-ferry-bus services to Lombok. You can travel directly to Mataram or Senggigi Beach for 13,000 rp or to Bangsal, from where the boats cross to the Gili Islands, for 15,000 rp.

Getting Around
To/From the Airport Ngurah Rai Airport is so close to Kuta you could actually walk if you were in the mood. The official taxi fare is 4500 rp from the airport to any place south of Jalan Bakung Sari (the southern part of Kuta), 6000 rp for anywhere north of Bakung Sari but south of Jalan Padma (central Kuta right up to the centre of Legian), 9000 rp north of Jalan Padma (the northern part of Legian) and 10,000 rp to the Oberoi Hotel (way north of Legian in Seminyak).

From Kuta to the airport you can generally bargain with bemo or taxi drivers to get these fares without too much effort but you will have to work hard to get lower fares. Theoretically, you could get to the airport from Kuta by regular public bemo for just a few hundred rp. Just try to do it! The Perama bus service to the airport costs 3500 rp.

Bemo & Taxi There are plenty of taxis around Kuta Beach (any car is a taxi) and even larger numbers of bemos (minibuses). Constant offers of 'transport' follow any pedestrian. None of the vehicles is metered so you have to negotiate the fare before you get on board. You should be able to get from the middle of Kuta to the middle of Legian for around 3000 rp.

Public bemos run all over Bali so theoretically you could take a bemo from Kuta to Denpasar, to the airport or even to Legian. Try it sometime! You can get a regular bemo from just beyond Bemo Corner into Denpasar for 400 rp but anywhere else you're almost certainly going to have to charter. Kuta bemo jockeys bargain hard but they're good humoured about it and once you've agreed on a price they usually stick to it. Note that there is no direct bemo public service to Sanur. By public bemo you have to go into Denpasar, change bus stations and take another bemo out.

Rental There are countless bicycle, motorbike and car rental places around Kuta. By the day you can rent a bike for about 3000 rp, a motorbike from around 8000 rp to 12,000 rp or a car from around 35,000 rp to 40,000 rp including insurance and unlimited km.

Tours There are countless tours organised from Kuta which can be booked through the many travel agencies. Tours further afield – to places like Lombok, Komodo or Sulawesi – are also offered. Agencies also rent cars, motorbikes and bicycles, sell bus and train tickets to Java and perform other travel agency services.

SANUR

Sanur Beach is the alternative to Kuta for those coming to Bali for sea, sand and sun. The resort of Nusa Dua is intended to be an up-market alternative to Sanur. Sanur is principally a locale for Hyatts, Sheratons and the like, and although it does have some more reasonably priced accommodation, prices are not down to the lower Kuta levels.

Sanur has a pleasant beach sheltered by a reef. At low tide it's very shallow, and you have to pick your way out over rocks and coral through knee-deep water. The Indonesians, both locals and 'domestic tourists', think it's ideal and you'll find many of them paddling here on Sundays and holidays, particularly at the northern end of the beach. At high tide the swimming is fine, and there is an array of water sports on offer – windsurfing, snorkelling, water-skiing, parasailing, paddle boards etc – all for a price. For surfers there is a good right-hand break on the reef, which works best in the wet season, from November to April.

What Sanur doesn't have, thankfully, is the noise, confusion and pollution of Kuta. You're not in constant danger of being mown down by motorbike maniacs, the traffic isn't horrendous and you're not constantly badgered to buy things – badgered yes, but not constantly.

Orientation

Sanur stretches for about three km along an

Kuta Banjars

Despite all the excesses Kuta is still a village, a place where little offerings are put out in front of house entrances and at tricky gang junctions. It's this part of Kuta which makes it so much more interesting than the antiseptic Nusa Dua.

The banjar is visible evidence of Kuta's thriving village life. A banjar is rather like a small town council and the bale banjar is a meeting place: a place for discussions, ceremonies, dancing or gamelan practice. If you hear a gamelan ringing out over Kuta some quiet evening it's probably a banjar practise session and nobody will mind if you wander in to watch and listen.

Most banjars are little more than an open pavilion or courtyard but they're easy to spot by the warning drum (kulkul) tower; Kuta banjars, with lots of tourist generated rupiah, can afford some pretty fancy towers. Check out the one at Banjar Pande Mas next to Made's Warung on Kuta Beach Rd, or the one at Banjar Buni Kuta next to The Pub. Best of all is the superb new multistorey tower at Banjar Tegal Kuta, further down the lane from Banjar Buni Kuta. ■

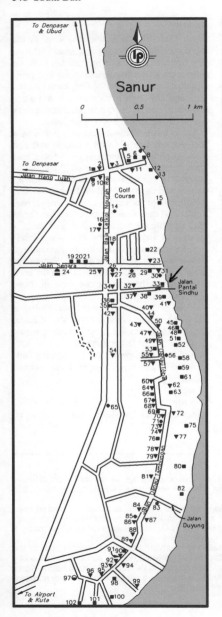

PLACES TO STAY

1 Sanur Village Club Hotel
4 Bali Eka Beach Inn
5 Watering Hole Homestay & Restaurant
6 Alit's Beach Bungalows & Restaurant
8 Ananda Hotel & Restaurant
9 Hotel Bali Continental
12 Diwangkara Beach Hotel
15 Hotel Bali Beach
19 Hotel Sanur-Indah
20 Hotel Taman Sari
21 Hotel Rani
22 Hotel Bali Beach - Cottage Section
29 Segara Village Hotel
33 Baruna Beach Inn
36 Abian Srama Inn
38 Queen Bali Hotel
39 Sindhu Beach Hotel
45 La Taverna Bali Hotel
46 Respati
48 Gazebo Beach Hotel
49 Made Homestay & Pub
51 Irama
52 Tandjung Sari Hotel
53 Kalpataharu Homestay & Restaurant
58 Besakih
59 Santrian Beach Cottages
61 Werdha Pura
63 Laghawa Beach Inn
66 Swastika Bungalows
69 Hotel Ramayana
75 Villa Batu Jimbar
76 Hotel Santai
80 Peneeda View
82 Bali Hyatt Hotel

east-facing coastline, with the landscaped grounds and restaurants of expensive hotels fronting right onto the beach. The conspicuous, '60s style Hotel Bali Beach is at the northern end of the strip, and the newer Surya Beach Hotel, invisible behind its walls and gardens, is at the southern end. West of these hotels the main drag, Jalan Danau Tamblingan (formerly Jalan Tanjung Sari), runs parallel to the beach, with the hotel entrances on one side and wall-to-wall tourist shops and restaurants down the other side.

98	Santrian Bali Beach Bungalows	73	Number One Club
100	Semawang Beach Inn	74	Penjor Restaurant
101	Hotel Sanur Beach	77	New Seoul Korean Restaurant
102	Surya Beach Hotel	78	Kulkul Restaurant
		79	Melanie Restaurant
▼	PLACES TO EAT	81	Restaurant Telaga Naga
		84	Paon Restaurant
2	Bali Raja restaurant	86	Legong Restaurant
3	Si Pino Restaurant	87	Whitesands Bar & Restaurant
10	Oasis & Borobudur Restaurants	88	Oka's Bar Restaurant
11	Bali	89	Bali Pub & Restaurant
16	Steak House	91	Rumah Makan Wayan
17	Kentucky Fried Chicken &	92	Kesumasari
	Swensens Ice Cream	93	Norman's Bar
18	Lenny's Restaurant	94	Alita Garden Restaurant
23	Swiss Restaurant	95	Balita Restaurant
25	Warung Mini	96	Sanur Kuring Restaurant &
27	The Corner Restaurant		Karaoke
31	Warungs	99	Trattoria da Marco
32	Carlo Restaurant		
34	Merry Bar & Restaurant		OTHER
37	Queen Bali Restaurant		
40	Bali Moon Restaurant	7	Boats to Nusa Lembongan
41	Mango Bar & Restaurant	13	Museum Le Mayeur
42	Aga Restaurant	14	Police Station
43	Swastika I Restaurant	16	Supermarket
44	Sindhu Corner Restaurant	24	Post Office
47	Raoul's & Dragon Restaurant	26	Apotik & Moneychanger
50	Kuri Putih Restaurant	28	US Consular Agency
54	Sita Restaurant	30	Sanur Beach Market
55	Ratu's Pizza	35	Night Market
57	Arena Restaurant	56	Sanur Foto Centre
60	Mina Garden Restaurant &	65	Petrol Station
	Yamcha Restaurant	67	Temptation
62	Laghawa Grill	71	Handicraft Market
64	Warung Aditya	83	Supermarket
68	Swastika II Restaurant	85	Double U Shopping Centre
70	Umasari Restaurant	90	Wisma Bahari Art Gallery
72	Blue Diamond Restaurant	97	Bemo Stop

To the west of this road are some small streets and lanes, then the main Sanur bypass road, Jalan Baja Letkol Ngurah Rai, which runs south then west to Kuta and the airport, and north towards Ubud.

Information
Sanur has travel agencies, moneychangers and other facilities just like Kuta. Most of them are along Jalan Danau Tamblingan.

Post & Telecommunications Sanur's post office is on the southern side of Jalan Segara, a hundred metres or so west of the bypass road. If you're an American Express customer you can have your mail sent to their office, c/o PT Pacto Ltd, PO Box 52, Sanur (☎ 88449), which is in the Hotel Bali Beach. Of course, you can also have mail addressed to the large hotels.

There's no Permuntel telephone office in Sanur – it's probably assumed that everyone who wants to make international phone calls can do so from their hotel room. There's a

Home Country Direct phone next to the Malaysian Airlines office in the Hotel Bali Beach. You can make reverse-charge (collect) calls or pay with your credit card; it's very easy to use.

Foreign Embassies The US consular agency is on Jalan Segara, 80 metres west of the Segara Village Hotel. There is a small sign next to the driveway. A number of other consulates and consular agencies are in Sanur, or not far away in the Renon area of Denpasar. See under Visas & Embassies in the Facts for the Visitor chapter for the addresses of other embassies.

Museum Le Mayeur

Sanur was one of the places in Bali favoured by Western artists during their prewar discovery of the island. It was a quiet fishing village at that time but few traces of the Sanur of 50 years ago remain. The exception is the former home of the Belgian artist Le Mayeur who lived here from 1932 to 1958. It must have been a delightful place then, a peaceful and elegant home right by the beach. Today it's squeezed between the Hotel Bali Beach and the Diwangkara Beach Hotel but it's still maintained by his widow, Ni Polok, once a renowned and beautiful Legong dancer.

The home displays paintings and drawings by Le Mayeur but unfortunately many of them are yellowed, dirty and badly lit. They are nevertheless interesting, impressionist-style paintings from his travels in Africa, India, Italy, France and the South Pacific. The more recent works, from the 1950s, are in much better condition, with the vibrant colours of Bali and the scenes of daily life which later became popular with Balinese artists. All the works have titles, descriptions, dates, etc in both Indonesian and English. The museum is also an interesting example of architecture in its own right. Notice the beautifully carved window shutters which recount the story of Rama and Sita from the *Ramayana*.

Admission is 200 rp (children 100 rp) and it's open from 8 am to 2 pm Sunday, Tuesday,

Wednesday and Thursday, from 8 to 11 am Friday and from 8 am to noon on Saturday. It's closed on Monday.

Kites

Asian children don't enjoy the same variety and quantity of toys that children in the West commonly have but they certainly do fly kites: almost anywhere in Asia the sky is likely to be full of kites of all sizes and types. Bali is no exception – you'll see children flying kites in towns and villages and even in the middle of the rice paddies. At Sanur, however, kite-flying is not just child's play. Here the local banjars compete in kite-flying competitions where size seems to be a major factor. July, August and September are the months for competitive kite flying.

The kites are enormous – traffic is halted when they're carried down the road and it takes half a dozen men to launch them, two men to carry the drum of heavy nylon cord, and a sturdy tree is needed to tie the kite to once it's up and flying. Kites can be up to 10 metres long, and the cord tensioning the main cross-piece (itself a hefty length of bamboo) makes a low 'whoop-whoop-whoop' noise during flight. Not unexpectedly, such big kites are a danger to aircraft – one of these monsters could bring down a 747 – and kite-flying has been restricted on the airport approaches, particularly across Pulau Serangan.

Many of the craft shops sell kites in the shape of birds, bats or butterflies. They come in a variety of sizes and fold up ingeniously so you can get them home. Look for ones with the feathers and other details carefully painted – there's a lot of junk around.

Other Attractions

Just wandering around Sanur, along the beach or through the rice paddies, is an interesting activity in itself. The rice farmers of Sanur are said to grow some of the finest rice in Bali. The beach at Sanur is always full of interesting sights such as the colourful outriggers known as *jukungs* ready to take you for a quick trip out to the reef. At low tide you can walk across the sand and coral to this sheltering reef. Villagers collect coral here to make lime for building.

Beyond the Hotel Sanur Beach, at Belanjong, there's a stone pillar with an inscription recounting military victories of over 1000 years ago. Tanjung Sari, with its coral pyramid, was once a lonely temple by the beach.

Places to Stay

There are no rock-bottom Kuta-style places in Sanur although there are a few cheapies. There's also a handful of mid- range places, a few of which are as good value as equivalent places at Kuta. Principally, however, Sanur is a high-price resort, the place for 'international standard' hotels where the majority of Bali's package tours go, and where prices don't include the 15.5% to 21.5% service charge. The prices quoted in the following sections don't include this additional charge.

Note also, that the prices given in the top-end section are the quoted walk-in rates, but hardly anyone just walks in to these places. It may actually be cheaper to book ahead through a travel agency, especially as part of a package.

Places to Stay – bottom end

The cheapest places are away from the beach at the northern end of town. On Jalan Segara, west of the main road, there are three lower priced places side by side – the *Hotel Sanur-Indah*, closest to Denpasar, is the most basic and the cheapest at about 12,000/12,500 rp for singles/doubles. The *Hotel Taman Sari*, in the middle, has doubles from 15,000 rp with fan to 45,000 rp with hot water and air-con. The *Hotel Rani* has rooms from 12,500/15,000 rp for singles/doubles, and some with air-con and hot water for about 40,000 rp.

You might also find a cheap room at *Made Pub & Homestay*, on the west side of Jalan Danau Toba almost opposite the Gazebo Beach Hotel. There are some small rooms downstairs from 15,000 rp for singles, and some bigger rooms upstairs for 30,000 rp a double.

Places to Stay – middle

At the northern end of Sanur Beach the *Ananda Hotel* (☎ 8827) is behind the restaurant of the same name, right by the beach. It's neat and clean and rooms with fan and cold water cost 25,000/30,000 rp for singles/ doubles.

The *Watering Hole Homestay*, (☎ 88289) on Jalan Hang Tuah (the Sanur to Denpasar road) opposite the Hotel Bali Beach entrance, has clean, pleasant rooms at 20,000/ 25,000 rp. It's a friendly, well-run place with good food and a bar. On Hang Tuah, on the other side of the bypass road, the *Hotel Bali Continental* has singles and doubles with air-con, TV and hot water for 50,000 rp.

The *Kalpatharu Homestay & Restaurant* (☎ 88457), on the west side of Jalan Danau Toba, is a pleasant place with a garden and swimming pool. It's clean and good value at 20,000/25,000 rp for budget rooms, 25,000/ 30,000 rp for better rooms, and 40,000/ 45,000 rp for rooms with air-con.

A little further south, on a sideroad which runs towards the beach between some government buildings, is the *Werdha Pura*. It's a government-run 'beach cottage prototype', with the type of service that will make you believe in private enterprise, but it's cheap enough at 25,000/50,000 rp for singles/ doubles and 60,000 rp for family rooms.

The more expensive mid-range places tend to quote their prices in US$ and add on about 15% for tax and service. Starting again from the northern end of town, the *Sanur Village Club* (one of the Bali Sanur Bungalows group), on Jalan Hang Tuah, costs US$35/40 with air-con but is not in a good location. The *Bali Eka Beach Inn* (☎ 88939) is on a small road off the northern side of Jalan Hang Tuah. It's clean and characterless, and costs US$35/40. *Alit's Beach Bungalows* are also on Hang Tuah, a bit closer to the beach, costing US$37/40 with air-con and hot water. On Jalan Pantai Sindhu, two streets further south, and right on the beach, is the *Baruna Beach Inn* with a great location and only seven rooms at US$28/30 including breakfast, tax and air-con. Rooms cost a few dollars extra in the high season. On the other side of the road, a bit further from the beach, the *Queen Bali Hotel* (☎ 88054) has standard rooms at US$25/30 and bungalows at US$30/35; extra beds are US$8. The price includes tax, breakfast, air-con and hot water. There's a bar and disco.

Continuing along Jalan Danau Tamblingan you'll find the *Laghawa Beach Inn* (☎ 88494, 87919) on the beach side of the road, with air-con singles/doubles for US$35/40 and air-con triples for US$45. Fan-cooled rooms are US$10 less and all prices include tax and continental breakfast. An extra bed costs US$7. The inn has an attractive garden setting, restaurant and bar and looks like quite good value for Sanur. On the other side of the road, with identical prices, the *Swastika Bungalows* has comfortable rooms, pretty gardens and two swimming pools. A few metres further south is the *Hotel Ramayana* (☎ 88429) with rooms at US$23 for singles or doubles, excluding tax and breakfast.

At the southern end of town, on a small road between the big hotels, the *Semawang Beach Inn* is close to the beach and offers good facilities and breakfast for US$27 (air-con) and US$20 (fan) for singles or doubles.

Places to Stay – top end

Sanur's first 'big' hotel and still one of the biggest is the massive *Hotel Bali Beach* (☎ 88511; PO Box 275, Denpasar). Dating from the Sukarno era of the mid-60s, today it's very out of place in Bali – a Miami Beach-style rectangular block squarely facing the beach. It's got all the usual facilities from bars, restaurants and a nightclub to swimming pools, tennis courts and even an adjacent golf course. The pool-side snack bar here is quite reasonably priced. Air-con rooms start at US$92 to over US$119 and there are suites from US$137 to US$358, some with kitchenettes. Adjoining the hotel to the south is the newer cottage section.

Almost all the more expensive hotels are on the beach front. Immediately north of the Bali Beach and adjacent to the Museum Le Mayeur is the partially secluded *Diwang-*

kara Beach Hotel (☎ 88577, 88591; PO Box 120, Denpasar). Air-con rooms cost from US$45 to US$55.

Going south from the Bali Beach hotels you come first to the *Segara Village Hotel* (☎ 88407/8, fax 87242). It's a more expensive place with motel-style rooms and two-storeyed cottages from US$50 to US$175. The hotel is in a pleasant landscaped area with swimming pools and a children's playground. The *Sindhu Beach Hotel*, (☎ 88351/2) right on the beach, has 50 air-con rooms from US$55 to US$80. The *La Taverna Bali Hotel* (☎ 88497; PO Box 40, Denpasar), also right on the beach, has air-con rooms from US$60 to US$70. There's also the smaller *Gazebo Beach Hotel* here with air-con cottages in a lush garden.

Sanur has several places to stay in the Bali Sanur Bungalows group. Heading south you come first to the *Irama* then to the *Respati*, both priced at US$40/45 for single/doubles. Further south you come to the *Besakih* and then to the *Peneeda View* bungalows, which are more expensive at US$50/60. Breakfast, tax and service are extra.

In between the Irama and the Besakih is the *Tandjung Sari Hotel* (☎ 88441) with air-con rooms from US$80 to US$100. Some of the bungalows in this pleasantly relaxed and fairly expensive place are interesting two-storeyed buildings.

Then it's the *Bali Hyatt* (☎ 88271/7; PO Box 392, Denpasar), one of the biggest hotels in Sanur and an interesting contrast with the Hotel Bali Beach built 10 years earlier. The lesson had been learnt in the '60s and a regulation was passed that no hotel could be 'taller than a palm tree'. The Hyatt, with its sloping balconies overflowing with tropical vegetation, blends in remarkably well. Look for the interesting pottery tiles used as decorations on various walls. Air-con rooms start at US$95. Sanur's flashiest and most popular disco is also here.

Further south is the big *Hotel Sanur Beach*, (☎ 88011, fax 87566) where air-con rooms cost from US$100 to US$120 and suites and bungalows from US$175 to US$850.

The *Santrian Bali Beach Bungalows* (☎ 88184, 89133; fax 88185) have air-con rooms from US$60 to US$80, plus two swimming pools and tennis courts. The newer *Sativa Sanur Cottages* (☎ 87881, fax 87276) are a bit off the beach, but attractively arranged around a swimming pool and gardens. Air-con rooms cost from US$59 to US$95.

Places to Eat

All the top-end hotels have their own restaurants, snack bars, coffee bars and bars of course – generally with top-end prices too! The food at Sanur is basically Western-style – there's even a place for homesick pasta lovers – *Trattoria da Marco* down at the southern end of the beach road. There's the *New Seoul Korean Restaurant* halfway down Jalan Danau Tamblingan on the beach side, and a *Japanese Restaurant* a bit further north. The *Swiss Restaurant*, on Jalan Segara just south of the Hotel Bali Beach, is very plush with thick carpet and a grand piano. Fondue is US$16 for two, other Swiss dishes from US$5 to US$10. There's a *Kentucky Ayam Goreng* and *Swensen's Ice Cream* next to the supermarket, on the bypass road opposite the golf course.

There are a number of quite reasonably priced places, very much in the Kuta restaurant mould. You'll find plenty of them down the main street, mostly on the western side. Just south of the Hotel Bali Beach there's the slightly more expensive beach-front *Sanur Beach Market*. Agung and Sue's *Watering Hole*, opposite the Hotel Bali Beach entrance, has good, food at affordable prices.

For seafood, *Lenny's* and the *Kulkul Restaurant* are worth trying. *Carlo Restaurant*, on Jalan Pantai Sindhu, is reasonably priced and has good food. *Kesumasari*, on the beach south of the Bali Hyatt, has good and commendably fresh food. If you continue to the southern end of the Sanur hotel strip, beyond the Hyatt, there are a number of inexpensive small restaurants and bars.

For cheaper eats try the rumah makans on the bypass road, but the cheapest, and possibly the tastiest, food is from the food carts

and stalls at the northern end of the beach, close to where boats leave for Nusa Lembongan.

Things to Buy

Like Kuta, Sanur has many shops, selling everything from T-shirts to fluoro-print beachwear, as well as a whole range of handicrafts from Bali and other Indonesian islands. The Sanur Beach market, just south of the Hotel Bali Beach, has a variety of stalls so you can shop around. There are plenty of other shops down the main street, as well as two small market areas, each with a cluster of shops. Temptation, near the Hotel Ramayana, has a curious collection of 'artyfacts', including an 'Egyptian mummy'. There are a few other art and antique shops, some with very interesting stock. The sellers are not afraid to ask for a high 'first price', so shop around for some idea of quality and price before you consider parting with your money.

The supermarket on the bypass road is a good place for those small odds and ends that you might need but don't know what to ask for. There's another supermarket at the southern end of town near the Bali Hyatt. There's also a traditional market between bypass road and Jalan Danau Toba near the northern end of the main street. It caters a bit for tourists, but still sells fresh vegetables, dried fish, pungent spices, plastic buckets and other household goods that the local people need for themselves.

Getting There & Away

Air See the Getting There & Away chapter for information about flying to or from Bali.

For those wanting to reconfirm prebooked flights or buy onward tickets, there's a Qantas office (☎ 88331/2/3) at the Hotel Bali Beach; it's open Monday to Friday from 8.30 am to 4.30 pm, Saturday from 8.30 am to 12.30 pm. You will also find a Garuda office here (☎ 88511) which is open Monday to Friday from 7.30 am to 4.30 pm and on Saturday from 9 am to 1 pm. The KLM office is open Monday to Friday from 8 am to 4.30 pm, Saturday 8 am to 1 pm. The Continental

Airlines agency is open Monday to Friday from 8 am to 4 pm, Saturday 8 am to noon. Singapore Airlines, Cathay Pacific, Thai International and Malaysian Airlines agencies are also in the Hotel Bali Beach and keep similar hours.

Bemo There are two different bemos operating between Sanur and Denpasar. Coming from Sanur the blue ones go past Kereneng station, across town to Tegal station (the Kuta station) and then back to Kereneng. The green bemos *sometimes* take this route around town but usually just go straight to the Kereneng station. The fare is 500 rp.

To get from Kuta to Sanur you have to go into Denpasar and then out again. You get one bemo from Kuta into the Tegal bemo station, then get a blue bemo to Sanur via Kereneng. If you get a green bemo at Tegal, it will stop at Kereneng and you'll have to get a third one out to Sanur. It's much faster and, between a few people, not that much more expensive to charter a bemo for a Kuta to Sanur trip, around 10,000 rp.

Boat Boats to Nusa Lembongan leave from the northern end of the beach, in front of the Ananda Hotel & Restaurant. Unless the boat captains' price-fixing cartel has collapsed, it costs 15,000 rp (including your surfboard) to get to the island.

Getting Around

To/From the Airport The taxi fare from the airport to Sanur is 12,000 rp, while in the other direction (from Sanur to the airport) the fare is between 8000 and 10,000 rp. A new 'super highway', Jalan Baja Lektol Ngurah Rai, runs from Nusa Dua in the south, past the airport and Kuta to Sanur and Denpasar. It makes transport along this route quite fast.

Bemo Small bemos shuttle up and down the beach road in Sanur at a cost of 200 rp. Make it clear that you want to take a public bemo, not charter it. Know where you want to go and accept that the driver may take a circuitous route to put down or pick up other passengers. There is a bemo stop at the south-ern end of town near where the main street rejoins the bypass road, and another stop at the northern end of town outside the entrance to the Hotel Bali Beach.

Rental There are numerous places around Sanur renting cars, motorbikes and bicycles, for about 40,000 rp, 10,000 rp and 3000 rp a day respectively. Tunas Tours & Travel, in the Hotel Bali Beach Arcade, rents mountain bikes for about US$8 a day and also organises bicycle tours of Bali.

PULAU SERANGAN

Very close to the shore, south of Sanur and close to the mouth of Benoa Harbour, is Pulau Serangan (Turtle Island). At low tide you can actually walk across to the island. Turtles are captured and fattened here in pens before being sold for village feasts. (See the Turtles aside in the Facts about Bali chapter for more information on the problems associated with the increasing slaughter of these turtles.)

The island has an important temple, Pura Sakenan, noted for its unusual shrines *(candi)*. Twice a year major temple festivals are held here, attracting great crowds of devotees. The giant puppet figures used in the Barong Landung dance are brought across to the island for these festivals.

Day trips to Serangan have become popular with the travel agencies at Kuta and Sanur, but Serangan has a very strong tourist-trap air and is not terribly popular with visitors. You're constantly hassled to spend, spend, spend. In fact you get pounced on as soon as the prahu beaches and you're followed, cajoled, pleaded with and abused until you leave.

One traveller who actually enjoyed Serangan said that the southern end of the island was less 'developed' and had nice beaches. The problem is to negotiate a return trip which gives you enough time to walk the length of the island, enjoy the beach, and then walk back. If you want to try this, a boat from Benoa village to the south of Serangan may be a better option, though still quite expensive (see the following section).

Getting There & Away

Like Kuta, Serangan has been affected by tourism – badly. It's not a place to waste time or money on but if you do decide to take a look you can either get there on an organised tour or charter a prahu yourself. If you decide to charter a boat, the starting price may be around 25,000 rp, but for a boat big enough for about six people, you should be able to negotiate the price down to around 10,000 rp. Allow about 20 minutes each way for the trip, and an hour to look around the island. Charters are available from Suwang, a small mangrove inlet near a rubbish dump. Pulau Serangan is hard work from start to finish.

JIMBARAN BAY

Just beyond the airport, south of Kuta, Jimbaran Bay is a superb crescent of white sand and blue sea. Jimbaran is basically a fishing village with, until recently, minimal tourist development.

Places to Stay

Jimbaran is being developed as a small, up-market resort area. Fortunately, there are now a couple of places where budget travellers can stay within walking distance of the beautiful bay. There is a basic losmen, the *Puri Bambu Bungalows*, on the western side of Jalan Ulu Watu. Further south, at Jalan Ulu Watu 28A, is *Puri Indra Prasta*. These bungalows have a restaurant, bar and swimming pool, and clean comfortable rooms from 20,000 to 25,000 rp for singles or doubles, including breakfast.

The first of the 1st-class hotels here, the *Pansea Puri Bali* (☎ 52227, fax 52220), has a full range of facilities and services, including two bars, two restaurants (one on the beach) and about 40 air-con bungalows and rooms. Depending on the season, these cost from US$110 to US$155 for singles or doubles, dinner and breakfast included. A bit to the north, the *Keraton Bali Cottages*, opened in 1991, are a really fine example of Balinese hotel architecture, beautifully decorated and tastefully landscaped, and somewhat cheaper at US$55 to US$80 depending on the room and the season.

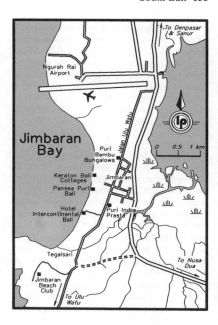

Further south you'll find the site of the large *Hotel Intercontinental Bali*, due to be opened in 1993. South of the village area, on a small road off to the west of Jalan Ulu Watu, is the *Jimbaran Beach Club* (☎ 80361). It's a bit isolated, and attracts mainly package-tour groups. Walk-in rates are from US$35 to US$45 for singles or doubles.

Places to Eat

The big hotels all have their own restaurants. You can eat in them even if you're not staying there, but expect to pay at least US$10 for lunch or dinner. There are some warungs in the main street, and you'll find cheap food in the market on market days.

BENOA PORT

The wide but shallow bay east of the airport runway, Benoa Harbour (Labuhan Benoa), is one of Bali's main ports. It's also the main harbour for visiting yachts and there's nearly always a few overseas vessels moored here.

Benoa is actually in two parts. Benoa Port is on the northern side, with a two-km long causeway connecting it to the main Kuta to Sanur road. It consists of little more than a wharf and a variety of port offices. Benoa village is on the point on the southern side of the bay.

Hydrofoil

The Nawala hydrofoil service to Lombok arrives and departs from Benoa Port. If you've booked your hydrofoil ticket through an agent such as Perama, the deal should include transport between the port and where you're staying. If not, a public bemo from Denpasar will cost around 500 rp from Suci bemo station, or 1000 rp from Tegal station. A chartered bemo direct to Kuta will cost around 4000 rp per person. Hydrofoils leave Benoa Port at 8.45 am and 3.30 pm, take about two hours to reach Lombok's Lembar Harbour, and cost 35,000 rp. From Lembar the hydrofoils leave at 10.45 am and 3.30 pm, take about the same time but cost only 32,000 rp. Initial demand for the service was low, and prices may eventually be lowered.

Bali Hai

The *Bali Hai* is a luxury tourist excursion boat that operates from Benoa Port. Its sightseeing, diving and surfing trips to various locations around Bali and the offshore islands are well promoted in the main tourist areas. One popular trip is for well-heeled surfers, who pay 115,000 rp to anchor offshore and paddle *in* to the reef breaks off Nusa Lembongan.

BENOA VILLAGE

To get to Benoa village, on the southern side of the bay, you have to take the highway to Nusa Dua and then the smaller road along the coast from there. Boats also shuttle back and forth between Benoa Harbour and Benoa village. There's an interesting Chinese temple in Benoa.

The village of Benoa has become much cleaner and more affluent in recent years and it's something of an activities centre for Nusa Dua. If you want to go windsurfing, parasailing, scuba diving or indulge in various other water sports, this is the place.

Places to Stay & Eat

The few places to stay are near the beach front on the road which heads south to Nusa Dua. They're all within a stone's throw of each other, so you won't have any trouble finding them. The cheapest place is the *Homestay Asa*, a bit off the road, which has clean, comfortable singles and doubles from 17,000 rp – good value for the area. The *Rasa Dua* has nice upstairs rooms for 30,000 rp and downstairs rooms for 20,000 rp. *Chez Agung Pension/Homestay* is now managed by the *Sorga Nusa Dua* next door (☎ 71604, fax 71143). Prices for singles/doubles are US$30/35 for standard rooms and US$40/45 for deluxe rooms. Rooms at the Sorga Nusa Dua are from US$50 to US$75, with air-con and hot water.

There are several restaurants in Benoa, like the *Dalang Sea View Restaurant*, the *Entari Restaurant*, the *Jeladi Suta Restaurant* or the *Rai Seafood Restaurant*. They're mostly on the beach front opposite the hotels, and they tend to be expensive by Bali's usual standards. You should be able to find a rumah makan in the village for cheaper food.

NUSA DUA

Nusa Dua, literally 'two islands', is Bali's top-end beach resort – a luxury tourist enclave, planned to ensure that the mistakes of Kuta would not be repeated! The two islands are actually small raised headlands, connected to the mainland by sand spits. Nusa Dua is south of Kuta and Sanur, on the eastern side of the sparsely populated Bukit Peninsula.

The beach here is very pleasant and there is often good surf, this is really a place for people who want to get away from Bali. There are no independent developments permitted within the compound so you have a km or so to walk if you want to get even so much as a Coke at less than international

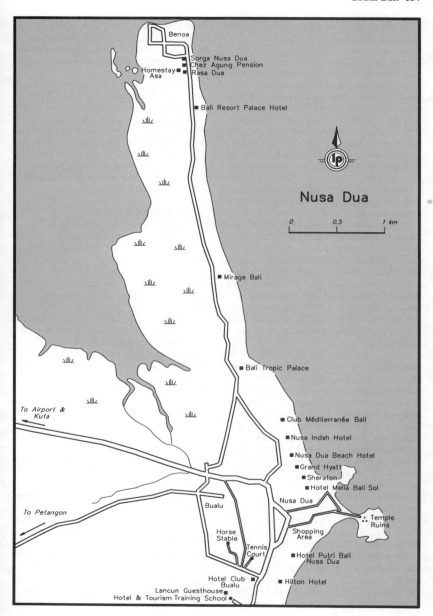

Benoa

Sorga Nusa Dua
Chez Agung Pension
Rasa Dua

Homestay
Asa

■ Bali Resort Palace Hotel

Nusa Dua

0   0.5   1 km

■ Mirage Bali

■ Bali Tropic Palace

To Airport &
Kuta

■ Club Méditerranée Bali

■ Nusa Indah Hotel

■ Nusa Dua Beach Hotel
■ Grand Hyatt
■ Sheraton
■ Hotel Melia Bali Sol

To Petangon

Bualu

Nusa Dua

Temple
Ruins

Horse
Stable

Shopping
Area

Tennis
Court

■ Hotel Putri Bali
Nusa Dua

Hotel Club
Bualu

■ Hilton Hotel

Lancun Guesthouse
Hotel & Tourism Training School

hotel prices, or if you want to get a bemo to the rest of Bali.

Places to Stay & Eat

The Nusa Dua hotels all have swimming pools, a variety of restaurants and bars, entertainment and sports facilities and various other international hotel mod cons.

Starting at the northern end of the beach, the *Bali Resort Palace Hotel* is the first you'll come across. It has about 200 rooms from US$80 to US$160, and a full range of facilities and restaurants. The next one south is the *Mirage Bali* with 100 expensive rooms. South again is the *Bali Tropic Palace*, then the *Club Méditerranée Bali* which is strictly a package-tour operation.

Next is the smaller *Nusa Indah Hotel*, then the *Nusa Dua Beach Hotel* (☎ 71210) which is huge (450 rooms) with all the luxuries you could expect and prices from around US$120 to US$160 for standard rooms, plus 15.5% service and tax. It's attractively designed using Balinese architecture and statuary, but then how seriously can you take a hotel that promotes itself as being the place where Ronald Reagan stayed when he came to Bali?

South of the Nusa Dua Beach Hotel is the new, 750-room *Grand Hyatt Nusa Dua*. Built on a massive budget, it is pressing for the title of one of the best hotels in Bali. Next is another international name, the *Nusa Dua Sheraton*, then the 500-room *Hotel Melia Bali Sol* (☎ 71510) with regular rooms from US$78 to US$90 and suites at US$138.

The shopping area near the Bali Sol has a variety of shops and restaurants. South of this is the *Hotel Putri Bali Nusa Dua* (☎ 71020, 71420) which has 425 rooms, plus suites, cottages and so on. South again is the Nusa Dua *Hilton*, and just inland from there, the smaller *Hotel Club Bualu* (☎ 71310). There are just 50 rooms at this hotel with prices from US$69 to US$112.

Adjacent to the Club Bualu is the closest you will come to budget accommodation in Nusa Dua. The *Lancun Guesthouse* (☎ 71983, 71985) is run by the Hotel & Tourism Training School, and has rooms for about US$25 a double, with bathroom and air-con. If it's empty you might be able to negotiate a cheaper rate, and the service could be anything from overattentive to nonexistent.

The hotels offer a large number of restaurants but there's no choice apart from the hotels, since it's a long walk to get out of the resort area. If you can make it to Bualu village, just to the west, you can find the places where the hotel staff eat, which should offer better value for money. There are some other eating places in the shopping area but you can't just stroll outside to other restaurants, as you can at Sanur.

Getting There & Away

The taxi fare from the airport is 12,000 rp. A bemo from Denpasar costs around 700 rp from Suci bemo station (1000 rp from Tegal station) to Bualu village, just outside the Nusa Dua compound. From there to the hotels is about a km. The bemo service operates on demand but there's usually one every hour, and more when the hotel staff are finishing their shifts – many people commute from Denpasar to Nusa Dua. There's a hotel bus service to Kuta for about 6000 rp return, or to Sanur or Denpasar for 10,000 rp return. You can easily charter a whole bemo between Kuta and Nusa Dua for around 8000 rp, but avoid being pressured into chartering a bemo by yourself if you're happy to wait for the public one.

ULU WATU

The southern peninsula is known as Bukit (*bukit* means 'hill' in Indonesian), but was known to the Dutch as Tafelhoek (Table Point). The road south from Kuta goes around the end of the airport runway, and the main route goes south then east to Nusa Dua. A couple of turn-offs to the west will take you to Jimbaran village, whose main road, Jalan Ulu Watu, continues right down to the end of the peninsula at Ulu Watu. The road is now sealed for the whole distance. At times the road climbs quite high, reaching 200 metres, and there are fine views back over the airport, Kuta and southern Bali.

When you see the Ugly Boys 'restaurant' on the left side near the top of a rise, you'll know you're getting close to the surf. The place is littered with surfboards (hire one for 10,000 to 15,000 rp per day if you know how to handle big waves) and Dexter here can give you some information about conditions.

Along the road you'll notice numerous limestone quarries where large blocks of stone are cut by hand. Many of the buildings in southern Bali are constructed from such blocks. Further inland there are some industrial developments, making preformed concrete products from the local limestone cement. This is a dry, sparsely inhabited area – a contrast to the lush, rice-growing country which seems to commence immediately north of the airport.

Pura Luhur Ulu Watu

The temple of Pura Luhur Ulu Watu perches at the south-western tip of the peninsula, where sheer cliffs drop precipitously into the clear blue sea – the temple hangs right over the edge! You enter it through an unusual arched gateway flanked by statues of Ganesh; there's a resident horde of monkeys in the compound. Ulu Watu is one of several important temples to the spirits of the sea to be found along the southern coast of Bali. Others include Tanah Lot and Rambut Siwi.

Ulu Watu, along with the other well-known temples of the south – Pura Sakenan on Pulau Serangan, Pura Petitenget at Krobokan and the temple at Tanah Lot – is associated with Nirartha, the Javanese priest credited with introducing many of the elements of the Balinese religion to the island. Nirartha retreated to Ulu Watu for his final days.

Surfing

Ulu Watu has another claim to fame. It's Bali's surfing Mecca, made famous through several classic surfing films. It's a popular locale for the surfers who flock to Bali from all over the world, but particularly from Aus-

tralia. At a dip in the road, just before the Ulu Watu car park, a sign indicates the way to the Suluban Surf Beach (Pantai Suluban). There will be a crowd of guys on motorbikes here, waiting to taxi you down towards the beach. It's two km down a narrow footpath – OK for motorbikes but nothing more. Take care on a motorbike – the path is narrow, some of the corners are blind and there have been some nasty accidents. From a motorbike park at the end of the track you continue on foot another 250 metres, down to the small gorge which gives access to the surf. There are half a dozen warungs on the northern side of the gorge, perched on a cliff with great views of the various surf breaks. All the serious surfers bring their own boards, but you can hire one here for about 5000 rp an hour. You can also get wax, ding repair stuff and a massage, depending on what you need most.

Places to Stay & Eat

The warungs around the cliff tops offer basic Indonesian food (nasi and mie) and Western fare (jaffles and pancakes) to the keen surfers who flock here. Food prices are reasonable, but it seems cruel to charge surfers 4000 rp for a large beer! The warungs are not really places to stay, but surfers are sometimes able to crash here to get an early start on the morning waves. One tiny losmen, the *Gobleg Inn*, is off the motorbike track to the surf. Run by Wayan Wena, it has only four rooms and asks 15,000 rp per person, including breakfast. The *Bali Cliffs Resort Hotel* is an expensive place, off to the south of the Ulu Watu road overlooking the Indian Ocean.

There are a few places to eat along the road into Ulu Watu. There's the *Ugly Boys* restaurant with basic food and normally priced beer, and the *Warung Indra* opposite – one letter from a hungry surfer raved on about their food for three pages! Further on is the *Corner Pub* and a place to buy petrol.

Ubud & Around

Perched on the gentle slopes leading up towards the central mountains, Ubud is the cultural centre of Bali and has attracted visitors interested in Bali's arts and crafts ever since Walter Spies established it as the centre for the cultured visitors of the '30s. Apart from the many places of interest in Ubud itself, there are also numerous temples, ancient sites and interesting craft centres around the town while the road up to Ubud from the southern tourist centres (Denpasar, Nusa Dua, Sanur and Kuta) leads through a dense corridor of craft shops and galleries.

Denpasar to Ubud

The road from Denpasar via Batubulan, Celuk, Sukawati, Batuan and Mas is the main tourist shopping route of Bali but there are also alternative, quieter routes between the two towns.

The construction of a new central bus and bemo station at Batubulan, east of Denpasar, has radically changed the transport system in the south. To get to Ubud from the beach resorts you first take a bemo to Batubulan. Bemos run directly from Sanur but from Kuta you must take one bemo to Tegal station and another to Batubulan station. The bemo fare from Batubulan to Ubud is about 700 rp and bemos shuttle back and forth so regularly it's no problem jumping on and off along the way. If you want to take a more obscure back route it's easier if you have your own transport.

The official taxi fare between the airport and Ubud is 34,000 rp. You can also charter a bemo between Ubud and Kuta or Sanur for around 20,000 rp.

From the southern beach centres to Ubud there are a couple of alternatives to the regular Batubulan, Celuk, Sukawati and Mas route. Both routes continue directly north from Batubulan, indeed the signpost at the junction points to Ubud via this route, rather than the usual main road. Three km from the junction you fork right at Belaluwan and enter Ubud through Pengosekan and Padangtegal.

If you took the left fork at Belaluwan (which really means continuing on the main road through Belaluwan rather than turning right on to a minor road) the road continues north through Sayan and you can then turn back down to Ubud at Kedewatan and enter the town through Campuan. The road via Sayan is very narrow at times and oncoming vehicles must stop and try to squeeze by each other.

BATUBULAN

Soon after leaving Denpasar the road is lined with outlets for Batubulan's main craft – stone sculpture. Batubulan means 'moon stone'. Stone carvers continue along the road to Tegaltamu, where the main road to Ubud does a sharp right turn while the back-road route continues straight on. Batubulan is where the temple gate guardians – seen all over Bali – come from. You'll also find them guarding bridges or making more mundane appearances in restaurants and hotels. The sculpting is often done by quite young boys and you're welcome to watch them chipping away at big blocks of stone. The stone they use is surprisingly soft and light, so if you've travelled to Bali fairly light it's quite feasible to fly home with a demonic stone character in your baggage!

Not surprisingly the temples around Batubulan are noted for their fine stone sculptures. Pura Puseh, just a couple of hundred metres to the east of the busy main road, is worth a visit.

Batubulan is also a centre for a variety of antique crafts, textiles and woodwork. A Barong & Rangda dance, popular with tourists, is held in Batubulan every morning. It's touristy and there's a stampede of souvenir sellers afterwards but if you don't get a

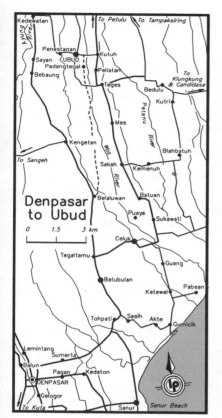

Denpasar to Ubud

0   1.5   3 km

finishes. Other centres for silverwork in Bali include Kamasan near Klungkung and Kuta.

SUKAWATI

Further on, before the turn-off to Mas and Ubud, are the villages of Sukawati and Batuan. Sukawati is a centre for the manufacture of those noisy wind chimes you hear all over the island and also specialises in temple umbrellas and *lontar* (palm) baskets, dyed with intricate patterns. Sukawati, a bustling market town with a morning fruit and vegetable market, also has a busy art and craft centre (the Pasar Seni). It's just across from the produce market and sells semi-finished artwork to craft shops who do the final finishing themselves.

The old palace is behind the produce market, and the town has a long tradition of dance and wayang kulit shadow puppet performance. The small village of Puaya, about a km west from the main road, specialises in making high-quality leather shadow puppets and masks.

There's an alternative but little-used route via the coast, bypassing Batubulan and Celuk and rejoining the main road to Ubud just before Sukawati. It passes through the coastal village of Gumicik (which has a good beach) and, just back from the coast, the village of Ketewel. A road branches off from Ketewel to the beach at Pabean, a site for religious purification ceremonies. Just north

chance to see a performance elsewhere then it's worth catching. Starting time is 9 am and the cost is about 6000 rp.

CELUK

Travelling from Batubulan to Celuk you move from stone to filigree for Celuk is the silversmithing centre of Bali. The craft shops that line the road here are dedicated to jewellery; a variety of pieces are on sale or you can order your own design. There are numerous jewellery specialists along with other craft shops and galleries. All are generally very busy after the morning dance in Batubulan

of Ketewel, before the main road, is Guang, another small woodcarving centre.

BATUAN

Batuan is a noted painting centre which came under the influence of Bonnet, Spies and the Pita Maha artists' co-operative at an early stage. Batuan painters produced dynamic black-ink drawings, good examples of which can be seen in Ubud's Puri Lukisan Museum. The big Batuan galleries have the usual range of work on display but some original work still comes from this village.

Today the distinct Batuan style of painting is noted for its inclusion of some very modern elements. Sea scenes are likely to include the odd windsurfer while tourists with video cameras or riding motorbikes pop up in the otherwise traditional Balinese scenery. Batuan is also noted for its traditional dance classes and is a centre for carved wooden relief panels and screens.

MAS

Mas means 'gold' but it's woodcarving, particularly mask carving, which is the craft here. The great Majapahit priest Nirartha once lived here and Pura Taman Pule is said to be built on the site of his home. During the three-day Kuningan festival, a Wayang Wong performance (an older version of the Ramayana ballet) is put on in the temple's courtyard.

The road through Mas is almost solidly lined with craft shops and you are welcome to drop in and see the carvers at work, and inspect the myriad items for sale. The price tags in dollars indicate that most business is done with the tour bus hordes but there are plenty of smaller carving operations in the small lanes off the busy main road. Many of these places virtually mass-produce carvings which are then sold to the numerous craft shops. The bigger and more successful craft outlets are often lavishly decorated with fine woodcarvings. The renowned artist Ida Bagus Tilem, whose father was also a noted woodcarver, has a particularly fine gallery. Mas sprawls virtually the whole five km

length of road from the Sakah turn-off to Teges.

If you want to stay in Mas, *Taman Harum* has elegant individual bungalows, some of them two-storeyed with balconies overlooking the rice paddies, and there's a swimming pool.

From Mas you can follow the main road the last few km into Ubud or take back-road routes and approach the town through Pengosekan, Padangtegal or even the Monkey Forest.

BLAHBATUH

Although the most direct route to Ubud is to turn off the main road at Sakah and head north through Mas, you can continue on a few km to the turn-off to Blahbatuh and go via Kutri and Bedulu before turning off again for Ubud. In Blahbatuh the Pura Gaduh has a metre-high stone head said to be a portrait of Kebo Iwa, the legendary strongman and minister to the last king of the Bedulu kingdom (see under Bedulu and Gunung Kawi in the Around Ubud section of this chapter). Gajah Mada, the Majapahit strongman, realised that he could not conquer Bedulu, Bali's strongest kingdom, while Kebo Iwa was there so he lured him away to Java (with promises of women and song) and had him killed.

The stone head is thought to be very old, possibly predating Javanese influence in Bali, but the temple is a reconstruction of an

Topeng mask

earlier temple destroyed in the great earthquake of 1917.

About a km west of Blahbatuh on the Petanu River is the Tegenungan Waterfall (also known as Srog Srogan) at Belang Singa village. There's a signpost to 'Air Terjun Tegenungan' from the village of Kemenuh on the main road, *(air terjun* means waterfall).

KUTRI

Just beyond Blahbatuh on the western side of the road is Pura Kedarman (also known as Pura Bukit Dharma). If you climb Bukit Dharma nearby *(bukit* means hill), you'll find a hill-top shrine with a stone statue of the eight-armed goddess Durga. The statue, in the act of killing a demon-possessed water buffalo, is thought to date from the 11th century and shows strong Indian influences.

Another theory is that the image is of Airlangga's mother Mahendradatta, who married King Udayana, Bali's 10th century ruler. When her son succeeded to the throne she hatched a bitter plot against him and unleashed evil spirits *(leyaks)* upon his kingdom. She was eventually defeated but this incident eventually led to the legend of the rangda, a widow-witch and ruler of evil spirits. The temple at the base of the hill has images of Durga and the body of a barong can be seen in the *bale barong* (literally 'barong building'); the sacred head is kept elsewhere.

From the hill-top lookout you can see down to Sanur on the coast or out to Nusa Lembongan and Nusa Penida. Just beyond Kutri is a T-junction where you turn west to Bedulu and Ubud or east to Klungkung. The road east crosses a series of deep gorges, the bridges rising high above the valleys below.

Ubud

In the hills north of Denpasar, Ubud is the calm and peaceful cultural centre of Bali. It has undergone tremendous development in the past few years but, unlike Kuta, hasn't been ruined by it. Ubud has managed to stay relaxed and beautiful, a place where the evenings are quiet and you can really tell you're in Bali. It's worth remembering that electricity only arrived in Ubud in the mid-70s, telephones in the late-80s. There's an amazing amount to do in and around Ubud so don't plan to do it in a day. You need at least a few days to appreciate it properly and Ubud is one of those places where days can quickly become weeks and weeks become months.

Orientation

The once small village of Ubud has expanded to encompass its neighbours — Campuan, Penestanan, Padangtegal, Peliatan and Pengosekan are all part of what we see as Ubud today. The crossroads, where the bemos stop, marks the centre of town. On the north (kaja) side is the Ubud Palace, on the south (kelod) side is the market. Monkey Forest Rd, beside the market, runs south to, of course, the Monkey Forest and Ubud's pura dalem (temple of the dead).

Continuing through Ubud, the road drops steeply down to the ravine at Campuan where you find Murni's Warung on one side of the suspension bridge, artist Antonio Blanco's house on the other and the Campuan Hotel on the site of Walter Spies' prewar home. From there the road bends north past many craft shops and galleries. Penestanan, famous for its painters, is just west of Campuan. Further west again is Sayan, where musician Colin McPhee lived in the '30s.

Entering Ubud from Denpasar the road passes through Peliatan before reaching the junction on Ubud's east side.

Information

Ubud is just high enough to be noticeably cooler than the coast. It's also noticeably wetter.

Tourist Office Ubud has a very friendly and helpful tourist office *(bina wisata)* on the main street. Ubud's survival has been largely due to local efforts. The Ubud tourist office is a local venture, not a government one. It

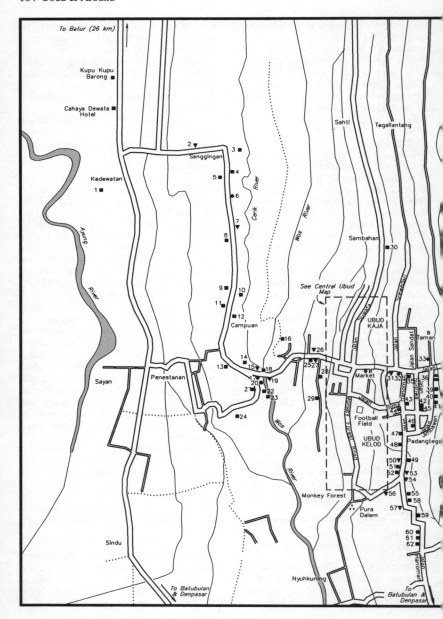

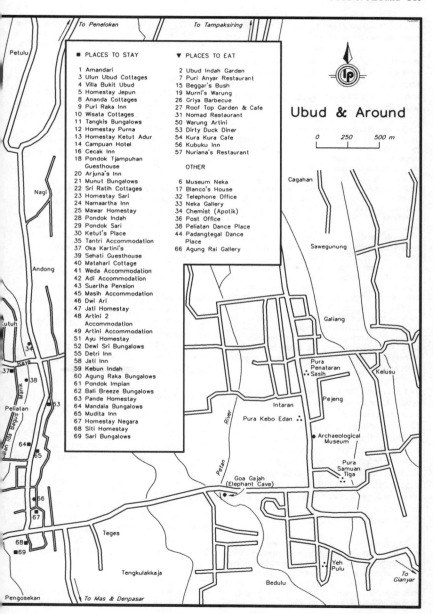

Ubud & Around

0   250   500 m

PLACES TO STAY

1 Amandari
3 Ulun Ubud Cottages
4 Villa Bukit Ubud
5 Homestay Jepun
8 Ananda Cottages
9 Puri Raka Inn
10 Wisata Cottages
11 Tangkis Bungalows
12 Homestay Purna
13 Homestay Ketut Adur
14 Campuan Hotel
16 Cecak Inn
18 Pondok Tjampuhan
   Guesthouse
20 Arjuna's Inn
21 Munut Bungalows
22 Sri Ratih Cottages
23 Homestay Sari
24 Namaartha Inn
25 Mawar Homestay
28 Pondok Indah
29 Pondok Sari
30 Ketut's Place
35 Tantri Accommodation
37 Oka Kartini's
39 Sehati Guesthouse
40 Matahari Cottage
41 Weda Accommodation
42 Adi Accommodation
43 Suartha Pension
45 Masih Accommodation
46 Dwi Ari
47 Jati Homestay
48 Artini 2
   Accommodation
49 Artini Accommodation
51 Ayu Homestay
52 Dewi Sri Bungalows
55 Detri Inn
58 Jati Inn
59 Kebun Indah
60 Agung Raka Bungalows
61 Pondok Impian
62 Bali Breeze Bungalows
63 Pande Homestay
64 Mandala Bungalows
65 Mudita Inn
67 Homestay Negara
68 Siti Homestay
69 Sari Bungalows

PLACES TO EAT

2 Ubud Indah Garden
7 Puri Anyar Restaurant
15 Beggar's Bush
19 Murni's Warung
26 Griya Barbecue
27 Roof Top Garden & Cafe
31 Nomad Restaurant
50 Warung Artini
53 Dirty Duck Diner
54 Kura Kura Cafe
56 Kubuku Inn
57 Nuriana's Restaurant

OTHER

6 Museum Neka
17 Blanco's House
32 Telephone Office
33 Neka Gallery
34 Chemist (Apotik)
36 Post Office
38 Peliatan Dance Place
44 Padangtegal Dance
   Place
66 Agung Rai Gallery

was set up in an effort to defend the village from the tourist onslaught – not by opposing tourism but by providing a service aimed at informing and generating a respect amongst visitors for Balinese culture and customs. The British-based magazine *New Internationalist* recounted some of the problems that faced the village:

The locals cursed the tourists, for they disturbed ceremonies and dressed impolitely. Guidebooks had told their readers about the family events, airlines had promoted Bali with all its glamorous ceremonies, photographers had made public exhibitions out of private occasions. All of this without asking permission. Foreigners were attracted. They came to Ubud full of expectations. They entered any private house as though the religious ceremonies there were tourist attractions. Conflict after conflict developed, anger mounted.

Boards were put on the gates or walls to warn tourists that the ceremony inside was a private event: 'No Tourist, Please', 'For Guest Only', 'This is a Religious Event', 'Entrance is Forbidden', 'Only for the Family Members'. It was really ugly to see religious offerings and decorations at a compound entrance disturbed by these emergency boards written in a foreign language. Tempers rose further when a group of tourists was ordered to leave a temple because they were disturbing the praying parishioners. The tourists blamed their guide for not informing them. The guide accused the locals of being unfriendly and unco-operative. The villagers chased the guide away.

In 1981, with the problems of the village so acute, a move was made to revive Ubud's former beauty by extensive tree-planting. Then the tourist office was established and its publications even included an English-language newspaper, probably the first such paper to be produced by a village in Indonesia. In many ways the offices have been very successful although it takes time for the message to get through – an article in the now defunct Australian newspaper *National Times* summed up the problem:

Some greenhorn visitors frequently think the tourist is a king who can do no wrong, possessing an unlimited right to see anything he or she wants to see and to grab as much as possible with as little expense as possible. 'Do you sell tickets for a wedding tour?' 'I want to see a cremation today.' 'Can you give me a good price?' 'How much do you charge to see a

tooth-filing ceremony?' ... I know the Balinese do not cry. But I do. I cry when visitors think that Bali is a huge open stage on which any local activity is exhibited to collect money...

Post The town has a pleasant little post office with a poste restante service – the letters sit in a box on the counter and you sort through them yourself. Have your mail addressed to Kantor Pos, Ubud, Bali, Indonesia. You can also get stamps at a couple of places around town, identified by a 'postal services' sign.

Telephone Telephone services in Bali in general and Ubud in particular have improved dramatically in the past few years. Many hotels and losmen now have telephones and you can make international direct-dial calls from Ubud. There's a telephone office on the main street, between the market and the post office turn-off.

Bookshops The Ubud Bookshop is an excellent bookshop on the main road right next to Ary's Warung in central Ubud. You'll also find a small but excellent selection of books in Murni's Warung and the Museum Neka. The Bookshop is a book exchange on the Monkey Forest Rd.

Other There's the usual varied selection of bicycle and motorbike hire places and a number of shops selling most items you might require. Ubud even has banks now but they're not as fast as the numerous money-changers and they do not offer as good an exchange rate.

Ubud's colourful produce market operates every third day. It starts early in the morning but pretty much winds up by lunch time. The main road in the centre operates one way on market day, you have to make a loop around the market and come up the Monkey Forest Rd if you're coming in from Denpasar.

Museums & Galleries

Ubud has two interesting museums, numerous galleries with art for sale and there are a number of artists' homes which you can visit to view their work.

Puri Lukisan Museum On the main street of Ubud the Puri Lukisan (Palace of Fine Arts) was established in the mid-50s and displays fine examples of all schools of Balinese art. It was in Ubud that the modern Balinese art movement started, where artists first began to abandon purely religious and court scenes for scenes of everyday life. Rudolf Bonnet, who played such an important role in this change, helped establish the museum's permanent collection in 1973. It's a relatively small museum and has some excellent art.

You enter the museum by crossing a river gully beside the road and wander from building to building through beautiful gardens with pools, statues and fountains.

In the late '80s the buildings and the gardens were beginning to look rather tired, worn and in need of rejuvenation. Fortunately a new building has been opened and the permanent collection is now better housed although the humid weather is still taking its toll on these important works. This gallery, along with the Museum Neka, is worth looking around before you make any decisions about buying art in Ubud.

The museum is open from 8 am to 4 pm daily and admission is 500 rp. There are exhibitions of art for sale in other buildings in the gardens and in a separate display just outside the main garden.

Museum Neka If you continue beyond the suspension bridge at Campuan for another a km or so, you'll find the Museum Neka. The museum, opened in 1982, is housed in a number of separate buildings and has a diverse and interesting collection, principally of modern Balinese art. Also on display is some of the work of other important Indonesian artists and Western artists who have resided or worked in Bali.

Balinese paintings have been defined as falling into four groups or styles, all of which are represented in the Museum Neka. First there are the classical or Kamasan paintings from the village of Kamasan near Klungkung. Then there are the Ubud paintings which basically fall into two subgroups. The older or traditional Ubud paintings are still heavily influenced by the prewar Pita Maha artists' circle while the postwar Young Artists' styles were influenced by Dutch artist Arie Smit, still an Ubud resident. The third group is the Batuan paintings which, in some respects, look like a blend of the old and new Ubud styles but are also notable for the modern elements which often sneak into their designs. Finally, there are the modern or 'academic' paintings, which can be loosely defined as anything which doesn't fall into the main Balinese categories.

The Balinese collection includes numerous works by I Gusti Nyoman Lempad, the Balinese artist who played a key role in the establishment of the Pita Maha group. Some of these works were from the collection of Walter Spies. Other works read like a role call of the best Balinese artists including Gusti Made Deblog, Gusti Ketut Kobot, Ida Bagus Made, Anak Agung Gede Sobrat, Made Sukada and many others. Works by artists from other parts of Indonesia include paintings by most of the country's best known painters including Abdul Aziz, Dullah, Affandi and Srihadi Sudarsono.

The museum's collection of work by Western artists is superb and covers almost every well-known name. Current residents like Arie Smit, Han Snel and Antonio Blanco are represented but there are also works by Theo Meier, Willem Hofker, Le Mayeur de Merpres, Walter Spies and Rudolf Bonnet. Miguel Covarrubias, whose book *Island of Bali* remains the best introduction to the island's art and culture, is represented as is Australian artist Donald Friend with, among others, his delightful painting of Batu Jimbar Village. Recent additions to the collection include works by Louise Koke who, with her husband Robert Koke, founded the original hotel at Kuta Beach in the 1930s.

Admission to the museum is 500 rp.

Galleries Ubud is dotted with galleries – they pop up on every street and down every alley. They're also enormously variable in the choice and quality of items on display. If you spend a little time studying the arts and crafts in Ubud you'll soon discover that even the most mundane 'me too' piece can vary widely in quality.

There are two 'must see' Ubud art galleries where the work displayed is generally of a very high quality and the prices are often similarly elevated. Suteja Neka not only operates the Museum Neka but also the Neka Gallery where the work is for sale. Across the road from the post office turn-off on the Denpasar side of Ubud, the extensive Neka Gallery displays fine pieces from all the schools of Balinese art as well as work by European residents like Han Snel and Arie Smit.

Ubud's other important commercial gallery is the Agung Rai Gallery at Peliatan, on the way out of Ubud to Denpasar. Again the collection extends for room after room and covers the full range of Balinese styles plus works by Western and Javanese artists like Antonio Blanco, Arie Smit, Han Snel, Theo Meier and Affandi. The gallery also has some important works which are not for sale, including paintings by I Gusti Nyoman Lempad and Walter Spies.

Artists' Homes The home of I Gusti Nyoman Lempad is on the main street of Ubud, just across from the market, and is open to the public although there are no works by the artist on display. He is well represented at the Puri Lukisan Museum and the Museum Neka.

Walter Spies and Rudolf Bonnet, the two Western artists who played a key role in changing the course of Balinese art from a purely decorative skill, both lived for some time at Campuan, near the suspension bridge. Spies' home is now one of the rooms at the Campuan Hotel and can be inspected if it is not in use; you can even stay there if you book well ahead.

These original visiting artists have been followed by a steady stream of Western dreamers, right down to the present day. Just beside the Campuan suspension bridge, across the river from Murni's Warung, the driveway leads up to Filipino-born artist Antonio Blanco's superbly theatrical house.

Entry to the beautiful house and gallery is 500 rp. Blanco's speciality is erotic art and illustrated poetry, though for Blanco, playing the part of the artist is probably just as important as painting.

Arie Smit and Han Snel are other well-known Western artists currently residing in Ubud. In the 1960s Smit sparked the Young Artists' school of painting in Penestanan, just west of Campuan. Han Snel's work is exhibited in a private collection at his restaurant and hotel, just off the main road through Ubud.

Adjoining Villages
The growth of Ubud has engulfed a number of nearby villages, though these have still managed to retain their distinct identities.

Peliatan Just over a km south-east of central Ubud, en route to Denpasar, Peliatan is the dance centre of Ubud and its dance troupe has performed overseas on many occasions. Many long-term visitors stay here to study Balinese or Indonesian dance. There are numerous craft shops and galleries in Peliatan and a variety of places to stay. The village can be a cheaper and quieter alternative to staying in Ubud itself.

Campuan Continuing through Ubud to the west, the road dives down to the deep gorge at Campuan, crossing the Wos River on a newer road bridge and a picturesque old suspension bridge. Right by the river is Murni's Warung (see the Places to Eat section in this chapter) while overlooking the river from the other side is the Hotel Campuan (sometimes spelt Tjampuhan in the old Dutch manner). This was the site of artist Walter Spies' home (now one of the hotel's rooms) and the centre for the Western circle of the '30s. Visitors can use the hotel's pool for a fee. Across the road from the hotel and across the river from Murni's Warung is the home and gallery of artist Antonio Blanco (see the earlier Artists' Homes section).

Campuan means 'where two rivers meet' and at the confluence of the Wos and Cerik rivers, far below the bridges, is the Pura

Gunung Labuh, a temple thought to date back as far as 1000 years. From beside the temple a walking track leads away to the north along the ridge between the rivers.

Penestanan The road bends sharply as it crosses the river at Campuan and then runs north, parallel to the river. If you take the steep uphill road which bends away from the main road you reach Penestanan, centre for the Young Artists' movement instigated by Arie Smit in the 1960s. There are more galleries, many of them specialising in paintings of the Young Artists' style, and numerous losmen around Penestanan. The road winds through the small village and rice paddies, past a small patch of forest and eventually meets the road through Sayan and Kedewatan.

Sayan & Kedewatan West of Penestanan is Sayan, site for Colin McPhee's home in the '30s, so amusingly described in *A House in Bali*. North of Sayan is Kedewatan, another small village where the road turns off past Museum Neka and back into Ubud via Campuan. Just west of the villages and the main road is the Ayung River (Yeh Ayung). The deep gorge of the swift-flowing river is now the site for the homes of a number of modern-day McPhees and for several up-market hotels, including one of the most expensive places you can stay in Bali.

Walks

Ubud is a place for leisurely strolls – wanders through the rice paddies, lazy rambles through the forests, walks to surrounding villages. There are lots of interesting walks in the area, including one to Ubud's famous Monkey Forest.

Around Town There's plenty to see simply wandering around the centre of Ubud. Look around the market in the early morning, it's across the road from the old palace in the centre of town and operates every third day. Or sip a coffee in the *Lotus Cafe* and gaze across the lotus-filled pond a little further up the road.

When you're wandering the streets of Ubud, look for the little black signs by each gateway. They detail the name of the occupant, his occupation and other vital details, like the number of children; LK stands for laki (boy), PR for prempuan (girl) and JML for jumlah (total). In one early morning stroll the biggest I saw were $8 + 6 = 14$ and $7 + 8 = 15$! Few families seem to have fewer than five or six children.

Tony Wheeler

Monkey Forest Just wander down the Monkey Forest Rd from the centre of Ubud and you'll arrive in a small but dense forest. It's inhabited by a handsome band of monkeys ever ready for passing tourists who just might have peanuts available for a hand-out. Peanut vendors are usually waiting to provide monkey sustenance but be warned, the monkeys have become far too used to visitors and can put on ferocious displays of temperament if you don't come through with the goods, and quick. If you're not planning on feeding them don't give any hint that you might have something interesting in a pocket or a bag. Although the forest is a regular thoroughfare you'll be asked for a donation (500 rp is more than sufficient) at the start of the forest.

Ubud's interesting old pura dalem (temple of the dead) is in the forest for this is the inauspicious, kelod side of town. Look for the rangda figures devouring children at the entrance to the inner temple. You can walk to Peliatan from Ubud via the Monkey Forest, which is more interesting and quieter than following the main road.

If you turn right down the track immediately after the Monkey Forest Hideway, there's a pool down the gorge on the left.

Nearby Villages Popular strolls to neighbouring villages include one to Peliatan, with its famous dance troupe, and to Penestanan, the 'village of young artists'. You can walk north from Penestanan and rejoin the main road near the Museum Neka, or walk south and cross the river to the Monkey Forest. If you continue through the Monkey Forest from Ubud you'll come to the small village of Nyuhkuning, which is noted for its woodcarving. Or follow the road down to

Pengosekan, south of Peliatan, another village with many painters.

Petulu In the late afternoon each day you can enjoy the spectacular sight of thousands of herons arriving home in Petulu. They nest in the trees along the road through the village and make a spectacular sight as they fly in and commence squabbling over the prime perching places.

Some recent road works have made it possible to visit the village as a pleasant round-trip walk or bicycle ride of about 10 km. From Ubud take the road beside the cinema and bemo stop (Jalan Suwatu) and walk straight north. It's surprising how quickly you get out of glitzy Ubud and into relatively unchanged countryside. Although people hail you in English, older women are often bare-breasted and the dogs definitely don't like foreigners.

The road continues through the village of Tunjungan, which seems to be totally devoted to the carving of garudas. Half a dozen shops by the roadside offer them in all sizes from a few cm high to giant two-metre garudas which probably weigh a ton. Shortly after Tunjungan there's a well signposted right turn to Petulu. It's about seven km from Ubud; there are roadside markers every km to help you gauge your progress.

Walk quickly under the trees if the herons are already roosting, the copious droppings on the road will indicate if it's wise not to hang around. Donations are requested at the other end of the village. About a km past the village you reach the Tegallantang to Ubud road, from where it's a couple of km back to the centre of Ubud. A number of woodcarving outlets and an umbrella shop mark the Petulu turn-off if you're coming up from Ubud on this road.

Pejeng If you take the road east out of Ubud and continue straight on past the T-junction there's a wonderful trail that leads through typical Balinese country to the superb gorge of the Petanu River that runs by the Goa Gajah (Elephant Cave). Following the trail beyond the river eventually brings you out at Pejeng, a very fine walk. You can visit the important temples at Pejeng (see the Ubud & Around map) and make your way back to Ubud via Yeh Pulu and Goa Gajah, or continue up the road to Tampaksiring.

Other Walks Take the trail up beside the river on the Ubud side of Murni's Warung to the beautiful hill at Campuan. Or walk down to the lovely Ayung River in the villages of Kedewatan or Sayan.

Places to Stay

Even in the mid-70s, when the tourist boom had definitely arrived down on the coast, Ubud had only a handful of accommodation possibilities. The construction boom which reached here in the '80s, however, is still continuing and today Ubud not only has a great many budget hotels but also a wide choice of mid-range and expensive places. Fortunately Ubud still does not have any of

---

Dogs

Dogs. If there's one thing wrong with Bali it has to be those horrible, mangy, flea-bitten, grovelling, dirty, noisy, disgusting *anjings* (that's the Indonesian word for dog) or, in high Balinese, *asu* or in low Balinese *cicing*. If you prefer, use asu when you're referring to dogs in a good way, cicing in a bad. Dogs are rarely referred to as asu!

Just why does Bali have so many dogs? Well, they're scavengers, garbage clearers, and they're simply accepted as part of the picture. It's widely, and probably correctly, thought that demons inhabit them, which is why you often see them gobbling down the offerings put out for the bad spirits. A popular theory is that they were created simply to keep things in balance – with everything so beautiful and picturesque the dogs were put there to provide a contrast. Ubud, incidentally, is particularly well endowed with anjings – terrible, apocalyptic dogs that howl all night long like it's the end of the world. ■

the big mass-tourism hotels found at Sanur or Nusa Dua but there are some very luxurious small hotels.

You'll find places fairly widely scattered around Ubud – there are places along the main road and on the roads leading off it. In particular the Monkey Forest Rd has become a real accommodation centre with places all the way down to the forest.

There are also lots of places in surrounding villages like Peliatan and Penestanan or simply scattered around the rice paddies. Several of the new top-end places are perched on the edge of the spectacular Ayung River Gorge, at Kedewatan and Sayan, a few km out of Ubud. If you're staying in one of the budget priced 'remote' losmen – and they can be very relaxing, peaceful places to stay – it's probably wise to have a torch (flashlight) with you if you want to avoid falling into a rice paddy on some starry, starry night.

Since Ubud is full of artists and dancers you can often find a losmen run by someone involved with the arts – this will enable you to pick up some of the guidelines for appreciating Balinese art. At most cheaper and mid-range places, breakfast is included in the price.

Places to Stay – bottom end

Ubud has a huge choice of places to stay and, since they tend to congregate, you can easily look at several before making a choice. What follows is just a sample; there are many other excellent places apart from those mentioned. These days prices tend to vary with demand but you can often find cheaper doubles with toilet and mandi for 10,000 rp and less. In the off-season you can still find a double for 6000 rp.

In Ubud There are lots of places in the bottom-end price bracket off the main road and down the Monkey Forest Rd. The small lanes and alleys between the football field and the market have much of Ubud's cheaper accommodation. There's nothing to choose between these numerous losmen. Just wander down the narrow lanes, have a look in a few, compare the prices and facilities and

make your choice. Prices depend on the demand at the time but you should be able to find doubles with breakfast at 10,000 rp or less.

Close to the top of Monkey Forest Rd, near the market, is one of Ubud's really long runners – *Canderi's* (or Candri's or Tjanderi's depending which sign or spelling style you choose). It's a fairly straightforward losmen-style place with singles from 8000 rp to 10,000 rp and doubles at 15,000 rp. Canderi's has been going almost as long as travellers have been staying in Ubud.

Other places along the Monkey Forest Rd include *Warsi's House* and *Karyawan Accommodation*, both simple, friendly and quite typical losmen-style places. The very clean and well-kept *Frog Pond Inn* is becoming surrounded by encroaching development but there's still a sign at the entrance suggesting that if there's nobody around you can simply select a vacant room and make yourself at home. Singles/doubles including breakfast cost 7000/10,000 rp.

Further down, *Ibunda's Inn* is a pleasant place with rooms at 15,000 rp or 25,000 rp with hot water. There are many other places along the road but right at the bottom, almost in the forest, is the secluded and pleasant *Monkey Forest Hideaway* (☎ 0361-95354). Doubles cost around 20,000 rp and some of the rooms, with their balconies overlooking the forest, are quite romantic.

On Jalan Suwata, *Suci Inn* is across from the banyan tree. Simple rooms with bathroom cost 8000 rp in the front, 10,000 rp in the back area. The rooms all have small verandahs looking out on the central garden and it's a friendly, relaxed place, pleasantly quiet yet very central. Next door to the Suci Inn is the *Hotel Ubud* one of Ubud's oldest places; for many years it was called the 'Hotel Oboed', the Dutch spelling indicating its age.

If you continue walking along Jalan Suwata for another 10 minutes you'll come to a small group of places to stay, the best known of which is *Ketut's Place* (☎ 0361-95304). See the Ubud & Around map. The rooms are in a family compound and cost

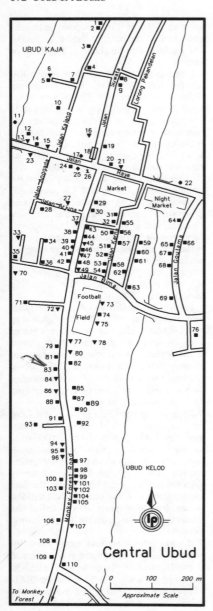

Central Ubud

	PLACES TO STAY
1	Kajeng Home Stay
2	Gusti's Garden Bungalow
3	Lecuk Inn
4	Arjana Accommodation
5	Siti Bungalows
7	Shanti's Homestay
8	Hotel Ubud
9	Suci Inn
10	Roja's Homestay
12	Mumbul Inn
14	Puri Saraswati
20	Sudharsana Bungalows
27	Suarsena House
29	Happy Inn
30	Canderi's Losmen & Warung
31	Yuni's House
32	Hibiscus Bungalows
34	Oka Wati's Sunset Bungalows
35	Igna 2 Accommodation
36	Sari Nadi Accommodation
38	Alit's House
39	Puri Muwa Bungalows
41	Dewa House
42	Igna Accommodation
43	Pandawa Homestay
44	Gayatri Accommodation
46	Badra Accommodation
48	Ibu Rai Bungalows
50	Gandra House
51	Sudartha House
52	Seroni Bungalows
53	Mertha House
54	Surawan House
55	Widiana's House Bungalows
56	Sania's House
57	Wija House
58	Ning's House
59	Sayong's House

10,000/15,000 rp for singles/doubles in the front and 25,000 rp (35,000 rp with hot water) for the individual cottages at the back. There's a pleasant garden in this comfortable and friendly place where Ketut Suartana puts on his regular Balinese feasts – see the Places to Eat section for more information.

There are many other places worth investigating in central Ubud. *Roja's Homestay*, off Jalan Kajang, is close to other low-priced losmen. The *Mumbul Inn* (☎ 0361-95364) is

▼ PLACES TO EAT

60	Dewi Putra House
61	Raka House
62	Devi House
63	Esty's House
64	Wayan Karya Homestay
65	Wena Homestay
66	Shana Homestay
67	Nirvana Pension
68	Agung's Cottages
69	Yoga Pension
71	Bendi's Accommodation
74	Wahyu Bungalows
76	Ramasita Pension
79	Accommodation Kerta
81	Karyawan Accommodation
82	Frog Pond Inn
83	Ubud Village Hotel
85	Puri Garden Bungalow
87	Adi Cottages
88	Pertiwi Bungalows
89	Rice Paddy Bungalows
90	Sri Bungalows
91	Villa Rasa Sayang
92	Nani House (Karsi Homestay)
93	Jati 3 Bungalows & Putih Accommodation
95	Jaya Accommodation
97	Ibunda Inn
98	Ubud Bungalows
99	Warsi's House
100	Dewi Ayu Accommodation
103	Ubud Tenau Bungalows
104	Fibra Inn
105	Ubud Inn
106	Lempung Accommodation
108	Pande Permai Bungalows
109	Monkey Forest Hideaway
110	Hotel Champlung Sari

6	Han Snel's Garden Restaurant
13	Mumbul's Cafe
15	Lotus Cafe
16	Coconut's Cafe
21	Restaurant Puri Pusaka
23	Menara Restaurant
24	Ary's Warung
28	Satri's Warung
33	Oka Wati's Warung
37	Ayu's Kitchen
45	Enny's Restaurant
47	Restaurant Dennis
49	Lilies Restaurant
70	Beji's Cafe
72	Bendi's Restaurant
73	Harry Chew's Restoran
75	Ubud Dancer Restaurant
77	Ibu Rai Restaurant
78	Cafe Bali
80	Dian Restaurant
84	Coco Restaurant
86	Cafe Wayan
94	Jaya Cafe
96	Yudit Restaurant & Bakery
101	Warsa's Cafe
102	Ubud Restaurant
107	Fruit Bat Restaurant

OTHER

11	Museum Puri Lukisan
17	Cinema
18	Bemo Stop
19	Palace & Hotel Puri Saren Agung
22	I Gusti Nyoman Lempad's home
25	Ubud Bookshop
26	Tourist Office (Bina Wisata)
40	Bookshop

near the Puri Lukisan Museum on the main road and has simple, spartan rooms at 10,000/20,000 rp for singles/doubles. More losmen can be found down towards Murni's Warung at Campuan or around the post office.

Around Ubud There are lots of places around Ubud, either in neighbouring villages or just out in the rice paddies. Cross the suspension bridge by Murni's, for example,

and take the steep path uphill by Blanco's house. There you'll find a pretty little group of homestays including the attractive *Arjuna's Inn*, run by the artist's daughter. There are more places further up in the rice paddies around Penestanan, like the nicely situated *Namaartha Inn*.

You'll find several places out of Ubud on the Peliatan road like the *Mudita Inn* with its shady garden. At the junction where the road bends sharp left to Denpasar you'll see a sign for the *Sari Bungalows*, just 100 metres or so off the road. It's a pleasantly quiet location and good value with singles at 3500 to 5000 rp and doubles from 6000 rp, all including a 'big breakfast'. Nearby is the *Siti Homestay* with a beautiful garden and charming owners.

Take the back road from Peliatan to Ubud and you'll pass the *Bali Breeze* and the pleasant *Jati Inn* which has two-storeyed rooms with great views across the rice paddies. There's been a lot of recent construction along this road and into Ubud through Padangtegal.

Places to Stay – middle

Places costing around 20,000 to 30,000 rp are becoming more common; they're usually priced in US$ and are almost always equipped with a swimming pool. Where the Campuan Hotel's prewar pool was once the only one in Ubud, there are now a great many pools dotted amongst the rice paddies. For most mid-range hotels, service, tax and breakfast are usually included in the price.

In Ubud The Monkey Forest Rd has a number of these newer mid-range places although some of them are very dull and featureless. Near the top of the Monkey Forest Rd and off to the right you'll find *Oka Wati's Sunset Bungalows* (☎ 0361-95063) a very pleasant and clean place right on the rice paddies. Prices range from US$20/25, US$25/30, US$35/40 and US$40/50 for singles/doubles. There's a swimming pool and a restaurant presided over by Oka Wati herself, a familiar face to visitors to Ubud since the early '70s.

A little further down, the *Ubud Village Hotel* (☎ 0361-95069) is one of the few new places built with some imagination and taste. The pleasantly decorated rooms, each with a separate garden entrance, cost US$30/35. There's a swimming pool with swim-up bar and other luxuries.

Also on Monkey Forest Rd and almost at the forest, the *Ubud Inn* (☎ 0361-95188) is one of the longer established places on this road. It has a variety of bungalows and rooms

dotted around a spacious garden area with a swimming pool. Rooms cost US$25/30 with fan, US$30/40 with air-con and there are some two-storeyed family rooms at US$45. The brick rooms have carved wood and thatched roofs and they're quite cool, each with a private bathroom. The upstairs verandah on the two-storeyed rooms is ideal for gazing out over the fast-disappearing rice paddies. Next door the *Fibra Inn* has rooms at US$25/30, and a swimming pool.

The newer Monkey Forest Rd hotels are not always so interesting. *Pertiwi Bungalows* (☎ 0361-95236) has comfortable rooms and a swimming pool but there's nothing very special about it. Nightly costs are US$30/35 or US$35/40 but service, tax and breakfast are all extra.

There are a number of places along the main road through Ubud but one of the nicest has to be artist Han Snel's *Siti Bungalows*, hidden away behind the Lotus Cafe. Some of the very pleasant individual cottages are perched right on the edge of the river gorge, looking across to the Puri Lukisan Museum on the other side. There are seven rooms, the nightly cost is US$40 and it's pleasantly quiet, back off the main road, yet close to the town centre.

Along the main road there are several places to stay associated with the old palaces of Ubud. The pleasant and well-kept *Puri Saraswati*, near the palace of that name, has rooms at US$15/20 and US$30/35. The *Hotel Puri Saren Agung*, near the bemo stop in the centre of Ubud, is part of the home of the late head of Ubud's royal family. The bungalows each have a private courtyard and displays of Balinese antiques.

Around Ubud On the main road but at the Peliatan end of Ubud is *Oka Kartini's*, another long-term survivor now with a swimming pool and other mod cons.

Close to the river junction in Campuan is *Murni's House*, run from Murni's Warung. There are apartments with verandahs for US$40 and also complete six-roomed houses for US$80. Right across the river from the warung, squeezed between the river and

Blanco's house, is the *Pondok Tjampuhan Guest House* with doubles at US$23. Many other mid-range places with pools have popped up recently, including the *Baliubud Cottages* just beyond Campuan in Penestanan and the *Dewi Sri Bungalows* down towards the Monkey Forest by the back route in Padangtegal.

Some distance out of town, opposite and a little before the Museum Neka, the relaxed and pretty *Ananda Cottages* has rooms at US$30/45 or two-storeyed family rooms for US$95; prices include breakfast.

Places to Stay – top end

Just up beyond the suspension bridge the long-established *Hotel Campuan* (or Tjampuhan if you prefer the old spelling) is beautifully situated overlooking the river confluence and Pura Gunung Labuh. The rooms are individual bungalows in a wonderful garden and cost US$45. The hotel is built on the site of artist Walter Spies' 1930's home and his small house is now one of the rooms. He was also responsible for the pool although it has been refurbished in the hotel's recent major renovation.

From the Campuan Hotel, the road out of Ubud passes the Neka Gallery, about a km further on, and just beyond the gallery is the turn-off to the *Ulun Ubud Cottages* (☎ 0361-95024). The bungalows are beautifully draped down the hillside overlooking the Cerik River and rooms cost US$40/55, US$45/65 or US$60/85 for singles/doubles. There are also larger, two-bedroom family bungalows at US$110. Rates include breakfast, taxes and service and there's a restaurant, bar and swimming pool.

Beyond Ulun Ubud Cottages, near the Kedewatan junction, is Ubud's most luxurious hotel, the *Amandari* (☎ 0361-95333). The standard rooms are US$200, US$250 or US$300 a night but if this doesn't seem good enough there are 'pool deluxe' rooms at US$500 a night or you can even have a room with your own private swimming pool at US$600 a night. Service (10%) and tax (5.5%) are extra. The 27 beautifully decorated rooms are huge and have superb views

over the rice paddies or down to the Ayung River. The hotel's large swimming pool seems to drop over the edge right down to the river. The Amandari is close to where prewar visitor Colin McPhee constructed the home he wrote about in *A House in Bali*.

If you head north from the Kedewatan junction you soon come to *Cahaya Dewata* (☎ 0361-95495) which overlooks the same magnificent river gorge. The rooms are US$40/45 for singles/doubles or US$60 for suites, plus service and tax. A little further along, about 800 metres north of the junction, is *Kupu Kupu Barong* (☎ 95470/8/9). Clinging precariously to the steep sides of the Ayung River Gorge, each of the beautiful two-storeyed bungalows have a bedroom and living room and cost US$195 or US$225 a night. Six of the 17 bungalows have two bedrooms, some of them have open-air spa baths. Tax and service charges are extra and children under 12 years of age are not welcome. The view from the pool and restaurant is also superb.

Back in Ubud, the *Hotel Champlung Sari* (☎ 0361-95418, 95473, 95349) overlooks the Monkey Forest. Rooms are US$50/60, US$60/70 or US$70/90 for singles/doubles and there's a swimming pool, restaurant, bar and all other mod cons. Despite these luxuries, the place is featureless and dull – a sad indicator that Ubud has been targeted for an injection of mass tourism.

Places to Eat

Ubud's numerous restaurants probably offer the best, most interesting and, if you search them out, most authentically Indonesian and Balinese food on the island. This is not to say you can't get excellent Western food if you want, simply that nasi campur (steamed rice mixed with a bit of everything) will also feature on the menu.

Monkey Forest Rd Start with the best by wandering down Monkey Forest Rd to *Cafe Wayan* which many Ubud regulars claim has the best food in town. There's a room in the front and a surprising number of tables in the open air at the back. The nasi campur at 2900 rp is terrific, the curry ayam (curried chicken) at 5250 rp is superb. Western dishes like spaghetti at 4500 rp also feature. Desserts include the famed coconut pie or you could even risk 'death by chocolate', a definite case of chocolate cake overkill.

The Monkey Forest Rd has several other interesting eating possibilities including, a little further down towards the forest, the popular and long-running *Ubud Restaurant* which also features some authentic local dishes. Or try the *Yudit Restaurant & Bakery* which has pretty good pizzas for 5000 rp and good bread, rolls and other baked goods. *Oka Wati's*, one of Ubud's long-term institutions and still a pleasant, friendly and economical place to eat, has no surprises on the menu but you can get a good mee goreng (fried noodles) and excellent pancakes.

There are a number of low-priced eating places along the market end of Monkey Forest Rd. *Canderi's Losmen and Warung* is another real institution. Travellers from the early '70s will remember when this was one of the very few places to eat in Ubud, back in the days when Ubud didn't even have electricity. *Lilies Restaurant* and *Restaurant Dennis* are other popular small places up at this end of the road or try *Bendi's* across from the football field or *Harry Chew's Restoran* near the northern side of the field.

Jalan Raya The main road through town also offers plenty of interesting dining possibilities including the popular and dirtcheap night market *(pasar malam)* which sets up at dusk beside the main market area. Just beyond the pasar malam is the *Nomad Restaurant*, notable for being one of the few places open really late at night although these days everything seems to be open a bit later in Ubud.

Right in the centre of town, the *Lotus Cafe* is a relaxed place for a light lunch or a snack any time. Compared to other places in Ubud it's definitely rather pricey but that doesn't seem to scare many people away; the Lotus is still the place to see and be seen in Ubud. Even a humble nasi campur is around 5000 rp at the Lotus, most main courses are 5000 to 7000 rp, a slice of cheesecake will set you back 3000 rp and even an ice juice is 2000 rp. The Lotus is closed on Mondays.

Across the road, *Ary's Warung* is just as glossy as the Lotus but somewhat cheaper; a nasi campur is 2700 rp. Or continue a few steps beyond the Lotus on the same side of the road to *Mumbul's Cafe*, a small place

---

A Balinese Feast

Finding real Balinese food in Bali is often far from easy but Ketut Suartana, who can be contacted at the Suci Inn (near the bemo station, off the main road opposite the market) or at Ketut's Place (further up the same road), puts on regular Balinese feasts at 10,000 rp per person. They're held in a pavilion in his parent's family compound where Ketut's Place is also located.

This is an opportunity to sample real Balinese food at its best. Typical meals include duck or Balinese satay, which is a minced and spiced meat wrapped around a wide stick and quite different from the usual Indonesian satay. A variety of vegetables will include several that we normally think of as fruits – like papaya, nangkur (jackfruit) and blimbing. *Paku* is a form of fern and *ketela potton* is tapioca leaves, both prepared as tasty vegetables. Red onions known as *anyang* and cucumber known as *ketimun* will also feature. Then there might be gado gado and mee goreng, both prepared in Balinese style, and a special Balinese dish of duck livers cooked in banana leaves and coconut. Of course there will be krupuks (prawn crackers) and rice. To drink there will be *brem* (Bali rice wine) and you'll finish up with Balinese coffee, peanuts and bananas or Balinese desserts like *sumping*, a leaf-wrapped sticky rice concoction with coconut and palm sugar or banana and jackfruit.

The dining area is hung with palm-leaf decorations, again as for a Balinese feast, and a gamelan player tinkles away in the background. It's fun, delicious and a rare chance to sample real Balinese food but it's also a great opportunity to learn more about Bali and its customs as Ketut talks about his house, his family and answers all sorts of questions about life in Bali. ■

with friendly service and excellent food. There's even a children's menu.

One of Ubud's real dining pleasures is *Han Snel's Garden Restaurant* off the main road and more or less directly behind the Lotus Cafe. The food is good, the quantities copious, the setting beautiful (frogs croak in the background) and the service impeccable. Main courses are generally 6000 to 7500 rp and desserts 2000 to 3000 rp. It's closed on Sundays.

Continue further down the main road towards Campuan to find the *Menara Restaurant* opposite the Lotus, the *Rumah Makan Cacik* which is popular even with local people, the *Griya Barbecue* for barbecued food and the *Roof Top Garden & Cafe* with good views from its elevated position.

Ubud has something of a reputation as an international jet-setters' hang-out and if they aren't at the Lotus then Murni's is where you're likely to find them. *Murni's Warung*, beside the Campuan suspension bridge, offers excellent food in a beautiful setting. The satay is served in a personal charcoal holder for 3900 rp, the nasi campur for 3400 rp is fantastic and you can get an excellent hamburger for the same price. To top it all the cakes are simply superb. Murni's also has some interesting arts and crafts on sale and a small but very good selection of books on Bali. It's closed on Wednesdays.

Other interesting places to try include the *Puri Pusaka*, opposite the market with a lengthy menu of Indonesian and Balinese specialities. Above the suspension bridge and across the river from Murni's, *Beggar's Bush* has a pleasant bar with draught Bintang beer. It's the local Hash House Harriers meeting point. There are also places along the road to Peliatan and, of course, countless warungs scattered everywhere.

Entertainment
Entertainment in Ubud means watching Balinese dances so head down to Kuta if you want discos and Western music. If you're in the right place at the right time you can still catch dances put on for temple ceremonies and an essentially local audience but even the strictly tourist dances are generally put on with a high degree of skill and commitment. Indeed the competition between the various Ubud dance troupes is so intense these days that local connoisseurs even whisper the unthinkable, that the Peliatan troupe is no longer necessarily the best!

Entry is usually 5000 rp, and this includes transport to performances further out from central Ubud, particularly at Bona village, 12 km away. You can buy tickets at the performance place but it's hard to escape the attentions of commissioned ticket sellers around Ubud market and down Monkey Forest Rd. Ubud's bina wisata (tourist office) has information on current performance nights but the following list gives a good idea of the possibilities:

Sunday	Kechak dance – Padangtegal, Ubud
	Kechak and Sanghyang dances – Bona
	Ladies' orchestra & dance – Peliatan
Monday	Legong – Puri Saren, Ubud
	Kechak and Sanghyang dances – Bona
	Ramayana ballet – Pura Dalem, Ubud
Tuesday	Mahabharata dance – Teges
	Ramayana ballet – Puri Saren, Ubud
Wednesday	Wayang kulit play – Oka Kartini, Ubud
	Kechak and Sanghyang dances – Bona
	Sunda Upabunda – Puri Saren, Ubud
	Legong – Banjar Tengah, Peliatan
Thursday	Gabor – Puri Saren, Ubud
Friday	Barong & Rangda – Puri Saren, Ubud
	Kechak and Sanghyang dances – Bona
	Legong dance – Peliatan
Saturday	Legong dance – Puri Saren, Ubud
	Legong dance – Pura Dalem, Puri Ubud

For descriptions of these dances, see the Music & Dance section in the Facts about Bali chapter.

Things to Buy
Ubud has a wide variety of shops and art galleries. It's also worth investigating smaller places or places further out from the centre. As in other places in Bali, so much is completely standard that it's a real pleasure when you find something really different. Murni's, down by the river, always seems to have something unusual – pretty cushion covers, carved and painted mirror frames, strange pottery.

Small shops by the market and along the Monkey Forest Rd often have good woodcarvings, particularly masks. M Nama, on the Peliatan corner, also has lots of interesting woodcarvings. There are some other good woodcarving places along the road from here to Goa Gajah. At Goa Gajah there is a host of stalls selling leatherwork. You'll find good places for paintings along the main road through Ubud or beyond the suspension bridge towards the Museum Neka. The main problem with Ubud is that there are so many places, it's difficult to find items that rise above the 'average'.

Getting There & Away

In Ubud bemos leave from the stop beside the cinema building in the middle of town. To get to Denpasar or the southern tourist centres you first take a bemo to Denpasar's Batubulan bus/bemo station for about 700 rp. From there bemos run to places all over Bali. There are direct bemos between Batubulan and Sanur but for Kuta you have to take a bemo from the Batubulan station to the Tegal station on the Kuta side of Denpasar for 500 rp and another bemo from there.

If you're staying in Ubud and have gone to Denpasar or Kuta for the day remember that bemo services tail off rapidly after about 4 pm. If you miss the last bemo you'll either have to stay overnight or charter a bemo.

A chartered bemo is the Balinese equivalent of a taxi and you will get regular offers of 'transport' from bemo operators. A typical charter fare to Kuta or the airport is about 20,000 rp while the official taxi fare from the airport to Ubud is 34,000 rp.

If tangling with bemos, either public or chartered, doesn't appeal you can take one of the tourist shuttle buses which operate to a fixed schedule directly between Ubud and other tourist centres. There are lots of signs around Ubud announcing departure times and ticket sales. Fares to Sanur, Kuta or the airport are 3000 rp; to Padangbai, Candidasa or Kintamani 6000 rp and to Singaraja and Lovina Beach 10,000 rp.

Getting Around

To get to the places around Ubud you can generally count on paying 200 to 350 rp by bemo. Count on about 30 rp a km with a 200 rp minimum. There are numerous places in Ubud renting mountain bikes at 3000 rp a day or 2500 rp a day for longer term rental. Places hiring out cars and motorbikes are equally plentiful.

Numerous tours (day trips or longer) are also operated from Ubud. A day tour typically costs US$5 to US$8.

Around Ubud

The Pejeng region around Ubud encompasses many of the most ancient monuments and relics in Bali, some of them well known and very much on the beaten track, others relatively unknown and little visited. The majority of them are found along the route from Ubud via Goa Gajah and Bedulu then up the road towards Gunung Batur via Gunung Kawi and Tampaksiring. Some of these sites are heavily overrun by the tourist hordes, others are just far enough off the beaten track to leave the crowds behind.

Getting Around

You can reach most of the places around Ubud by bemo and on foot. If you're planning to see a lot of them it's a good idea to start at Tampaksiring (14 km from Ubud), then any walking you have to do is back downhill. It's only two km from Tirta Empul at Tampaksiring to Gunung Kawi – you can follow the path beside the river.

From Gunung Kawi you can take bemos back down to Pejeng, Bedulu, Goa Gajah and on to Ubud. Pejeng to the Bedulu turnoff is only about a km and from there it's a half km or so to Yeh Pulu and a similar distance to Goa Gajah. Alternatively from Pejeng you can cut across directly to Ubud, a pleasant walk with fine views. See under Walks in the Ubud section for more details.

If you have your own transport you can make a loop trip by turning north from the T-junction just east of Ubud (ie away from Peliatan) and following the road north to the fork just beyond Tegalalang. From there take the right fork to Kedisan where you turn east to Tampaksiring. You can then return from Tampaksiring by the regular road through Pejeng.

GOA GAJAH

Only a short distance beyond Peliatan, on the road to Pejeng and Gianyar, a car park on the northern side of the road marks the site of Goa Gajah (Elephant Cave). The cave is carved into a rock face, reached by a flight of steps down from the other side of the road. There were never any elephants in Bali; the cave probably takes its name from the nearby Petanu River which at one time was known as Elephant River.

You enter the cave through the cavernous mouth of a demon. The gigantic fingertips pressed beside the face of the demon push back a riotous jungle of surrounding stone carvings. Inside the T-shaped cave you can see fragmentary remains of *lingams*, the phallic symbols of the Hindu god Shiva, and their female counterpart the *yoni*, plus a statue of the elephant-headed god Ganesh.

Goa Gajah was certainly in existence at the time of the Majapahit takeover of Bali. One tale relates that it was another example of the handiwork of the legendary Kebo Iwa but it probably dates back to the 11th century and shows elements of both Hindu and Buddhist use.

In front of the cave are two square bathing pools with water gushing into them from waterspouts held by six female figures. The cave was discovered in 1923 but it was not until 1954 that the fountains and pool were unearthed. You can clamber down through the rice paddies to the Petanu River where there are crumbling rock carvings of stupas (domes for housing Buddhist relics) on a cliff face and a small cave.

Admission to Goa Gajah is 500 rp (children 100 rp). The *Puri Suling* restaurant overlooks the cave.

YEH PULU

Although it's only a km or so from Goa Gajah to Yeh Pulu, few visitors go there – it's amazing to see the difference between a place with a car park beside it and a place you have to walk to through the rice paddies! Yeh Pulu is easy to find too. Off the road beyond Goa Gajah you'll find a sign pointing to a path. The track follows a small cliff face most of the way, and is as picturesque as any tramp through the paddies in Bali – there are ups and downs, small streams gurgling by and Heath Robinson bamboo contraptions channelling water across gullies from one series of paddies to another.

Eventually, a small gateway leads to the ancient rock carvings at Yeh Pulu. Only excavated in 1925 these are some of the oldest relics in Bali. The carved cliff face is about 25 metres long and is believed to be a hermitage dating from the 14th century. Apart from the figure of elephant-headed Ganesh, the son of Shiva, there are no religious scenes here. The energetic frieze includes various scenes of everyday life – two men carrying an animal slung from a pole, a man slaying a beast with a dagger (and a frog imitating him by disposing of a snake in like manner – clearly the Balinese sense of humour is not new!), and a man on horseback either pulling a captive woman along behind him or with a woman holding the horse's tail?

On the way through the rice paddies to Yeh Pulu you pass a bathing place with female fountain figures remarkably similar to those at Goa Gajah. The Ganesh figures of Yeh Pulu and Goa Gajah are also quite similar, indicating a close relationship between the two sites. *Yeh* is the Balinese word for water and, as at Goa Gajah, water and fountains play an important part at Yeh Pulu.

BEDULU

Just beyond Goa Gajah is the road junction where you can turn south to Gianyar or north to Pejeng and Tampaksiring. It's hard to imagine Bedulu, the small village at the junction, as the former capital of a great kingdom. The legendary Dalem Bedaulu ruled the Pejeng dynasty from here and was the last

Balinese king to withstand the onslaught of the powerful Majapahits from Java. He was eventually defeated by Gajah Mada in 1343. The capital shifted several times after this, ending up at Gelgel and then later at Klungkung.

A legend relates how Bedaulu possessed magical powers which allowed him to have his head chopped off and then replaced. Per-forming this unique party trick one day the servant entrusted with lopping off his head and then replacing it unfortunately dropped it in a river and, to his horror, watched it float away. Looking around in panic for a replace-ment he grabbed a pig, cut off its head and popped it upon the king's shoulders. There-after the king was forced to sit on a high throne and forbade his subjects to look up at

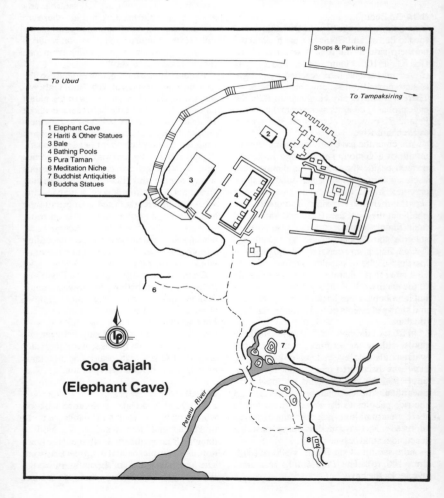

Shops & Parking

← To Ubud

To Tampaksiring →

1 Elephant Cave
2 Hariti & Other Statues
3 Bale
4 Bathing Pools
5 Pura Taman
6 Meditation Niche
7 Buddhist Antiquities
8 Buddha Statues

Goa Gajah

(Elephant Cave)

Petanu River

him; Bedaulu means 'he who changed heads'.

AROUND BEDULU

There are several interesting sites around Bedulu and up the road towards Pejeng.

Pura Samuan Tiga

The Pura Samuan Tiga (Temple of the Meeting of the Three) is about 100 metres east of the Bedulu junction. Follow the sign to the government rest house to find this important 11th century temple. The annual Odalan festival takes place here on the full moon of the 10th month of the lunar calendar, rather than on the shorter 210-day Balinese calendar. Throngs of Balinese flock to the huge temple courtyard from all over the island.

Bedulu Arkeologi Gedong Arca

The Bedulu Archaeological Museum (Bedulu Arkeologi Gedong Arca) is about two km north of Bedulu and includes a collection of pre-Hindu artefacts including stone sarcophagi from the time before cremations were practised in Bali. It's a rather dry and dusty museum, unlikely to be of interest to anyone other than serious students of archaeology. It's open from 8 am to 2 pm Monday and Thursday and from 8 am to 1 pm other days except Sunday when it is closed.

PEJENG

Continuing up the road to Tampaksiring you soon come to Pejeng and its famous temples. Like Bedulu this was once an important seat of power, the capital of the Pejeng kingdom which fell to the Majapahit invaders in 1343.

Pura Kebo Edan

The Crazy Buffalo Temple (Pura Kebo Edan) with its nearly four-metre-high statue of Bima, liberally endowed with six penises, is on the western side of the road as you come in to Pejeng. There's considerable conjecture over what this fearsome image is all about. The dead body which the image tramples upon appears to relate to the Hindu Shiva cult but it may also have Tantric Buddhist over-

tones. Other figures flank the main one and male and female buffaloes lie before it. It's said that *dukans* (witch doctors) gather here on certain nights.

Pura Pusering Jagat

The large Navel of the World Temple (Pura Pusering Jagat) is said to be the centre of the old Pejeng kingdom. Dating from 1329, this temple is also said to be visited by dukans during the full moon and by young couples who pray at the stone lingam and yoni (Hindu phallic symbols).

Pura Penataran Sasih

In the centre of Pejeng, Pura Penataran Sasih was once the state temple of the Pejeng kingdom. In the inner courtyard, high up in a pavilion where you really cannot see it very well, is the huge bronze drum known as the 'Moon of Pejeng'. It is believed to be more than 1000 years older than the kingdom of Pejeng itself, a relic from the Bronze Age in Indonesia. The hourglass-shaped drum is more than three metres long, the largest single piece cast drum in the world.

A Balinese legend relates how the drum came to earth as a fallen moon, landing in a tree and shining so brightly that it prevented a band of thieves from going about their unlawful purpose. One of the thieves decided to put the light out by urinating on it but the moon exploded, killed the foolhardy thief and fell to earth as a drum – with a crack across its base as a result of the fall.

TAMPAKSIRING

Continuing up the road to Tampaksiring you pass through pleasant paddy fields along the steady upward climb which continues all the way to the rim of the crater at Penelokan. Tampaksiring is a small town with a large and important temple and the most impressive ancient monument in Bali.

Gunung Kawi

On the southern outskirts of Tampaksiring a sign points off the road to the right to Gunung Kawi. From the end of the access road a steep stone stairway leads down to the river, at one point making a cutting through an embankment of solid rock. There, in the bottom of this lush green valley with beautiful rice terraces climbing up the hillsides, is one of Bali's oldest, and certainly largest, ancient monuments.

Gunung Kawi consists of 10 rock-cut candi, memorials cut out of the rock face in imitation of actual monuments – in a similar fashion to the great rock-cut temples of Ajanta and Ellora in India. Each candi is believed to be a memorial to a member of the 11th century Balinese royalty but little is known for certain. They stand in seven-metre-high sheltered niches cut into the sheer cliff face. There are four on the west side of the river which you come to first. To reach the five on the eastern side, you have to cross the river on a bridge. A solitary candi stands further down the valley to the south; this is reached by a trek through the rice paddies.

Legends relate that the whole group of memorials was carved out of the rock face in one hard working night by the mighty fingernails of Kebo Iwa. It's uncertain who the real builders were but they may date from the Udayana dynasty of the 10th and 11th centuries. It's said that the five monuments on the eastern bank are to King Udayana, Queen Mahendradatta (see the Kutri section in this chapter), their son Airlangga and his brothers Anak Wungsu and Marakata. While Airlangga ruled eastern Java, Anak Wungsu ruled Bali. The four monuments on the western side are, by this theory, to Anak Wungsu's chief concubines. Another theory is that the whole complex is dedicated to Anak Wungsu, his wives, concubines and, in the case of the remote 10th candi, to a royal minister.

Each of the sets of memorials has a group of monks' cells associated with it, including one on the eastern side with perhaps Bali's one and only 'No shoes, sandals, boots may be worn' sign. There are other groups of candi and monks' cells in the area of Bali encompassed by the ancient Pejeng kingdom, but none so grand as these.

Entry to Gunung Kawi is 500 rp. It's

another two km to the Tirta Empul temple at Tampaksiring.

Tirta Empul

After Tampaksiring, the road branches. The left fork runs up to the grand palace once used by Sukarno while the right fork leads to the temple at Tirta Empul and continues up to Penelokan. You can look back along the valley and see Gunung Kawi from this road, just before you turn into Tirta Empul. The holy springs at Tirta Empul are believed to have magical powers so the temple here is an important one.

Each year an inscribed stone is brought from a nearby village to be ceremonially washed in the spring. The inscription on the stone has been deciphered and indicates that the springs were founded in 962 AD. The actual springs bubble up into a large, crystal-clear tank within the temple and gush out through waterspouts into a bathing pool. According to legend, the springs were created by the god Indra who pierced the earth to tap the 'elixir of immortality' or *amerta*. Despite its antiquity, the temple is glossy and gleamingly new – it was totally restored in the late '60s.

The springs of Tirta Empul are a source of the Pakerisan River, which rushes by Gunung Kawi only a km or so away. Between Tirta Empul and Gunung Kawi is the temple of Pura Mengening where you can see a freestanding candi similar in design to those of Gunung Kawi. There is a spring at this temple which also feeds into the Pakerisan. Overlooking Tirta Empul is the Sukarno Palace, a grandiose structure built in 1954 on the site of a Dutch rest house. Sukarno, whose mother was Balinese, was a frequent visitor to the island. It's said he used a telescope to spy on women bathing at the Tirta Empul pool below.

The car park outside Tirta Empul is surrounded by the familiar unholy confusion of souvenir and craft shops. Chess sets and bone carving are popular crafts here. There is an admission charge to Tirta Empul and you have to wear a temple scarf. It's a good idea to come early in the morning or late in the afternoon to avoid the tour-bus hordes.

Places to Stay & Eat

Although Tampaksiring is an easy day trip from Ubud or even Bangli, it's possible to stay here. In the village itself there's the small *Homestay Gusti* and the *Homestay Tampaksiring*. Both charge about 4000/5000 rp for singles/doubles.

Apart from the usual selection of warungs there's also the expensive *Tampaksiring Restaurant* for tourist groups; it's some distance below the village.

UBUD TO BATUR

The usual road from Ubud to Batur is through Tampaksiring but there are other lesser roads up the gentle mountain slope. If you head east out of Ubud and turn away from Peliatan, towards Petulu at the junction, this road will bring you out on the crater rim just beyond Penelokan towards Batur. It's a sealed road all the way except for a few km near the top where it's cobbled and fairly rough. Along this road you'll see a number of woodcarvers producing beautiful painted birds, frogs, garudas and tropical fruit. Tegalalang and the nearby village of Jati, just off the road, are noted woodcarving centres. Further up, other specialists carve stools and there are a couple of places where whole tree trunks are carved into whimsical figures.

Another route from Ubud to Batur can be followed by taking the road through Campuan and Sanggingan and then turning up the hill, instead of down towards Denpasar, at Kedewatan. On this route you pass through Payangan, the only place in Bali where lychees are grown. It's possible to get bemos some distance up the road on both these routes but finding public transport at the top can be difficult. The roads, once quite rough, are not bad now.

Of course you could walk up to Batur from Ubud too. If you take the path from near the temple down by the Campuan suspension bridge and follow it steadily uphill you'll pass unspoilt villages like Bangkiang Sidem, Keliki and Sebali. Just walking through is pleasant and from Sebali you can cut across to Tegalalang and get a bemo back to Ubud. And if you keep walking? Well it's 30 km to Batur, uphill all the way.

East Bali

The eastern end of Bali is dominated by mighty Gunung Agung, the 'navel of the world' and Bali's 'mother mountain'. Towering at 3142 metres, Agung has not always been a kind mother – witness the disastrous 1963 eruption. Today Agung is again a quiet but dominating mountain and the mother temple Pura Besakih, perched high on the slopes of the volcano, attracts a steady stream of devotees...and tourists.

The east has a number of places of great interest. Here you'll find Klungkung, the former capital of one of Bali's great kingdoms. From Klungkung the road runs close to the coast past interesting fishing villages like Kusamba, past the bat-infested cave temple of Goa Lawah, the beautiful port of Padangbai, the turn-off to the pretty little Bali Aga village of Tenganan, the popular beach centre of Candidasa, before it finally reaches Amlapura, another former capital.

At Amlapura you can about-turn and retrace your route or take an alternative route higher up the slopes of Agung to Rendang. From Rendang you can turn north to Besakih, south to Klungkung or continue west on a pretty but lesser-used route to Bangli. As a third alternative you can continue right around the coast from Amlapura to Singaraja in the north. See the North Bali chapter for more details on this lightly populated coastal route.

The 1963 Eruption

The most disastrous volcanic eruption in Bali this century took place in 1963 when Agung blew its top in no uncertain manner and at a time of considerable prophetic importance: 8 March 1963 was the culmination of Eka Desa Rudra, the greatest of all Balinese sacrifices and an event which only takes place every 100 years on the Balinese calendar. At the time of the eruption, it had been more than 100 Balinese years (115 years on the lunar calendar) since the last Eka

Desa Rudra. Naturally the temple at Besakih was a focal point for the festival but Agung was already acting strangely as preparations were made in late February. Agung had been dormant since 1843 but by the time the sacrifices commenced, the mountain was belching smoke and ash, glowing and rumbling ominously.

On 17 March 1963 it exploded in a catastrophic eruption that killed more than 1000 people and destroyed entire villages. Streams of lava and hot volcanic mud poured right down to the sea at several places, completely covering roads and isolating the eastern end of the island for some time. The entire island was covered in ash and crops were wiped out everywhere. The torrential rainfall that followed the eruptions compounded the damage as boiling hot ash and boulders known as *lahar* were swept down the mountain side, wreaking havoc on many villages like Subagan, just outside Amlapura and Selat, further along the road towards Rendang. The whole of Bali suffered a drastic food shortage and many Balinese, whose rice land was completely ruined, had to be resettled in Sulawesi.

Although Besakih is high on the slopes of Agung, only about six km from the crater, it suffered little damage from the eruption. Volcanic dust and gravel flattened timber and bamboo buildings around the temple complex but the stone structures came through unscathed. The inhabitants of the villages of Sorga and Lebih, also high up on Agung's slopes, were all but wiped out. Most of the people killed at the time of the eruption were burnt and suffocated by searing clouds of hot gas that rushed down the volcano's slopes. Agung erupted again on 16 May, with serious loss of life although not on the same scale as the March eruption.

The Balinese take signs and portents seriously – that such a terrible event should happen as they were making a most important sacrifice to the gods was not taken lightly.

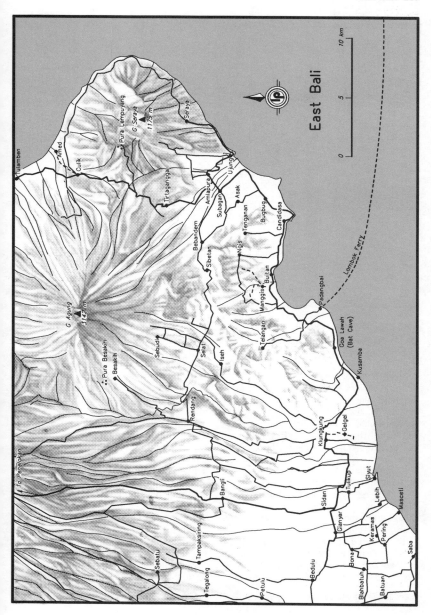

East Bali

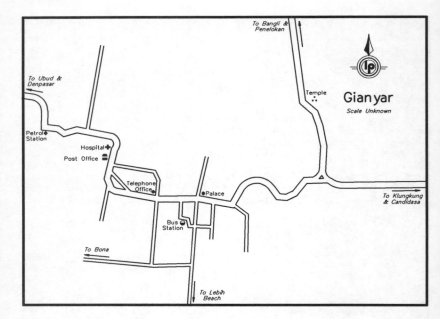

The interrupted series of sacrifices finally recommenced 16 years later in 1979.

Getting There & Away
Buses to eastern Bali generally depart from the Batubulan station in Denpasar. Fares include: Gianyar 700 rp, Klungkung 1000 rp, Padangbai 1500 rp, Amlapura 2500 rp and Bangli 1000 rp. To get to Besakih take a bus to Klungkung and then a bemo from there for 600 rp.

Klungkung to Amlapura costs about 900 rp, then from Amlapura to Singaraja buses cost 2500 rp. From Culik, a little beyond Tirtagangga, to Kubutambahan, costs 1800 rp and takes about 3½ hours. Local bemos run from Amlapura to Tirtagangga.

To reach the centres in eastern Bali from Ubud you can either take a bemo to Gianyar or take a bemo to Batubulan, the main bus/bemo station just outside Denpasar.

GIANYAR
Gianyar is the administrative centre of the Gianyar District which also includes Ubud, but is of minimal interest in its own right. On the main road from Denpasar, and still in the heavy traffic region of southern Bali, the town has a number of small textile factories on the Denpasar side. You're welcome to drop in, see the materials being woven and even make a purchase. It takes about six hours to weave a complete sarong. At the height of the tourist season the regular arrival of buses and free-spending visitors can push prices up to higher levels than in Denpasar.

Right in the centre of town, across from the large open space known as the alun alun, the old palace is little changed from the time the Dutch arrived in the south and the old kingdoms lost their power. The Gianyar royal family saved their palace by capitulating to the Dutch, rather than making a heroic last stand like the other Balinese kingdoms. Despite its relatively original appearance, the palace, dating from 1771, was destroyed in a conflict with the neighbouring kingdom of Klungkung in the mid-1880s and was rebuilt only to be severely damaged again in the 1917 earthquake. Nevertheless, it's a fine example of traditional palace architecture, surrounded by high brick walls. The royal family of Gianyar still live in the palace, so without a formal invitation you can do no more than look in through the gates.

Gianyar's warungs are noted for their fine roast piglet, babi guling. Eat early though, as the warungs are usually cleaned out by late morning.

BONA

The village of Bona, on the back road between Gianyar and Blahbatuh, is credited with being the modern home of the Kechak dance. Kechak and other dances are held here every week and are easy to get to from Ubud. Tickets (including transport) from Ubud cost around 5000 rp.

Bona is also a basket-weaving centre and many other articles are also woven from lontar (palm leaves). Nearby Belega, en route to Blahbatuh, is a centre for bamboo work.

LEBIH & THE COAST

South of Gianyar the coast is fringed by black-sand beaches and small coastal villages like Lebih. The Pakerisan River, which starts up in the hills at Tampaksiring, reaches the sea near Lebih. Here, and at other coastal villages south of Gianyar, funeral ceremonies reach their conclusion when the ashes are consigned to the sea. Ritual purification ceremonies for temple artefacts are also held on these beaches.

Further west is Masceti, where the Pura Masceti is one of Bali's nine directional temples. On the beach the local villagers have recently erected a huge and somewhat horrific 'swan' (chicken?) in an attempt to create a tourist attraction! Masceti is reached via Bona, Keramas and Pering. Further west again is Saba, another small coastal village. One of the best beaches along this stretch of coast is found to the east of Lebih at Siyut, reached via Tulikup.

SIDAN

Continuing east from Gianyar you come to the turn-off to Bangli at Sidan, just a few km out of town. Follow this road for about a km until you reach a sharp bend. Here you'll find the Sidan Pura Dalem, a good example of a temple of the dead. Note the sculptures of Durga with children by the gate, and the separate enclosure in one corner of the temple – this is dedicated to Merajapati, the guardian spirit of the dead. If you continue up the Bangli road there's another interesting pura dalem at Penunggekan, just before you reach Bangli. See the Bangli section for more details.

KLUNGKUNG

Klungkung was once the centre of Bali's most important kingdom and a great artistic and cultural focal point. The Gelgel dynasty, the most powerful kingdom in Bali at that time, held power for about 300 years, until the arrival of the Dutch. It was here that the Klungkung school of painting was developed. This style, where subjects were painted in side profile (like wayang kulit figures), is still used today, but most of the paintings are produced in Kamasan, a few km outside Klungkung.

Klungkung is a major public transport junction – from here you can find buses to Besakih or further east to Padangbai, Candidasa and Amlapura. Modern Klungkung is a dusty, busy market town with pony-drawn carts (dokars) providing an exotic touch. The bus and bemo station is a major gathering point, particularly at night when a busy night market (pasar malam) operates there.

Kertha Gosa

The Kertha Gosa (Hall of Justice) stands beside the road as you reach the centre of town from Denpasar. It's in the grounds of the Taman Gili, the remains of the palace of the Dewa Agungs. The Kertha Gosa, an open pavilion surrounded by a moat, is a superb example of Klungkung architecture; the roof

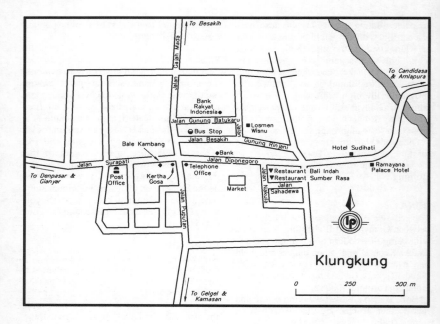

To Besakih

Jalan Mada

To Candidasa & Amlapura

Bank Rakyat Indonesia●

Jalan Gunung Batukaru

●Bus Stop

Jalan Besakih

Losmen Wisnu

Gunung Rinjani

Hotel Sudihati

Bale Kambang

●Bank

Jalan Diponegoro

Telephone Office

Ramayana Palace Hotel

Jalan

Surapati

To Denpasar & Gianyar

Post Office

Kertha Gosa

Market

Jalan Nakula

▼Restaurant Bali Indah

▼Restaurant Sumber Rasa

Jalan Sahadewa

Jalan Puputan

Klungkung

0   250   500 m

To Gelgel & Kamasan

is completely painted inside with fine paintings in the Klungkung style. The paintings, done on asbestos sheeting, were installed in the 1940s, replacing the cloth paintings which had deteriorated. Further repainting and restoration took place in the '60s and '80s but the style of the paintings appears to have been fairly consistent. Virtually the only record of the earlier paintings was a photograph of the ceiling taken by Walter Spies in the '30s. Given Bali's humid climate there is, of course, rapid deterioration and already the current paintings are looking very second-hand.

This was effectively the 'supreme court' of the Klungkung kingdom, where disputes and cases which could not be settled at the village level were eventually brought. The defendant, standing before the three priests who acted as judges (kerthas), could gaze up at the ceiling and see wrongdoers being tortured by demons and the innocent enjoying the pleasures of Balinese heaven.

The capital of the kingdom was shifted to Klungkung from nearby Gelgel in the early 1700s and the Kertha Gosa was probably constructed around the end of that century. The building was damaged in 1908 and rebuilt in 1920, under the Dutch, to deal with questions of traditional law (adat). Colonial law was handled by the Dutch.

Bale Kambang

Adjoining the Kertha Gosa in the Taman Gili is the beautiful Bale Kambang (Floating Pavilion). Its ceiling is also painted in Klungkung style, having been repainted in 1945. Around the Kertha Gosa and the Bale Kambang note the statues of top-hatted European figures, an amusing departure from the normal statues of entrance guardians. Admission to the palace and Kertha Gosa is 500 rp (children 200 rp).

Places to Stay & Eat

Few travellers stay overnight in Klungkung

as it's only 40 km from Denpasar, even less from Ubud and, in the other direction, only another 16 km to Padangbai or 25 km to Candidasa. If you do want to stop for the night there are a couple of possibilities, the nicest of which is the *Ramayana Palace Hotel* on the Candidasa side of town. It's a pleasant place and set far enough back from the busy main road to be quiet. There's a restaurant and the fairly spartan rooms cost 8000/12,000 rp for singles/doubles.

Less attractive alternatives include the *Losmen Wisnu* near the bus station in the centre. The upstairs rooms are much brighter than those downstairs. The very basic *Hotel Sudihati* is between the town centre and the Ramayana Palace Hotel.

Apart from the Ramayana Palace's restaurant there are several places to eat including the Chinese *Restaurant Bali Indah* and *Restaurant Sumber Rasa*. They're both neat and clean and across from the market.

Things to Buy
There are a number of good shops along Jalan Diponegoro in Klungkung selling Klungkung-style paintings and some interesting antiques. Klungkung is also a good place for buying temple umbrellas – several shops sell them.

Kamasan Paintings
The village of Kamasan, a few km from Klungkung, has long been a bastion of traditional painting, the origins of which can be traced back at least 500 years. Highly conventionalised, the symbolism of equating right and left with good and evil, as in wayang kulit performances, is evident in the compositions and placement of figures in Kamasan paintings. Subject matter derives largely from Balinese variations of the ancient Hindu epics, the *Ramayana* and the *Mahabharata*. Kakawins, poems written in the archaic Javanese language of Kawi, provide another important source, as does indigenous Balinese folklore with its pre-Hindu/Buddhist beliefs in demonic spirit forces. The style has also been adapted to create large versions of the zodiacal and lunar calendar, especially the 210-day wuku calendar which still regulates the timing of Balinese festivals.

The earliest paintings were done on bark cloth, said to have been imported from Sulawesi, although a coarse handspun cloth and later machine-made cloth were used as backing for the bark cloth. Kamasan art is essentially linear – the skill of the artist is apparent in its composition and in the sensitivity of its lines. The colouring was of secondary importance and was left to apprentices, usually the artist's children. Members of the family would assist in preparing the colours, stiffening the cloth with rice paste and polishing the surface smooth enough to receive the fine ink drawing.

Paintings were hung as ceremonial backdrops in temples and houses and were also sufficiently prized by the local rulers to be acceptable gifts between rival royal households. Although they were traditionally patronised by the ruling class, paintings also helped fulfil the important function of imparting ethical values and customs *(adat)* to the ordinary people, in much the same way as traditional dance and wayang puppetry. In fact, it is from the wayang tradition that Kamasan painting takes its essential characteristics – the stylisation of human figures, their symbolic gestures, the depiction of divine and heroic characters as refined, and of evil ones as vulgar and crude, as well as the primary function of narrating a moral tale.

It's worth noting that there are striking similarities between Kamasan paintings and a now almost totally abandoned form of wayang theatre, the *wayang beber*. The slender horizontal format of Balinese paintings almost certainly derives from the *wayang bebe*, which is a large handscroll, held vertically and unrolled and expounded upon by the puppet-master, accompanied by the gamelan orchestra. The wayang beber was still being performed during the Dutch occupation, but a performance now is very rare, although craftsmen in eastern Java are still producing scenes from such scrolls for the tourist trade.

The wayang style can be traced back to 9th-century Javanese sculpture, and its most mature form can be seen at the 14th-century temple complex at Panataran in eastern Java. The relief sculptures at Panataran display the characteristic wayang figures, the rich floral designs, the flame-and-mountain motifs – all vital elements of Balinese painting.

In Kamasan, at Banjar Siku, there's a gallery where you can buy good quality Kamasan paintings. ∎

Getting There & Away

Bemos bound for Candidasa and Amlapura all pass through Klungkung. Bemos also shuttle up and down the mountain road from Klungkung to Besakih.

KUSAMBA

Beyond Klungkung the road crosses lava flows (now overgrown) from the '63 eruption of Agung before turning back towards the coast and the fishing village of Kusamba. If you turn off the main road and go down to the beach, you'll see lines of colourful fishing prahus (outriggers) lined up on the beach. Fishing is normally done at night and the 'eyes' on the front of the boats help navigation through the darkness. You can charter a boat out to Nusa Penida, clearly visible opposite Kusamba. Regular supply trips are made to the island; you could try to get on one of these cargo prahus. The crossing takes several hours.

Just beyond Kusamba you can see the thatched roofs of salt-panning huts along the beach. Saltwater-saturated sand from the beach is dried out around these huts and then further processed inside the huts. You can see the same process being carried out beside the Kuta to Sanur road. Although salt processed by machine is cheaper, connoisseurs still demand real sea salt.

GOA LAWAH

Beyond Kusamba the road continues close to the coast and after a few km you come to the Goa Lawah (Bat Cave). The cave in the cliff face here is packed, crammed, jammed full of bats. There must be untold thousands of the squeaking, flapping creatures, tumbling and crawling over one another. Occasionally, one launches out of the cave only to zip straight back when it realises it's still daytime.

The cave, part of a temple, is said to lead all the way to Besakih but it's unlikely anybody would be too enthusiastic about investigating! The bats provide sustenance for the legendary giant snake Naga Basuki, which is said to live in the cave. A distinctly batty aroma exudes from the cave, and the roofs of the temple shrines in front of the cave are also liberally coated with bat droppings.

Entry to the bat cave temple is 500 rp (100 rp children) including hire of a temple scarf. It costs another 150 rp to park in the car park. The souvenir sellers who besiege visitors are very pushy.

PADANGBAI

Padangbai is the port for the ferry service between Bali and Lombok. Along with Benoa it's the principal shipping port in the south of the island. The town is a couple of km off the main road, a scruffy little place on a perfect little bay, one of the very few sheltered harbours in Bali. It's very picturesque with a long sweep of sand where colourful outrigger fishing boats are drawn up on the beach. Like some other coastal towns there's a large Muslim population.

Padangbai can be an interesting place to spend a day or so if you don't want to simply arrive in the morning and depart straight for Lombok. If you walk around to the right from the wharf and follow the trail up the hill, you'll eventually come to the idyllic *Pantai Kecil* (Little Beach) on the exposed coast outside the bay. Out on the northern corner of the bay is the temple of Pura Silayukti, where Empu Kuturan, who introduced the caste system to Bali in the 11th century, is said to have lived.

Cruise ships visiting Bali use Padangbai but have to anchor offshore outside the harbour as only small ships can actually enter the bay. When the cruise ships are in, Padangbai is temporarily transformed into a cacophonous souvenir market with sellers flocking in from all over the island.

Information

There are no banks or moneychangers in Padangbai so, whether you plan to stay or continue to Lombok, make sure you've changed enough money before you arrive. Otherwise you may have to backtrack to Klungkung to the nearest bank or continue to Candidasa to find a moneychanger. Johnny, at Johnny's Warung, will sometimes

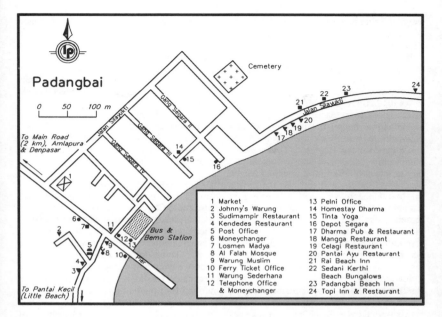

Padangbai

0   50   100 m

To Main Road
(2 km), Amlapura
& Denpasar

Cemetery

To Pantai Kecil
(Little Beach)

Bus &
Bemo Station

1 Market
2 Johnny's Warung
3 Sudimampir Restaurant
4 Kendedes Restaurant
5 Post Office
6 Moneychanger
7 Losmen Madya
8 Al Falah Mosque
9 Warung Muslim
10 Ferry Ticket Office
11 Warung Sederhana
12 Telephone Office
   & Moneychanger
13 Pelni Office
14 Homestay Dharma
15 Tinta Yoga
16 Depot Segara
17 Dharma Pub & Restaurant
18 Mangga Restaurant
19 Celagi Restaurant
20 Pantai Ayu Restaurant
21 Rai Beach Inn
22 Sedani Kerthi
   Beach Bungalows
23 Padangbai Beach Inn
24 Topi Inn & Restaurant

change US$ or A$ (cash, not travellers' cheques) into rupiah at a discount.

Diving & Surfing

There's some excellent diving on the coral reefs around Pulau Kambing, off Padangbai. Gili Toapekong, which has a series of coral heads at the top of a sheer drop-off, is perhaps the best site. The currents here are strong and unpredictable and there are also sharks – it's recommended for experienced divers only.

There's a good surf break off the western point of the harbour.

Places to Stay

Most visitors to Padangbai stay at one of the pleasant beach-front places – the gentle arc of beach with colourful fishing boats drawn up on the sand is postcard perfect. To get to these places you can either head straight down to the pier and turn left through the bus and bemo station or you can take the signposted turn-off to the left as you enter the town.

First there's the *Rai Beach Inn* which has a collection of two-storeyed cottages looking rather like traditional rice barns. There's an open sitting area downstairs and a sleeping area with verandah upstairs. Rooms cost 20,000 rp and the only drawback with these cottages is that the high wall which surrounds each one provides a bit too much isolation. You miss the opportunity to sit outside and chat with your neighbours which is one of the more pleasant aspects of staying in a traditional losmen. The inn also has straightforward single-storeyed rooms with bathroom at 15,000 rp.

Next along the beach is the *Sedani Kerthi Beach Bungalows* with simple rooms at 8000 rp and also double-storeyed thatched cottages, very similar in style to the Rai Beach Inn. The third place in the central beach-front cluster is the *Padangbai Beach Inn* where rooms are 6000/8000 rp for singles/doubles. The rooms are straight out of the standard losmen design book but, as they all face the sea, they're the best situated rooms in Padangbai.

If you continue along the beach right to the end of the bay, you'll find the *Topi Inn & Restaurant*. It's a new addition to the Padangbai beach scene with rooms upstairs at 7000/10,000 rp for singles/doubles.

The beach-front places keep most visitors to Padangbai happy but there are several other alternatives. Back towards the main street of town the *Homestay Dharma* is a plain family compound with very neat and tidy rooms at 8000 rp for a double. *Losmen Madya*, on the main street, was the town's original place to stay and has rooms at around 10,000 rp although there's no real reason to stay here in preference to the more pleasantly situated places on the beach. *Johnny's Warung*, behind the post office, also has accommodation.

Places to Eat

Restaurants have been proliferating in Padangbai even faster than hotels. Right across from the Rai Beach Inn there's a line-up of simple beach-front warungs where Ibu Komang, the 'mama' of the *Pantai Ayu Restaurant* wins the popularity contest hands down. Everyone gets a cheery welcome and the food is simple and well prepared.

Other places in this group on the beach are the long-running *Celagi Restaurant*, the *Mangga Restaurant* and the *Dharma Pub & Restaurant*. The Dharma seems to be popular with visiting dive groups. Continue down the beach to the end of the bay and the *Topi Restaurant* is the fanciest place in Padangbai with an open, sand-floored dining area and a colourful menu featuring fish dishes plus the Indonesian regulars.

Along the main street there are a host of small Indonesian restaurants including the *Warung Muslim* in front of the mosque. Round by the post office there's *Kendedes Restaurant*, the *Sudimampir Restaurant* and *Johnny's Warung*.

Getting There & Away

See the Getting There & Away chapter for information on the ferry service between Padangbai and Lombok. The ticket office is down by the pier. Buses meet the ferries and go straight to Denpasar.

On the beach just east of the pier car park you'll find the twin-engined fibreglass boats that run across the strait to Nusa Penida (3000 rp).

There are also connections from Padangbai right through to Surabaya and Yogyakarta in Java. Padangbai is a couple of km off the main Klungkung to Amlapura road, 54 km from Denpasar.

BALINA BEACH (BUITAN)

It's 11 km from the Padangbai main road turn-off to Candidasa and between the two is Balina Beach, the tourist name bestowed on the village of Buitan. The original resort development here was intended to be the major scuba-diving centre for Bali. The resort has diving equipment for hire and organises snorkelling and diving trips all around Bali including Nusa Penida and the northern coast. The development is unusual in its association with the nearby village of Manggis; villagers from Manggis also manage the handicraft centre near the beach.

Diving

Diving trips from the Hotel Balina Beach, including transport and a full tank, range from US$30 to US$40 on the trips closer to Balina, from US$50 for Nusa Penida and from US$60 to Pulau Menjangan on the northern coast. You can also go on the same trips to snorkel, for a lower cost. Snorkelling trips start from US$10.

Places to Stay

Balina Beach Bungalows (☎ 0361-88451) has rooms at a host of prices from as low as US$15/18 for singles/doubles and up to US$40/45 for fancier rooms or US$55 for a large family unit. All prices include breakfast but the 15.5% service and tax charges are extra. This is a quite large and attractive development and the beach here is reasonably good.

Directly opposite the Balina Beach Bungalows is *Puri Buitan* (☎ 0361-87182), a new development with fan-cooled rooms at US$30/35 plus tax and service.

If you walk east along the beach for 200 metres, you'll find *Cangrin Beach Homestay* and *Sunrise Homestay*, which have standard losmen rooms for about 20,000 rp a double.

TENGANAN

From Padangbai the road moves inland through a beautiful stretch of scenery: while clambering up the hills you can catch glimpses of fine beaches back on the coast. At the turn-off to Tenganan a little posse of motorbike riders waits by the junction, ready to ferry you up to Tenganan. There's also a walking path to Tenganan from Candidasa but the trail is sometimes hard to follow.

Tenganan is a Bali Aga village, a centre of the original Balinese prior to the Majapahit arrival. Unlike the other well-known Bali Aga centre, Trunyan, this is a reasonably friendly place and also much more interesting. Tenganan is a walled village and consists basically of two rows of identical houses stretching up the gentle slope of the hill. The houses face each other across a grassy central area where the village's public buildings are located. The Bali Aga are reputed to be exceptionally conservative and resistant to change but even here the modern age has not been totally held at bay. A small forest of television aerials sprouts from those oh-so-traditional houses! The most striking feature of Tenganan, however, is its exceptional neatness, the hills behind providing a beautiful backdrop.

Tenganan is full of strange customs, festivals and practices. Double ikat cloth known as *gringsing* is still woven here – the pattern to be produced is dyed on the individual threads, both warp (lengthwise) and weft (crosswise), *before* the cloth is woven. This is the only place in Indonesia where the double ikat technique is practised. All other ikat produced in the archipelago is single ikat, where only the warp or weft, never both, is dyed. Double ikat cloth is only produced in small quantities and at great expense, so don't come here expecting to find a bargain piece to purchase.

A magical cloth known as *kamben gringsing* is also woven here – a person wearing it is said to be protected against black magic! A peculiar, old-fashioned version of the gamelan known as the gamelan selunding is still played here and girls dance an equally ancient dance known as the Rejang.

At the annual Usaba Sambah festival, held around June or July, men fight with their fists wrapped in sharp-edged pandanus leaves – similar events occur on the island of Sumba, far to the east in Nusa Tenggara. At this same festival, small, hand-powered Ferris wheels are brought out and the village girls are ceremonially twirled round. There are other Bali Aga villages in the vicinity including Asak where an even more ancient instrument is played – the *gamelan gambang*.

In recent years, festivals have often been cancelled in Tenganan because the village's population has been in steep decline. If a villager marries outside the Tenganan circle he or she loses their Bali Aga status. With

---

The Legend of Tenganan

There's a delightful legend about how the villagers of Tenganan came to acquire their land. The story pops up in various places in Indonesia, but in slightly different forms. The Tenganan version relates how Dalem Bedaulu (the king with a pig's head – see the Bedulu section for details) lost a valuable horse and offered to reward the villagers of Tenganan who had found its carcass. They asked that they be given the land where the horse was found – that is, all the area where the dead horse could be smelt.

The king sent a man with a keen nose who set off with the village chief and walked an enormous distance without ever managing to get away from the foul odour. Eventually accepting that enough was enough the official headed back to Bedulu, scratching his head. Once out of sight the village chief pulled a large hunk of dead horse out from under his clothes. ■

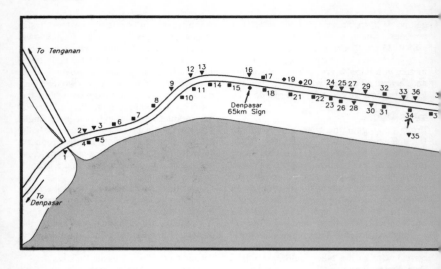

■ PLACES TO STAY

4 Bali Samudra Indah Hotel
5 Homestay Catra
6 Saputra Beach Inn
7 Bambu Garden Bungalows & Restaurant
8 Homestay Sri Artha
10 Candidasa Beach Bungalows
11 Homestay Geringsing
14 Homestay Segara Wangi
15 Homestay Ayodya
17 The Watergarden (Taman Air)
18 Puri Bali
21 Wiratha's Bungalows
22 Pandan Losmen & Restaurant
23 Candidasa Beach Bungalows II
26 Homestay Lilaberata
31 Agung Bungalows

32 Homestay Sasra Bahu
34 Pondok Bamboo Seaside Cottages
37 Puri Amarta Beach Inn
39 Natia Homestay
40 Cantiloka Beach Inn
42 Homestay Ida
43 Homestay Kelapa Mas
46 Dewi Bungalows
47 Rama Bungalows
48 Sindhu Brata Homestay
49 Pandawa Homestay
54 Srikandi Bungalows
55 Barong Beach Inn
56 Ramayana Beach Inn
57 Nani Beach Inn
58 Genggong Cottages
59 Puri Oka
60 Puri Pudok Bungalows

such a small population pool and declining fertility, this village and its unique culture may eventually be wiped out.

If you walk right up through the village to the road off to the right you'll see a sign pointing to the home of I Made Muditadnana, who produces lontar books – the traditional Balinese palm-leaf books. He's a friendly man and well worth visiting but if you're thinking of buying one of his books check the prices at the village handicraft shops first!

CANDIDASA

Candidasa has had a remarkably rapid rise to fame but, like Kuta 10 years earlier, is now

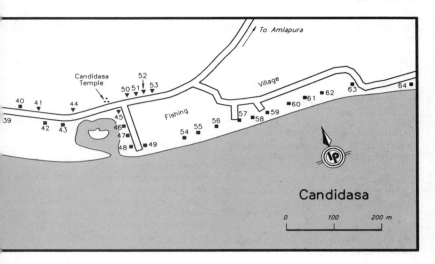

61	Asoka Beach Bungalows	29	Hawaii Restaurant
62	Sekar Orchid Bungalows	30	Tirtanadi (The TN) Restaurant
63	Puri Bagus Beach Hotel	33	Sanjaya Beer Garden
64	Bunga Putri Homestay	35	Pondok Bamboo Restaurant
		36	Kubu Bali Restaurant
▼	PLACES TO EAT	38	Murni's Cafe
		41	Legend Rock Cafe
1	Restaurant Agung	44	Warung Rasmini
2	Restaurant Flamboyant	45	Kusuma Restaurant
3	Molly's Garden Cafe	50	Raja's Restaurant
9	Arie's Restaurant	51	Pizzeria Candi Agung
12	Candidasa Restaurant	52	Ngandi Restaurant
13	The Coffee Shop	53	Mandara Giri Pizzaria
16	TJ's Restaurant		
24	Camplung Restaurant		OTHER
25	Tunjung Restaurant		
27	Restaurant Chandra	19	Bookshop
28	Restaurant Sumber Rasa	20	Pandun Harum

hopelessly overbuilt and rapidly becoming unattractive and squalid. This decline is not helped by the beach, which has been all but washed away since hotel construction got into high gear.

The road reaches the sea just beyond the turn-off to Tenganan, about 13 km before Amlapura, and runs close to the coast through the small village of Candidasa. The proliferation of hotels has now spread back to well beyond the Tenganan turn-off and hotel signs start appearing a couple of km before Candidasa itself. In 1983 Candidasa was just a quiet little fishing village. Two years later a dozen losmen and half a dozen restaurants had sprung up and suddenly it was *the* new beach place in Bali. Now it's shoulder to shoulder development and suffering all the Kuta-style problems.

Beyond Candidasa the road spirals up to the Pura Gamang Pass (*gamang* means 'to get dizzy'), from where there are fine views down to the coast.

Information

Candidasa has the full complement of shops, moneychangers, travel agencies, bicycle, motorbike and car rental outlets, film developers and other facilities. There are a couple of bookshops and book exchanges and a number of postal agencies where you can buy stamps and mail cards and letters.

Things to See & Do

Even with the tide out Candidasa's beach is nothing special:

Even the tourist brochures admit that Candidasa's beach disappears at high tide. If they wanted to be scrupulously honest they could add that even at low tide there isn't much of it. So how did a beach resort end up without a beach? The answer lies a few hundred metres offshore where the Candidasa reef used to be. Building all of Candidasa's hotels required large amounts of cement. An essential ingredient of cement is lime, and coral is a convenient source of limestone. So the Candidasa reef was ripped out, ground down and burnt to make the lime for the cement used to build the hotels. Without the protection of the reef the sea soon washed the beach away. A series of remarkably ugly T-shaped piers have been built to try to conserve what little beach is left, but don't come to Candidasa in search of a beach – there really isn't one.

Candidasa's temple is on the hillside across from the lagoon at the northern end of the village strip. The fishing village, just beyond the lagoon, has colourful fishing prahus drawn up on the beach. In the early morning you can watch them coasting in after a night's fishing. The owners regularly canvas visitors for snorkelling trips to the reef and the nearby islets.

If you follow the beach from Candidasa towards Amlapura a trail climbs up over the headland with fine views over the rocky islets off the coast. From the headland you'll notice that although the islets look as if they're in a straight line, they're actually made up of one cluster of smaller ones plus the solitary larger island off to the east. The diving around these islands is good.

Looking inland there's no sign at all of the village below or the road – just an unbroken sweep of palm trees. On a clear day, Agung rises majestically behind the range of coastal hills. Around the headland there's a long sweep of wide, exposed, black-sand beach.

Places to Stay

When places first popped up at Candidasa they were almost all out of the standard losmen mould – simple rooms with bathrooms and a small verandah area out front. Now mass tourism has arrived and there are a number of larger and more luxurious places with air-conditioning, swimming pools and the other accoutrements of the modern travel industry. A number of smaller, more exclusive hostelries have also popped up but shoestring travellers needn't worry, for there are still plenty of low-cost places to choose from. Accommodation now extends from before the Tenganan turn-off right through the tourist part of the village to the original fishing village, hidden in the palm trees where the road turns away from the coast. Basic doubles can be found from less than 10,000 rp but, like Kuta or Ubud, there are so many places to choose from that the best advice is simply to wander around and have a look at a few rooms.

Places to Stay – bottom end

Look into a few places before making a decision about where to stay. Starting at the Denpasar side don't confuse the *Candidasa Beach Bungalows* with the larger, mid-range *Candidasa Beach Bungalows II* in the centre of the village strip. At the original, the rooms are pleasant if a little tightly packed together. Next to it is the cheaper *Homestay Geringsing*. The *Wiratha's Bungalows* has simple but well-kept singles/doubles with private mandi for 8000/10,000 and 11,000/13,000 rp. The more expensive 20,000/22,000 rp rooms are not worth the extra money. Rooms at the *Puri Bali* are simple, clean and good value.

Continuing along the road there's the *Pandan Losmen* and the popular but rock-bottom *Homestay Lilaberata*. The *Pondok Bamboo Seaside Cottages* is a fancier place with singles/doubles at 26,000/32,000 rp and a beach-front restaurant. *Puri Amarta Beach Inn* has regular losmen-style rooms at 6000 rp plus larger ones at 10,000 rp. At the *Homestay Natia* next door, smaller rooms are 6000 rp although there are a couple of larger rooms on the sea front at 18,000 rp.

Homestay Ida, close to the lagoon, definitely doesn't fit the usual pattern, with pleasantly airy bamboo cottages dotted around a grassy coconut plantation. Smaller rooms are 20,000 rp, the larger rooms with mezzanine level are 40,000 rp, all including breakfast. Fortunately the owners don't seem intent on cramming more and more rooms onto the spacious site.

Next door is the *Homestay Kelapa Mas* which is also well kept and a little more spacious than usual. The rooms facing the seafront are particularly nicely situated. Prices start from 10,000 rp for the smallest rooms and continue upwards through 15,000, 25,000 and 30,000 rp.

Beyond the Kelapa Mas is the lagoon and there are plenty of small losmen further along the beach. These include *Dewi Bungalows*, *Rama Bungalows* and the *Sindhu Brata Homestay*, three fairly standard losmen right beside the lagoon. Further along the beach the *Puri Oka* offers standard rooms at 25,000 rp and there's a swimming pool. Right at the end of the beach the *Bunga Putri (Princess Flower) Homestay* is picturesquely situated looking back down the coast.

Places to Stay – top end

More expensive places are a relatively recent addition to the Candidasa scene. Coming from Denpasar, *Candi Beach Cottages* is a couple of km before the Candidasa village. It runs a bus to the village twice a day for its guests. Singles/doubles cost from US$60/70 to US$80/90 plus 15.5% tax and service, depending on the room and the season. It's a pleasant new hotel with air-con rooms, pool, tennis courts and full facilities. The distance from Candidasa itself means the beach is a bit better here.

About a km from the centre are the *Rama Ocean View Bungalows* (☎ 0361-51864/5) with similar facilities and style at US$60 to US$65 plus tax and service. *Nirwana Cottages*, immediately before the Rama Ocean View, is a smaller resort with 12 very comfortable individual cottages at US$35 and US$45, a swimming pool and a restaurant.

Continuing towards the centre the *Bali Samudra Indah Hotel* (☎ 0361-23358, 31246) is right beside the Tenganan turn-off at the start of the Candidasa village. This is a rather featureless place aimed squarely at the package-tour market. The hotel's amusing brochure claims that each room's 'comprehensive facilities' include 'hot and cold running water, telephone, discotique!' It goes on to announce that the large swimming pool has a 'sunken bar.' Rooms are US$15/20, US$25/30 or US$35/40 for singles/doubles including breakfast; service and tax are extra.

Right in the centre of Candidasa the *Candidasa Beach Bungalows II* takes considerable liberty with the word 'bungalow': it's a three-storeyed hotel which gives the distinct impression that the maximum number of rooms has been crammed into the minimum amount of space. Singles are US$28 and doubles or twins US$33 to US$40. Breakfast is included but service and tax are extra.

On the side of the road away from the beach *The Watergarden* or *Taman Air* (☎ 0361-35540) is a smaller, low-key resort, like Nirwana Cottages. The rooms are very pleasant and there's a verandah area like a jetty, which projects out over the fish-filled ponds that wind around the buildings. Nightly costs are US$40/45 plus 15.5% tax and service. Taman Air is associated with TJ's restaurant next door.

Finally the *Puri Bagus Beach Hotel* (☎ 0361-51223/6) is right at the end of the beach, hidden away in the palm trees which surround the original fishing village, beyond the lagoon. The nicely designed rooms cost US$55/60 plus service and tax.

Places to Eat

Restaurants in Candidasa are dotted along the main road although, curiously, there are not many right on the waterfront. The fish is usually good.

Working along the road from the Denpasar end some of the more interesting places include *The Coffee Shop*, a quietly relaxed place for lunch or a snack. There's a choice of teas at 500 to 700 rp, wine by the glass for 3500 rp and a range of fresh salad baguettes for 5500 rp.

TJ's Restaurant is related to the popular TJ's in Kuta and certainly looks similar, but the only Mexican dish on the menu here is guacamole. The fish is good at 3750 rp, there's an excellent nasi campur for 3500 rp and from 6.30 to 9.30 pm the 'jukung salad bar' is open, at 3750 rp.

The *Camplung Restaurant, Restaurant Sumber Rasa* and the *Hawaii Restaurant* are all long-term survivors at Candidasa. Straightforward and reasonably priced Indonesian food is the order of the day at Hawaii. The *Puri Amarta*, another place which has been around since Candidasa's early development as a tourist destination, has quite good food in its roadside restaurant.

On the beach side of the road, *Tirtanadi (The TN) Restaurant* is a cheerful place with a long cocktail list. On the other side of the road is the *Kubu Bali Restaurant*, a big place built around a pond with a bright and busy open kitchen area out front where Indonesian/Chinese dishes are turned out with great energy and panache.

Just beyond the lagoon the *Pizzeria Candi Agung* and the *Mandara Giri Pizzaria* display different approaches to spelling although pizza is definitely on the menu at both!

Entertainment

Barong & Rangda, Topeng and Legong dance performances take place at 9 pm at the Pandan Harum in the centre of the Candidasa strip. Entry is 4000 rp.

Getting There & Away

Candidasa is on the main route between Amlapura and Denpasar so any bus or bemo coming by will get you somewhere! The tourist shuttle buses which have become so popular of late also operate to Candidasa. The fare to Denpasar or Kuta airport is 8000 rp, to Ubud 6000 rp or to Singaraja or Lovina Beach 12,000 rp.

AMLAPURA

Amlapura is the main town in the eastern end of Bali and the capital of the Karangasem District. At Amlapura the main road turns north and then bends round west to follow the coast to Singaraja and the north coast. From Ujung, south of Amlapura, there's now a smaller road which follows the coast around Gunung Seraya before rejoining the main road at Culik.

The Karangasem kingdom broke away from the Gelgel kingdom in the late 17th century and 100 years later had become the most powerful kingdom in Bali. Amlapura used to be known as Karangasem, the same as the district, but it was changed after the '63 eruption of Agung in an attempt to get rid of any influences which might provoke a similar eruption!

Information

Amlapura is the smallest of the district capitals, a sleepy place which doesn't seem to have fully woken up from its period of enforced isolation after the '63 eruption of Agung cut the roads to the west of the island. There are banks in Amlapura but it's probably easier to change money in Candidasa.

The Palaces

Amlapura's three palaces are decaying reminders of Karangasem's period as a kingdom. They date from the late 19th and early 20th centuries but only one of the palaces is open for general inspection. You can study the Puri Gede and Puri Kertasura from the outside but special arrangements must be made for an internal inspection.

Admission to Puri Agung (also known as Puri Kanginan) costs 200 rp. There's an

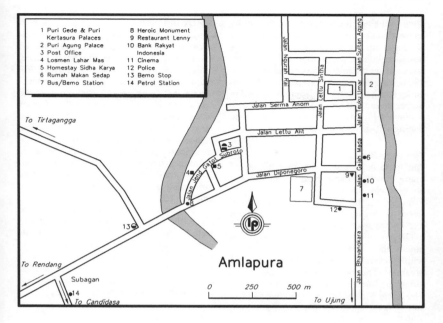

1 Puri Gede & Puri Kertasura Palaces
2 Puri Agung Palace
3 Post Office
4 Losmen Lahar Mas
5 Homestay Sidha Karya
6 Rumah Makan Sedap
7 Bus/Bemo Station
8 Heroic Monument
9 Restaurant Lenny
10 Bank Rakyat Indonesia
11 Cinema
12 Police
13 Bemo Stop
14 Petrol Station

To Tirtagangga

Jalan Serma Anom
Jalan Lettu Alit
Jalan Diponegoro

To Rendang
Subagan
To Candidasa

Amlapura

0   250   500 m

To Ujung

impressive three-tiered entry gate and beautiful sculptured panels on the outside of the main building. After you pass through the entry courtyard a left turn takes you to the Bale London, so called because of the British royal crest on the furniture. The decrepit building is not open to the public, as a solitary elderly member of the old royal family still lives there.

A right turn from the entrance leads to the main palace courtyard. The main building is known as Maskerdam, after Amsterdam in the Netherlands, because it was the Karangasem kingdom's acquiescence to Dutch rule which allowed it to hang on long after the demise of the other Balinese kingdoms. This may be your best opportunity to view a Balinese palace but it's certainly not impressive. A number of old photographs and paintings of the royal family are displayed on the verandah. You can buy an explanation sheet at the palace entry desk.

Inside you can see into several rooms including the royal bedroom and a living room with furniture which was a gift from the Dutch royal family. On the other side of this main courtyard is the Balai Kambang, surrounded by a pond like the similar but better preserved Bale Kambang in the palace grounds at Klungkung. The Balai Pemandesan was used for royal tooth-filing and cremation ceremonies, while the Balai Lunjuk was used for other religious ceremonies.

There are other courtyards around the main one. It's said that about 150 members of the old family and their servants still live in this slowly deteriorating relic of a now-forgotten era of Balinese history.

Ujung Water Palace

A few km beyond Amlapura, on the road down to the sea, is the Ujung Water Palace, an extensive, picturesque and crumbling complex. It has been deteriorating for some time but a great deal more damage has been done to it since the mid-70s, principally by an earthquake in 1979. The last king of Karangasem, Anak Agung Anglurah, was obsessed with moats, pools, canals and fountains and he completed this grand palace in 1921. You can wander around the pleasant park, admire the view from the pavilion higher up the hill above the rice paddies or continue a little further down the road to the fishing village on the coast.

Places to Stay

Amlapura has a few places to stay but not many travellers pause here – Candidasa is not far away and it's only another six km to Tirtagangga. If, for some reason, you're intent on staying here there are two options a few steps apart, just as you enter town.

On your left, opposite the heroic war monument, the *Losmen Lahar Mas* has rooms with toilet and shower at 10,000 rp including breakfast. The rooms surround a large common-room area and are quite comfortable. The Lahar Mas backs on to the rice paddies and visitors report that it's a pleasant place with friendly people.

On the other side of the road, a short distance in towards the centre, *Homestay Sidha Karya* was Amlapura's original losmen but most visitors deserted it as soon as there was accommodation at Tirtagangga. Rooms at the homestay are slightly cheaper than the Lahar Mas. A third possibility is the *Losmen Kembang Ramaja*, just out of Amlapura on the Rendang road.

Places to Eat

There's the usual collection of rumah makans and warungs around the bus station plus the *Restaurant Lenny* and the *Rumah Makan Sedap* on Jalan Gajah Mada. Amlapura tends to shut down early so don't leave your evening meal until too late.

Getting There & Away

Although Amlapura is the 'end of the road' for bus services from Denpasar, there are buses from here to Singaraja and the north coast.

TIRTAGANGGA

Amlapura's water-loving rajah, having constructed his masterpiece at Ujung, later had another go at Tirtagangga. This water palace, built around 1947, was damaged in the 1963 eruption of Agung and during the political events that wracked Indonesia around the same time. Nevertheless, it's still a place of beauty and solitude and a reminder of the power the Balinese rajahs once had. The palace has a swimming pool as well as the ornamental ponds. Entrance to the water palace is 200 rp (children 100 rp) and another 700 rp (children 200 rp) to use the fine swimming pool (500 rp for the lower one, children 100 rp).

The rice terraces around Tirtagangga are reputed to be some of the most beautiful in Bali. They sweep out from Tirtagangga almost like a sea surrounding an island. Note how some of the terraces are faced with stones. A few km beyond here, on the road around the east coast to Singaraja, there are more dramatically beautiful terraces.

Information

Tirtagangga is such a popular little enclave these days that there's even a moneychanger, but don't count on it always being in operation. Candidasa is the nearest reliable place to change money.

Places to Stay & Eat

Right by the water palace is the peaceful *Losmen Dhangin Taman Inn* with rooms at 7000, 8000, 10,000 and 15,000 rp including breakfast. The most expensive rooms are large and have an enclosed sitting area. You can sit in the courtyard, gazing across the rice paddies and the water palace while doves coo in the background. The losmen owner here is very amusing and the food is not bad although the warung nearest the losmen also does excellent food. This was the original Tirtagangga losmen.

Actually within the palace compound the *Tirta Ayu Homestay* has pleasant individual bungalows at 20,000 rp including admission to the water palace swimming pools. The restaurant has a superb outlook over the palace pools.

Alternatively you can continue 300 metres beyond the water palace and climb the steep steps to the *Kusuma Jaya Inn*. The 'Homestay on the Hill' has a fine view over the rice paddies and rooms at 8000 to 15,000 rp including breakfast and dinner. Lunch is also available and the owners have information about local walks.

Across the road from the palace the *Rijasa Homestay* is a small and simple place with extremely neat and clean rooms at 5000/7000, 6000/8000 and 10,000/15,000 rp, all including breakfast and tea. A few steps back towards Amlapura the *Taman Sari Inn* has rooms at 7000 rp and 8000 rp but looks rather derelict.

Getting There & Away

Tirtagangga is about five or six km from the Amlapura turn-off on the main road that runs around the eastern end of Bali. Bemos from Amlapura cost 250 rp. Buses continue on the main road to Singaraja.

TIRTAGANGGA TO TULAMBEN

Soon after leaving Tirtagangga, the road starts to climb. Look for the sign to Pura Lempuyang, one of Bali's nine 'directional temples'. From the turn-off, there is a steep and winding road for eight km which stops just short of the temple. Lempuyang is perched on a hilltop at 768 metres.

Further on, the main road climbs over a small range of hills and passes by some of the most spectacular rice terraces in Bali. They're the last rice paddies for some distance, however, for this part of Bali is relatively dry and barren.

The road gets back down towards sea level at Culik and thereafter closely follows the coast, though rarely right beside it. There's a good beach near Culik but the main feature of this route is the superb view of Gunung Agung. On this stretch of coast, Bali's mightiest mountain descends to meet the sea, its slopes beckoning climbers. The road crosses a great number of dry riverbeds, most of them too wide to be easily bridged and, in

the dry season at least, showing no sign of water. They're probably similar to many rivers in Australia, running briefly during the heavy rains of the wet season but remaining dry for the rest of the year.

TULAMBEN

The small village of Tulamben has the only places to stay around the east coast. The beach here is composed of pebbles rather than sand but the water is clear and the snorkelling good. In June and July there's good windsurfing but Tulamben's prime attraction is the huge WW II wreck of a US cargo ship.

The recently constructed losmen at Tulamben make this an interesting place to pause on your way around the barren east coast.

The Wreck of the Liberty

On 11 January 1942 the armed US cargo ship USAT *Liberty* was torpedoed by a Japanese submarine about 15 km south-west of Lombok. It was taken in tow by the destroyers HMNS *Van Ghent* and USS *Paul Jones* with the intention of beaching it on the coast of Bali and retrieving its cargo of raw rubber and railway parts. When its condition looked perilous the crew were evacuated and, although it was successfully beached, the rapid spread of the war through Indonesia prevented the cargo from being saved.

Built in 1915, the *Liberty* sat on the beach at Tulamben, a prominent east coast landmark, until 1963 when the violent eruption of Gunung Agung toppled it beneath the surface. Or at least that's one version of the story. Another relates that it sank some distance offshore and the lava flow from the eruption extended the shoreline almost out to the sunken vessel. Whatever the course of events it lies just 40 or 50 metres offshore, almost parallel to the beach with its bow only a couple of metres below the surface.

It's within easy reach of snorkellers although scuba divers, who make frequent trips from Candidasa, Balina Beach and other diving centres, get the best views of this very impressive wreck. The bow is in quite good shape, the midships region is badly mangled and the stern is intact. Snorkellers can easily swim around the bow which is heavily encrusted with coral and a haven for colourful fish. The ship is more than 100 metres long – this is a *big* wreck – and as you follow it back, it soon disappears into the depths. Scuba dives are generally made at depths from 10 to 30 metres.

To find the wreck simply walk about 100 metres north of the Gandu Mayu Bungalows, the northernmost beach losmen, to the small white building by the beach. It's liberally plastered with dive-shop stickers and when there's a dive group on the wreck you'll see Balinese girls shuttling back and forth from the losmen car park toting air tanks elegantly balanced on their heads. Swim straight out from the white building and you'll suddenly see this huge wreck rearing up from the depths.

Places to Stay & Eat

Until the late '80s there was no place to stay on the east coast from Tirtagangga to Yeh Sanih. Now the original losmen constructed here has been joined by two more.

Paradise Palm Beach Bungalows, the village's first accommodation, is a cheerful little losmen right on the beach. Singles/ doubles cost 10,000/15,000 rp with breakfast. The rooms are neat, clean and well kept with bamboo chairs and a table on the verandahs. The garden is lovely and, at night, there is electricity.

Alternatives are the *Bali Timur Bungalows* at 10,000 rp, just on the Amlapura side, and the *Gandu Maya Bungalows* at 12,000 rp, on the other side. Because the Gandu Maya is closest to the wreck, dive trips usually stop there.

TULAMBEN TO YEH SANIH

Beyond Tulamben the road continues to skirt the slopes of Agung, with frequent evidence of lava flows from the '63 eruption. Beyond Agung, Gunung Abang and then the outer crater of Gunung Batur also slope down to the sea. Shortly before Yeh Sanih there's a famous (but not very interesting) horse bath

at Tejakula. You can turn inland to the interesting village of Sembiran just before Yeh Sanih.

AMLAPURA TO RENDANG

The Amlapura to Rendang road branches off from the Amlapura to Denpasar road just a km or two out of Amlapura. The road gradually climbs up into the foothills of Gunung Agung, running through some pretty countryside. It's a quieter, less-travelled route than the Amlapura to Denpasar road, which is very busy between Klungkung and Denpasar. At Rendang you meet the Klungkung to Besakih road close to the junction for the very pretty minor road across to Bangli.

The road runs through Bebandem (which has a busy market every three days), Sibetan and Selat before reaching Rendang. Sibetan and Rendang are both well known for the salaks grown there. If you've not tried this delicious fruit with its curious 'snakeskin' covering then this may be the time to do so. It's worth diverting a km or so at Putung to enjoy the fantastic view down to the coast. Only here do you realise just how high up you have climbed.

Shortly before Selat you can take a road that runs south-west through Iseh and Sideman and meets the Amlapura to Klungkung road. The German artist Walter Spies lived in Iseh for some time from 1932. Later, the Swiss painter Theo Meier, nearly as famous as Spies for his influence on Balinese art, lived in the same house.

Although the route from Amlapura to Rendang is fine with your own transport it can be time-consuming by bemo, requiring frequent changes and lots of waiting. Taking the busier coastal route to Gianyar is much faster.

Places to Stay

Three km along the Rendang (or Bebandem) road from the junction as you leave Amlapura, *Homestay Lila* is a very pretty little place in the rice paddies. It's quiet and well away from everything, an ideal place to relax. The individual bungalows have bathrooms and a verandah out front, but no electricity. Singles/doubles cost 6000/10,000 rp including breakfast – there's nowhere else to eat in the area but the homestay also prepares other meals. It's a half-hour walk from the homestay to Bukit Kusambi.

Further along towards Rendang, 11 km beyond Bebandem, you can turn off the road a km or so to the superbly situated *Putung Bungalows*. On the edge of a ridge, the bungalows overlook the coast far, far below. You can see large ships anchored off Padangbai and across to Nusa Penida. There are two-storeyed bungalows, with a bathroom and small sitting area downstairs and also 'losmen-class' rooms. Prices start at 20,000 rp. Putung Bungalows also has a restaurant.

BANGLI

Half-way up the slope to Penelokan the town of Bangli, once the capital of a kingdom, is said to have the best climate in Bali. It also has a very fine temple and quite a pleasant place to stay. Bangli is a convenient place from which to visit Besakih, and makes a good base for exploring the area. However, there's one catch in Bangli – the dogs are even worse than Ubud.

Pura Kehen

At the top end of the town, Pura Kehen, the state temple of the Bangli kingdom, is terraced up the hillside. A great flight of steps leads up to the temple entrance and the first courtyard, with its huge banyan tree, has colourful Chinese porcelain plates set into the walls as decoration. Unfortunately most of them are now damaged. The inner courtyard has an 11-roofed meru (Balinese shrine) and a shrine with thrones for the three figures of the Hindu trinity – Brahma, Shiva and Vishnu. This is one of the finest temples in Bali. There's a large arts centre just round the corner from the Pura Kehen.

Bukit Demulih

Three km from Bangli, along the Tampaksiring road, is Bukit Demulih, a hill just off the south side of the road. If you can't find the sign pointing to it, ask local children to direct you. You can make the short climb to the top

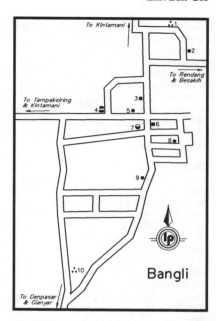

1	Pura Kehen
2	Arts Centre
3	Losmen Dharmaputra
4	Post Office
5	Cinema
6	Artha Sastra Inn
7	Bus Stop
8	Market
9	Telephone Office
10	Pura Dalem Penunggekan

where there's a small temple and good views back over Bangli, or you can walk along the ridge line to a viewpoint where all of southern Bali spreads out below. You can see the long sweep of Sanur Beach with the Hotel Bali Beach, a minuscule rectangular box, far away.

Pura Dalem Penunggekan

Just below Bangli, beside the road to Gianyar, there's an interesting temple of the dead, the Pura Dalem Penunggekan. The reliefs on the front illustrate particularly vivid scenes of wrongdoers getting their just deserts in the afterlife. In one panel, a demon rapes a woman while other demons simultaneously stab and castrate a man. Elsewhere in the same panel demons gouge out eyes and a particularly toothy demon takes a bite out of some ne'er-do-well. On an adjoining panel unfortunate sinners are hung by their heels from a tree branch and roasted over a fire.

Places to Stay & Eat

The *Artha Sastra Inn* is a former palace residence and still run by the grandson of the last king of Bangli. Rooms, some with private bathrooms, cost from 10,000 to 20,000 rp. It's a pleasant, friendly place, quite popular and very centrally located – right across from the bus station and main square.

The *Losmen Dharmaputra*, a short distance up the road towards Kintamani, is a YHA affiliate. It's cheaper but also fairly basic. Rather drab singles/doubles cost 6000/8000 rp and you can also get food there.

Bangli has a good night market (pasar malam) in the square opposite the Artha Sastra and there are some great warungs but they all close early.

BESAKIH

Perched nearly 1000 metres up the side of Gunung Agung is Bali's most important temple, Pura Besakih. In all, it comprises about 30 separate temples in seven terraces up the hill, all within one enormous complex. The temple was probably first constructed more than 1000 years ago; 500 years later, it became the state temple of the powerful Gelgel and Klungkung kingdoms. Today, it's the 'mother temple' of all Bali – every district in Bali has its own shrine or temple at Besakih and just about every Balinese god you care to name is also honoured there. Apart from its size and majestic location, Besakih is also probably the best kept temple you'll see on the island. This is not a temple simply built and then left to slowly decay.

As well as being the Balinese mother temple, Besakih is also the 'mother' of Balinese financial efforts. You pay to park, pay to enter, pay to rent a scarf and then brave the usual large collection of souvenir sellers. And, after all that, it's quite possible you'll find the inner courtyards are all closed to visitors!

The temple is definitely impressive, but you do not need a guide to see it. So if someone latches on to you and begins to tell you about the temple, let them know quickly whether you want their services. Without a firm no, they'll continue being a guide and expect to be paid at the end; whatever you pay them, however, is certainly not going to be enough – they have no qualms about asking for more.

Places to Stay

About five km below Besakih the *Arca Valley Inn* has rooms and a restaurant. It's prettily situated in a valley by a bend in the road. This is a good place to stay if you want to climb Gunung Agung from Besakih and want an early start. There is also a losmen close to the temple entrance.

Getting There & Away

The usual route to Besakih is by bus or bemo to Klungkung from where there are regular bemos up the hill to the temple for 750 rp.

If you have your own wheels, take the left fork about a km before the temple ignoring the 'No Entry' sign. This fork brings you to a car park close to the entrance. The right fork ends about half a km from the temple, leaving you with a long walk up the entrance road or a little hassling with the motorbike gang who'll offer to ferry you up there. The first price is usually 1000 rp. You can't take your own bike up the entrance road.

The 'guardhouse' on the right fork is a bit of a scam as well. Here they'll try and get you to sign a visitor's book where you'll find that lots of previous foreign guests have dispensed little donations, like 50,000 rp! Taking the left fork not only brings you out closer to the temple, it also bypasses the souvenir sellers and 'donation' collectors.

GUNUNG AGUNG

You can climb 3142-metre-high Gunung Agung, Bali's highest and most revered mountain, from the village of Sorga or from Pura Besakih. To get to Sorga, turn off the Amlapura to Rendang road at Selat and follow the road up the slopes of the mountain to Sebudi and finally Sorga. This area was devastated by the 1963 eruption. From Sorga the road ends and the walking begins, first to the temple of Pasar Agung and then to the holy spring of Tirta Mas. From the spring it takes about two hours to reach the summit. You can either make an early start from Sorga and climb all the way to the top in one go or start late in the afternoon and camp at Tirta Mas. The spring is just below the tree line and a good base for an early ascent the next morning.

If you want to climb Gunung Agung from Besakih you must leave no later than 6.30 am. From either starting point it's a pretty tough climb. It's easy to get lost on the lower trails so it's worth hiring a guide. They're available in Sorga or at Besakih. The cost could be anything from 15,000 to 30,000 rp depending on the size of your party, plus a few thousand rp as a tip. Take plenty of food and water, an umbrella, waterproof clothing, a warm woollen sweater and a torch (flashlight) with extra batteries – just in case you don't get back down by nightfall.

The following is one climber's account of the ascent from Besakih:

We were approached by a young man named Gede who told us that he could take us up Gunung Agung the next day. It's unwise to attempt Agung without a guide, as there are numerous trails leading in all directions in the early stages of the climb. In the later stages there are also a few choices, some of them less dangerous, some more time-consuming. Generally, the guides will have been to the top on a number of occasions. They are all particularly fit and strong and will carry your day pack for you.

The cost of a guide depends on how many are going to climb and on how hard you bargain. We met a party of three on their way down who had started climbing at 1 am and given up at 7 am, only an hour or two from the top. Their guide had cost 22,000 rp.

Our day pack contained three litres of water, three packs of Marie biscuits, half a dozen bananas and a few fistfuls of boiled sweets as we set out from our losmen at 5.15 am. It was cold so we were glad of our woollen sweaters. After walking through the temple we hit upon a very narrow path. It was very dark and humid here and we would have been lost without our torches. Our guide was setting a roaring pace, so it wasn't long before our sweaters became a burden. Gradually the path steepened and although it was now daylight, the vegetation was very thick and we often lost sight of our guide as he surged ahead. Eventually, the way became so steep that we had to grab onto roots or branches to pull ourselves up the track.

After about three hours of oppressive humidity there was a rather sudden change in terrain. The vegetation all but disappeared and we found ourselves at the base of a slope made entirely of small fragments of volcanic rock. With perseverance, we made it through this slippery section to a point where we had to haul ourselves up onto a ledge above the slope. Briefly, the ground levelled out for the first time in around three hours – a great relief! (This was where we met the vanquished trio who had started out at 1 am. To have come so far and then turned back must have been very painful.) I found it hard to imagine that the climb could become more difficult, yet our guide assured us that 'most' people turned back somewhere between our present position and the top.

A 10-minute rest was followed by a new phase in the ascent. We spent the next hour scrambling up what seemed like an endless slope. With no path to follow, it was a matter of clawing our way from one rock to the next, and there was only one way to go – up. Looking back down the 'hill' only brought fear to my heart as I became convinced I would fall off the mountain into oblivion. Unfortunately, the lichen-covered rock was not as sturdy as it looked. On many occasions during that hour I would grab a rock only to find it crumble in my hand. It's important to be alert on this section, which is probably the steepest part of the climb.

Finally, we reached the top of the lichen field and the summit was in view – or so we thought. The way was no longer as steep, but had become very narrow. This was the beginning of the summit ridge, which was no wider than two metres and in some places less than a metre. It took another half hour to reach the summit along this ridge. From both sides of the ridge the mountain dropped away with alarming steepness. The wind was also very strong and we began to notice the altitude, needing to catch our breath every five minutes or so. With the thought of plunging off the mountain into infinity ever present, we pressed on.

There was only room for one person to stand on the actual summit. The wind was positively biting but the view was breathtaking. It was also brief. From Besakih we had climbed some 2200 vertical metres to an altitude of 3142 metres (10,300 feet). We reached the summit at around 10 am and had looked at the view for no more than a few seconds when the clouds rolled in. An icy dew formed on our arms and legs. Our guide showed us his thermometer – it was 3°C! There was nowhere to hide from the cold and the wind, so we headed off along the ridge toward the crater some 10 to 15 minutes away.

I peered nervously over the edge into the gaping abyss. There appeared to be no bottom. My nose, ears and hands were stinging and I wanted desperately to get off the summit ridge and out of the cold.

We arrived back in Besakih at 3 pm after some four hours of slipping and sliding our way down Agung. Our knees were swollen and painful, our arms and legs were covered in small cuts and abrasions and we were covered from head to toe in grime. To an inexperienced mountaineer like myself this had been an epic climb. I number it among the great experiences of my life but wouldn't do it again if you paid me.

Mark Balla

South-West Bali

Most of the places regularly visited in south-western Bali, like Sangeh or Tanah Lot, are easy day trips from Denpasar. The rest of the west tends to be a region travellers zip through on their way to or from Java. In the latter half of the last century this was an area of warring kingdoms, but with the Dutch takeover, the princes' lands were redistributed among the general population. With this bounty of rich agricultural land the region around Tabanan quickly became one of the wealthiest parts of Bali.

Further west two spectacular roads head inland across the central mountains to the north coast. Even further west the rugged hills are sparsely populated and the agricultural potential is limited by the low rainfall. Much of the area is a virtual wilderness and is part of the Bali Barat National Park (see the North Bali chapter for details). There are periodic rumours of the continued existence of the Balinese tiger, but no evidence to support them.

Along the southern coast there are long stretches of wide black-sand beach and rolling surf. Here the main road runs close to the coast but never actually on it, so you rarely catch a glimpse of the sea. Countless tracks run south of the main road, usually to fishing villages which rarely see a tourist despite being so close to a main transport route.

Getting There & Away

Buses to western Bali generally leave from the Ubung station in Denpasar. Costs are around 3500 rp to Gilimanuk, 3000 rp to Negara and 900 rp to Mengwi.

SEMPIDI, LUKLUK & KAPAL

Kapal is the garden gnome and temple curlicue centre of Bali. If you're building a new temple and need a balustrade for a stairway, a capping for a wall, a curlicue for the top of a roof, or any of the other countless standard architectural motifs then the numerous shops which line the road through Kapal will probably have what you need. Or if you want some garden ornamentation, from a comic book deer to a brightly painted Buddha then again you've come to the right place.

Lukluk's pura dalem (temple of the dead) and Sempidi's three pura desa (temples of the spirits) are all worth inspecting but Kapal's Pura Sadat is the most important temple in the area. Although it was restored after WW II (it was damaged in an earthquake earlier this century), the Sadat is a very ancient temple, possibly dating back to the 12th century.

TANAH LOT

The spectacularly placed Tanah Lot is possibly the best known and most photographed temple in Bali. It's almost certainly the most visited – the tourist crowds here are phenomenal, the gauntlet of souvenir hawkers to be run is appalling and the commercial hype is terrible. Signs direct you to the best place to photograph the sunset, and the faithful line up, cameras poised, ready to capture the hallowed moment.

It's easy to see why Tanah Lot is such an attraction – its setting is fantastic. The temple is perched on a little rocky islet, connected to the shore at low tide but cut off as the tide rolls in. It looks superb whether delicately lit by the dawn light or starkly outlined at sunset.

It's also an important temple – one of the venerated sea temples respected in similar fashion to the great mountain temples. Like Pura Luhur Ulu Watu, at the southern end of the island, Tanah Lot is closely associated with the legendary priest Nirartha. It's said that Nirartha passed by here and, impressed with the tiny island's superb setting, suggested to local villagers that this would be a good place to construct a temple. There's a small charge to enter the temple.

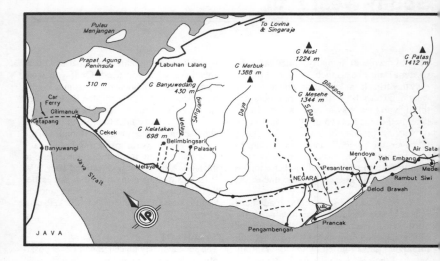

Getting There & Away

Tanah Lot is reached by turning off the Denpasar to Gilimanuk road at Kediri and taking the road straight down to the coast. From Denpasar you'll have to take a bemo from Ubung to Kediri (600 rp) then another to the coast (about 250 rp). There is no regular service out of Tanah Lot and, after sunset, when all the visitors have disappeared, you may find the car park empty. Your only options may be to charter a bemo or walk. If you have your own wheels, leave early to miss the tourist jam.

MENGWI

The huge state temple of Pura Taman Ayun, surrounded by a wide moat, was the main temple of the kingdom which ruled from Mengwi until 1891. The kingdom split from the Gelgel dynasty, centred near Klungkung in eastern Bali. The temple was originally built in 1634 and extensively renovated in 1937. It's a very large, spacious temple and the elegant moat gives it a very fine appearance. The first courtyard is a large, open grassy expanse and the inner courtyard has a multitude of merus (multi-tiered shrines).

In a beautiful setting across the moat from the temple is a rather lost-looking arts centre. Built in the early '70s it became an almost instant white elephant and today is beginning to take on the ageless look of all Balinese architecture. There's also a small museum. The *Water Palace Restaurant* overlooking the moat is not a bad place for lunch.

BLAYU

In Blayu, a small village between Mengwi and Marga, traditional songket sarongs are woven with intricate gold threads. These are for ceremonial use only, not for everyday wear.

MARGA

Near Mengwi stands a peculiar memorial to Lt Colonel I Gusti Ngurah Rai who, in 1946, led his men in a futile defence against a larger and better armed Dutch force. The Dutch, trying to recover Bali after the departure of the Japanese, had called in air support but the Balinese refused to surrender. The outcome was similar to the puputans of 40 years before; all 94 of Ngurah Rai's men were killed. Denpasar's airport is named in his memory.

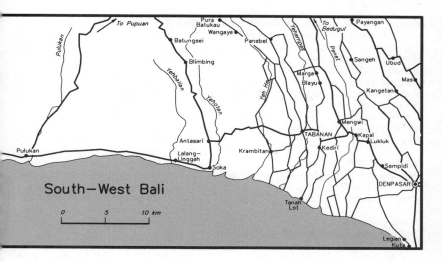

SANGEH

About 20 km north of Denpasar, near the village of Sangeh, stands the monkey forest of Bukit Sari. It is featured, so the Balinese say, in the *Ramayana*. To kill the evil Rawana, king of Lanka, Hanuman had to crush him between two halves of Mahameru, the holy mountain. Rawana, who could not be destroyed on the earth or in the air, would thus be squeezed between the two. On his way to performing this task, Hanuman dropped a piece of the mountain near Sangeh, complete with a band of monkeys. Of course, this sort of legend isn't unique – Hanuman dropped chunks of landscape all over the place!

There's a unique grove of nutmeg trees in the monkey forest and a temple, Pura Bukit Sari, with an interesting old garuda statue. Plus, of course, there are lots of monkeys. They're very worldly monkeys, well aware of what the visiting tourists have probably bought from the local vendors – peanuts! Take care, for the monkeys will jump all over you if you've got a pocketful of peanuts and don't dispense them fast enough. The Sangeh monkeys have also been known to steal tourists' hats, sunglasses and even, as they

run away, their thongs! A new variation on this mischief has been created by some local people, who reclaim the items from the monkeys and then charge a ransom for their return.

There are also plenty of Balinese jumping on you, clamouring to sell you anything from a sarong to a carved wooden flute. This place is geared to tourists.

Getting There & Away

You can reach Sangeh by bemos which run direct from Denpasar but there is also a road across from Mengwi and from Ubud.

TABANAN

Tabanan is in the heart of the rice belt of southern Bali, the most fertile and prosperous rice-growing area on the island. It's also a great centre for dancing and gamelan playing. Mario, the renowned dancer of the prewar period, who perfected the Kebyar dance and is featured in Covarrubias' classic guide to Bali, was from Tabanan.

AROUND TABANAN

Near Tabanan is Kediri, where Pasar Hewan is one of Bali's busiest markets for cattle and other animals. A little beyond Tabanan a road turns down to the coast through Krambitan, a village noted for its beautiful old buildings, including two 17th century palaces.

About 10 km south of Tabanan is the village of Pejaten, which is a centre for the production of traditional pottery, including elaborate, ornamental roof tiles. Porcelain clay objects, made for purely decorative use, can be seen in the Pejaten Ceramics Workshop.

TABANAN TO NEGARA

There's some beautiful scenery but little tourist development along the 74 km of coast between Tabanan and Negara.

Lalang-Linggah

The *Balian Beach Club* overlooks the Balian River (Yehbalian) and is surrounded by coconut plantations. There are bunk beds for 6000 rp plus bungalows at 8000/10,000 rp or a pavilion for 25,000 rp. To get to Lalang-Linggah from Denpasar, take any Negara or Gilimanuk bus and ask the driver to stop at the 49.6 km post.

Medewi

About 30 km from Soka, and 25 km before Negara, a large but faded sign announces the sideroad south to 'Medewi Surfing Point'. The turn-off is just west of Pulukan village. Medewi is noted for its *long* left-hand wave – if you catch one of these on a good day you should bring a packed lunch.

There are now two places to stay near the beach. The *Hotel Nirwana*, on the west side of the road, has rooms for 15,000 to 20,000 rp. The restaurant has standard fare for slightly higher than standard prices. The *Medewi Beach Cottages* on the other side of the road are new, luxurious and cost 45,000/65,000 rp for singles/doubles. For bottom-end accommodation, there's a losmen on the main road.

Rambut Siwi

Between Air Satang and Yeh Embang, a short diversion off the main road leads to the beautiful coastal temple of Pura Luhur at Rambut Siwi. Picturesquely situated on a cliff top overlooking a long, wide stretch of beach, this superb temple with its numerous

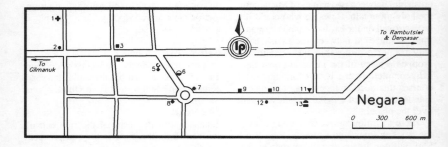

1 Hospital	8 Bank
2 Telephone	9 Hotel Ana
3 Losmen & Rumah Makan Taman Sari	10 Hotel & Restaurant Wirapada
4 Hotel Ijo Gading	11 Rumah Makan Puas
5 Mosque	12 Petrol Station
6 Bus station	13 Post Office
7 Market	

shady frangipani trees is one of the important coastal temples of southern Bali. There are two caves in the base of the cliff. It is said that one cave houses a dragon and the other extends through the mountains to Singaraja. The caves are sacred and visitors are asked not to enter.

Delod Brawah

Beyond Rambut Siwi, and seven km before Negara, is the turn-off to Delod Brawah. The beach here, four km off the main road, is reputed to be good for windsurfing.

NEGARA

Negara, the capital of the Jembrana District, comes alive each year when the bullock races take place between July and October. These normally docile creatures charge down a two-km stretch of road pulling tiny chariots. Riders often stand on top of the chariots forcing the bullocks on. The winner, however, is not necessarily first past the post. Style also plays a part and points are awarded for the most elegant runner!

Places to Stay & Eat

Hotel Ana, on Jalan Ngurah Rai, the main street through town, is a standard losmen with rooms at around 3000, 5000 and 7000 rp. Nearby is the *Hotel & Restaurant Wirapada* (☎ 41161), at Jalan Ngurah Rai 107, which costs 12,500 rp including breakfast or 18,500 rp for a room with a shower. The Wirapada serves good food, as does the *Rumah Makan Puas*, a little further east on the same street.

The Denpasar to Gilimanuk road, which bypasses the town centre, has several accommodation possibilities. *Hotel Ijo Gading*, at Jalan Nakula 5, is clean and friendly and has singles/doubles from 7500 to 10,000 rp. The *Losmen & Rumah Makan Taman Sari*, at Jalan Nakula 18, has rooms from 6000 rp.

GILIMANUK

At the far western end of the island, Gilimanuk is the terminus for ferries which shuttle back and forth across the narrow strait to Java. There's a bus station and a market on the main street about a km from the ferry port. Most travellers buy combined bus and ferry tickets and don't need to stop in Gilimanuk. There's little of interest here for the traveller anyway, it's just an arrival and departure point.

Gilimanuk is off the main road. About a km on the Denpasar side from the junction is a curious pagoda-like structure with a spiral stairway around the outside. In the same area, Cekek is supposed to be the headquarters and information office for the Bali Barat National Park. Although there's an impressive visitors' centre with a large car park and a children's playground, it seems to be locked up and deserted. If you want information about the park, go to the office at Labuhan Lalang, further north, which is the most interesting part of the park anyway.

For more information about the park, or the route from Gilimanuk to the north coast, see the North Bali chapter.

Places to Stay

Most people simply zip straight through Gilimanuk, but if you do have a reason to stay, there are several places along Jalan Raya, the main road into the port. Within a km or so of the ferry port you'll find *Homestay Gili Sari*, *Homestay Surya* and *Lestari Homestay*.

Central Mountains

Bali, as you'll quickly realise from a glance at one of the three-dimensional terrain models so common in Balinese hotels, has lots of mountains. Most are volcanoes, some dormant, some definitely active. The mountains divide the gentle sweep of fertile rice land to the south from the narrower strip to the north. In eastern Bali there's a small clump of mountains right at the end of the island, beyond Amlapura. Then there's the mighty volcano Gunung Agung (3142 metres), the island's mother mountain. North-west of Agung is the great crater of Batur with its lake and smaller volcano inside. In central Bali, around Bedugul, is another group of mountains, while yet another series of mountains stretches off to the sparsely inhabited western region.

The popular round trip to the north coast crosses the mountains on one route (from Bangli or Tampaksiring to Penelokan, Kintamani and Gunung Batur), and returns on another (from Singaraja on the coast back through Lake Bratan and Bedugul to Denpasar), thus covering most of the mountain region.

It's often said that the Balinese look away from the sea (the home of demons and monsters) and towards the mountains (the abode of the gods). But although they may look towards the mountains, the Balinese don't actually live on them. The true Balinese heartland is the gentle, fertile land rising up to the mountains. The mountain villages tend to be strange, often chilly and cloudy places.

PENELOKAN

The roads up to Batur from Bangli and from Tampaksiring meet just before reaching the crater rim at Penelokan, a spectacular place. The road runs along the narrow rim of the crater, with superb views across to Gunung Batur and down to Lake Batur at the bottom of the crater. Penelokan appropriately means 'place to look'. At the far end of the crater road, at Penulisan, you can look back into the crater or turn the other way and see Bali's northern coastline spread out at your feet, far below.

At Penelokan, where a sideroad runs down into the crater to Kedisan, the views are particularly stunning. Penelokan is a popular place to stay, but those intending to tour the lake or climb the mountain might find it more convenient to stay at Kedisan or Tirta, at the bottom of the crater.

Information

If you arrive in your own vehicle you will be charged a fee as you enter Penelokan. It's not clear whether this is for parking or for entry to the area, but it costs 1000 rp for a car with one person. Keep the ticket if you plan to drive back and forth around the crater rim or you may have to pay again.

Even apart from this fee, Penelokan has a reputation as a money-grubbing place where you're constantly importuned to buy things and where you need to keep an eye on your gear. Many visitors come to Gunung Batur on day trips organised by their (expensive) hotels, stopping for lunch at Penelokan. Hence the selling style of the hawkers, who have trained themselves to make their pitch and close the deal quickly. The only thing sure to discourage them is the arrival of a bus-load of tourists more affluent than yourself.

It can get surprisingly chilly up here so come prepared. Clouds often roll in over the crater, sometimes getting hung up along the rim and making all the crater rim towns cold and miserable places to be.

Places to Stay

There are several places to stay in Penelokan, a couple teetering right on the edge of the crater. Apart from the views, these are just basic losmen with basic prices, though prices will change depending on what the owners reckon the market will bear.

If you arrive from the south, the first place

in Penelokan is the *Caldera Batur*, which has a great view and may even rent rooms if you can find any staff. A little further along, the *Lakeview Restaurant & Homestay* (☎ 32023), which clings to the crater rim, has economy rooms for US$8 and more comfortable bungalow-style rooms with bathroom for US$15. The economy rooms are impossibly small – if the beds weren't so tiny and narrow they wouldn't be able to get two in a room. Ah, but the view, the view...!

Continuing past the road down into the crater, you come to *Losmen & Restaurant Gunawan*. Again, the view is terrific, the economy rooms are tiny at 10,000 rp and the better, bungalow-style rooms cost from 15,000 rp.

Places to Eat

Along the road between Penelokan and Kintamani you'll find a crowd of restaurants which are geared to bus-loads of tour groups. All the restaurants have fine views and all prepare buffet-style lunches at international tourist prices. The restaurants, from Penelokan to Kintamani, include the *Lakeview, Batur Garden, Gunawan, Puri Selera, Puri Aninditha* and the *Kintamani Restaurant*. Lunch costs from around 10,000 rp if you order from the menu. Of course there are also cheap warungs along the main road like the *Warung Makan Ani Asih* or the *Warung Makan Sederhana*.

Getting There & Away

To get to Penelokan from Denpasar, you can either get a Kintamani-bound bemo from Batubulan station (1700 rp) which will pass through Penelokan, or you can take one of the more frequent bemos to Gianyar (700 rp) or Bangli (1000 rp) first and then another from there up the mountain. To get to Penelokan from Ubud, go first to Gianyar. Bemos shuttle back and forth fairly regularly between Penelokan and Kintamani (300 rp) and less frequently down to the lakeside at Kedisan (500 rp).

The two main routes up the mountains to Penelokan (through Gianyar and Tampaksiring) meet just before you get to Penelokan. There are, however, lesser roads which are being improved and are OK for motorbikes and the standard Suzuki rental cars, but have very little public transport. (See the Ubud to Batur section in the Ubud & Around chapter for details.) You could, for example, follow the road which starts out around the crater rim then drops down to Rendang, joining the Rendang to Besakih road at Menanga. If the weather's clear you'll have fine views of Gunung Agung along this route.

Most of the rivers and streams in this area run from north to south, and most of the roads run between them. The few east to west roads tend to be very rough with lots of creek crossings and plenty of opportunities to get lost. Consequently the country to the west of Batur, though not remote, is seldom visited.

Getting Around

From Penelokan you can hike around the crater rim to Gunung Abang (2152 metres), the high point of the outer rim. You could also continue hiking, in an anticlockwise direction, all the way round to Penulisan and take a bemo back to your starting point.

BATUR & KINTAMANI

The village of Batur used to be down in the crater. A violent eruption of the volcano in 1917 killed thousands of people and destroyed more than 60,000 homes and 2000 temples. Although the village was wiped out, the lava flow stopped at the entrance to the villagers' temple. Taking this as a good omen, they rebuilt their village, only to have Batur erupt again in 1926. This time the lava flow covered all but the loftiest temple shrine. Fortunately, the Dutch administration anticipated the eruption and evacuated the village, partly by force, so very few lives were lost. The village was relocated up on the crater rim, and the surviving shrine was also moved up and placed in the new temple, Pura Ulun Danu. Construction on the new temple commenced in 1927. Gunung Batur is the second most important mountain in Bali – only Agung outranks it – so the temple here, one of the island's nine directional temples, is of considerable importance.

The villages of Batur and Kintamani now virtually run together – it's impossible to tell where one ends and the other begins. Kintamani is basically one main street spread out along the rim of the crater. Although often cold and grey, it is a major centre for growing oranges and you'll often see them on sale. Kintamani is famed for its large and colourful market, held every three days. Like most markets throughout Bali it starts and ends early – by 11 am it's all over. The high rainfall and cool climate up here make this a very productive fruit and vegetable growing area. Kintamani is also a contender for the hard-fought title of 'miserable howling dog capital of Bali'.

Places to Stay & Eat

There are a number of losmen along the main street of this volcano-rim town, but most are pretty drab and don't have the spectacular setting of the places at Penelokan. The only reason to stay here is to do a trek down the outer rim and into the crater itself.

Starting from the Penelokan end of town is *Losmen Superman's*, on the left side of the road, where cheap rooms with bathroom cost 4000 rp.

Further north, on the same side of the road, is the *Hotel Miranda*. Rooms here cost from 5000 to 6000 rp for singles/doubles, the most expensive have bathrooms. It's a bit better than the general run of Kintamani accommodation and has good food and an open fire at night. Made Senter, who runs it, is very friendly and informative and also acts as a guide for treks into the crater and around Gunung Batur.

Continuing along the road for a few hundred metres you come to *Losmen Sasaka*. It appears to be new, even modern, but a closer look reveals that the washbasin has no taps, the toilet has to be flushed with a bucket and the hot-water tap is mostly for decoration. The rooms cost 15,000 rp.

Further along again, a sign points off the road to the *Puri Astini Inn* – it says 200 metres, but the distance is probably more like four times that, down quite a rough track. The original rooms in Astini 1 have a minimal bathroom, no view and cost 12,000 to 20,000 rp including breakfast. The four new rooms in Astini 2 are better and have great views if the weather is clear, but cost a little more. The inn is a bit hard to get to unless you've got your own wheels, but it's a convenient spot from which to start a trek into the crater, and Putu Arya here is a trekking guide.

Getting There & Away

From Denpasar (Batubulan station) a bemo to Kintamani is about 1700 rp, though there will be more frequent bemos from Gianyar or Bangli. Buses run between Kintamani and Singaraja on the north coast for 1800 rp.

For lesser-used routes from Ubud to Penelokan, see the Around Ubud section of the Ubud & Around chapter.

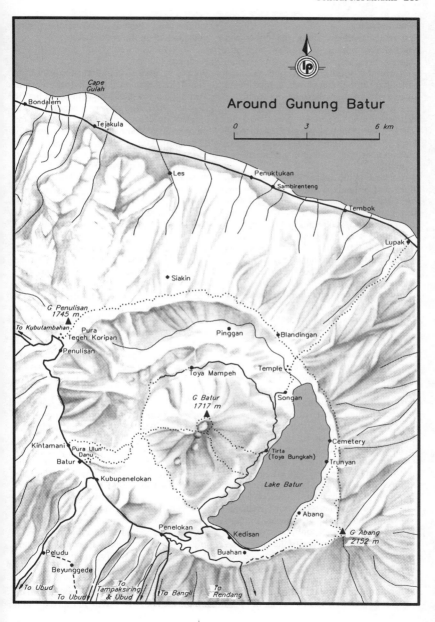

Around Gunung Batur

0   3   6 km

Cape Gulah
Bondalem
Tejakula
Les
Penuktukan
Sambirenteng
Tembok
Lupak
Siakin
G Penulisan 1745 m
To Kubutambahan
Pura Tegeh Koripan
Pinggan
Blandingan
Penulisan
Toya Mampeh
Temple
G Batur 1717 m
Songan
Kintamani
Pura Ulun Danu
Cemetery
Batur
Tirta (Toya Bungkah)
Trunyan
Kubupenelokan
Lake Batur
Penelokan
Abang
Peludu
Kedisan
G Abang 2152 m
Beyunggede
Buahan
To Ubud
To Ubud
To Tampaksiring & Ubud
To Bangli
To Rendang

PENULISAN

The road continues along the crater rim beyond Kintamani, gradually climbing higher and higher. Sometimes, if you come up from the south, you'll find yourself ascending through the clouds around Penelokan and Kintamani then coming out above them as you approach Penulisan. If it's clear, there are more fine views down over the crater, this time looking across the land to the north of Gunung Batur. Sometimes you can even see as far as Gunung Rinjani on Lombok.

At a bend in the road at Penulisan, a steep flight of steps leads to Bali's highest temple, Pura Tegeh Koripan, at 1745 metres. Inside the highest courtyard are rows of old statues and fragments of sculptures in the open bales (buildings). Some of the sculptures date back as far as the 11th century. The views from this hilltop temple are superb: facing north you can see down over the rice terraces clear to the Singaraja coast.

Towering over the temple, however, notice the shrine to a new and powerful god – Bali's television repeater mast!

GUNUNG BATUR & LAKE BATUR

The views from the crater at Penelokan, Batur, Kintamani and Penulisan may be superb, but the most exciting activities are to descend into the massive outer crater, take a boat across the crater lake and/or to climb the dormant Gunung Batur volcano.

A hairpin-bend road winds its way down from Penelokan to Kedisan on the shore of the lake. From Kedisan you can take a boat across the surprisingly large and very deep lake to Trunyan, the Bali Aga village on the eastern side. To get to the hot springs at Tirta, take a boat or take the quaint little road which winds around the lakeside from Kedisan, over many turns and switchbacks, through the lava field. The road continues to Songan, under the north-eastern rim of the crater, and a sideroad goes around to the north side of Gunung Batur until it is stopped by a huge 'flow' of solidified black lava. You can climb to the summit of Gunung Batur in just a few hours from either Kedisan or Tirta, or make longer treks over and around the central volcano and up the crater rim.

Kedisan

Places to Stay Coming into Kedisan from Penelokan you reach a T-intersection. Turning left towards Tirta you come first to the *Segara Bungalows*, where basic singles/doubles cost from 6000/8000 rp and more comfortable rooms with hot water at 12,000/20,000 rp, including breakfast. A bit further on is the *Surya Homestay & Restaurant* with rooms from 8000 to 12,000 rp. The cheapest rooms are not fancy, but definitely OK. Turning right as you come into town will bring you to the *Segara Homestay* which has similar prices (and the same owner) as the Segara Bungalows.

Getting Around Getting across the lake from Kedisan was once one of Bali's great rip-offs. After negotiating a sky-high price, your boatmen would then want to renegotiate halfway across. Meanwhile, your motorbike was being stripped back at Kedisan. It got so bad that the government took over and set prices. The boats leave from a jetty near the middle of Kedisan, where there is a boat office, a fenced car park and the usual assortment of rumah makans and warungs. Your car or motorbike will be safe here!

The set prices are expensive, however. The listed price for a boat for a round trip stopping at Trunyan, the cemetery and the air panas (hot springs) at Tirta, then returning to Kedisan is posted at 32,500 rp, plus 500 rp per person for entrance to the cemetery and 75 rp insurance. The first boat leaves at 8 am and the last at 4 pm; the later departures won't leave much time for sightseeing.

If you want to do it on the cheap don't consider the alternative of hiring a dugout canoe and paddling yourself – the lake is much bigger than it looks from the shore and it can quickly get very choppy if a wind blows up. A better alternative is to walk. The road continues from Kedisan to Buahan and from there you just follow the good footpath around the lakeside to Trunyan, an easy hour or two's walk. From Trunyan you should be able to negotiate a cheaper boat to the cemetery and hot springs.

Buahan

A little further around the lake is Buahan, a small place with market gardens right down to the lake shore. *Baruna Cottages* is a very peaceful and pleasant place to stay. It's new, clean and has a restaurant; singles/doubles with mandi cost 5000/8000 rp. You can walk around the lake shore from here to Trunyan in about 1½ hours.

Trunyan

The village of Trunyan, on the shore of Lake Batur, is squeezed tightly between the lake and the outer crater rim. This is a Bali Aga village, inhabited by remnants of the original Balinese, the people who predate the Majapahit arrival. Unlike the other well-known Bali Aga village, Tenganan, this is not an interesting and friendly place. It's famous for its four-metre high statue of the village's guardian spirit, Ratu Gede Pancering Jagat, but you're unlikely to be allowed to see it. About all you do get to do at Trunyan is sign the visitors' book, make a donation and be told you can't visit the temple.

Kuban

A little beyond Trunyan, and accessible only by the lake (there's no path) is the village cemetery. The people of Trunyan do not cremate or bury their dead – they lie them out in bamboo cages to decompose. Despite their secretiveness in the village they're quite happy for you to visit the cemetery. Unless you're a serious anthropologist, this tourist trap is only for those with morbid tastes.

Tirta (Toyah Bungkah)

Directly across the lake from Trunyan is the small settlement of Tirta, also known as Toyah Bungkah, with its famous hot springs – *tirta* and *toyah* both mean 'holy water'. The hot springs (air panas) bubble out in a couple of spots and are used to feed a bathing pool before flowing out into the lake. For 500 rp you can join half the village for a hot bath –

women on one side, men on the other, soap and shampoo under the shower heads where the water flows out. The water is soothingly hot, ideal for aching muscles after a volcano climb.

Many travellers now stay in Tirta rather than Penelokan. It's more convenient if you want to climb Gunung Batur in the early morning, places to stay are a bit cheaper and you don't get hassled as much.

Places to Stay There are quite a few places to stay in Tirta, and more are being built. If there are empty rooms all over town and the asking price seems a bit high, you may be able to negotiate.

Under the Volcano Homestay in the village has rooms at 5000/8000 rp for basic singles/doubles; better rooms cost up to 15,000 rp. It's quite a pleasant place with a popular restaurant. *Awangga Bungalows*, at the other end of the village near the lake, advertises itself as the 'cheapest', with simple rooms from 5000 rp including breakfast. The nearby *Losmen Tirta Yatra* and *Setana Boga Guesthouse* are right by the lake. Other cheap places include the *Walina Losmen* from 6000 rp and the *Amerta Homestay & Restaurant*, near the hot springs, which has singles/doubles at 6000/8000 rp.

The small and basic *Siki Inn* has rooms from 8000 rp, and also offers a tourist shuttle-bus service to other parts of Bali. (The list of destinations and fares is in the restaurant.) *Kardi's Mountain View Losmen*, at 8000 rp for room only, is back from the lake, on the far side of the village. *Alina* has rooms at 8000 rp and comfortable bungalows at 15,000/20,000 rp; the amazing bathrooms have been done out to resemble fairy grottos! *Nyoman Pangus Homestay & Restaurant*, on the right as you come in from Kedisan, is clean and friendly with rooms at 10,000 to 15,000 rp.

The *Balai Seni Toyabungkah* (Toya Bungkah Arts Centre), up the hill on the western side of the village, is a pleasant place with rooms at 15,000 rp and bungalows at 25,000 rp, definitely a cut above the other small losmen. There's an excellent library there. The three *Putu Bungalows* behind Nyoman Mawa's restaurant are new, and the only rooms with Bali-style decorations. Doubles cost 25,000 rp, and you'll have to ask around to find someone to take your money and let you in.

Places to Eat Fresh fish from the lake is the local speciality, usually barbecued with onion and garlic. The fish are tiny but tasty, and you get three or four for a meal. There are a number of warungs and restaurants, mostly with similar menus and prices. *Nyoman Pangus Restaurant* (it used to be called a warung) does a good version of the barbecued fish. It has an interesting visitors' book with some very critical reviews of Lonely Planet guidebooks! On the other side of the road, the *Under the Volcano* restaurant has good, cheap food, as does the restaurant at *Alina* at the other end of town. The arts centre restaurant has a slightly higher standard at correspondingly higher prices.

Climbing Gunung Batur

Soaring up in the centre of the huge outer crater is the cone of Gunung Batur (1717 metres). It has erupted on several occasions this century, most recently in 1963 and 1974. There are several routes up, and some interesting walks around the summit. You can take one route up and another one down, then get a bemo back to your starting point. A bemo from Kedisan to Tirta will cost about 300 rp. You should start very early in the morning, before mist and cloud obscure the view. Ideally you should get to the top for sunrise – it's a magnificent sight.

You will be hassled by people offering to guide you up the mountain, sometimes asking outrageous prices. A few of the losmen also offer guides. If you have a reasonable sense of direction, and it's not totally dark when you start climbing, you won't need a guide for the usual routes up and down. About 5000 rp would be a fair price for guiding you up one of these routes and back. If you want to explore the crater, or take an unusual route up the mountain, then

you may need a guide with more expertise than the kids who hassle you in town. The best source of information is Jero Wijaya, who can be found at Awangga Bungalows. He has some useful hand-drawn maps showing the whole crater area, with a variety of treks on Gunung Batur, up to the outer rim and beyond to the east coast. His knowledge of the history and geology of the area is way ahead of some of the local amateur guides, who can do little more than show you the path.

The most straightforward route is probably from Tirta. Walk out of town on the road to Kedisan and turn right at one of the signs pointing to Gunung Batur. There are quite a few paths at first, but just go uphill, tending south-west. After half an hour or so you'll be on a ridge with quite a well-defined track; keep going up. It gets pretty steep towards the top, and it can be hard walking over the loose volcanic sand – climbing up three steps and sliding back two. It takes about two hours to get to the top.

There are several refreshment stops along the way, and people with ice buckets full of cold drinks. It'll cost you more than 2000 rp for a small coke, but it's been carried a long way. The warung at the top has tea (500 rp), coffee (700 rp), jaffles (2000 rp) and a brilliant view (free).

At the summit it's possible to walk right around the rim of the volcanic cone, or descend into the cone from the southern edge. Wisps of steam issuing from cracks in the rock, and the surprising warmth of the ground, indicate that things are still happening down below. Some people bring eggs and cook them for breakfast in the steaming fissures – they take about seven minutes.

Other popular routes are from Kedisan or from Purajati, the ruined village on the Kedisan to Tirta road. These routes are well used and should be easy to follow across the lava flows to the west of Gunung Batur, then up to the smaller cone, created by the most recent eruption. Another possibility is to ascend from Kintamani, first descending the outer crater rim and then climbing the inner cone. For an interesting round trip, you can climb Gunung Batur from Tirta, follow the rim around to the other side, then descend on the regular route back to Kedisan. Climbing up, spending a reasonable time on the top and then strolling back down can all be done in four or five hours.

Songan

The road continues from Tirta around the lake to Songan, quite a large village which extends to the edge of the outer crater. Not many tourists come this far, but there's one place to stay, the *Restttt Inn Homestay & Restaurant* (that's how they spell it), on the left side of the road past the main part of the village, which looks quite OK and costs 12,000 rp for a room with a mandi.

From the temple at the crater edge you can climb to the top of the crater rim in just 15 minutes and from there you can see the east coast, only about five km away. It's an easy downhill stroll to the coast road at Lupak but, unless you want to walk back, remember to take your stuff with you – there's no direct public transport back to Tirta.

LAKE BRATAN AREA

The serenely calm Lake Bratan is on the most direct road from Denpasar to Singaraja. This route to the north coast is quicker than the one via Kintamani, but it makes a good round trip to go one way via Kintamani, stopping at Gunung Batur, and the other way via Bedugul and the Lake Bratan area. Approaching Bedugul from the south, you gradually leave the rice terraces behind and ascend into the cool, damp mountain country. There are several places to stay near the lake, and Bedugul can be an excellent base for walking trips around the other lakes and surrounding hills. There is also an interesting temple, botanical gardens, an excellent golf course and a variety of activities on Lake Bratan itself.

Taman Rekreasi Bedugul

The Bedugul Leisure Park (Taman Rekreasi Bedugul) is at the southern end of the lake. It's along the first road to the right as you come in to Bedugul from the south, and it costs 200 rp to get into the lakeside area.

Along the waterfront are restaurants, souvenir shops, a hotel, and facilities for a number of water activities. You can hire a canoe and paddle across to the temple, or hire a motorboat (17,500 rp for half an hour, maximum four people) for a trip around the lake. Waterskiing and parasailing are also available.

It's possible to hire a prahu for 5000 rp an hour (but we got the same rate for a half day) and paddle across Lake Bratan from the lakeside just below the Lila Graha to some caves which the Japanese used during WW II. You can also walk there in about an hour. From there a very well-marked path ascends to the top of Gunung Catur. It takes about two hours for the climb up and an hour back down. The final bit is steep and you should take some water but it is well worth the effort. There is an old temple on the summit with lots of monkeys.
Anne Whybourne & Peter Clarke, Australia

Pura Ulu Danau

At Candikuning, on the shores of the lake a few km north of Bedugul, is the Hindu/Buddhist temple of Ulu Danau. It's very picturesque, with a large banyan tree at the entrance, attractive gardens and one courtyard isolated on a tiny island in the lake. The temple, founded in the 17th century, is dedicated to Dewi Danau, the goddess of the waters. It is the focus of ceremonies and pilgrimages to ensure the supply of water. Ulu Danau has classical Hindu thatched-roof merus and an adjoining Buddhist stupa. Admission is 200 rp (children 100 rp).

Botanical Gardens

Between Bedugul and Candikuning is the market of Bukit Mungsu, noted for its wild orchids. From the intersection, conspicuously marked with a large, phallic sculpture of a sweet corn cob, a road leads west up to the entrance of the Kebun Raya Eka Karya (*kebun raya* is Indonesian for 'botanical gardens'). The gardens were established in 1959 as a branch of the national botanical gardens at Bogor, near Jakarta. They cover more than 120 hectares on the lower slopes of Gunung Pohon, and have an extensive collection of trees and some 500 species of orchid in the Lila Graha. It's a very peaceful place, cool and shady with very few visitors.

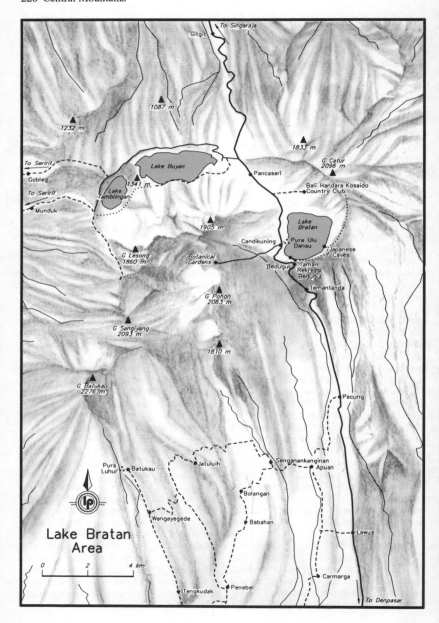

Lake Bratan
Area

0   2   4 km

Unfortunately there is almost nothing in the way of visitor information, and the gardens are not as attractively laid out or as well established as those at Bogor or Cibodas in Java – so, if you've seen those two superb gardens you may be disappointed.

Around the Lakes

North of Candikuning, the road descends past the Bali Handara Kosaido Country Club, with its beautifully situated, world-class golf course. Green fees are US$42 for 18 holes, and you can hire a half-set of clubs for US$9.

If you continue to Lake Buyan, there's a fine walk around the southern side of Buyan, then over the saddle to the adjoining, smaller Lake Tamblingan. From there you can walk uphill, then west to the village of Munduk (about two to three hours) and then take the road around the northern side of the lakes back to Bedugul. Alternatively, you can follow the road west from Munduk, and then north, descending through picturesque villages to Seririt on the north coast.

Heading north from the Lake Bratan area, on the scenic main road, you come to the coastal town of Singaraja, about 30 km away (see the North Bali chapter). On the way there's a beautiful waterfall west of the road just past Gitgit village, about 10 km north of Bedugul. To get there, find the 'air terjun' sign, then walk for about a km through rice fields and jungle. It's a great place for a swim or a picnic, and entry costs 200 rp.

Places to Stay & Eat

There are several places to stay along the road and around the lake. In the Taman Rekreasi Bedugul, at the southern end of the lake, you'll find the *Bedugul Hotel & Restaurant* (☎ 26593) with lakeside rooms at 21,500 and 25,000 rp, and bungalows from 39,500 rp. On the main road just by the turn-off is the *Hadi Raharjo*, a fairly basic losmen with rooms at 10,000 rp.

Continuing north, the road climbs up the hillside to the *Bukit Mungsu Indah Hotel* turn-off. 'Deluxe' rooms cost from US$20 to US$23, and 'executive' rooms from US$27

to US$43. Prices include breakfast, TV, hot water, a fireplace and a great view, but tax is extra. On the road up to the botanical gardens (turn left at the giant sweet corn) you'll find the unprepossessing *Losmen Mawa Indah* which asks 10,000 rp for singles and doubles, but may lower prices if you negotiate.

The main road turns right and drops down towards the lake, passing the turn-off up a steep driveway to the *Lila Graha*, with rooms and bungalows from 25,000/30,000 rp for singles/doubles. It is well located, clean and comfortable, and the accommodation incorporates an old Dutch resthouse. On the other side of the road right by the lake is the *Hotel Ashram*, with rooms from 15,000 to 40,000 rp.

Top-end accommodation is at the *Bali Handara Country Club*, north of Candikuning, where a 'standard cottage' costs US$49, and an 'executive suite', US$350, plus 15.5% tax and service. Meals here cost from US$12, but the view from the bar might be worth the price of a drink.

In Candikuning you'll find the *Restaurant Pelangi, Rumah Makan Mini Bali* and others in the same area. The eating places at the Taman Rekreasi are OK, but a bit expensive.

Getting There & Away

Bedugul is on the main north-south road so is easy to get to from either Denpasar or Singaraja. It costs 1700 rp from Denpasar's Ubung bus station, and about the same from the western bus station in Singaraja. The road is sealed all the way and signposted, so it's easy to follow if you have your own transport.

GUNUNG BATUKAU

West of the Mengwi-Bedugul-Singaraja road rises 2276-metre Gunung Batukau, the 'coconut-shell mountain'. This is the third of Bali's three major mountains and the holy peak of the western end of the island.

Pura Luhur

Pura Luhur, on the slopes of Batukau, was the state temple when Tabanan was an independent kingdom. The temple has a seven-roofed meru to Maha Dewa, the mountain's guardian spirit, as well as shrines for the three mountain lakes: Bratan, Tamblingan and Buyan.

There are several routes to Pura Luhur but none of them are particularly high-class roads – it's a remote temple. You can reach it by following the road up to Penebel from Tabanan. Or turn off the Mengwi to Bedugul road at Baturiti near the 'Denpasar 40 km' sign and follow the convoluted route to Penebel. Wangayagede, the nearest village to the temple, is surrounded by forest and is often damp and misty.

Jatuluih
Also perched on the slopes of Gunung Batukau, but closer to Bedugul and the Mengwi to Bedugul road, is the small village of Jatuluih, whose name means 'truly marvellous'. The view truly is – it takes in a huge chunk of southern Bali.

ROUTES THROUGH PUPUAN
The two most popular routes between the south and north coast are the roads via Kintamani or Bedugul, but there are two other routes over the mountains. Both branch north from the Denpasar to Gilimanuk road, one from Pulukan and the other from Antosari, and meet at Pupuan before dropping down to Seririt, to the west of Singaraja. They're interesting and little-used alternatives to the regular routes.

The Pulukan to Pupuan road climbs steeply up from the coast providing fine views back down to the sea. The route runs through spice-growing country and you'll often see spices laid out on mats by the road to dry – the smell of cloves rises up to meet you. At one point, the narrow and winding road actually runs right through an enormous banyan tree which bridges the road. Further on, the road spirals down to Pupuan through some of Bali's most beautiful rice terraces.

The road from Antosari starts through rice paddies, climbs into the spice-growing country, then descends through the coffee-growing areas to Pupuan.

If you continue another 12 km or so towards the north coast you reach Mayong, where you can turn east to Munduk and on to Lake Tamblingan and Lake Buyan. The road is rough but passable, and offers fine views of the mountains, lakes and out to the northern coast.

North Bali

Northern Bali, the district of Buleleng, makes an interesting contrast with the south of the island. It's separated from the south by the central mountains – a short distance, but it keeps many of the tourist hordes at bay. There's a string of popular coastal beaches west of Singaraja, but these are nothing like the first-class tourist ghettos of Sanur or Nusa Dua. There's also a good variety of places to stay and eat, but nothing like the hassle and confusion of Kuta, and nowhere near the expense of Sanur. Many travellers arriving from Java go straight from Gilimanuk to the north coast, rather than taking the south-coast road which would leave them in Denpasar or, horror of horrors, Kuta Beach. Apart from the peaceful beaches, there are a number of other features worth visiting.

The north coast has been subject to European influence for longer than the south. Although the Dutch had established full control of northern Bali by 1849, it was not until the beginning of this century that their power extended to the south. Having first encountered Balinese troops in Java in the 18th century, the Dutch were the main purchasers of Balinese slaves, many of whom served in the Dutch East India Company armies. Although the Netherlands did not become directly involved with the island's internal affairs, as it had in Java, in 1816 it made several unsuccessful attempts to persuade the Balinese to accept Dutch authority. Various Balinese kings continued to provide the Dutch with soldiers but, in the 1840s, disputes over the looting (salvaging?) of shipwrecks, together with fears that other European powers might establish themselves in Bali, prompted the Dutch to make treaties with several of the Balinese rajahs. The treaties proved ineffective, the plundering continued and in 1844 disputes arose with the rajah of Buleleng over the ratification of agreements.

In 1845 the rajahs of Buleleng and Karangasem formed an alliance, possibly to conquer other Balinese states or, equally possibly, to resist the Dutch. In any case, the Dutch attacked Buleleng and Karangasem in 1846, 1848 and 1849, seizing control of the north in the third attempt. The western district of Jembrana came under Dutch control in 1853 and the rajah of Gianyar surrendered his territory in 1900, but it was not until 1906 that the south was finally subdued. The last confrontation was in 1908, when Klungkung rebelled – unsuccessfully.

From the time of their first northern conquests, the Dutch interfered increasingly in Balinese affairs. It was here that Balinese women first covered their breasts – on orders from the Dutch to 'protect the morals of Dutch soldiers'.

SINGARAJA

Singaraja was the centre of Dutch power in Bali and remained the administrative centre for the islands of Nusa Tenggara (Bali through to Timor) until 1953. It is one of the few places in Bali where there are visible reminders of the Dutch period, but there are also Chinese and Muslim influences from Singaraja's time as a centre of administration and trade. With a population of around 50,000 Singaraja is a busy town, but orderly, even quiet compared with Denpasar. Dokars are still a common means of transport on the pleasant tree-lined streets, and there are some interesting Dutch colonial houses. The 'suburb' of Beratan, south of Singaraja, is the silverwork centre of northern Bali.

For years the port of Singaraja was the usual arrival point for visitors to Bali – it's where all the prewar travel books started. Singaraja is hardly used as a harbour now, due to its lack of protection from bad weather. Shipping for the north coast generally uses the new port at Celukanbawang, and visiting cruise ships anchor at Padangbai in the south. Singaraja has a conspicuous

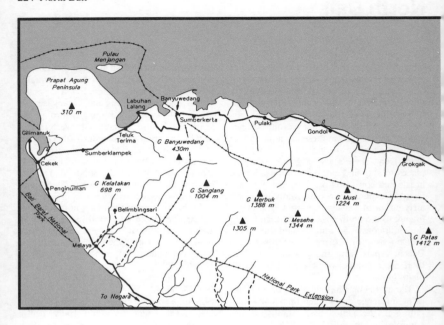

monument on its waterfront, with a statue pointing to an unseen enemy out to sea. It commemorates a freedom fighter who was killed here by gunfire from a Dutch warship early in the struggle for independence.

Singaraja is still a major educational and cultural centre. Apart from two university campuses there is the Gedung Kirtya Historical Library, with a magnificent collection of around 3000 old Balinese manuscripts inscribed on lontar (palm). These lontar books include literary, mythological, historical and religious works. Even older written works, in the form of inscribed metal plates called *prasastis*, are kept here. You're welcome to visit, but you'll find this a place for scholars rather than tourists.

Places to Stay

There are plenty of places to stay and eat in Singaraja but few people bother – the attractions of the beaches, only 10 km away, are too great. It's a pity because Singaraja is not a bad place to stay for a day or so – at least there are not too many tourists.

As in Denpasar, most of the hotels are principally used by local business travellers. You'll find a string of hotels along Jalan Jen Achmad Yani, starting in the east with the *Hotel Sentral*, where basic singles/doubles cost 6500/9000 rp or 20,000/25,000 rp with air-con. The *Hotel Garuda* (☎ 41191), further west at No 76, has rooms from 7500 to 12,500 rp including breakfast, while the *Hotel Duta Karya*, across the road, costs 7500/10,000 rp for singles/doubles, or 35,000 rp with air-con. Further west again, and handy to the bus station, are the *Hotel Saku Bindu* and the *Hotel Gelar Sari*.

On Jalan Imam Bonjol, the street that continues south to Bedugul and Denpasar, you'll find the *Hotel Segara Yoga*, with clean, fan-cooled rooms from 8000/12,000 rp. Further south this street becomes Jalan Gajah Mada, with the *Tresna Homestay* (☎ 21816) on the western side. It's cheap, with very basic

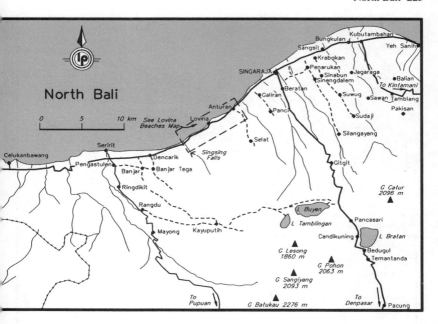

rooms at 3000 rp and better rooms at 5000/8000 rp for singles/doubles. The proprietors are very friendly and interesting, and the place is filled with an amazing collection of antiques and old junk, some of it for sale.

Places to Eat

There are plenty of places to eat in Singaraja, including a batch of places in the small Mumbul market on Jalan Jen Achmad Yani. You'll find the popular *Restaurant Gandhi* here, with a good Chinese menu and glossy, clean surroundings. Across the road is the *Restaurant Segar II*, where a good Chinese meal will run to about 5000 rp. There are also a few restaurants along Jalan Imam Bonjol, and some warungs near the two bus stations.

Getting There & Away

Singaraja is the north coast's main transportation centre and there are bus stations on the eastern and western sides of town. From the western station, minibuses to Denpasar

(Ubung station) via Bedugul leave about every half hour from 6 am to 4 pm and cost around 2500 rp. Buses to Lovina cost 400 rp and to Gilimanuk, 2500 rp (about two hours). From the eastern station, minibuses to Kintamani are 1800 rp, and to Amlapura (via the coast road) about 2500 rp. On many routes there are also full-sized buses which are typically more crowded, less frequent, and about 500 rp cheaper.

There are also direct buses to Surabaya (Java). You'll find a number of ticket offices near the junction of Jalan Jen Achmad Yani and Jalan Diponegoro, but you can also arrange tickets from the Lovina Beach places. There are no direct buses to Yogyakarta but it is possible to arrange to connect with a direct Denpasar to Yogyakarta bus in Gilimanuk.

LOVINA

West of Singaraja is a string of coastal villages – Pemaron, Tukad Mungga, Anturan,

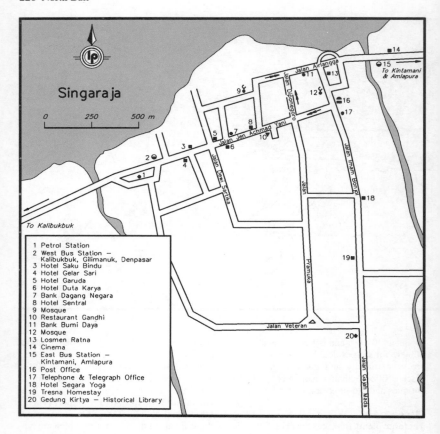

Singaraja

0   250   500 m

1 Petrol Station
2 West Bus Station —
   Kalibukbuk, Gilimanuk, Denpasar
3 Hotel Saku Bindu
4 Hotel Gelar Sari
5 Hotel Garuda
6 Hotel Duta Karya
7 Bank Dagang Negara
8 Hotel Sentral
9 Mosque
10 Restaurant Gandhi
11 Bank Bumi Daya
12 Mosque
13 Losmen Ratna
14 Cinema
15 East Bus Station —
   Kintamani, Amlapura
16 Post Office
17 Telephone & Telegraph Office
18 Hotel Segara Yoga
19 Tresna Homestay
20 Gedung Kirtya — Historical Library

Lovina, Kalibukbuk and Bunut Panggang –
which have become popular beach resorts
collectively known as Lovina. They developed much later and more slowly than Sanur
and Kuta and, by comparison, the area is
relaxed and unhassled. The shops, bars and
other tourist facilities don't dominate the
place as they do at Sanur and, to an even
greater extent, Kuta. The local hustle is 'You
want to see the dolphins?', but apart from
that you are not endlessly harassed to buy
things, have a massage, or do anything more
than simply laze on the beach. It's a popular
stop for those who have come overland

through Java and beyond, and want to take it
easy for a few days. It's a good place to meet
travellers, as there's quite an active social
scene.

The beaches here are black volcanic sand,
not the white stuff you find in the south. It
doesn't look as appealing but it's perfectly
clean and fine to walk along. Nor is there any
surf – a reef keeps it almost flat calm most
of the time.

The beach also provides plenty of local
entertainment, with goats and ducks making
a morning and evening promenade along the
sand. The sunsets here are every bit as spec-

tacular as those at Kuta and are accompanied by a programme of 'local' entertainment: as the sky reddens, the bats come out to play and the lights of the fishing boats appear as bright dots across the horizon. Earlier in the afternoon, at fishing villages like Anturan, you can see the prahus (outriggers) being prepared for the night's fishing. It's quite a process bringing out all the kerosene lamps and rigging them up around the boat.

Orientation & Information

Going along the main road, it's hard to know where one village ends and the next one begins, so note the km posts which show distances from Singaraja. These are marked on the map. The tourist area stretches out over seven or eight km, but the main focus is at Kalibukbuk, about 10½ km from Singaraja. This is where you'll find the tourist office and the police station, which share the same premises. The tourist office is open Monday to Thursday from 7 am to 2 pm, Friday from 7 to 11 am, and Saturday from 7 am to 12.30 pm. If you need information outside these times the police may be able to help.

There are a couple of good bookshops on the other side of the road, beside the Badai Restaurant. Opposite the Badai you'll find Beny Tantra's T-shirt shop. It's not cheap, but it's worth a look because his designs are so good, brilliant in fact. He'll also make them to order.

There's no post office at Lovina, but you can buy stamps and post letters at the Hotel Perama. Local and long-distance telephone calls can be made at Aditya Bungalows – just ask at the front desk.

Dolphins

From the moment you set foot in Lovina you'll be inundated with offers to see the dolphins; to the extent that you might feel like refusing on principle. In fact it's quite an experience, and not to be missed.

You take a boat out before dawn, and see the sun burst over the volcanoes of central Bali. Then you notice that, despite the ungodly hour, dozens of other boats have gathered beyond the reef and lie there waiting. Suddenly a dolphin will leap from the waves, to be followed by several more and then a whole school, vaulting over the water in pursuit of an unseen horde of shrimps. The boats all turn and join the

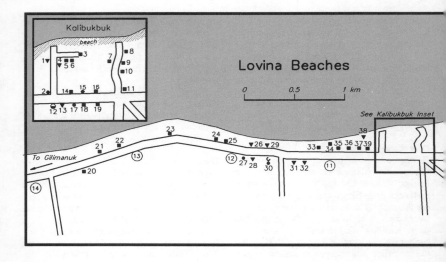

■ PLACES TO STAY

3 Nirwana Cottages & Restaurant
5 Susila Beach Inn 2
6 Angsoka Cottages & Restaurant
7 Astina Cottages
8 Rini Hotel
9 Puri Bali Bungalows
10 Rambutan Cottages & Restaurant
11 Ayodya Accommodation
14 Chono Beach Cottages
16 New Srikandi Hotel, Bar & Restaurant
18 Wisata Jaya Homestay
19 Khie Khie Hotel & Restaurant
20 Ayu Pondok Wisita
21 Krisna Beach Inn
22 Samudra Cottages
23 Toto Pub

24 Parma Beach Homestay
25 Aditya Bungalows & Restaurant
33 Puri Tasik Madu
34 Mangalla Homestay & Restaurant
35 Susila Beach Inn
36 Purnama Homestay
37 Permata Cottages
39 Arjuna Homestay
41 Kali Bukbuk Beach Inn
42 Yudhistra Inn
43 Banyualit Beach Inn
44 Mas Bungalows
45 Janur's Dive Inn
46 Adi Homestay
47 Lila Cita
48 Celuk Agung Cottages

chase, sometimes surrounded by dozens of dolphins, till the animals unaccountably cease their sport, and the boats wait quietly for the next sighting.

So why are tourists hassled so much to take dolphin trips? When the boat owners realised that the dolphins were becoming a tourist attraction, they formed a cartel and fixed the price of a dolphin trip at 8000 rp per person, including 2000 rp commission for the hotels which booked their guests on a trip. Then some freelancers started selling dolphin trips on their friends' boats, and claiming the 2000 rp commission for themselves. A new 'service' industry was born. Flogging dolphin trips to tourists must seem better than, for example, working as a labourer, who might be paid only 2000 rp for

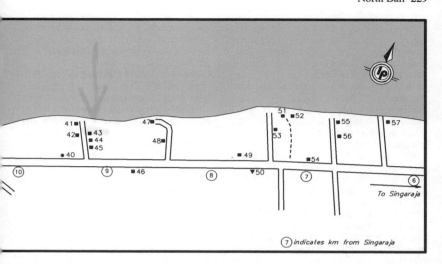

7 indicates km from Singaraja

49 Hotel Perama & Postal Agency
51 Simon's Seaside Cottages
52 Homestay Agung & Restaurant
53 Mandhara Cottages
54 Bali Taman Beach Hotel
55 Jati Reef Bungalows
56 Permai Beach Bungalows
57 Baruna Beach Cottages

▼ PLACES TO EAT

1 Bali Bintang Restaurant
4 Kakatua Bar & Restaurant
13 Badai Restaurant
26 Johni's Restaurant
28 Restaurant Adi Rama

29 Marta's Warung
31 Superman Restaurant
32 Singa Pizza Restaurant
38 Bali Ayu Restaurant
50 Harmoni Restaurant

OTHER

2 Beny Tantra's Shop
12 Bus Stop
15 Tourist Office & Police Station
17 Moneychanger
27 Spice Dive
30 Mosque
40 Radio Mast

a day's hard work. Unfortunately, as you will notice, competition between the touts is now so intense as to be a public nuisance, and the touts can be almost hostile towards tourists who book dolphin trips through a hotel instead of with them. Lovina has lost its reputation as a place where tourists don't get hassled.

Diving
Generally, the water is very clear and the reef is terrific for snorkelling. It's not the best coral you'll find but it's certainly not bad and getting out to it is very easy. In many places you can simply swim out from the beach. Elsewhere you can get a prahu to take you out to the reef, and the skipper should know where the best coral is. All the hotels seem

to have their own boat, or access to one, but plenty of touts on the beach will offer you snorkelling trips, usually just after you have declined an invitation to see the dolphins. It costs about 4000 rp per person for an hour, including the use of mask, snorkel and fins. Out on the reef the water is calm, clear and relatively shallow, and even beginner swimmers can have a good look around with the boat's outrigger to hang on to for security. It's great for kids.

For those with a scuba qualification, there's also a diving operation here. Spice Dive, in humble premises on the south side of the main road near Johni's restaurant, runs trips out to Lovina reef (from US$45), to the wreck at Tulamben (US$55) and to the island of Pulau Menjangan in the Bali Barat National Park (US$60). Menjangan offers probably the best diving in Bali, but transport costs make it an expensive dive with operators from anywhere else in Bali. From Lovina, a trip to Menjangan is good value if you can arrange a group of around six people. If you're interested, talk to Imanuel or Nancy at Spice Dive – they're friendly and very informative.

Places to Stay

There are now so many places to stay along the Lovina beach strip that it's impossible to list them all, or to keep the list up to date. For most of the year it's easy to find a place to stay, but because these are strung out over several km it may be hard to get to a particular place in the peak periods. The first hotel is north of the main road just after the six km marker, the last is nearly 14 km from Singaraja. Places are usually clustered in groups on one of the sideroads to the beach, then there might be nothing for a half km or so.

During peak times (mid-July to the end of August and mid-December to mid-January) accommodation can be tight and prices are somewhat higher. At other times prices may be more negotiable, particularly if there are a lot of empty rooms around. Generally the cheapest places are away from the beach, some on the south side of the main road.

Upstairs rooms are cooler and a bit more expensive, especially if they have a view. There's a 5% tax on accommodation.

Singaraja to Anturan Starting from the Singaraja end, the first place is the slightly higher priced *Baruna Beach Cottages*, with individual cottages and rooms in a larger two-storeyed block. All have bathrooms, and prices range from US$40 with fan, and from US$52 with air-con, including breakfast. There's a swimming pool, and a bar/restaurant on the beach. You can also rent windsurfers (12,000 rp per hour) and other water-sports equipment.

On the next sideroad, the *Jati Reef Bungalows*, in the rice paddies close to the beach, look a bit like concrete bunkers. Comfortable double rooms with private, open-air bathrooms cost around 15,000 rp. Further inland are the new *Permai Beach Cottages* where basic rooms cost from 10,000 rp and rooms with hot water and air-con cost from 30,000 rp. The reef off the beach here is reputed to be the best along the Singaraja to Lovina coastal strip.

Fronting onto the main road, but extending all the way down to the beach, is the new and expensive *Bali Taman Beach Hotel* (☎ 41125). Standard singles/doubles cost US$15/20 and air-con rooms cost an extra US$25.

Anturan Continuing along the road, you come to the turn-off to the scruffy little fishing village of Anturan, where there are three places to stay, and lots of local colour. *Mandhara Cottages* is a neat little complex where singles/doubles with bathroom cost 8000/10,000 rp including breakfast. Walking east along the beach for about 100 metres will bring you to *Simon's Seaside Cottages*, an old establishment which has been completely rebuilt and where comfortable rooms cost US$20. There's actually a little track leading from the main road directly to Simon's, but it's hard to spot. Next door to Simon's is the neat and clean *Homestay Agung*, with rooms from 7000 to 10,000 rp – the more expensive rooms are interesting two-storeyed places, with bedroom upstairs and bathroom downstairs. The food at Agung can be quite good.

Anturan to Kalibukbuk Continuing west from Anturan you pass the *Hotel Perama* (☎ 21161) on the main road, with rooms for 10,000 rp and a good restaurant. This is also the office for the Perama bus company, and a good source of information for tours. The next turn-off goes down to the *Lila Cita*, right on the beach front. It's simple, but the owners are friendly and welcoming and it's a popular place. Singles/doubles cost 8000/10,000 rp, or 15,000/20,000 rp with private mandi, and the sea is just outside your window. On the way there you'll pass the *Celuk Agung Cottages*, with rooms from 27,000 rp, or 50,000 rp with air-con. The complex has satellite TV, tennis courts and a pool.

Back on the main road, on the side away from the beach, is the *Adi Homestay*, with rooms from 6000 rp including breakfast.

The next sideroad down to the beach has quite a few places to stay. The pleasant *Kali Bukbuk Beach Inn* has rooms from 15,000 to 30,000 rp. On the other side, back a bit from the beach, is the similarly priced *Banyualit Beach Inn*. Other places here include *Yudhistra*, *Mas Bungalows* and *Janur's Dive Inn*.

Kalibukbuk A little beyond the 10-km marker is the 'centre' of Lovina – the village of Kalibukbuk. Here you'll find *Ayodya Accommodation*, a traditional place in a big old Balinese house. It's clean, friendly and extremely well run. Rooms cost from 4000 to 8000 rp and are bare and functional, but you sit outside and take your meals there. It's very pleasant in the evening, with the bamboo gamelan tinkling in the background, although the traffic noise can be annoying.

Follow the track beside Ayodya down towards the beach and you'll come to the delightful *Rambutan Cottages*. The beautifully finished rooms cost 15,000 rp downstairs and 20,000 rp upstairs, 5000 rp more in peak seasons. Next along are the *Puri Bali Bungalows* where singles/doubles cost 8000/

10,000 rp, good value for this location. Closest to the beach is the super-clean and well-run *Rini Hotel*. Rooms cost from 15,000 to 30,000 rp and there's a good restaurant. Families and children are welcome. Opposite Rini are the *Astina Cottages*, in a pretty garden setting, with a variety of rooms and bungalows from 7000 to 10,000 rp; prices are a bit higher in the peak season.

Along the main road west of Ayodya, among the bars, restaurants and other facilities, you'll find the *Khie Khie Hotel & Restaurant*. It has a pool and rooms from 12,500 to 15,000 rp. A bit further along is the small *Wisata Jaya Homestay*, one of the cheapest around, with basic but satisfactory rooms for 5000 rp. On the other side of the road is the *New Srikandi Hotel Bar & Restaurant*, with singles/doubles at 5000/7000 rp. Further along, *Chono Beach Cottages* has rooms from 10,000 to 17,000 rp.

The next turn-off, just beyond the 11-km marker, takes you down a driveway to *Nirwana Cottages* (☎ 41288). This is the biggest development at Lovina, with a large slab of beach-front property extending to the back of Astina Cottages. It's a great location, and the restaurant overlooking the beach is one of the best places to enjoy the sunset. Double rooms cost from 11,000 to 19,000 rp, and delightful, double-storeyed Bali-style cottages from 34,000 rp – ideal for families. Prices are higher in peak season. Some people think the rooms and the restaurant are overpriced, but it's a well-run place and the location is unbeatable.

Right behind Nirwana are the *Angsoka Cottages,* a small (but expanding) place with simple rooms from 6000 rp – excellent value for money. The newer rooms cost more: up to 50,000 rp for a bungalow with air-con. If you want to stay in Kalibukbuk, it's worth asking at Angsoka. There should be something to suit your budget. The small *Susila Beach Inn 2*, beside the Angsoka, is a straightforward losmen with cheap rooms from about 6000 rp.

Back on the main road there's a string of cheaper places with prices from about 5000 rp. These include the *Arjuna Homestay,* the

Permata Cottages, Purnama Homestay and *Susila Beach Inn*, which are all grouped together on the northern side the road. Some of the places here extend through to the beach so you can get away from the road noise. Further along is the slightly more expensive *Mangalla Homestay*, then the *Puri Tasik Madu*.

Beyond Kalibukbuk Continuing further along there's the top-end *Aditya Bungalows & Restaurant*, with beach frontage, pool, shops and a variety of rooms with TV, phone, fridge etc. Some of the rooms are right on the beach and costs range from US$13 to US$40. Next, there's the friendly *Parma Beach Homestay*, with cottages from 5000 rp, set in a garden extending down to the beach. The *Toto Pub* is another bottom-end place with a top location; it's at the end of town but right on the beach. Very basic rooms are 7000 rp for a double. The *Samudra Cottages* have a secluded location even further along the road, but are expensive at about 30,000 rp for rooms with air-con. The *Krisna Beach Inn* is the next one out, with rooms from 5000 rp, and there are more places extending further west.

Places to Eat
Most of the places to stay along the beach strip also have restaurants and snack bars and you're generally welcome to visit other losmen for a meal, even if you're not staying there. Many of the restaurants are also bars, depending on the time of night, and you can stop at any of them just for a drink. With all these places, plus a handful of warungs, there are dozens of places to eat. Some of them are listed here, but you'll do well just looking around and eating anywhere that takes your fancy.

Starting from the Singaraja end, the small *Homestay Agung* has a good reputation for its food, and people from other losmen often drop in. On the main road nearby there's the *Harmoni Restaurant* which has great fresh fish and other seafood dishes.

At Kalibukbuk village the *Khie Khie Restaurant* has a good seafood menu, and a bit

further along is the popular *Badai Restaurant*. It has a relaxed, friendly feel and is a convivial meeting place for travellers in the evening. The food is pretty good too, with some excellent 'order a day in advance' dishes like fish curry, duck, or Hidangan Jawa (like a rijstaffel). The Badai also has a useful bulletin board.

The restaurant at *Nirwana*, overlooking the beach, is pricey but popular. It's worth at least one visit for a drink at sunset. On the road down to Nirwana there's also the *Bali Bintang Restaurant* on one side and the *Kakatua Bar & Restaurant* on the other. The Bintang is good, relatively cheap and happy to tackle food not featured on the menu. The Kakatua (Cockatoo) also offers a good meal in a very convivial atmosphere.

Further along is *Singa Pizza Restaurant*, the *Superman Restaurant*, *Marta's Warung* and then *Johni's Restaurant*. All these places are popular, and their menus and prices are similar so it's impossible to single out individual places. There are also some small warungs in this area which serve tasty food at good prices, even if the surroundings are not quite as salubrious.

Entertainment
Some of the hotel restaurants have special nights with an Indonesian buffet meal and Balinese dancing. At about 3500 rp for entertainment and all you can eat, this can be very good value. *Rambutan* does a good one on Wednesdays and Sundays. *Aditya*, the *New Srikandi* and *Angsoka* also have buffet nights which are well advertised by leaflets that circulate around the beach and the bars.

There is something of a social scene in Lovina – it could even be described as a romantic place. On the beach and in the bars you can meet young people from all over the world, including quite a few Indonesians.

Warning Balinese guys can be very charming and, as elsewhere in Bali, they are not averse to accepting gifts from foreign girlfriends. There's nothing wrong with this, but a few of these guys are con artists who are mainly interested in the girl's money. The routine often involves taking a new girl-friend to see 'his' village – usually it's not the guy's own village but the girl doesn't know that. She may be shocked by the poor circumstances of her new lover, particularly when she hears about his sick mother who can't pay for an operation, the brother who needs money for his education or the important religious ceremony that they can't afford. If the girl does not give him money on some such pretext, the guy may well try to steal it from her. After he has her money the guy dumps the girl, often in a very hurtful fashion, to clear the way for another unsuspecting tourist. Of course most guys are OK, and no doubt there have been thousands of delightful holiday romances in Bali, but don't let the romantic atmosphere cloud your better judgement.

Getting There & Away

To get to Lovina from the south of Bali you first have to get to Singaraja, then take a bemo out from there. The regular bemo fare from Singaraja to the middle of Lovina's beach strip is 400 rp. See the Singaraja section for details.

There are direct public buses between Surabaya (Java) and Singaraja, but if you're coming in from Surabaya you can get off along the beaches rather than have to backtrack from Singaraja. If you're heading west you can flag down a bus or bemo in the main drag and save going into Singaraja then back out. Drivers will probably stop anywhere, but the main stop is around the Badai Restaurant; you can buy bus/bemo tickets near here as well.

The Perama bus company's office (☎ 21161) and bus stop is at the Perama Hotel in Anturan, about eight km from Sinaraja. Perama's tourist shuttle buses are more expensive than regular public transport, but are often worth the extra for the sake of convenience. Fares are 10,000 rp to Kuta or Ubud, 12,000 rp to Candidasa or Padangbai, 16,000 rp to Lombok, 16,000 rp to Surabaya and 25,000 rp to Yogyakarta.

WEST OF SINGARAJA

There are numerous places of interest along the north coast, both west and east of Singaraja. The road west of Singaraja follows the coast through Lovina then cuts through the Bali Barat National Park to join the south coast road near Gilimanuk, the port for ferries to Java. There are several places along this road, or near to it, which are worth a visit.

Waterfalls

At the village of Labuhan Haji, five km from the middle of the Lovina beach strip, there's a sign to Singsing Air Terjun (Daybreak Waterfall). About one km from the main road there's a warung on the left and a car park on the right – you may be asked to pay 100 rp for parking. Walk past the warung and along the path for about 200 metres to the lower falls. The waterfall is not huge, dropping about 12 metres into a deep pool which is good for a swim. The water isn't crystal clear either, but it's much cooler than the sea and very refreshing. Local kids will leap from a tree high up on the hill into the deep water – for a fee or just for fun.

You can clamber further up the hillside to the second waterfall (Singsing Dua), which is slightly bigger and has a mud bath which is supposedly good for the skin. This one also cascades into a deep pool in which you can swim. It's a pretty setting and makes a nice day trip from Lovina. The falls are more spectacular in the wet season.

Banjar

Buddhist Monastery Bali's only Buddhist monastery (wihara) is about half a km beyond the village of Banjar Tega, which is about three km up a steep track from the main coast road. It is vaguely Buddhist-looking, with colourful decoration, a bright orange roof and statues of Buddha, but overall it's very Balinese with the same decorative carvings and door guardians. It's quite a handsome structure, in a commanding location with views down the valley and across the paddy fields to the sea. The road continues past the monastery, winding further up into the hills.

Hot Springs The hot springs (air panas) are only a short distance west of the monastery if you cut across from Banjar Tega, rather than return to the main road. From the monastery, go back down to Banjar Tega and turn left in the centre of the village. The small road runs west for a km or so to the village of Banjar. From there it's only a short distance uphill before you see the 'air panas one km' sign on the left. Follow the road to the car park where you'll be shown a place to park. Buy your ticket from the little office (400 rp, children 200 rp) and cross the bridge to the baths. There are changing rooms under the restaurant, on the right side.

Eight carved stone nagas (mythological serpents) spew water from a natural hot spring into the first bath, which then overflows (via the mouths of five more nagas), into a second, larger pool. In a third pool, water pours from three-metre-high spouts to give you a pummelling massage. The water is slightly sulphurous and pleasantly hot, so you might enjoy it more in the morning or the evening than in the heat of the day. You must wear a swimsuit and you shouldn't use soap in the pools, but you can do so under an adjacent outdoor shower.

The whole area is beautifully landscaped with lush tropical plants. The restaurant, a striking example of modern Balinese architecture, is not too expensive and has good Indonesian food.

Getting There & Away The monastery and hot springs are both signposted from the main road. If you don't have your own transport, it's probably easiest to go to the hot springs first. Heading west from Singaraja, continue beyond the turn-off to Banjar Tega to the Banjar turn-off (around the 18 km marker) where there are guys on motorbikes who will take you up to the air panas for 1000 rp or so. From the springs you can walk across to the monastery and back down to the main road.

Seririt

Seririt is little more than a junction town for the roads that run south over the mountains to Pulukan or Bajera, on the way to Denpasar. The road running west along the coast towards Gilimanuk is quite good. In parts it is quite scenic, even spectacular, and it's certainly not overrun with tourists.

Seririt has a petrol station and a reasonable selection of shops. If you need to stay there, the *Hotel Singarasari*, near the bus and bemo stop, has singles/doubles for 5000/7000 rp, or 17,000/20,000 rp with air-con. There are places to eat in the market area, just north of the bemo stop.

Celukanbawang

Celukanbawang, the main port for northern Bali, has a large wharf. Bugis schooners, the magnificent sailing ships which take their name from the seafaring Bugis people of Sulawesi, sometimes anchor here. There's also a small beach – so it's very picturesque. The *Hotel Drupadi Indah*, a combination losmen, cinema, bar and restaurant, is the only place to stay.

Pulaki

Pulaki is famous for its Pura Pulaki, a coastal temple which was completely rebuilt in the early '80s. The temple has a large troop of monkeys. Pulaki itself seems to be entirely devoted to grape growing and the whole village is almost roofed over with grapevines. For some reason grape growing has become popular at several locations on the north coast in recent years. A local wine is made which tastes a little like sweet sherry – mixed with lemonade it's drinkable, sort of. The grapes are also exported as dried fruit. One km past Pulaki are the Pemuteran hot springs, a few hundred metres off the road.

BALI BARAT NATIONAL PARK

The Bali Barat (West Bali) National Park covers nearly 20,000 hectares of the western tip of Bali. In addition, 50,000 hectares are protected in the national park extension, as well as nearly 7000 hectares of coral reef and coastal waters. On an island as small and densely populated as Bali, this represents a major commitment to nature conservation. The management of the area is to be integrated with a conservation and environment plan for all of Bali. Information and facilities for visitors are quite limited, but this may improve as the area becomes better known.

The main north coast road connects with Gilimanuk through the national park, and you don't have to pay any entrance fees just to drive through. If you want to visit any places of interest (they're called 'visitor objects'), then you have to pay separately for each one.

Banyuwedang Hot Springs

Coming from the north coast, this is the first 'visitor object' you will encounter. There is a Balinese temple here and, according to one brochure, the hot springs will 'strengthen the endurance of your body against the attack of skin disease'. Entrance costs 450 rp, including 50 rp insurance, 250 rp for children.

Labuhan Lalang & Pulau Menjangan

Labuhan Lalang is the place to get a boat to Pulau Menjangan (Deer Island), an unspoilt and uninhabited island reputed to offer the best diving in Bali. The office at the entrance has some information and a good relief model of the national park. They also sell the 400 rp ticket to enter the foreshore area. There's a jetty for the boats to Menjangan, a warung with the usual sort of menu, and a pleasant white-sand beach 200 metres to the east. There are coral formations close to the shore which are good for snorkelling and, since this area of Bali is sparsely populated and now protected in the national park, the variety of fish and coral is amazing.

Excursions from Labuhan Lalang to Pulau Menjangan start at 35,000 rp, including the half-hour boat trip, three hours on or around the island, and the return trip. If you want to stay longer, each additional hour costs about 5000 rp. Both snorkelling and scuba diving are excellent around the island, with superb unspoiled coral, caves, lots of tropical fish and a spectacular drop-off. Boats usually visit the same areas, where fixed moorings have been installed to prevent the coral being damaged by anchors. Diving is usually best in the early morning, when the water is clear-

est. Diving trips to the island can be arranged by various dive operators in Bali, but it's a long way to come for a day trip from the south. The closest dive operation is Spice Dive at Lovina Beach. There is a short nature trail on the island, and most trips allow some time to walk around and look at the flora and fauna, particularly the wild deer after which the island is named.

Teluk Terima

Teluk literally means bay or inlet, but Teluk Terima refers more generally to an area just west of Labuhan Lalang. The 'tourist object' here (400 rp admission) is Jayaprana's grave, a 10-minute walk up some stone stairs from the south side of the road. The foster son of a 17th century king, Jayaprana, planned to marry Leyonsari, a beautiful girl of humble origins. The king, however, also fell in love with Leyonsari and had Jayaprana killed. In a dream, Leyonsari learned the truth of Jayaprana's death, and killed herself rather than marry the king. This Romeo and Juliet story is a common theme in Balinese folk- lore, and the grave is regarded as sacred even though the ill-fated couple were not deities. From the site, there's a fine view to the north and, according to a national park pamphlet, '...you will feel another pleasure which you can't get in another place'.

Jungle Treks

Three-hour guided treks around the Teluk Terima area can be arranged through the national park office at Labuhan Lalang. The treks cost about 5000 rp, and the best times to go are in the early morning and around dusk. The peninsula north of the Terima to Gilimanuk road, Prapat Agung, is within the park, and a 25-km walking track skirts the coast. There are no facilities and it's a hot walk, so take plenty of liquids.

Places to Stay

At Labuhan Lalang there are some basic bungalows on the foreshore area near the boat jetty. Both singles and doubles cost 7500 rp, but there are only a few of them so they may be full – ask at the warung. A little further west at Teluk Terima, *PT Margarana Accommodation* is just off the road at the 13-km marker before Gilimanuk. It has a small restaurant and clean rooms with showers for 15,000 rp.

Getting There & Away

The road east follows the coast to Lovina and Singaraja. The road west goes to Cekek, where there is a T-intersection – if you turn right, it's a couple of kilometres to Gilimanuk, while turning left will take you to Negara and Denpasar. (See the South-West Bali chapter for more information on these places.) You should be able to flag down public transport in either direction.

EAST OF SINGARAJA

There are a number of places of interest close to the coast road between Singaraja and the turn-off to Kintamani, including some of northern Bali's best known temples. The north-coast sandstone used in temple construction is very soft and easily carved, allowing local sculptors to give free rein to their imaginations. You'll find some delightfully whimsical scenes carved into a number of the temples here. Overall, the exuberant, even baroque, style of the north makes temples in the south appear almost restrained in contrast.

Although the basic architecture of the temples is similar in both regions, there are some important differences. The inner courtyard of southern temples usually houses a number of multi-roofed shrines (merus) together with other structures, whereas in the north, everything is grouped on a single pedestal. On the pedestal you'll usually find 'houses' for the deities to use on their earthly visits and also for storing important religious relics. Also, there will probably be a padmasana or 'throne' for the sun god.

At Kubutambahan there is a turn-off to the south which takes you up to Penulisan and Kintamani, or you can continue east to the lovely spring-fed pools at Yeh Sanih. From there the road continues right around the east coast to Amlapura – see the East Bali chapter for details.

Sangsit

At Sangsit, only a few km beyond Singaraja, you'll find an excellent example of the colourful architectural style of northern Bali. Sangsit's Pura Beji is a subak temple, dedicated to the spirits that look after irrigated rice fields. It's about a half km off the main road towards the coast. The sculptured panels along the front wall set the tone with their Disneyland demons and amazing nagas.

The temple is just the same on the inside, with a variety of sculptures covering every available space. Like many other northern temples the inner courtyard is spacious and grassy, shaded by a frangipani tree.

If you continue beyond Sangsit to Bungkulan, you'll find another fine temple with an interesting kulkul (warning drum).

Jagaraga

The village of Jagaraga, a few km off the main road, has an interesting pura dalem. The small and otherwise unprepossessing temple has delightful sculptured panels along its front wall, both inside and out. On the outer wall look for a vintage car driving sedately past, a steamer at sea and even an aerial dogfight between early aircraft. Jagaraga is also famous for its legong troupe, said to be the best in northern Bali.

It was the capture of the local rajah's stronghold at Jagaraga that marked the arrival of Dutch power in Bali in 1849. A few km past Jagaraga, along the right-hand side as you head inland, look for another small temple with ornate carvings of a whole variety of fish and fishermen.

Sawan

Several km further inland, Sawan is a centre for the manufacture of gamelan gongs and complete gamelan instruments. You can see the gongs being cast and the intricately carved gamelan frames being made. It's very much a local cottage industry and, as the craft workers don't get many visitors, they're usually pleased to see you and show you around.

Kubutambahan

Only a km or so beyond the Kintamani turn-off at Kubutambahan is the Pura Maduwe Karang. Like Pura Beji at Sangsit, the temple is dedicated to agricultural spirits, but this one looks after unirrigated land. The temple is usually kept locked but if you ask at the shop opposite, you may get the key.

This is one of the best temples in northern Bali and is particularly noted for its sculptured panels, including the famous bicycle panel depicting a gentleman riding a bicycle with flower petals for wheels. It's on the base of the main plinth in the inner enclosure, but there are other panels worth inspecting in this peaceful and pleasant temple.

Yeh Sanih

About 15 km east of Singaraja, Yeh Sanih (also called Air Sanih) is a popular local spot where freshwater springs are channelled into some very pleasant swimming pools before flowing into the sea. Yeh Sanih is right by the sea and the area with the pools is attractively laid out with pleasant gardens, a restaurant and a couple of places to stay. It's well worth a visit and admission to the springs and pool is 150 rp (children 100 rp). On the hill overlooking the springs is the Pura Taman Manik Mas temple.

Places to Stay & Eat There are a couple of places to stay near the springs. In fact, the *Bungalow Puri Sanih* is actually in the springs complex. It has a very pretty garden

Temple guardian, Kubutambahan

and doubles cost 10,000 to 20,000 rp – the most expensive rooms are little two-storeyed bungalows. Just beyond the springs, *Yeh Sanih Seaside Cottages* has pleasant rooms at 25,000/30,000 rp for singles/doubles.

The Puri Sanih also has a restaurant overlooking the springs and the gardens. There are a number of warungs across the road from the springs, and a restaurant up on the hillside which you reach up some steep stairs.

Nusa Penida

Nusa Penida, an administrative region within the Klungkung district, comprises three islands – Nusa Penida itself, the smaller Nusa Lembongan to the north-west, and tiny Nusa Ceningan between them. Nusa Lembongan attracts many visitors for its surf, seclusion and snorkelling. The island of Nusa Penida is right off the tourist track and has few facilities for visitors, while Nusa Ceningan is virtually uninhabited.

Economic resources are limited on Nusa Penida. It has been a poor region for many years and there has been some transmigration from here to other parts of Indonesia. Thin soils and a lack of water do not permit the cultivation of rice, but other crops are grown, some for export to mainland Bali. Fishing is another source of food, and some sardines and lobster are also sold to Bali. The cultivation of seaweed is a recent development but now quite well established, and the underwater fences on which it is grown can be seen off many of the beaches. After harvesting, the seaweed is spread out on the beach to dry, then exported to Japan and Europe where it is used as a thickening agent in processed foods and cosmetics.

NUSA LEMBONGAN

Most visitors to Nusa Lembongan come for the surf that breaks on the coral reef offshore, and stay around the beach at Jungutbatu. The reef protects the beach, a perfect crescent of white sand with clear blue water, and there are superb views across the water to Gunung Agung on mainland Bali. There's also good snorkelling on the reef, with some spots accessible from the beach. To reach other snorkelling spots you need to charter a boat, which costs about 5000 rp per hour. Apart from the attractions of the beach, the coral and the surf, there's not much else to do.

There's no jetty – the boats usually beach at the village of Jungutbatu and you have to jump off into the shallows. Your boat captain might be able to leave you at the eastern end of the beach where most of the bungalows are, but otherwise you'll have to walk a km to reach them.

Apart from the few basic bungalows and restaurants there are virtually no tourist facilities. There's no post office and the bank doesn't change travellers' cheques. The notice board at the Main Ski restaurant advertises excursions and day trips to various locations around the three islands, as well as the cost of bicycle and motorbike hire. The restaurant owners also know the name and address of a local doctor who seems to specialise in coral cuts and surfing injuries.

Lembongan Village

It's about three km south-west along the sealed road from Jungutbatu to Lembongan village, the island's other town. Leaving Jungutbatu you pass a Balinese-style temple with an enormous banyan tree, then climb up a knoll with a nice view back over the beach. After crossing the knoll you descend to the outskirts of Lembongan village and soon get the feeling that tourists are a rarity here. The people aren't hostile, but neither do they display the welcoming smiles that greet you elsewhere in Bali. It's an antiquated, vaguely spooky place. Following the road downhill brings you to the lagoon which separates Nusa Lembongan from Nusa Ceningan. It's possible to continue right around the island, following the rough track which eventually comes back to Jungutbatu.

The Underground House As you enter Lembongan you'll pass a warung on the right with a couple of pool tables. For 1000 rp the kids here will offer to take you through the labyrinthine underground 'house', 100 metres back off the road. It's a crawl and scramble through the many small passages, rooms and chambers, supposedly dug by one man.

The story goes that the man lost a dispute

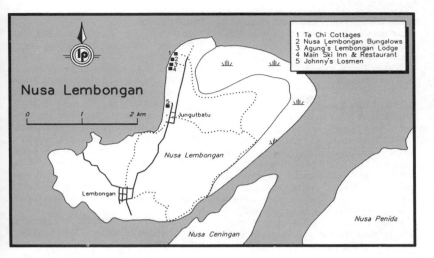

1 Ta Chi Cottages
2 Nusa Lembongan Bungalows
3 Agung's Lembongan Lodge
4 Main Ski Inn & Restaurant
5 Johnny's Losmen

Nusa Lembongan

0   1   2 km

Jungutbatu

Nusa Lembongan

Lembongan

Nusa Ceningan

Nusa Penida

with an evil spirit and was condemned to death, but pleaded to be allowed to finish his house first. The spirit relented, and the man started excavating his cave with a small spoon. He always started a new room before he finished the last one, so of course the house was never completed, and thus his death sentence was postponed indefinitely.

The kids provide a candle but it would be a good idea to bring your own torch (flashlight). Be very careful as there are big holes in unexpected places. On your way back to the road, have a look down the well and see from how far down the villagers must draw their water.

Surfing

There are three main breaks on the reef. Off the beach where the bungalows are is Shipwreck, a right-hand break named for the remains of a wreck which is clearly visible from the shore. To the west of this is Lacerations, which breaks over shallow coral, and further west again is Playground. You can paddle out to Shipwreck, but for the other two it's better to hire a boat. Prices are negotiable depending on time and numbers, but it's about 2500 to 3000 rp to be taken out and

back, with an hour's surfing in between. Strangely, the surf can be crowded even when the island isn't, as charter boats often bring groups of surfers for day trips from the mainland.

Places to Stay & Eat

In the village, *Johnny's Losmen* was the first place on Lembongan to accommodate visitors. It's basic but quite OK, and cheap at 3000/4000 rp for singles/doubles, although not many people stay here. These days most of the accommodation is further along the beach to the north-east, and that's where most of the visitors go.

Heading in that direction you'll pass some miscellaneous bungalows (which may get a name and a restaurant soon), before you get to the conspicuous *Main Ski Inn & Restaurant*. The two-storeyed restaurant, right on the beach, is a little more expensive than some of the others, but serves good food and has a great view. Binoculars are provided so you can watch the surf while you're waiting for lunch. Upstairs rooms are 10,000/12,000 rp for singles/doubles, rooms downstairs are 8000/10,000 rp.

Agung's Lembongan Lodge has double

rooms from 5000 rp, and a restaurant with cheap but tasty food. Next to that is the *Nusa Lembongan Restaurant & Bungalows*. Finally there's *Ta Chi* with rooms from 10,000 to 12,000 rp and reputedly the best cook on the island.

Getting There & Away

From Sanur Boats leave from the northern end of Sanur Beach, in front of the Ananda Hotel. The boat captains – that's what they're called – have fixed the tourist price to Lembongan at 15,000 rp. The strait between Bali and the Nusa Penida islands is very deep and huge swells develop during the day, so the boats leave before 8.30 am. Even so, you may get wet with spray, so be prepared. The trip takes at least 1½ hours, more if conditions are unfavourable. The return trip is a bit cheaper at about 12,000 rp.

From Kuta Some agencies in Kuta sell a ticket through to Lembongan via Sanur for 15,000 rp. This is pretty good value as it gets you, in effect, free transport to Sanur.

From Kusamba Most boats from Kusamba go to Toyapakeh on Nusa Penida, but sometimes they go to Jungutbatu on Lembongan. Although it might be a bit cheaper to go to Lembongan than Penida, you may have to wait a long time for the boat to fill up before it leaves.

From Nusa Penida There are boats which take the local people between Jungutbatu and Toyapakeh on Nusa Penida, particularly on market days. You'll have to ask around to find when they leave, and discuss the price. The public boats will be chock full of people, produce and livestock. A charter boat will run to about 25,000 rp, which would be OK between six or eight people.

Getting Around

The island is fairly small and you can easily walk around it in a few hours. You can also hire a motorbike or get a lift on the back of one.

NUSA PENIDA

Clearly visible from Sanur, Padangbai, Candidasa or anywhere else along Bali's south-east coast, the hilly island of Nusa Penida has a population of around 40,000 and was once used as a place of banishment for criminals and other undesirables from the kingdom of Klungkung. Nusa Penida is also the legendary home of Jero Gede Macaling, the demon who inspired the Barong Landung dance. Many Balinese believe the island to be a place of enchantment and evil power *(angker)* – paradoxically, this is an attraction. Although foreigners rarely visit here, thousands of Balinese come every year for religious observances aimed at placating the evil spirits.

The island has a number of interesting temples dedicated to Jero Gede Macaling, including Pura Ped near Toyapakeh and Pura Batukuning near Sewana. There is also a huge limestone cave, Goa Karangsari, on the coast about four km from Sampalan. The mountain village of Tanglad in the south-east, with its throne for the sun god, Surya, is also interesting.

The north coast has white-sand beaches and views over the water to the volcanoes on Bali. This coastal strip, with the two main towns of Toyapakeh and Sampalan, is moist and fertile, almost lush. The south coast has limestone cliffs dropping straight down to the sea – a spectacular sight if you're coming that way by boat. The interior is a hilly, rugged landscape, not barren but with sparse-looking crops and vegetation and unsalubrious villages. Rainfall is limited here, and there are large square concrete tanks called *cabangs* in which water is stored for the dry season. The hillsides are terraced, but they are not like the wet rice paddies of Bali. The terraces are supported with stone walls and the crops include sweet potatoes, cassava, corn and soybeans, but not rice, which is brought in from the mainland.

The population is predominantly Hindu, but the culture is distinct from that of Bali. The language is an old form of Balinese no longer heard on the mainland, and there are also local types of dance, architecture and

Top: Lake Batur sunrise, Bali (JL)
 Left: Gunung Batur – dormant but not extinct, Bali (JL)
Right: Gunung Batur, Bali (PL)

Top: The famous bicycle rider sculpture, Pura Maduwe Karang, Kubutambahan (TW)
Left: View of Gunung Agung from Toyapakeh, Nusa Penida (JL)
Right: Young man on Nusa Lembongan (JL)

Nusa Penida

0   2   4 km

craft, including a unique type of red ikat weaving. The people have had little contact with foreign visitors and the children are more likely to stare than shout 'hello mister'. They are not unfriendly, just bemused. Many people do not speak Indonesian and almost no-one speaks English.

Sampalan

There's nothing inspiring about Sampalan, but it's pleasant enough, with a market, warungs, schools and shops strung out along the coast road. The market area, where the bemos congregate, is on the northern side of the road, by definition almost in the middle of the town. Buyuk Harbour, where the boats leave for Padangbai, is a few hundred metres west of the market. The town's only losmen is opposite the police station, a few hundred metres in the opposite direction.

Goa Karangsari

If you follow the coast road south-east from Sampalan for about six km, you'll see the cave entrance up the hill on the right side of the road, just before the village of Karangsari. You might have to ask for directions. The entrance is a small cleft in the rocks, but the cave is quite large, extending for over 200 metres into the hillside. Many small bats live in the cave – they're noisy but harmless. During the Galungan festival there is a torch-lit procession into the cave, followed by ceremonies at a temple by the lake in one of the large chambers. If you want to do more than put your head in the entrance, bring a good torch.

Toyapakeh

If you come by boat from Nusa Lembongan you'll probably be dropped on, or just off, the beach at Toyapakeh. It's a pretty town with lots of shady trees. The beach has clean white sand, clear blue water, a neat line of prahus and Bali's Gunung Agung as a back-drop. Step up from the beach and you're at the roadhead, where there will be bemos to take you to Ped or Sampalan. Few travellers stay here, but if you want to, you'll find the *Losmen Terang* on your right, which has rooms for about 5000 rp.

Pura Dalem Penetaran Ped

This important temple is near the beach at the village of Ped, a few km east of Toyapakeh. It houses a shrine for Jero Gede Macaling, the source of power for the practitioners of black magic, and it's a place of pilgrimage for those seeking protection from sickness and evil. The temple structure is crude, even ugly, which gives it an appropriately sinister ambience.

Getting There & Away

The strait between Nusa Penida and southern Bali is very deep and subject to heavy swells – hence the big surf on the reefs around Nusa Penida. If there is a strong tide running, the boats may have to wait. You may also have to wait a while for a boat to fill up, unless you are prepared to pay extra for a charter.

From Padangbai Fast, twin-engined fibre-glass boats now operate between Padangbai and Nusa Penida. The boats are about eight or 10 metres long and look pretty seaworthy, and some are well-supplied with life jackets, which is unusual for small Indonesian craft, as well as reassuring. The trip takes less than an hour and costs 3000 rp. It's an exciting ride as the boat bounces across the water beneath the looming volcano of Agung. At Padangbai, the boats land on the beach just east of the car park for the Bali to Lombok ferry. On Nusa Penida, the boats land at the beach at Buyuk Harbour, just west of Sampalan, but some may also go to Toyapakeh.

From Kusamba Prahus carry produce and supplies between Nusa Penida and Kusamba, which is the closest port to Klungkung, the district capital. The boats leave when they're full, weather and waves permitting, and cost about 2500 rp one-way. They are slower than the boats from Padangbai, and may be heavily loaded (over-loaded?) with provisions.

From Nusa Lembongan The boats that carry local people between the islands usually land at Toyapakeh. Ask around the beach-front area to find when the the next boat is leaving, and discuss the price. You may have to wait quite a while, or charter a boat.

Getting Around

There are regular bemos on the sealed road between Toyapakeh and Sampalan, on to Sewana and up to Klumpu, but beyond these areas the roads are rough or nonexistent and transport is uncertain. If you want to charter a bemo, try to find Wayan Patra, from Banjar Sentral Kanjin in Ped. He knows Nusa Penida well, and speaks English. You may be able to get someone to take you on the back of a motorbike, although this can be a high-risk form of transport. You could also try bringing a bicycle from the mainland, but remember Nusa Penida is hilly. If you really want to explore the island, you'll probably have to walk.

LOMBOK

West Lombok

AMPENAN, MATARAM, CAKRANEGARA & SWETA

Although officially four separate towns, Ampenan, Mataram, Cakranegara and Sweta actually run together, so it's virtually impossible to tell where one stops and the next starts. Collectively they're the main 'city' on Lombok, but these days many visitors head straight to Senggigi or the Gili Islands and don't stay in the town at all. You can now change money and arrange airline tickets at Senggigi, and it's within easy commuting distance if you need to do any other business in town. There are some interesting shops and markets, and a few things to see, but once that's out of the way most visitors head off to other places on the island.

Ampenan

Once the main port of Lombok, Ampenan is now not much more than a small fishing harbour. It's a bit run-down and dirty, but it's also full of hustle and bustle and colour and life. The long main road through Ampenan, Mataram and Cakranegara does not actually reach the coast at Ampenan, but simply fades out just before it gets to the port's grubby beach.

Ampenan has a curious mixture of people. Apart from the Sasaks and Balinese, there is also a small Arab quarter known as Kampung Arab (*kampung* means 'district' or 'quarter'). The Arabs living here are probably descendants of Arab merchants and Sasak women, and are devout Muslims.

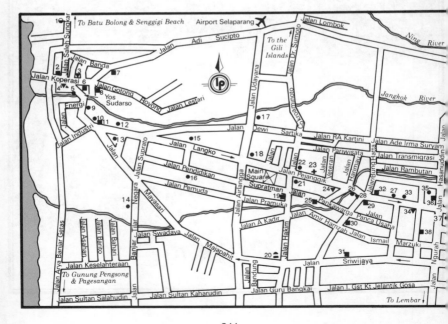

They marry among themselves, are well educated and relatively affluent. They're also extremely friendly towards foreigners.

Most of the Chinese living in Lombok today are based in Ampenan or Cakranegara – many shops and restaurants in Cakranegara are run or owned by the Chinese. The Chinese first came to Lombok with the Dutch as a cheap labour force, but the Dutch later fostered them as economic intermediaries between themselves and the Indonesian population. The Chinese soon became a privileged minority and were allowed to set up and develop their own businesses. When the Dutch were ousted from Indonesia in 1949, the Chinese stayed and continued to expand their business interests. Many of those in eastern Lombok however, were killed in the aftermath of the attempted '65 coup. The massacres were perhaps as much anti-Chinese as anti-Communist.

Mataram

Mataram is the administrative capital of the province of Nusa Tenggara Barat (West Nusa Tenggara) which comprises the islands of

■	PLACES TO STAY
2	Losmen Pabean
6	Zahir Hotel
7	Losmen Wisma Triguna
8	Losmen Horas & Latimojong
11	Wisma Melati
19	Hotel Kambodja
25	Losmen Rinjani
29	Mataram Hotel
30	Hotel Granada
31	Puri Indah Hotel
32	Selaparang Hotel
36	Hotel Pusaka
38	Hotel Shanti Puri

▼	PLACES TO EAT
3	Timur Tengah
4	Cirebon & Pabean
24	Garden House Restaurant
28	Rumah Makan Flamboyan
34	Sekawan Depot Es

	OTHER
1	Ampenan Bemo Stop
5	Ampenan Market
9 & 10	Merpati Offices
12	Tourist Office
13	Telephone Office
14	Museum Negeri
15	Bank Negara Indonesia
16	Mataram University
17	Immigration Office
18	Bank Indonesia
20	Main Post Office
21	Governor's House
22	Governor's Office
23	Hospital
26	Bali Ferry Office
27	Perama Office
33	Bank Eskpor-Impor
35	Motorbike Rental
37	Cakra Market
39	Mayura Water Palace
40	Selamat Riady
41	Pura Meru
42	Sweta Bemo/Bus Station
43	Sweta Market

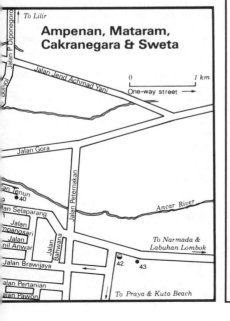

Ampenan, Mataram, Cakranegara & Sweta

Lombok and Sumbawa. Some of the public buildings, such as the Bank of Indonesia, the new post office and the governor's office and residence, are impressive. There are also some substantial houses around the outskirts of town – these are the homes of Lombok's elite.

Cakranegara

Now the main commercial centre of Lombok, Cakranegara is usually referred to as Cakra. Formerly the capital of Lombok under the Balinese rajahs, Cakra today is a cacophony of bemos and motorbikes and people trying to keep their heads above the exhaust fumes. It has a thriving Chinese community as well as many Balinese residents. It's also a craft centre and is particularly well known for its basketware and weaving. Check out the bazaar and watch the silver and goldsmiths at work. You may also be able to find some of the idiosyncratic clay animal figures and ceramics produced on Lombok.

Sweta

Seven km from Ampenan and only about 2½ km beyond Cakra is Sweta, the central transport terminal of Lombok. This is where you catch bemos, buses and minibuses to other parts of the island. There are several warungs here, and numerous food, tobacco and drink vendors. Stretching along the eastern side of the terminal is a vast, covered market, the largest on Lombok. If you wander through its dim alleys you'll see stalls spilling over with coffee beans, eggs, rice, fish, fabrics, crafts, fruit and hardware. There's also a bird market.

Orientation

The 'city' is effectively divided into four functional areas: Ampenan the port, Mataram the administrative centre, Cakranegara the trading centre and Sweta the transport centre. The towns are spread along one main road which starts as Jalan Pabean in Ampenan, quickly becomes Jalan Yos Sudarso, then changes to Jalan Langko, then to Jalan Pejanggik and finishes up in Sweta as Jalan Selaparang. It's a one-way street, running east from the port through Cakranegara. Just as it's difficult to tell where one town merges into the next, it's also difficult to tell where the road changes names. Indeed, it seems that they overlap, since some places appear to have more than one address.

A second one-way street, Jalan Sriwijaya/Jalan Majapahit, brings traffic back in the other direction. Bemos run a shuttle service between the bemo stop in Ampenan and the big station in Sweta about seven km away. Getting back and forth is therefore dead easy. You can stay in Ampenan, Mataram or Cakra since there are hotels and restaurants in all three places. Budget travellers tend to head towards Ampenan because it has a little enclave of cheap hotels and places to eat, but Mataram and Cakra are handy to shopping and transport, and the mid-range hotels there are good value.

Mataram has a small commercial 'centre' near the river and a larger shopping area past the Jalan Selaparang/Jalan Hasanuddin intersection. You'll find the Cakra market just east of here, south of the main road. The Mataram government buildings are chiefly found along Jalan Pejanggik. The main square, Lampangan Mataram, is on the south side of Jalan Pejanggik. Art exhibitions, theatre, dance and wayang kulit performances are held in the square, but you'll only find out about these shows by word of mouth. Alternatively, look for the swarms of police and military personnel that are the most obvious sign of such an occasion.

Information

Tourist Office The main Lombok government tourist office, the Kantor Dinas Pariwisata Daerah (☎ 21866, 21730), is in Mataram at Jalan Langko 70, on the north side, almost diagonally opposite the telephone office. The people at the tourist office are helpful and reasonably well informed. They have a good pamphlet with tourist information and maps of Lombok, Sumbawa and Ampenan-Mataram-Cakranegara-Sweta. They're not very good maps, but they're the only ones around – every other tourist map seems to have been copied from these.

The Perama office (☎ 22764, 23368) is at Jalan Pejanggik 66. The staff are very helpful and provide good information, organise shuttle bus connections, change money and arrange day trips around Lombok.

Money There are a number of banks along the main drag, all in large buildings. Most will change travellers' cheques, although it can take some time. The Bank Ekspor-Impor seems to have longer opening hours than other banks: weekdays from 7.30 am to noon and from 1 to 2 pm, Saturdays from 7.30 to 11.30 am. The moneychanger, in the Mataram shopping centre (Kompleks APHM) on the south side of Jalan Pejanggik, is efficient, open for longer hours, and has rates only slightly less than at the banks. You can also change travellers' cheques at the airport and at the Perama office.

Remember that there are only minimal banking facilities elsewhere on the island so make sure you have enough cash with you. On the Gili Islands in particular there is nowhere to change travellers' cheques. In more remote parts of Lombok changing large denominations can be difficult, so don't carry big notes.

Post Mataram's main post office, on Jalan Majapahit (or is it Sriwijaya?), has a poste restante service. It's open from 8 am to 2 pm Monday to Thursday, and Saturday, and from 8 to 11 am on Friday. Mail sent from Lombok goes to Bali first, so it can take some time to get through.

If you want to mail things from Lombok you have to get customs clearance before they can be sent. You may need forms CP2 and five copies of form C2 and CP3 from the post office. From most post offices the maximum parcel size is three kg, but you can send 10 kg from the main post office.

Telecommunications The Permuntel telephone office, at the Ampenan end of Mataram on Jalan Langko, also has telegram and fax services. The international telephone service is very efficient, and you can usually get an overseas call through in minutes. A three-minute call costs around 25,000 rp to Australia, New Zealand or the USA, and 29,000 rp to the UK or Europe.

Immigration Lombok's kantor imigrasi (immigration office) is on Jalan Udayana, the road out to the airport.

Bookshops There are a number of bookshops along the main road through the towns. Toko Buku Titian in Ampenan has some English magazines and maps. The bookshop in Kompleks APHM, the Mataram shopping centre on the south side of Jalan Pejanggik, is also good. The daily *Jakarta Post* usually arrives at 2 pm the day after publication.

Weaving Factories
One of the last weaving factories still operating in Mataram is Selamat Riady, off Jalan Hasanuddin, where women weave delicate gold and silver thread sarongs and exquisite ikats on looms that look like they haven't altered since the Majapahit dynasty. A bemo will drop you within a few metres of the factory and you're welcome to wander around. The factory is open from 7.30 am. Rinjani Hand Woven at Jalan Pejanggik 44-46, beside the Selaparang Hotel, also has an interesting collection of woven materials.

Pura Segara
This Balinese sea temple is on the beach a few km north of Ampenan. Along the beach you can watch the fishing boats come and go. Nearby are the remnants of a Muslim cemetery and an old Chinese cemetery – worth a wander through if you're visiting the temple. You fly right over them on the approach to the airport from Bali.

Museum Negeri
The Museum Negeri Nusa Tenggara Barat is on Jalan Panji Tilar Negara in Ampenan. With exhibits on the geology, history and culture of Lombok and Sumbawa, it's well

worth browsing around if you have a couple of free hours. If you intend buying any antiques or handicrafts have a look at the krises, songket, basketware and masks to give you a starting point for comparison. It's open from 8 am to 2 pm Tuesday to Thursday, from 8 to 11 am Friday, and from 8 am to noon on weekends. Admission is 200 rp, 100 rp for children.

Mayura Water Palace

Just beyond the market, on the main road through Cakra, stands the Mayura Water Palace. It was built in 1744 and was once part of the royal court of the Balinese kingdom in Lombok. The centrepiece is the large artificial lake covered in water lilies. In the centre of the lake is an open-sided hall connected to the shoreline by a raised footpath. This Bale Kambang (Floating Pavilion) was used as both a court of justice and a meeting place for the Hindu lords. There are other shrines and fountains dotted around the surrounding park. Entrances to the walled enclosure of the palace are on the northern and western sides.

Today the Balinese use the palace grounds to graze their livestock and as a place to unleash their fighting cocks and make offerings to the gods. It's a pleasant retreat from Cakra, although less than a century ago it was the site of a bloody clash with the Dutch.

In 1894 the Dutch sent an army to back the Sasaks in a rebellion against their Balinese rajah. The rajah quickly capitulated but the crown prince decided to fight on while the Dutch-backed forces were split between various camps.

The Dutch camp at the Mayura Water Palace was attacked late at night by a combined force of Balinese and western Sasaks. The camp was surrounded by high walls, and the Balinese and Sasaks took cover behind them as they fired on the exposed army, forcing the Dutch to take shelter in a nearby temple compound. The Balinese also attacked the Dutch camp at Mataram, and soon after the entire Dutch army on Lombok was routed and withdrew to Ampenan where, according to one eyewitness, the soldiers 'were so nervous that they fired madly if so much as a leaf fell off a tree'. The first battles resulted in enormous losses of men and arms for the Dutch.

Although the Balinese had won the battle they had just begun to lose the war. Now they would not only

have to continue to fight the eastern Sasaks but also the Dutch, who were quickly supplied with reinforcements from Java. The Dutch attacked Mataram a month after their initial defeat, fighting street to street not only against Balinese and west Sasak soldiers but also the local population. The Balinese crown prince was killed in the battle for the palace and the Balinese retreated to Cakranegara, where they were well armed and where the complex of walls provided good defence against infantry. Cakra was attacked by a combined force of Dutch and eastern Sasaks and, as happened in Mataram, Balinese men, women and children staged repeated suicidal lance attacks, to be cut down by rifle and artillery fire. The rajah and a small group of *punggawas* (commanders) fled to the village of Sasari near the pleasure gardens at Lingsar. A day or two later the rajah surrendered to the Dutch, but even his capture did not lead the Balinese to surrender.

In late November the Dutch attacked Sasari and a large number of Balinese chose the suicidal puputan. With the downfall of the dynasty the local population abandoned its struggle against the Dutch. The conquest of Lombok, thought about for decades, had taken the Dutch barely three months. The old rajah died in exile in Batavia in 1895.

Pura Meru

Directly opposite the water palace and just off the main road is the Pura Meru, the largest temple on Lombok. It's open every day, and a donation is expected (about 500 rp or 'up to you'). It was built in 1720 under the patronage of the Balinese prince, Anak Agung Made Karang of the Singosari kingdom, as an attempt to unite all the small kingdoms on Lombok. Though now rather neglected looking, it was built as a symbol of the universe and is dedicated to the Hindu trinity of Brahma, Vishnu and Shiva.

The temple has three separate courtyards. The outer courtyard has a hall housing the wooden drums that are beaten to call believers to festivals and special ceremonies. In the middle court are two buildings with large raised platforms for offerings. The inner court has one large and 33 small shrines, as well as three meru (multi-roofed shrines). Each shrine is looked after by members of the Balinese community. The three meru are in a line: the central one, with 11 tiers, is Shiva's house; the one in the north, with nine tiers, is Vishnu's and the seven-tiered one in the south is Brahma's. A festival is held here each June.

Places to Stay – bottom end
The most popular cheap places to stay are in Ampenan. Although there is plenty of accommodation elsewhere, few travellers bother to go further afield unless they intend to head straight out to beautiful Senggigi Beach, just 10 km to the north. It's easy to commute into town from there for business.

Jalan Koperasi branches off Jalan Yos Sudarso in the centre of Ampenan. Only a short stroll from the centre is the *Hotel Zahir* (☎ 22403) at Jalan Koperasi 12. It's a straightforward place with singles/doubles at 4000/5000 rp, or 5000/6000 rp with bathroom. Prices include breakfast, and tea or coffee throughout the day. The rooms at this popular, convenient and friendly losmen each have a small verandah and face a central courtyard. The owners can arrange motorbike rental for about 7500 rp per day.

Continue along the road to Jalan Koperasi 65 where *Losmen Horas* (☎ 21695) is very clean and well kept. Singles/doubles with spotless bathrooms cost 4000/6000 rp. Virtually next door is the *Latimojong* at number 64. It's dirt cheap at 1500/2500 rp, but extremely basic and definitely a bottom-end place. Continuing further east you come to *Losmen Wisma Triguna* (☎ 21705), which is operated by the same people as the Horas. It's a little over a km from central Ampenan and a quiet, relaxed place. Spacious rooms opening on to a bright verandah or the garden cost 6000/8000 rp, including breakfast. The people at Horas or Wisma Triguna can help you organise a climb up Gunung Rinjani, and will rent camping equipment and arrange a guide.

Back in the centre of town is *Losmen Pabean* (☎ 21758) at Jalan Pabean 146, also known as Jalan Yos Sudarso. It's better inside than it looks from the outside. Rooms are 3500/5500 rp for singles/doubles; triples cost 7500 rp.

In Mataram, *Hotel Kambodja* (☎ 22211) on the corner of Jalan Supratman and Jalan Arif Rahmat is pleasant and has rooms at 6500/7500 rp.

Hotel Pusaka (☎ 23119), at Jalan Hasanuddin 23, has doubles from 12,500 up to 35,000 rp with air-con. The cheap rooms are pretty basic and the mid-range rooms are quite good at 17,000 rp a double. Close by, at Hasanuddin 17 is the *Losmen Merpati* with rooms at 3000/4000 rp, 5000/6000 rp and 6000/7000 rp. The cheapest rooms are depressingly basic.

Places to Stay – middle
There are quite a few good value, mid-range places in the Mataram-Cakra area. The *Selaparang Hotel* (☎ 22670), at Jalan Pejanggik 40-42 in Mataram, is close to the Perama office. Air-con rooms cost 35,000/40,000 rp for singles/doubles, and fan-cooled rooms about half this. Across the road at 105 is the *Mataram Hotel* (☎ 23411) with double rooms at 18,000 rp, or rooms with air-con, TV, hot water and other mod cons for up to 35,000 rp. Both these mid-range hotels have pleasant little restaurants. At Jalan Pejanggik 64, just west of the Perama office, is the *Hotel Hertajoga* (☎ 21775). It's good value, with fan-cooled rooms at 10,000/13,500 rp, and 15,000/18,500 rp with air-con.

Just south of the main drag, at Jalan Maktal 15, is the *Hotel & Restaurant Shanti Puri* (☎ 22649). Cheap singles/doubles are 5000/6000 rp, and very comfortable rooms cost up to 10,000/12000 rp. It's run by a friendly and helpful Balinese family who can also arrange motorbike and car hire. Also in Mataram, the *Wisma Chandra* (☎ 23979) at Jalan Caturwarga 55, has singles/doubles at 7000/9000 rp, triples at 15,000 rp. Rooms with air-con cost 15,000/17,500/20,000 rp. Prices include breakfast.

Places to Stay – top end
The heavily advertised *Hotel Granada* (☎ 22275) is a top-end place on Jalan Bung Karno, a little south of the shopping centre in Mataram. There's a swimming pool and all rooms are air-conditioned. The prices include breakfast but not the 10% tax, and start at around 50,000 rp a double. If you

want this kind of comfort, the *Puri Indah* (☎ 27633) on Jalan Sriwijaya also has a restaurant and a pool but is much better value at 15,000/20,000 rp, or 20,000/30,000 rp for air-con singles/doubles.

At the other end of Mataram, almost in Ampenan, the *Wisma Melati* (☎ 2364) is quiet and comfortable, with carpets, air-con, telephone etc. Standard rooms are 26,000/ 29,000 rp, superior rooms 44,000/52,000 rp for singles/doubles.

Places to Eat

Ampenan has several Indonesian and Chinese restaurants including the very popular *Cirebon*, at Jalan Pabean 113, with a standard Indonesian/Chinese menu and most dishes at 1500 to 2500 rp. Next door at 111 is the *Pabean* with similar food. Closer to the Ampenan bemo stop is the *Rumah Makan Arafat*, at No 64, with good, cheap Indonesian food. Other alternatives are the *Setia* at Jalan Pabean 129, the *Depot Mina* at Jalan Yos Sudarso 102 and the *Timur Tengah* at Jalan Koperasi 22, right across from the Hotel Zahir.

There are a couple of interesting restaurants at the Mataram shopping centre off Jalan Pejanggik, several hundred metres down the road from the governor's residence on the same side. The *Garden House Restaurant* is a pleasant open-air place with inexpensive nasi campur, nasi goreng and other standard meals. There's also a variety of ice cream dishes, plus casatta and tutti frutti! The nearby *Taliwang* offers local dishes. Continue further along the main road towards Cakra and you come to the more expensive *Rumah Makan Flamboyan*, a nice place with seafood and Chinese dishes.

In Cakra the *Sekawan Depot Es* has cold drinks downstairs and a seafood and Chinese restaurant upstairs. Around the corner on Jalan Hasanuddin is the *Rumah Makan Madya*, which serves very good, cheap food in authentic Sasak style. A little further north, the *Rumah Makan Akbar* also looks good. There are a number of other restaurants in this area, a handful of bakeries and, of course, plenty of places to buy food at the market.

Things to Buy

There are a surprising number of antique and handicraft shops in Lombok. Rora Antiques, in Ampenan at Jalan Yos Sudarso 16A, sells some excellent woodcarvings, baskets and traditional Lombok weavings (songket and so on). Renza Antiques, at Jalan Yos Sudarso 92, is also a good place to browse.

Musdah at Dayan Penen, Jalan Sape 16 also has an interesting collection of masks, baskets, krises and carvings for sale in a private residence. Describing how to get to there is virtually impossible but a series of signs leads you from the Hotel Zahir or other accommodations on Jalan Koperasi.

Another good place to look for handicrafts and other local products is the Sweta market, next to the Sweta bemo station.

Bargaining It's more difficult to bargain in Lombok than it is in Bali. You need to take your time – don't rush or be rushed. Bargaining is a ritual and a pastime as much as a commercial negotiation. It's also harder to make an accurate evaluation of things, particularly antiques. You'll hear a lot of talk about special Lombok prices – these are supposed to be much cheaper than Bali prices – but unless you know what you're doing you can pay as much, if not more, than you would in Bali. Be very sure you want to buy before making an offer. Try to get the dealer to put a price on the object before starting to bargain. Always bargain for what you buy, particularly for items like cloth, basketware or antiques. If you manage to get the price down to half the asking price then you're doing very well, although it's more likely that you will end up paying about two-thirds of the starting price or only get a nominal amount knocked off.

Getting There & Away

Air See the introductory Getting There & Away chapter for details of flights to and from Lombok. There's a Merpati office (☎ 23762) which can book and reconfirm

Garuda flights, at Jalan Yos Sudarso 6 in Ampenan. There's another Merpati office (☎ 21037) a little closer to the centre of Ampenan at Jalan Yos Sudarso 22, and a third one (☎ 22670, 23235) at the Selaparang Hotel, Jalan Pejanggik 40-42 in Mataram.

Bus The Sweta bus station is at the inland end of the Ampenan-Mataram-Cakra-Sweta development and is the main bus terminus for the entire island. It's also the eastern terminus for the local bemos which shuttle back and forth between Ampenan at one end and Sweta at the other. There's an office in the middle of the place, with a notice board on which you can check the fare before you're hustled on board one of the vehicles. Some distances and approximate bemo fares from Sweta to other parts of Lombok include:

Destination	Fare
East (Jurusan Timor)	
Narmada (6 km)	200 rp
Mantang (17 km)	450 rp
Kopang (25 km)	550 rp
Terara (29 km)	800 rp
Sikur (33 km)	800 rp
Masbagik (36 km)	850 rp
Selong (47 km)	1400 rp
Labuhan Lombok (69 km)	2000 rp
South & Central	
(Jurusan Selatan dan Tenggara)	
Kediri (5 km)	500 rp
Gerung (12 km)	500 rp
Lembar (22 km)	1000 rp
Praya (27 km)	700 rp
North (Jurusan Utara)	
Pemenang (31 km)	700 rp
Tanjung (45 km)	800 rp
Gondang (53 km)	1000 rp
Amor-Amor (64 km)	1100 rp
Bayan (79 km)	1600 rp

Boat See the Getting There & Away chapter for details of the ferry services to and from Lombok. The ferry docks at Lembar, 22 km south of Ampenan. The Bali ferry office is at Jalan Pejanggik 49 in Mataram.

The office for the Nawala hydrofoil service (☎ 21655) is at Jalan Langko 11A in Mataram.

Getting Around
To/From the Airport Lombok's Selaparang Airport is only a couple of km from Ampenan, and a taxi there costs about 4500 rp. Alternatively, you can walk out of the airport car park to the main road, and take one of the frequent No 7 bemos which run straight to the Ampenan bemo stop for 150 rp. It's not even necessary to go into town from the airport if you want to head out to Senggigi Beach or to the Gili Islands. See those sections for more details.

Bemo & Dokar Ampenan-Mataram-Cakra-Sweta is surprisingly sprawling, so don't plan to walk from place to place. Bemos shuttle back and forth along the main route between the Ampenan stop at one end and the Sweta station at the other. The fare is a standard 150 rp regardless of the distance. There are also plenty of dokars to rent for shorter trips around town, although these are not permitted on the main streets.

Chartering a bemo in Lombok is easy. Count on about 35,000 rp a day, or more for a long trip. Check the bemo over carefully as some are in decidedly poor condition. The Lombok section of the Getting Around chapter has more details. The bemo stop in Ampenan is a good place to charter a bemo.

Motorbike Motorbike rental on Lombok is usually less formal and not as straightforward as it is in Bali (see the Getting Around chapter), but it's still relatively easy to do. At the Cakranegara end of Mataram, go to Jalan Gelantik, off Jalan Selaparang near the junction with Jalan Hasanuddin. The motorbike owners who hang around there have bikes to rent for 8000 to 12,000 rp a day. As usual, the more you pay the better you get and it's wise to check a bike over carefully before saying yes. In fact this is even more important in Lombok because you can be a long way from help should you suffer a breakdown or puncture in a remote area. Some hotels also may have a motorbike to rent.

Car Car hire is also less formal than on Bali – basically you arrange to borrow a car from a private owner. They rarely insist on a licence, but may want you to leave a passport for security. There is usually an insurance cover for damage to other people or property, but the car itself is usually uninsured and you drive it at your own risk. It costs from about 35,000 to 50,000 rp per day for a Suzuki Jimny type vehicle, depending on where you get it and how you bargain. If you take it for a few days or a week you should get a discount. Between four people it can be quite a cheap way to get around. Hotels in town or at Senggigi can often arrange car hire. Metro Photo (☎ 22146) at Jalan Yos Sudarso 79 in Ampenan can arrange pretty cheap rental cars.

There are some 'official' car rental companies, but these tend to be more expensive. Rinjani Rent Car (☎ 21400), in Mataram opposite the Hotel Granada on Jalan Bung Karno, has Suzuki Jimnys for 50,000 rp per day without insurance. Yoga Rent Car (☎ 21127), in the Kompleks APHM shopping centre in Mataram, has similar cars for 45,000 rp per day.

Bicycle You can rent bicycles from the Losmen Horas or Wisma Triguna in Ampenan. It costs about 2000 rp a day for an old one, up to twice that for a new one.

GUNUNG PENGSONG

This Balinese temple is built – as the name suggests – on top of a hill. It's nine km south of Mataram and has great views of rice fields, the volcanoes and the sea. Try to get there early in the morning before the clouds envelop Gunung Rinjani. Once a year, generally in March or April, a buffalo is taken up the steep 100-metre slope and sacrificed to celebrate a good harvest. The Bersih Desa festival also occurs here at harvest time – houses and gardens are cleaned, fences whitewashed, roads and paths repaired. Once part of a ritual to rid the village of evil spirits, it is now held in honour of the rice goddess Dewi Sri. There's no set admission charge, but you will have to pay the caretaker 200 rp or so, especially if you use the car park.

LEMBAR

Lembar, 22 km south of Ampenan, is the main port on Lombok. The ferries and hydrofoils to and from Bali dock here, and there are regular buses and bemos between Lembar and Sweta during the day.

Places to Stay & Eat

There's only one place to stay in Lembar, the *Serumbum Indah*, which has a restaurant and singles/doubles from 12,500/15,000 rp. It's not very convenient, being about two km north of the harbour on the main road, and the owners aren't used to foreign visitors.

There's a canteen at the harbour where you can buy snacks and drinks while waiting to catch the ferry.

Getting There & Away

See the Getting There & Away chapter for information on the Bali to Lombok ferry and hydrofoil services. You can buy your tickets at the wharf on the day, or from the offices in Mataram.

Regular buses and bemos from Sweta cost 1000 rp during the day. You are dropped off almost directly in front of the Lembar ferry office. If you arrive in Lembar on the afternoon ferry from Bali, buy a bemo ticket on the journey over. Although you'll be paying more than the normal price, you'll have guaranteed transport to Ampenan, Mataram or Cakranegara. Bemo drivers meeting travellers off this ferry often jack up their prices to more than 1000 rp after dark. A minibus from the Zahir Hotel in Ampenan often meets the ferry.

SOUTH-WESTERN PENINSULA

If you approach Lembar by ferry you'll see a hilly and little-developed peninsula on your right. A road from Lembar runs on to this peninsula in Lombok's south-west, but it's pretty rough after Sekotong, and impassable for ordinary cars after Taun. Bangko Bangko is at the end of the track, and from there it's a two or three km walk to a beach

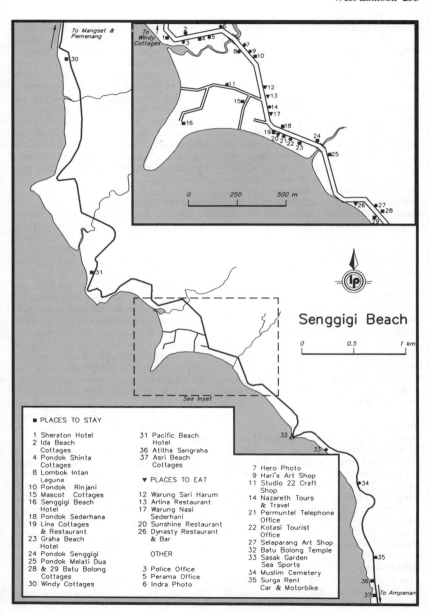

■ PLACES TO STAY

1 Sheraton Hotel
2 Ida Beach
  Cottages
4 Pondok Shinta
  Cottages
8 Lombok Intan
  Laguna
10 Pondok Rinjani
15 Mascot Cottages
16 Senggigi Beach
   Hotel
18 Pondok Sederhana
19 Lina Cottages
   & Restaurant
23 Graha Beach
   Hotel
24 Pondok Senggigi
25 Pondok Melati Dua
28 & 29 Batu Bolong
   Cottages
30 Windy Cottages

31 Pacific Beach
   Hotel
36 Atitha Sangraha
37 Asri Beach
   Cottages

▼ PLACES TO EAT

12 Warung Sari Harum
13 Arlina Restaurant
17 Warung Nasi
   Sederhani
20 Sunshine Restaurant
26 Dynasty Restaurant
   & Bar

   OTHER

3 Police Office
5 Perama Office
6 Indra Photo

7 Hero Photo
9 Hari's Art Shop
11 Studio 22 Craft
   Shop
14 Nazareth Tours
   & Travel
21 Permuntel Telephone
   Office
22 Kotasi Tourist
   Office
27 Selaparang Art Shop
32 Batu Bolong Temple
33 Sasak Garden
   Sea Sports
34 Muslim Cemetery
35 Surga Rent
   Car & Motorbike

which has great surf but no places to stay or eat. There are a number of picturesque islands off the north coast of the peninsula and one of them, Gili Nanggu, has some tourist bungalows. You can get a boat there from Lembar.

SENGGIGI

On a series of sweeping bays, between seven and 12 km north of Ampenan, Senggigi has become the most popular tourist area on Lombok. These days many travellers head straight for this string of beaches without stopping in Ampenan-Mataram-Cakra-Sweta. Promotional work for the big, expensive Senggigi Beach Hotel has focused much more interest on Senggigi and on Lombok as a whole. There are now a few other fancy places in Senggigi, and the Lombok government is encouraging more four- and five-star developments. Fortunately, however, there is still some budget accommodation there.

Senggigi has fine beaches, although they slope very steeply into the water. There's some snorkelling off the point and in the sheltered bay around the headland. There are beautiful sunsets over the Lombok Strait and you can enjoy them from the beach or from one of the beach-front restaurants. The nightlife can be pretty active, with home-grown rock bands playing to enthusiastic crowds of locals and visitors.

Information

You can change money or travellers' cheques at the Graha Beach Hotel, in the middle of the Senggigi strip. The staff can also make bookings and confirm flights for Garuda and Merpati. There's a Perama office further north which runs tours and tourist transport and will also provide information and change money. Other facilities include a Permuntel telephone office and some photo-processing places.

Batu Bolong

This temple is on a rocky point which juts into the sea about a km south of Senggigi Beach, eight km north of Ampenan. The rock

on which it sits has a natural hole in it which gives the temple its name – *batu bolong* means literally 'rock with hole'. Being a Balinese temple, it's oriented towards Gunung Agung, Bali's holiest mountain, across the Lombok Strait. There's a fantastic view and it's a good place to watch the sunsets. Periodically the local people make offerings here, and legend has it that beautiful virgins were once thrown into the sea from the top of the rock. Locals like to claim that this is why the temple was built and why there are so many sharks in the water near Batu Bolong.

Places to Stay – bottom end

Senggigi is moving up-market. Although there's plenty of mid-range accommodation, and an increasing number of expensive places, there's not that much for shoestring travellers. The most popular travellers' centre at Senggigi is the *Pondok Senggigi*. It's expanded a bit, but still has some cheaper rooms at 6000/8000 rp for singles/doubles. There's a good restaurant, and rooms with Western-style bathrooms for 15,000/ 18,000 rp. The rooms run off a long verandah with a pleasant garden area in front. Along the other side of the garden are comfortable individual bungalows at 20,000/ 25,000 rp. The Pondok Senggigi sometimes has live music and alot of people hang around the restaurant area which isn't separated from the rooms, so security is not great. We've had a report that women travellers have been harrassed here.

One of the cheapest places to stay is *Pondok Sederhana*, north-west of Pondok Senggigi. These rooms, staggered up the hillside, are a bit grotty but the position is good and the prices, from about 5000 rp with shared mandi and toilet, are hard to beat.

The *Pondok Shinta Cottages* are a bit isolated, but if that appeals to you they're cheap at 8000/10,000 rp, including breakfast and tax.

Places to Stay – middle

About the first place you'll strike coming in from Ampenan is *Asri Beach Cottages*, with standard rooms at 10,000 rp and bungalows at 15,000 rp, including tax and breakfast. They're basic but clean, and near the beach. Just north of Asri is *Atitha Sangraha*, a nice new place with spotlessly clean cottages near the beach at 14,500/16,500 rp for singles/doubles.

Batu Bolong Cottages (☎ 24598), have bungalows on both sides of the road. On the beach side they cost from 29,000 rp, and on the other side from 23,000 rp, including tax.

The better rooms at *Pondok Senggigi* are good value mid-range accommodation, and the small *Pondok Melati Dua* next door has standard rooms at 16,500/22,000 rp and cottages at 18,700/27,500 rp, including tax and breakfast.

Lina Cottages, with rooms at 20,000/25,000 rp, is reasonable value and its restaurant has a good reputation. A little further north, *Pondok Rinjani* has cottages with private bathrooms at 15,000/20,000 rp plus tax. It's OK, but if you're a light sleeper you'll notice that there's a mosque next door.

Windy Cottages are out by themselves, north of Senggigi in an area known as Mangset. It's a great location if you want to get away from it all, and the restaurant has good food. There are only eight rooms, at 10,000/15,000 rp for singles/doubles.

Places to Stay – top end

Senggigi's first big 'international standard' hotel is right on the headland. Operated by Garuda, the *Senggigi Beach Hotel* (☎ 23430) charges from US$52/62 for an air-con room and up to US$120 for a deluxe bungalow. The hotel has a beautiful setting, a swimming pool and other mod cons. At least as classy is the new *Lombok Intan Laguna* (☎ 23659), a large and handsome luxury hotel with deluxe bungalows from US$90 and a presidential suite for US$550, plus 21% tax and service.

Mascot Cottages (☎ 23865), near the Senggigi Beach Hotel, are pleasant individual cottages from US$23/26 for singles/doubles, plus 21% service and tax. The *Graha Beach Hotel* (☎ 23782), just north of the Pondok Senggigi on the other side of the

road, has singles/doubles at US$40/45, with air-con, TV and a beach-front restaurant.

Ida Beach Cottages (☎ 21013, 21353) is very pleasant, with air-con, telephone, TV, hot water and great views. Standard rooms cost US$45 and suites up to US$90, including tax and service. There's a swimming pool and restaurant, and children are welcome.

At the northern end of Senggigi, the *Pacific Beach Hotel* is another 'international standard' place with air-con, TV, hot water, swimming pool and prices in US$. Standard rooms cost US$25/30 for singles/doubles; add US$5 for deluxe rooms, or US$20 for 'VIP' rooms, plus 21% tax and service. Even further north in Mangset you'll find *Bunga Beach Cottages*, another new place with a splendid beach-front position and 28 comfortable, air-conditioned bungalows at 70,000/80,000 rp.

Other top-end places under construction include the *Sheraton*, the *Senggigi Palace Hotel* and the *Senggigi Resort Hotel*.

Places to Eat

Most of the places to stay have their own restaurants and, of course, you can eat at any one you like. The open-air restaurant at *Pondok Senggigi* is far and away the number one dining attraction, and is deservedly popular from breakfast time until late at night. The restaurant at *Lina Cottages* has some very tasty dishes and is also popular. The *Senggigi Beach Hotel* restaurant is noted for its high prices, while the one at the *Graha Beach Hotel* is noted for its slow service.

At the bottom end of the scale, the small *Warung Nasi Sederhani* is mainly for local people, but tourists are quite welcome to enjoy its standard Indonesian food at rock-bottom prices. In the same area, the *Sunshine Restaurant* has a typical tourist menu and good Chinese food. Further north is the *Arlina Restaurant* and the *Warung Sari Harum*, another good-value place.

Coming in from the south you'll pass the *Dynasty Restaurant & Bar* which seems to be poorly patronised. There's a pool table and cheap beer, and Chinese dishes cost from about 3500 rp, which is pretty standard. At the other end of the Senggigi strip, the restaurant at *Windy Cottages* serves good food at reasonable prices in a delightful seaside setting.

Entertainment
There's quite a music scene in this part of Lombok. The local bands do good rock and reggae music with an Indonesian flavour, as well as covers of popular Western numbers. Cassettes of Indonesian bands are available, and you'll probably hear them in bemos and buses. *Pondok Senggigi* and the *Graha Beach Hotel* both have live music on occasions, with both tourists and young locals crowding the dance floor. As the lead singer of one band said, attempting to reach the British, US, Australian and Indonesian members of his audience, 'It's super mega bloody bagus!'.

Getting There & Away
A public bemo from Ampenan to Senggigi is about 250 rp. (There's a bemo stop on the coast road just north of Ampenan.) To get to Senggigi from the airport, first get a bemo to Lendang Bajur, just north of the airport on the road to Pemenang. From Lendang Bajur you can catch a bus to Senggigi, making the total fare about 500 rp. A taxi from the airport to Senggigi will cost around 7500 rp.

NARMADA
Laid out as a miniature replica of the summit of Gunung Rinjani and its crater lake, Narmada is a hill about 10 km east of Cakra, on the main east-west road crossing Lombok. It takes its name from a sacred river in India and the temple here, Pura Kalasa, is still used. The Balinese Pujawali celebration is held here every year in honour of the god Batara, who dwells on Gunung Rinjani. At the same time the faithful, who have made the trek up the mountain and down to Lake Segara Anak, hold a ritual called pekelan in which they dispose of their gold trinkets and artefacts by ceremonially throwing them into the lake.

Narmada was constructed by the king of Mataram in 1805, when he was no longer able to climb Rinjani to make his offerings to the gods. Having set his conscience at rest by placing offerings in the temple, he spent at least some of his time in his pavilion on the hill, lusting after the young girls bathing in the artificial lake.

It's a beautiful place to spend a few hours, although the gardens are neglected. Don't go there on weekends, when it tends to become very crowded. Apart from the lake there are two other pools in the grounds. Admission is 250 rp, 125 rp for children, and there's an additional charge to swim in the pool.

Along one side of the pool is the remains of an aqueduct built by the Dutch and still in use. Land tax was tied to the productivity of the land so the Dutch were keenly interested in increasing agricultural output. They did this by extending irrigation systems to increase the area under cultivation. The Balinese had already built extensive irrigation networks, particularly in the west of Lombok.

The construction of roads and bridges was also given high priority, because from both a political and an economic point of view it was in the Dutch interest to establish a good communication system. A large number of roads and tracks were constructed which, like the aqueducts, were built and maintained with the unpaid labour of Lombok peasants.

Places to Eat
Right at the Narmada bemo station is the local market, which sells mainly food and clothing and is well worth a look. There are a number of warungs scattered around offering soto ayam (chicken soup) and other dishes.

Getting There & Away
There are frequent bemos from Sweta to Narmada, costing around 200 rp. When you get off at the bemo station at Narmada, you'll see the gardens directly opposite. If you cross the road and walk 100 metres or so south along the sideroad you'll come to the entrance. There are parking fees for bicycles, motorbikes and cars.

LINGSAR
This large temple complex, just a few km north of Narmada, is said to have been built in 1714. The temple combines the Bali

Hindu and Wektu Telu religions in one complex. Designed in two separate sections and built on two different levels, the Hindu pura in the northern section is higher than the Wektu Telu temple in the southern section.

The Hindu temple has four shrines. On one side is Hyang Tunggal, which looks towards Gunung Agung and is the seat of the gods in Bali. The shrine faces north-west rather than north-east as it would in Bali. On the other side is a shrine devoted to Gunung Rinjani, the seat of the gods in Lombok. Between these two shrines is a double shrine symbolising the union between the two islands. One side of this double shrine is named in honour of the might of Lombok, and the other side is dedicated to a king's daughter, Ayu Nyoman Winton who, according to legend, gave birth to a god.

The Wektu Telu temple is noted for its small enclosed pond devoted to Lord Vishnu. It has a number of holy eels that can be enticed from their hiding places along the water ducts by persistent tapping on the walls and the use of hard-boiled eggs as bait. Apart from their outstanding size, they're rather unprepossessing – like huge swimming slugs. The stalls outside the temple complex sell boiled eggs – expect to pay around 200 rp or so. Next to the eel pond is another enclosure with a kind of large altar or offering place, bedecked in white and yellow cloth and mirrors. The mirrors are offered by Chinese business people asking for good luck and success. Many local farmers also come here with offerings, or to feed the holy eels.

On the right as you enter the temple, running almost its entire length and hidden behind a wall, is a women's washing place. It's mainly a series of individual fountains squirting holy water and, once again, there are holy eels here. There's a men's mandi at the back. You can bathe here, but Narmada is probably a better place to swim.

Once a year at the beginning of the rainy season – somewhere between October and December – the Hindus and the Wektu Telus make offerings and pray in their own temples, then come out into the communal compound and pelt each other with ketupat – rice wrapped in banana leaves. No-one quite knows what this ceremony is for. Some say it's to bring the rain, others to give thanks for the rain. Be prepared to get attacked with ketupat from both sides if you visit Lingsar at this time!

Getting There & Away
There are frequent bemos from Sweta to Narmada for 200 rp. At Narmada, you can catch another bemo to Lingsar for the same price, and walk the short distance from there to the temple complex. Watch for the school on the main road – it's easy to miss the temple, which is set back off the road behind the school.

There is a large square in front of the temple complex, with a couple of warungs to the right before you enter the main area. There's a small stall closer to the temple where you can buy snacks, and hard-boiled eggs for the holy eels. If the temple is locked ask at one of the warungs for a key.

SURANADI
A few km east of Lingsar, Suranadi has one of the holiest temples on Lombok. This small temple, set in pleasant gardens, is noted for its bubbling, icy cold spring water and restored baths with ornate Balinese carvings. The eels here have also been sanctified. Drop a hard-boiled egg into the water and watch the eels swim out of the conduits for a feed.

You can also swim here so bring your swimsuit. It is polite to ask permission before jumping in.

Hutan Wisata Suranadi

Not far from Suranadi, on the road towards Sesaot, there's a small jungle sanctuary, the Hutan Wisata Suranadi (*hutan* means 'forest' or 'jungle'). There are various types of trees, some with botanical labels, as well as walks of up to 1½ hours. Along the way you can see many types of birds and butterflies as well as some brown monkeys.

Places to Stay & Eat

The *Suranadi Hotel* (☎ 23686) has rooms at a variety of prices from US$12, and cottages from about US$30, plus 21% tax and service. It's an old Dutch building, originally an administrative centre, although it's no great example of colonial architecture. There are two swimming pools, tennis courts, a restaurant and a bar. People not staying at the hotel can use the swimming pool for 1000 rp (children 250 rp).

Apart from the restaurant in the hotel, there are also a few warungs in the main street.

SESAOT

About five km from Suranadi, and also worth a visit, is Sesaot, a small quiet market town on the edge of a forest where wood-felling is the main industry. There's regular transport from Suranadi to Sesaot and you can eat at the warung on the main street, which has simple but tasty food.

Go up the main street and turn left over the bridge. There are some nice places for picnics, popular with locals on holidays, and you can swim in the river. The water is very cool and is considered holy as it comes straight from Gunung Rinjani. You can continue up the road about three km to Air Nyet, a small village with more places for swimming and picnics.

Central, South & East Lombok

Central Lombok, the first section of this chapter, is the name of one of the six administrative districts (kabupaten) of West Nusa Tenggara Province, but here it is used in a more general sense to cover the inland towns and villages between Gunung Rinjani and the south coast. The second section of this chapter deals with the beautiful beach areas on the south coast while the third section covers the east coast, an area scarcely visited by foreigners except those using the ferry port at Labuhan Lombok.

Central Lombok

Most of the places in central Lombok are more or less traditional Sasak settlements, and several of them are known for particular types of local handicrafts. The area on the southern slopes of Gunung Rinjani is well watered and lush, and offers opportunities for scenic walks through the rice fields and the jungle. South of the main east-west road, the country is drier, and some quite large dams have been built to provide irrigation during the dry season.

KOTARAJA

Basketware from Lombok has such a fine reputation in the archipelago that many Balinese make special buying trips to Lombok, reselling the basketware to foreigners in Bali at inflated prices. The villages of Kotaraja and Loyok in eastern Lombok are noted for their handicrafts, particularly basketware and plaited mats, but there are only a couple of places where visitors can buy the stuff. There is some very good quality work, but it seems that most of it is sold directly for export. Exquisitely intricate jewellery, vases, caskets and other decorative objects also come from Kotaraja.

Kotaraja means 'city of kings', although no kings ruled from here. Apparently, when

the Sasak kingdom of Langko, located at Kopang in central Lombok, fell to the Balinese invaders, the rulers of Langko fled to Loyok, the village south of Kotaraja. After the royal compound in that village was also destroyed, two sons of the ruler of Langko went to live in Kotaraja. The aristocracy of Kotaraja can trace their ancestry back to these brothers, although the highest caste title of raden has now petered out through intermarriage.

Places to Stay
The only option in Kotaraja itself is to stay with the kepala desa. Otherwise, you can stay nearby at Tetebatu or Lendang Nangka.

Getting There & Away
Kotaraja is 32 km from Sweta. If you go by bemo you have to change a couple of times. From Sweta you take a bemo to Narmada for 200 rp, and from there another bemo to Pomotong (also spelt Pao' Motong) for about 600 rp. From Pomotong you can either get a dokar to Kotaraja (400 rp), or wait for one of the infrequent bemos which are a bit cheaper. You might also get a lift on the back of a motorbike. There is a direct bus from Sweta to Pomotong but, as you may have to wait around for a while, it may actually be quicker and easier to take a bemo.

LOYOK
Loyok, a tiny village just a few km from Kotaraja, is also noted for its fine handicrafts despite being very much off the trampled track. Most of the craftspeople work from their homes, but the dokar drivers will be able to take you to where the basket weavers work. There's a place in the main street where you can buy some of the excellent basketware.

Getting There & Away
To get to Loyok, you can get a bemo from Pomotong to take you as far as the turn-off

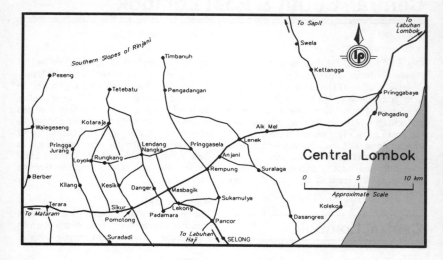

to the village, and then either walk the rest of the way or get a dokar for 250 rp per person. If you're setting out from Kotaraja for Loyok you've got the same options – either take a dokar or walk. It's a very pretty drive, with traditional thatched Sasak huts and lush rice terraces along the way.

PRINGGASELA

This village, east of Kotaraja, is another centre for traditional craftwork. You can stay in Lenek, near Pringgasela, at the *Wisma Longgali Permai*, which costs about 7500 rp for a room.

TETEBATU

A mountain retreat at the foot of Gunung Rinjani, Tetebatu is 50 km from Mataram and about four km north of Kotaraja. Like Loyok it was originally an offshoot settlement of Kotaraja. It's quite a bit cooler here, and it can be misty and rainy, particularly between November and April.

There are magnificent views over southern Lombok, east to the sea and north to Gunung Rinjani. You can climb part way up Rinjani from here but the formerly magnificent stands of mahogany trees have virtually disappeared. Other destinations for walks include Jukut Waterfall, six km to the east, and the hutan (forest), four km north-west, where lots of jet-black monkeys will shriek at you.

Places to Stay & Eat

The original place to stay is *Wisma Soedjono*, an old colonial house that was once a country retreat for a Dr Soedjono. A number of rooms and bungalows have been added as well as a restaurant and a good-sized swimming pool. In the simplest rooms, prices start at 7500/11,000 rp for singles/doubles, and peak at 25,000/35,000 rp for 'VIP' accommodation. The better rooms have Western-style toilets and showers with hot water, and all prices include tax and continental breakfast. The staff provide good information about walks in the area. Food here is excellent, but costs extra – you can even get a packed lunch if you want to spend the day out walking. In fact, everything here costs extra – even parking a motorbike while you have lunch will cost money.

A cheaper place is *Diwi Enjeni*, on the south side of town. It seems to be stuck out in the rice fields by itself, but has a nice outlook. Bungalows with outside mandi cost 4000/5000 rp for singles/doubles, including breakfast and tax. Bungalows with a private mandi cost about 1500 rp more. There's a restaurant here, and another one, the *Restaurant Alan*, is on the opposite side of the road. There are also two or three warungs in the town.

Getting There & Away

Getting to Tetebatu involves a number of changes if you haven't got your own wheels. Take a direct bus from Sweta to Pomotong or, if you can't wait that long, take a bemo to Narmada for 200 rp, and then another to Pomotong for 600 rp. From Pomotong take a bemo (250 rp) or a dokar (400 rp) to Kotaraja, and from there another bemo or dokar to Tetebatu. If you're not in a hurry and you're not carrying too much, you can walk from Pomotong to Tetebatu. It's an easy 2½ to three hours, through attractive country patched with rice fields.

LENDANG NANGKA

Lendang Nangka is a small village seven km from Tetebatu. Hadji Radiah is a local primary school teacher who has been encouraging people to stay in Lendang Nangka, which is a traditional Sasak village with similar surroundings to those of Tetebatu. In and around the village you can see blacksmiths who still make knives, hoes and other tools using indigenous techniques. Jojang, the biggest spring in Lombok, is a few km away or you can walk to a waterfall

Lendang Nangka

Radiah's House ●

School

Mosque

To Masbagik

Monument

● Market

To Bagek Bontong

with beautiful views, or see the black monkeys in a nearby forest.

In August you should be able to see the traditional Sasak form of boxing at Lendang Nangka. It's a violent affair with leather-covered shields and bamboo poles. Local dances are a possibility at Batu Empas, one km away. At the village of Pringgasela the girls weave Sasak cloths, blankets and sarongs. It's a few km east of Lendang Nangka – take a dokar or walk.

Since Radiah originally wrote to us for the first edition of the *Bali & Lombok* guide book, his family homestay has become quite popular among travellers who want an experience of typical Lombok village life. He speaks English very well, and is a mine of information on the surrounding countryside and customs. He has a map for local walks and enjoys acting as a guide – he may even drive you around to nearby villages and sights on his motorbike.

Places to Stay

Staying with Radiah will cost you about 10,000/14,000 rp for a single/double, including three excellent meals per day of local Sasak food, and tea or coffee. You will get customary Sasak cake and fruit for breakfast – it's good value and highly recommended. His house is fairly easy to find in Tetebatu (see the map, but everyone knows him), and has 12 bedrooms for guests, each with a bathroom and toilet. If his place is full, he may be able to find accommodation for you in one of the nearby villages – the idea is to avoid a big concentration of visitors in one place.

Getting There & Away

Take a bemo from Sweta to Masbagik (42 km, 850 rp) and then take a dokar to Lendang Nangka (about four km, 350 rp). Lendang Nangka is about five km from Pomotong and connected by a surfaced road – take a dokar for 400 rp (500 rp if you have a heavy load).

RUNGKANG

This small village, less than a km east of Loyok, is known for its pottery, which is made from a local black clay. The pots are often finished with attractive cane work, which is woven all over the outside for decoration and for greater strength. Similar pottery is made in a number of other villages in the area south of the main road.

SUKARARA

Twenty-five km south of Mataram, not far off the Kediri to Praya road, is the small village of Sukarara. On the way to this traditional weaving centre you'll pass picturesque thatched-roof villages surrounded by rice fields. More unusual are the houses built from local stone found in Sukarara. In this area, watch for Sasak women in their traditional black costume with brightly coloured edgings.

Lombok is renowned for its traditional weaving, the techniques for which have been handed down from mother to daughter for generations. Each piece of cloth is woven on a handloom in established patterns and colours. Some fabrics are woven in as many as four directions and interwoven with gold thread. They can be so complicated that they take one person three months to complete. Many incorporate flower and animal motifs including buffaloes, dragons, lizards, crocodiles and snakes. Several villages, including Sukarara and Pringgasela, specialise in this craft.

Nearly every house in Sukarara has an old wooden handloom. Along the main street there are half a dozen places with looms set up outside, and displays of sarongs hanging in bright bands. You can stop at one, watch the women weaving and buy direct. One place worth trying is the Taufik Weaving Company on Jalan Tenun. The manager's name is Widasih and he has sarongs, songkets, Sasak belts, tablecloths and numerous other pieces.

Before you go to Sukarara it may be a good idea to check prices in the Selamat Riady weaving factory in Cakranegara, and get some idea of how much to pay and where to start bargaining. There's such a range of quality and size that it's impossible to give a guide to prices, but the best pieces are magnificent and well worth paying for. If you're accompanied to Sukarara it will inevitably cost you more through commissions. Although the village is a regular stop for tour groups, the people are very friendly and if you eat or drink at the warung you'll be surrounded by locals.

Places to Stay

Stay with the kepala desa or make a day trip. You could also check with the woman who runs the warung – she sometimes puts people up for the night and has a fine selection of cloth for sale.

Getting There & Away

Get a bemo from Sweta towards Praya, and get off at Puyung (about 600 rp). From Puyung you can hire a dokar for about 200 rp to take you the two km to Sukarara.

PENUJAK

This small village, six km south of Praya, is well known for its traditional *gerabah* pottery made from a local red clay. You'll see the pottery places from the road, and you can watch the pots being made by hand and fired in traditional kilns. There's a lot worth buying, but the bigger pieces would be hard to carry.

Pots range in size up to a metre high, and there are kitchen vessels of various types, and decorative figurines, usually in the shape of animals. Look for the water containers in a characteristic local design, with a filling hole in the bottom and a drinking spout on the side. They're almost spill-proof, and the clay is slightly porous so some moisture seeps through to the outside, providing natural evaporative cooling. The local industry has formed a partnership with a New Zealand organisation to develop export markets for its products, so hopefully this distinctive pottery will become more widely known.

LENANG

Just east of the road between Puyung and Praya, Lenang is not really a tourist destination. It is, however, a centre for 'white magic'

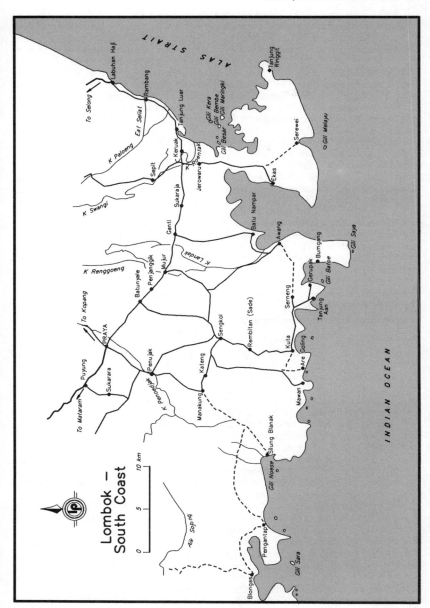

Lombok –
South Coast

– Pak Aripin is famous throughout Lombok for healing broken bones, virtually while you wait. Hopefully, you won't need to visit him.

REMBITAN (SADE)

The village of Rembitan, also known as Sade, is a slightly sanitised Sasak village where tourists are welcome to look around, with one of the local kids as a guide. It's a few km south of Sengkol and has a population of about 750. You can check the vital statistics of the village on the charts displayed on the porch of the village meeting house. Masjid Kuno, an old thatched-roof mosque, tops the hill around which the village houses cluster.

The area from Sengkol down to Kuta Beach is a centre of traditional Sasak culture, and there are many relatively unchanged Sasak villages where the people still live in customary houses and engage in indigenous craftwork.

South Lombok

The best known place on the south coast is Lombok's Kuta Beach, a magnificent stretch of sand with impressive hills rising around it. At the moment, it has far less tourists than the better known Kuta Beach in Bali, but there are plans to develop not only Kuta, but a whole stretch of the superb south coast with four- and five-star hotels. People flock to Kuta for the annual nyale fishing celebration, usually falling in February or March each year, but otherwise it's very quiet. Stinging seaweed is said to make swimming unpleasant at times, but the south coast has great potential for surfing and windsurfing if you know when and where to go.

East of Kuta is a series of beautiful bays punctuated by headlands. All the beach-front land has been bought by the government for planned tourist resorts. Segar Beach is about two km east around the first headland, and you can easily walk there. An enormous rock about four km east of the village offers superb views across the countryside if you climb it early in the morning. The road goes five km east to Tanjung Aan (Cape Aan) where there are two classic beaches with very fine, powdery white sand. You can see the beginnings of the expensive hotels planned for this area. Both the excellent quality of the road and the new hotel developments are said to be related to the political connections of the developers.

The road continues another three km to the fishing village of Gerupak, where there's a market on Tuesday. From there you can get a boat cross the bay to Bumgang. Alternatively, turn north just before Tanjung Aan and go to Serneng. Beyond here the road deteriorates, but you can get to Awang with a motorbike or on foot, then continue into south-eastern Lombok.

West of Kuta are more fine beaches at Mawan and Silung Blanak, both known for their surfing possibilities. There are no facilities and no direct roads suitable for ordinary vehicles. You'll have to go into Sengkol first, then out again to the coast.

KUTA BEACH
Information

There are no banks or moneychangers in Kuta, so bring enough rupiah to keep you going. There's a market twice a week, on Sunday and Wednesday.

Nyale Fishing Festival

Once a year a special Sasak celebration is held in Kuta for the opening of the nyale fishing season. On the 19th day of the 10th month in the Sasak calendar – generally February or March – hundreds of Sasaks gather on the beach. When night falls, fires are built and the young people sit around competing with each other in rhyming couplets called *pantun*. At dawn the next morning, the first nyale are caught, after which it is time for the Sasak teenagers to have fun. In a colourful procession boys and girls put out to sea – in different boats – and chase one another with lots of noise and laughter.

Places to Stay & Eat

The road from the north turns east along the

coast, just after the village. Along this beach-front road you'll find most of Kuta's accommodation, which is all of a similar price and quality. After the police station you pass *Rambutan*, with rooms at 7500 rp, including tea but not breakfast. The *Wisma Segara Anak* next door has a restaurant, and rooms at 6000/8000 rp for singles/doubles and bungalows at 8000/10,000 rp including breakfast. Next along, *Pondok Sekar Kuning* (Yellow Flower Cottage), has double rooms downstairs for 8000 rp, and upstairs, with a nice view, for 10,000 rp. *Anda Cottages*, next door, is the original place at Kuta. It has some trees and shrubs which make it more pleasant, a good restaurant with Indonesian, Chinese and Western dishes, and rooms from 9000 to 12,500 rp including breakfast.

A bit further along is *New Paradise Bungalows*, with good food and singles/doubles at 8000/10,000 rp, and the *Rinjani Agung Beach Bungalows* with standard rooms at 8000/10,000 rp and 'suit rooms' for another 10,000 rp including breakfast. The old *Mascot Cottages* may be open again when you get there, or continue to the *Cockatoo Cottages & Restaurant*, the last place along the beach, with a nice restaurant area and rooms for 10,000/15,000 rp, including breakfast.

There are a few cheap, basic homestays in the village, and also the *Losmen Mata Hari*, near the market on the road to Mawan. It has a restaurant and nine small, clean rooms with private shower at 8000/10,000 rp, including breakfast.

There's a big new place at Tanjung Aan, but its opening was apparently delayed by the authorities. It now seems to have been acquired by the government's Lombok Tourist Development Corporation (Pemerintah Pengembangan Parawisata Lombok), and it's anyone's guess when it will open or what it will charge. There's no doubt about the location though – it's magnificent.

Getting There & Away
Getting to Kuta by public transport is diffi-cult. It's no trouble getting a bemo to Praya, but beyond there you might have to wait a

while for another one to Sengkol (500 rp) and then another down to Kuta (300 rp). Market day in Sengkol is Thursday, so there may be more transport then.

You could also inquire at the Perama office in Mataram – it's only a matter of time before their convenient tourist shuttle bus service is extended to the south coast.

If you have your own transport it's easy – the road is sealed all the way. The final five km to Kuta is a steep and winding descent which suddenly leaves the hills to arrive at the coast.

East Lombok

Few travellers see any more of the east than Labuhan Lombok, but improvements to the road around the north coast make a round-the-island trip quite feasible. Similarly, the once-remote south eastern peninsula is becoming more accessible, particularly to those with their own transport.

LABUHAN LOMBOK
There are fantastic views of mighty Gunung Rinjani from the east coast port of Labuhan Lombok. Ferries run from here to Sumbawa, the next island to the east. It's a friendly, sleepy little place with a mixed bag of con-crete houses, thatched shacks and stilt bungalows. You can climb the hill on the south side of the harbour and watch the boats plying between here and Sumbawa.

If you're just passing through Labuhan Lombok on your way to Sumbawa there's no need to stay overnight. You can catch an early bus from Sweta (5.30 am at the latest) and get to the port in time for the Sumbawa ferry. The Ampenan losmen are quite used to getting their guests on the road by that time.

Places to Stay & Eat
In the village of Labuhan Lombok you can stay at the basic *Losmen Dian Dutaku*, on the main road coming into town, with rooms at 2600/3600 rp for singles/doubles. On Jalan Khayangan, the road that runs round to the

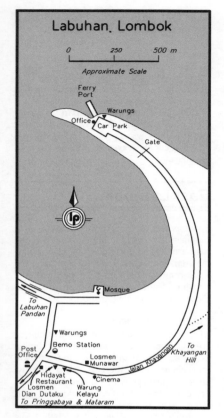

Labuhan Lombok

Labuhan Lombok and Sweta. The 69-km trip costs about 2000 rp and should take a bit less than two hours. If you're zipping straight across Lombok and bound for Bali, you can take a bus via Sweta to Lembar. Other road connections go to Masbagik (1000 rp), Pancordao and Kopang (1500 rp).

Passenger ferries leave Labuhan Lombok for Poto Tano (Sumbawa) at 8, 9.30 am, noon, 3 and 5 pm. In the other direction, boats depart Poto Tano at 7, 9 am, noon, 2.30 and 5 pm. Departure times may change, depending on demand and goodness knows what other local considerations. The trip takes about 1½ hours and costs around 2500 rp in ekonomi A, 1500 rp in ekonomi B, 500 rp for a bicycle, 3000 rp for a motorbike and 27,000 rp for a car. The boats depart from a new port on the north side of the harbour. It's about two or three km from the port to the town of Labuhan Lombok, on the road which skirts the east side of the bay. It will be too hot to walk, so take a bemo for 250 rp. The ticket office is beside the car park.

There are a couple of food stalls at the port, and one or two warungs serving nasi campur. Men come on board the boat selling fried rice wrapped in banana leaves, and hard-boiled eggs. Take a water bottle with you – it can be a bloody hot ride! The ferries can get very crowded, especially at times such as Ramadan when local people are travelling. Arrive at the dock early to get a seat, or bring a hat for sun protection and stretch out on the roof.

NORTH OF LABUHAN LOMBOK

North of Labuhan Lombok there are some fishing villages where foreigners are still a curiosity. Pulu Lampur, 14 km north, has a black-sand beach and is popular with locals on Sundays and holidays. At Teranset, near Pulu Lampur, you might be able to stay with Pak Moti. He's well known locally and has some rooms for about 10,000/15,000 rp, including three meals.

Labuhan Pandan is another few km to the north. There's not much there, but it's a good place to charter a boat to the offshore islands. You can't stay on them, but the uninhabited islands of Gili Sulat and the Gili Petangan

ferry port, there's the *Losmen Munawar*, with rooms at 2500/5000 rp; it's pretty basic but quite OK.

There are a couple of warungs around the bemo station, but the menu is restricted and the food is not that good. You can always buy a fish at the market and get it cooked at a warung. The *Hidayat Restaurant*, across the road from the bemo station, is a friendly place. Alternatively there's the fairly clean *Warung Kelayu* right next door.

Getting There & Away

There are regular buses and bemos between

group have lovely white beaches, good coral for snorkelling, and an unspoilt natural environment. It's quite expensive to get a boat out and back, and to wait long enough for you to explore the island. Try to do it with a group, and take drinking water and a picnic lunch. Some of the tour operators in Mataram may run day trips to the islands, but it would be a long day and very expensive. Some new tourist bungalows are being developed near the seashore just south of Labuhan Pandan, and they'll probably cost about 15,000/25,000 rp for singles/doubles with three meals.

SOUTH OF LABUHAN LOMBOK

On the coast, south of Labuhan Lombok, is Labuhan Haji, formerly a port for those departing on a *haji*, or pilgrimage to Mecca. There's a beach here, but some people find it a bit dirty. It's accessible from Selong by bemo and dokar. Tanjung Luar is another coastal village a little further south.

Sukaraja, a few km inland, is another slightly sanitised Sasak-style village which tourists are welcome to visit.

The south-eastern peninsula was inaccessible until recently, but a road now extends south from Jerowaru to Ekas, and there are plans to continue it to Serewei Beach. To get to the peninsula, take a bemo to Keruak (1000 rp from Sweta), then perhaps a motorbike from there. There are plans for tourist bungalows on the peninsula, unless the government decides that this coastline is too good for budget travellers and reserves the whole area for five-star hotels.

Tanjung Ringgit, on the east coast of the peninsula, has some large caves which, according to local legend, are home to a demonic giant. Tanjung Ringgit is a day's walk from the nearest road.

North Lombok

It's now possible to go by road around the north coast, but it's pretty rough between Bayan and Sambelia. You'll need a reliable motorbike, or a vehicle with good ground clearance – you're unlikely to make it in a normal car. You can do it on public transport, but east of Bayan that probably means standing in the back of a truck rather than sitting on a bus or a bemo. The road is being improved all the time, and a trip around the north coast will probably become a regular item for more adventurous visitors to Lombok.

From Mataram, a good road heads north through Lendang Bajur and the scenic Pusuk Pass (Baun Pusuk) to Pemenang, where you can turn off to Bangsal to get a boat to the Gili Islands (see the Gili Islands chapter). There are plans to continue the road north of Senggigi and Mangset, making an alternative route around the coast to Pemenang. When completed, this road will offer spectacular coastal scenery, but for now you must take the inland route through the Pusuk Pass. North of Pemenang, the road runs close to the coast almost as far as Bayan, but there is no tourist development along this stretch – yet.

SIRA
Just a few km north of Pemenang, on the coast facing Gili Air, Sira has a wonderful white-sand beach and good snorkelling on the nearby coral reef. There is a proposal to develop a big three-star hotel here but at the moment there's no accommodation, so you'll have to make a day trip. It's a short bemo ride from Pemenang.

Further round the coast, just past Gondang, is Teluk Pandau beach. It's also slated for development, hopefully of a type that budget travellers can afford.

BAYAN
Bayan, the birthplace of the Wektu Telu religion, is still an isolated village but the main road now extends to it. Traditional Hindu dances are still performed in Bayan, but getting to see them is a case of stumbling in at the right time, or asking around to find out when they're on. Bayan is also one of the main starting points for the climb up Gunung Rinjani.

Places to Stay & Eat
You can stay with the kepala desa for around 5000 rp per person per night, including two meals. There are a couple of warungs in Bayan, one on the road to Senaru just off to the right. You can get fried chicken and rice here for 1500 rp.

Getting There & Away
There are several buses daily from Sweta to Bayan, the first leaving at around 9 am. It's a three-hour trip, and you should try to get on an early bus. There may be more frequent buses to intermediate places like Pemenang. Approximate distances and fares from Sweta are: Pemenang (31 km) 700 rp; Tanjung (45 km) 800 rp; Bayan (79 km) 1600 rp.

The north coast road reaches the east coast at Sugian, and connects through Sambelia and Labuhan Pandan to Labuhan Lombok.

BATU KOQ
Batu Koq is the usual starting point for a climb up Gunung Rinjani, and the highest village at which you can stay. The local school teacher used to be the person to see for accommodation, food and information, but there are now several homestays in the village, which charge about 5000 rp per person. There are a couple of warungs near where the bus stops and the odd shop where you can buy last minute bits and pieces. Once you get to Batu Koq, numerous children will rush out shouting their 'Hello Misters' and take you to the school teacher.

Make sure you go to the magnificent waterfall near Batu Koq – it can be heard from far away. It's a pleasant hour's walk

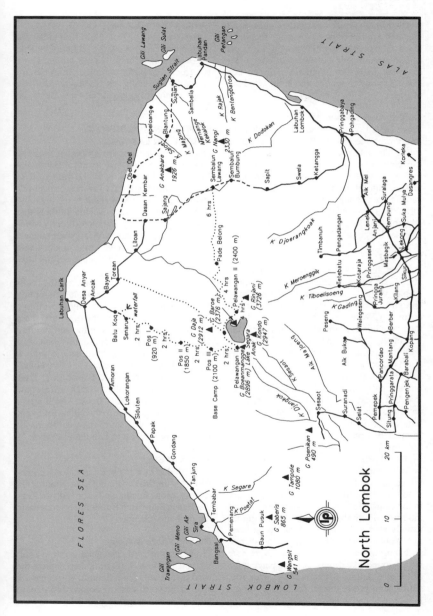

North Lombok

partly through forest, and partly alongside an irrigated water course. Watch for the sleek black monkeys swinging through the trees. Splash around near the waterfall – the water cascades down the mountain slope so fast that it's strong enough to knock the wind out of you.

Getting There & Away
From Bayan, you have to walk the four or five km up the road to Batu Koq, or take a truck. The latter is a far better alternative, especially if you arrive in Bayan at around midday when it's hot and dusty. There's not much shade along this road and you'll be carrying a fair amount of junk, as well as three days' worth of food for the walk up Rinjani. Trucks go up and down here with 'regular irregularity'.

SENARU
Perched high in the foothills of Rinjani, about nine km from Bayan, this small traditional village has an air of untainted antiquity. The villagers of Senaru did not encounter Westerners until the 1960s. Until then they lived completely isolated from the rest of the world. You may be able to stay with the schoolmaster or at the warung, but don't expect any privacy in either place.

The village is surrounded by a high wooden paling fence and comprises about 20 thatched wooden huts in straight lines, some on stilts, others low to the ground. On the left, just before you come to the village, is a small coffee plantation. There's a waterfall 2½ km from Senaru. Unless accompanied by a local person it's polite to ask permission before entering Senaru. Nobody in the village speaks English.

Many of the men from this village work in the nearby forests as woodcutters. Part of the ritual of climbing Rinjani is that guides usually stop at Senaru to stock up on betel nut. Young boys in the village thresh rice with long wooden mallets which reverberate with a sound like drums. A large percentage of the population, which is fewer than 500, suffer from goitre due to the lack of iodine in their diet and water.

Getting There & Away
It's only a km or so from Batu Koq to Senaru so you can easily walk, or you may be able to get a lift on the back of a motorbike. There is a truck that picks up timber from Senaru regularly – usually on Sundays – so you might be able to get a ride down to Bayan on it.

SEMBALUN BUMBUNG & SEMBALUN LAWANG
High up on the eastern slopes of Gunung Rinjani is the cold but beautiful Sembalun Valley. The inhabitants of the valley claim descent from the Hindu Javanese, and a relative of one of the Majapahit rulers is said to be buried here. While it seems unlikely that Java ever controlled Lombok directly, similarities in music, dance and language suggest that Lombok may have come under some long-lasting Javanese influence several hundred years ago.

In the valley, five km apart, are the traditional Sasak villages of Sembalun Bumbung and Sembalun Lawang. It's only a 45-minute walk from one village to the other and there are many pleasant walks in the surrounding area. From Sembalun Bumbung there is a steep 1½ hour climb to a saddle with a beautiful panoramic view. After five hours' walk from Sembalun Bumbung, first through rainforest, later through coffee, paw paw, rice and vegetable fields, you'll arrive at a small village close to the village of Sapit. From Sapit, you can take a bemo to Pringgabaya and on to Labuhan Lombok.

Places to Stay
In Sembalun Lawang you can stay at a home-stay or with the kepala desa for about 5000 rp per person. Accommodation with the kepala desa in Sembalun Bumbung is more basic but probably cheaper.

Getting There & Away
From the south, you can get a bemo to Sapit but you'll have to walk from there, unless the road is finished. From Senaru, you can walk around the north-eastern slopes of Rinjani to Sembalun Lawang but you'll have to start

early. It's a long way and would take around 12 hours. From Bayan there are sometimes trucks to Sembalun Lawang, or you can walk via Liloan and Sajang, which would take a whole day.

GUNUNG RINJANI

Both the Balinese and Sasaks revere Rinjani. To the Balinese it is equal to Gunung Agung, a seat of the gods, and many Balinese make a pilgrimage here each year. In a ceremony called pekelan the people throw jewellery into the lake and make offerings to the spirit of the mountain. Some Sasaks make several pilgrimages a year – full moon is the favourite time for paying their respects to the mountain and curing their ailments by bathing in its hot springs.

Rinjani is the highest mountain in Lombok, and the third highest in Indonesia. At 3726 metres it soars above the island and dominates the landscape. Early in the morning it can be seen from anywhere on the island, but by mid-morning on most days the summit is shrouded in cloud. The mountain is actually an active volcano, although its last eruption was in 1901. There's a huge crater containing a large green crescent-shaped lake, Segara Anak, which is about six km across at its widest point. There's a series of natural hot springs on the north-eastern side of the caldera, a testimony to the fact that Rinjani is still geologically active. These springs, known as Kokok Putih, are said to have remarkable healing powers, particularly for skin diseases. The lake is 200 metres below the caldera rim, and in the middle of its curve there's a new cone, Gunung Baru-jari, only a couple of hundred years old.

Climbing Rinjani

Many people climb up to Rinjani's caldera every year. These are mostly local people making a pilgrimage or seeking the curative powers of the hot springs. Many foreign visitors climb up to the caldera too, though very few people go the extra 1000 or so metres to the very summit of Rinjani. Even the climb to the crater lake is not to be taken lightly. Don't try it during the wet season as

the tracks will be slippery and very dangerous, and in any case you would be lucky to see any more than mist and cloud. You need at least three full days to do it, and probably another day to recover. Don't go up during the full moon because it will be very crowded.

There are several routes up Rinjani, but most visitors go from Bayan in the north, ascending via Batu Koq and Senaru and returning the same way. The other main route is from Sembalun Lawang on the eastern side, which is accessible by walking from either Sapit or Bayan. The northern route is more accessible as you can get to Bayan by road. It's an easier climb from the east, but it's also easier to get lost.

Guides & Equipment You can do the trek from Bayan without a guide, but in some places there's a confusion of trails branching off and you could get lost. The other advantage of guides is that they're informative, good company, and also act as porters, cooks and water collectors. When you're doing this walk with a guide make sure you set your own pace – some guides climb Rinjani as often as 20 or 30 times a year and positively gallop up the slopes! A guide will cost about 10,000 to 12,500 rp per day, porters about 8000 rp per day.

It's worthwhile talking to the people at the losmen Wisma Triguna in Ampenan. For

about US$80 (!) they will organise the complete trip for you – food, tent, sleeping bag and a guide. But if you don't want to come at that they can tell you how to go about it on your own. They'll explain what food to take, and will rent you a two- or three-person tent (12,500 rp for up to five days), a stove (2500 rp) and a sleeping bag (10,000 rp). A sleeping bag and tent are absolutely essential.

Food & Supplies You need to take enough food to last three days – including food for your guide. It's better to buy most of it in Ampenan, Mataram or Cakra as there's more choice available. Take rice, instant noodles, sugar, coffee, eggs (get a container to carry the eggs in – the Wisma Triguna will lend you one), tea, biscuits or bread, some tins of fish or meat, onions, fruit, and anything else that keeps your engine running.

Bring plenty of matches, a torch (flashlight), a water container and some cigarettes. A guide should provide water and containers for you, but it's a good idea to have your own handy. Even if you don't smoke, the guides really appreciate being given cigarettes. If you have any food left over, leave it at the school.

The Northern Route This is the most popular route taken by visitors, ascending via Batu Koq and Senaru and returning the same way. It takes about four days.

Day 1 Depart Batu Koq at about 8 am for Senaru (altitude 600 metres). From there it's about two hours to the first post, Pos I (920 metres), then another two hours to Pos II (1850 metres), where there is a hut and a water supply. A further two hours brings you to the base camp at Pos III (2100 metres), where there is also water. The climb is relatively easy going through dappled forest, with the quiet broken only by the occasional bird, animal, bell or woodchopper. At base camp pitch the tent, collect wood and water and, if you have enough energy left, climb up to the clearing and watch the sunset. The ground is rock hard at base camp and it's very cold, so bring thick woollen socks, a sweater

and a ground sheet with you. If a flock of 30-odd locals arrives unexpectedly out of the gloom, the chances of having the lake and the hot springs to yourself are slim indeed.

Day 2 Set off at about 8 am again, and after approximately two hours you will arrive at Pelawangan I, on the rim of the volcano, at an altitude of 2600 metres. Rinjani is covered in dense forest up to 2000 metres, but at around this height the vegetation changes from thick stands of mahogany and teak trees to the odd stand of pine. As you get closer to the rim the pines become sparser and the soil becomes rubbly and barren. The locals cut down the mahogany and teak trees with axes and then carry the huge logs down the steep slopes, by hand! Monkeys, wild pigs, deer and the occasional snake inhabit the forest. Once you get above the forest and up to the clearing the going is hot as there's not much shade – the land here is harsh and inhospitable – but you have superb views across to Bali and Sumbawa.

From the rim of the crater, it takes up to six hours to get down to Segara Anak and around to the hot springs, though some people will say it takes as little as two. The descent from the rim into the crater is quite dangerous – for most of the way the path down to the lake clings to the side of the cliffs and is narrow and meandering. Watch out for rubble – in certain spots it's very hard to keep your footing. Close to the lake a thick forest sweeps down to the shore. There are several places to camp along this lake, but if you head for the hot springs there are many more alternatives. The track along the lake is also narrow and very slippery – be careful and take it slowly. There are several species of small water bird on the lake, and the lake has been stocked with fish over the last few years.

After setting up camp at the lake, it's time to soak your weary body in the springs and recuperate. It's not as cold here as it is at base camp, but it is damp and misty from the steaming springs. Despite the hundreds of local people around, it can still be an eerie place. Watch your step on the paths –

Top: Narmada, Lombok (JL)
Bottom: Kuta Beach, Lombok (TW)

Top: Tanjung Aan, Lombok (JL)
Left: Pots, Lombok (JL)
Right: Rice barn, Sade, Lombok (TW)

although this is a holy place, some people have few inhibitions or qualms about relieving themselves when and wherever they need to.

Day 3 Once again, departure time is approximately 8 am, and you walk more or less all day, arriving at Batu Koq in the late afternoon. It's a hard walk, between eight and 10 hours.

Day 4 If you get back to Batu Koq late in the afternoon, it's preferable to stay there overnight. Even if you can get a lift down to Bayan by truck, the last bus from there to the Sweta terminal departs around 6 pm and there's a good chance you'll miss it. This means that you'll be stuck in Bayan after a tiring trip with nowhere to stay except with the kepala desa. If you stay overnight at Batu Koq it's still a good idea to leave early in the morning before the sun gets too hot. You may have to walk all the way down to Bayan, but there's a bus to Sweta from there at about 8.30 am and a few others during the day.

The Eastern Route You can climb to the crater of Rinjani directly from either Sembalun Bumbung or Sembalun Lawang, but you must come prepared with sleeping bag, tent, food and other supplies. You can hire a guide in Sembalun Lawang – and you'll probably need one to get through the maze of trails as you climb west from the village. It will take about six hours to get to the

village of Pade Belong, and another four hours to get to Pelawangan II on the crater rim at 2400 metres. Near here there's a crude shelter and a trail junction, with one track climbing southwards to the summit of Rinjani and the other heading west, to much more comfortable camp sites near the hot springs or the lake, about four hours away.

Going the other way, you can get from the crater rim down to Sembalun Lawang in about seven hours. It's quite possible to ascend by the northern route and descend by the eastern route, or vice versa, but you'll have to work out how to get yourself, and particularly your guide, back to your starting point.

Other Routes up Rinjani You can climb up to the crater from Torean, a small village just south-east of Bayan. The trail follows Sungai Kokok Putih, the stream that flows from Lake Segara and the hot springs, but it's hard to find; you'll need a guide.

You can also climb the south side of Rinjani, from either Sesaot or Tetebatu. Either route will involve at least one night camping in the jungle, and you may not see any views at all until you get above the tree line. Again, a guide is essential.

To the Very Top
The path to the summit branches off the Sembalun Lawang track near Pelawangan II. From the shelter there, allow four hours to reach the summit. Start early in the morning

---

A Solo Climb
It's easy enough to do the climb without a guide, although we thought climbing to the rim from the north and not bothering with the actual peak was just as good value and easy to do. But a traverse across the mountain is also perfectly feasible. Sign the book in Senaru and collect water, because it's scarce along the track. Hundreds of paths lead uphill from Senaru so if you get lost ask *several* locals and take the most logical advice. One guy pointed back to Bayan when I asked him which was the path to Gunung Rinjani!

The track is erratically numbered from 0 to 200 (200 is the crater rim). You can camp at about 65-75, 110, 170 and 185. The last is an excellent spot above the bushline with fabulous views and only half an hour from the rim for sunrise the next morning. Water is only available at 114 and 185.

From the crater rim to Segara Anak is steeply downhill. From here across the top and down to Sapit takes two to three days. A tent and sleeping bag are essential. ■

Mark Austin, New Zealand

because you have to get to the top within an hour or so of sunrise if you want to see more than mist and cloud.

The first two days were pretty much as described, but on the third day we warmed up in the springs before making a three-hour climb to a shelter by the path just before the junction with the summit route. This shelter is just a hollow scooped out of the ground and lined with dry grass. A few old sheets of iron serve as a roof. It fits three people, or maybe an intimate four.

There is wood that can be used for a fire – which is useful, because as soon as the sun goes down it gets very cold.

The next morning we watched the sun rise over Sumbawa from the junction of the paths, before starting the final ascent. The view from the rim is great, but it's nothing compared with the view from the very top! From the top, you look down into the crater which fills up with 'cotton wool' cloud streaming through the gap in the crater wall at the hot springs. In the distance, you look over Bali in one direction and Sumbawa in the other.

It's a difficult three-hour climb from the shelter; the air gets thinner and the terrain is horrible to walk on. It's powdery to start with, then you find loose stones on a steep slope (offering little support for your weight). It's a case of climbing one step up, then sliding two-thirds of a step back down, and the peak always looks closer than it is! Climbing without strong-toed shoes or boots would be masochistic.

Richard Tucker, England

The Gili Islands

Off the north-west coast of Lombok are three small, coral-fringed islands – Gili Air, Gili Meno and Gili Trawangan – each with superb, white sandy beaches, clear water, coral reefs, brilliantly coloured fish and the best snorkelling on Lombok. Although known to travellers as the 'Gili Islands', *gili* actually means 'island', so this is not a local name. In fact, every island is called 'Gili' something.

The islands have become increasingly popular with visitors, but any development is being carefully monitored and controlled to ensure they retain much of their unspoilt quality. The islanders are all Muslims, and visitors should respect their sensibilities. In particular, topless (for women) or nude sunbathing is offensive to them, although they won't say so directly. Away from the beach, it is polite for both men and women to cover their shoulders and knees.

Although the attractions of sun, sand and sea are common to all three islands, to some extent each one has developed an individual character. Unfortunately it is difficult (or expensive) to go directly from one island to another – there are no regular public boats so you have to charter one for yourself. Alternatively, you have to get a public boat back to the mainland, then wait for another boat out to the island you want to go to.

Apart from the hill on Gili Trawangan, all three islands are pancake flat. There are no roads, cars or even motorbikes, so getting around is as easy as walking. Fishing, raising cattle and goats, making palm oil and growing corn, coconuts, tapioca and peanuts are the main economic activities, along with developing tourism.

There are few facilities on these islands, although some of the places to stay have their own electricity generators and there are small shops with a bare minimum of supplies. You can change cash (not travellers' cheques) on Trawangan but there's no other place to change money on the islands, so bring enough rupiah with you.

Accommodation & Food

Most places to stay come out of a standard mould – a plain little bungalow on stilts with a small verandah out the front. Inside there will be one or two beds with mosquito nets, and the verandah will probably have a table and a couple of chairs. Mandi and toilet facilities are usually shared. The local tourist corporation has set the price of accommodation at around 10,000/15,000 rp for singles/doubles, including three meals and tea or coffee on call. The food is simple but fresh and healthy. You can live well here and it's certainly cheap!

Getting There & Away

From Ampenan or the airport you can get to one of the islands, and be horizontal on the beach within a couple of hours. The trip involves several stages unless you opt to simply charter a bemo from Ampenan – not a bad move between a group of people.

Usually, the first step in Ampenan is a bemo from the airport or the city to Rembiga for about 200 rp. From Rembiga it's 600 rp for a bus to Pemenang. Alternatively, you may be able to get a bemo from Sweta direct to Pemenang for about 700 rp. The 25-km trip takes one to 1½ hours. It's a scenic journey past many small villages and through lush green forest where you'll see monkeys by the roadside. The road also climbs to the Pusuk Pass, from which you get views down to the north coast. From Pemenang it's a km or so off the main road to the harbour at Bangsal, 200 rp by dokar.

A small information office at Bangsal Harbour has a list of the official fares out to the islands – 700 rp to Gili Air, 900 rp to Gili Meno, 1200 rp to Gili Trawangan. It's a matter of sitting and waiting until there's a full boat load, about 20 people. If you have almost that number waiting, the boat will leave if you can pay the extra fares between you. As soon as you do this, you'll be amazed at how many local people appear from

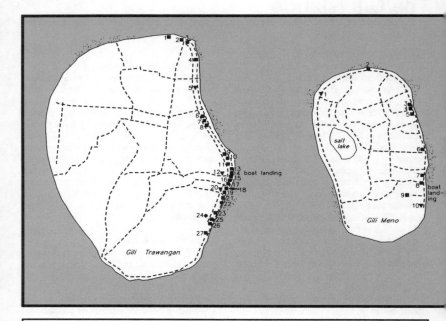

GILI TRAWANGAN

1   Nusa Tiga Homestay
2   CoralBeach Homestay
3   Pasir Putih II
4   Alex Accommodation
5   Excellent Restaurant
6   Good Heart Homestay
7   Homestay Makmur I
8   Passir Putih I
9   Danau Hijau Bungalows
10 Creative Losmen
11 Melati Losmen
12 Rudy's Cottage Restaurant
13 Dua Sekawan I
14 Pak Majid's Losmen
15 Simple Bungalow
16 Dua Sekawan II
17 Trawangan Beach Cottage & Restaurant
18 Mountain View Cottage & Restaurant, Perama Office
19 Fantasi Bungalows
20 Borobudur Restaurant
21 Holiday Inn Cottages
22 Sandy Beach
23 Paradise Cottages & Restaurant
24 Albatross Diving Adventures
25 Homestay Makmur II
26 Majestic Cottages
27 Rainbow Cottages

nowhere to fill the boat. It's a good idea to get to Bangsal by 10 am. If you have to hang around that's no problem as it's a pleasant place to while away some time, and the shaded warungs like the *Parahiangan Coffee House* have good food and coffee.

If you take a Perama minibus from Senggigi, Mataram or elsewhere, it should connect with a boat to the islands; the boat trip will be included in the price of your ticket.

The official prices for chartering a boat are 12,500 rp to Gili Air, 15,000 rp to Gili Meno

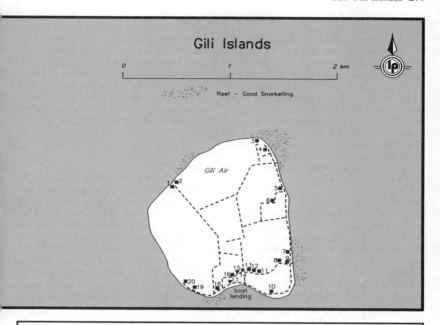

Gili Islands

0 1 2 km

Reef — Good Snorkelling

Gili Air

boat landing

GILI MENO

1 Good Heart Restaurant
2 Blue Coral Bungalows
3 Pondok Meno
4 New Cottages (Being Built)
5 Janur Indah Cottages
6 Janur Indah Bungalows
7 Matahari Bungalows
8 Malia's Child Bungalows
9 Gazebo Hotel
10 Kontiki Cottage Restaurant

GILI AIR

1 Hink Bungalows
2 Muksin Cottages
3 Hans Bungalows & Restaurant

4 Gusung Indah Bungalows
5 Fantastick Bungalows
6 Gili Air Cottages
7 Gita Gili Sunrise
8 Nusa Tiga Bungalows
9 Gili Beach Inn Bungalows
10 Paradiso Bungalows
11 Sederhana Losmen
12 Bupati's Place Cottages
13 Garden Cottages
14 Village Office
15 Gado Gado Pub
16 Bamboo Cottages
17 Fanta Pub
18 Gili Indah Cottages & Restaurant, Perama Office
19 Sunset Cottages
20 Salabose Cottages

and 20,000 rp to Gili Trawangan. In practice, you can usually beat those prices down a bit. The trip out to Gili Trawangan takes about an hour, less to the other islands. If you want to try the other beaches, it's quite expensive to charter boats around the islands but not too bad if you can get a group together. From Gili Trawangan it's 12,000 rp to Gili Meno and 15,000 rp to Gili Air. Between Gili Air and Gili Meno it's 12,500 rp.

GILI AIR

Gili Air is the closest island to the mainland. It's also the smallest and has the largest population, with about 600 people. There are beaches around most of the island and a small village at the southern end. Homes and small farms are dotted amongst the palm trees, along with a few losmen and a couple of 'pubs'. Because the buildings are so scattered, the island has a pleasant, rural character and is delightful to wander around. There are plenty of other people to meet, but if you stay in one of the more isolated places, socialising is optional.

Places to Stay

Most of the accommodation is scattered around the southern end of the island near the harbour, although there are losmen near the east, north and west coasts. The cheapest rooms have a shared outdoor mandi and cost 10,000/15,000 rp for singles/doubles and 20,000 rp for triples, all with three meals. Rooms are 6000/9000/13,500 rp if you have breakfast only. More expensive rooms with private mandi are 12,500/22,500/26,000 rp with three meals, or 8000/11,000/16,000 rp for breakfast only. This means it costs roughly 4000 rp for lunch and dinner, which is pretty cheap considering the good quality and quantity of the food, although you may prefer the freedom to eat wherever you wish.

Gili Indah, one of the bigger places on Gili Air, is where you'll find the Perama office. The office has useful information and you maybe able to change foreign cash. Up north, at the other end of the island, *Hans Bungalows* are well away from everything and have a beautiful view of the beach, but may be more expensive than the standard price. There are about 15 other places to stay, all so similar that it wouldn't be fair to mention any one in particular. Pick one that appeals to you in a location you like, or one that's been recommended on the travellers' grapevine.

GILI MENO

Gili Meno, the middle island, has the smallest population – about 300. It is also the quietest of the islands, with fewer tourist facilities and fewer tourists. If you want to play Robinson Crusoe, this is the place to do it. There's a salt lake in the middle of the island which produces salt in the dry season and mosquitoes in the wet season. The mozzies are probably no worse than in other places at that time of year, but the usual precautions are called for – mosquito net, repellent, long sleeves and long pants around dusk.

Places to Stay

The accommodation here is mostly on the east beach with a couple of places up north. The *Gazebo Hotel* is pretty up-market by Gili standards, with a fancy balcony restaurant and tastefully furnished and decorated Bali-style bungalows. Rooms with private bathroom, air-con and electricity (if it's working) cost about US$30 including breakfast. Another posh place is being built at the northern end of the east coast, with a tennis court no less! The other half-dozen places offer standard Gili bungalows, though perhaps a little more spacious, and charge the usual Gili prices – 10,000/15,000 rp for singles/doubles and 20,000 rp for triples with three meals. Rooms with private bathroom cost a bit more, and rooms with breakfast only, a bit less.

GILI TRAWANGAN

The largest island, with a local population of about 400, Gili Trawangan also has the most visitors and the most facilities, although it is still undeveloped by Western standards. The accommodation and restaurants/bars are all along the east coast beach, and this compact layout gives the island a friendly village atmosphere. Most of the places to stay also serve food, but there are a few convivial restaurants, like the *Excellent* and the *Mountain View*, which are more like bars in the evening. There's usually music and dancing at one of them.

The white-sand beach is the main daytime attraction, and the snorkelling is superb, with beautiful coral and lots of colourful fish. You can rent a mask and snorkel for 2000 rp per day, and fins for the same amount. There's a diving operation here too, Albatross Diving Adventures, though much of the coral in deeper water has been damaged by explosives used for fishing. Fortunately, this destructive fishing technique has now been totally banned.

Gili Trawangan also has a hill at its southern end, where you can find traces of two Japanese WW II gun emplacements and enjoy the view across the strait to Bali's Gunung Agung, particularly at sunset. Sunrise over Gunung Rinjani is also impressive. One local described Trawangan's three main attractions as 'sunrise, sunset, sunburn'! It's certainly hot enough, and it can get rather dusty in the dry season.

Places to Stay

The accommodation and prices here are even more standardised than those on the other islands. Typical bungalows run to 10,000/15,000 rp for singles/doubles and 20,000 rp for triples. A couple of places, like *Rainbow Cottages*, have private mandis and cost more. Some others don't provide lunch or dinner, so they're a bit cheaper. Pick a place you like the look of (some have prettier gardens), or one recommended by a recent visitor (you can't beat that travellers' grapevine), or go with one of the friendly people who will meet you when the boat comes in. The places in the middle of the beach strip may be a bit better for meeting people, while those at the northern and southern ends of the beach offer more peace and quiet.

Glossary

Adat – tradition; manners and customs

Air panas – hot springs

Aling aling – guard wall behind the entrance gate to a Balinese family compound. Demons can only travel in straight lines so the aling aling prevents them from coming straight in through the front entrance.

Alun alun – main public square of a town or village

Anjing – dog

Angklung – the portable form of the gamelan used in processions as well as in other festivals and celebrations

Arak – colourless, distilled palm wine; the local firewater

Arja – a refined form of Balinese theatre, like an opera

Arjuna – a hero of the *Mahabharata* epic and a popular temple gate guardian image

Bahasa – language

Bale – house, building, pavilion

Bale banjar – the communal meeting place of the village banjar (a sort of community club which organises activities including the gamelan)

Bale gede – the reception room or guest house in the home of a wealthy Balinese

Bale kambang – floating pavilion

Bali Aga – the 'original' Balinese; these people managed to resist the new ways brought in with the Majapahit migration

Balian – see Dukun

Banjar – local division of a village represented by all the married adult males

Banyan – holy tree; see Waringin

Bapak – father; also a polite form of address to any older man

Baris – warrior dance

Barong – mythical lion-dog creature, star of the Barong & Rangda dance and champion of the good

Barong Landung – literally 'tall barong', these enormous puppet figures are seen at the annual festival on Pulau Serangan

Barong Tengkok – name for the portable gamelan used for wedding processions and circumcision ceremonies on Lombok

Baruna – god of the sea

Batara – title used to address a deceased spirit, particularly that of an important person

Batik – process of printing fabric by coating part of the cloth with wax, then dyeing it and melting the wax out. The waxed part is not coloured and repeated waxings and dyeings builds up a pattern. Although a Javanese craft, the Balinese also produce batik.

Bayu – god of the air

Bedaulu, Dalem – legendary last ruler of the Pejeng dynasty

Bemo – popular local transport in Bali and Lombok, traditionally a small pick-up truck with a bench seat down each side in the back. Traditional bemos are becoming scarce and are being replaced by small minibuses.

Bima – another hero of the *Mahabharata*, biggest and strongest of the Pandava brothers

Boma – son of the earth, a temple guardian figure

Brahma – the creator, one of the trinity of Hindu gods

Brahmana – the caste of priests and highest of the Balinese castes; although all priests are Brahmanas, not all Brahmanas are priests

Brem – rice wine

Bu – shortened form of ibu (mother)

Bukit – hill; also the name of the southern peninsula of Bali

Bupati – government official in charge of a district (kabupaten)

Buta – demon or evil spirit

Camat – government official in charge of a subdistrict (kecamatan)

Candi – shrine, originally of Javanese design; also known as prasada

Candi Bentar – split gateway entrance to a temple

Caste – the Balinese caste system is nowhere near as important or firmly entrenched as India's caste system. There are four castes: three branches of the 'nobility' (Brahmana, Wesia, Satria) and the common people (Sudra).

Catur Yoga – ancient manuscript on religion and cosmology

Cidomo – horse-drawn cart on Lombok

Cokorda – male title of a person of the Satria caste

Dalang – the puppet master and storyteller in a wayang kulit performance; a man of varied skills and considerable endurance

Danau – lake

Desa – village

Dewa – a deity or supernatural spirit

Dewi – goddess

Dewi Danau – goddess of the lakes

Dewi Sri – goddess of rice

Dokar – horse-drawn cart; still a popular form of local transport in many towns and larger villages throughout Bali – known as a cidomo on Lombok

Dukan – 'witch doctor', actually a faith healer and herbal doctor

Durga – goddess of death and destruction and consort of Shiva

Durian – 'the fruit that smells like hell and tastes like heaven'

Gajah Mada – famous Majapahit prime minister who defeated the last great king of Bali and extended Majapahit power over the island

Gambang – gamelan orchestra from Jakarta

Galungan – great Balinese festival, an annual event in the 210-day Balinese wuku calendar

Gamelan – traditional Balinese orchestra, usually percussion with large xylophones and gongs

Ganesh – Shiva's elephant-headed son

Gang – alley or footpath

Garuda – mythical man-bird creature, the vehicle of Vishnu and the modern symbol of Indonesia

Goa – cave

Gringsing – rare double-ikat woven cloth (made only in the Bali Aga village of Tenganan)

Gunung – mountain

Gusti – the polite title for members of the Wesia caste

Hanuman – the monkey god who plays a major part in the *Ramayana*

Homestay – a small, family-run losmen

Ibu – mother; also polite form of address to any older woman

Ida Bagus – honourable title for a male Brahman

Iders-iders – long scrolls painted in the wayang style which are used as temple decorations

Ikat – cloth where a pattern is produced by dyeing the individual threads before weaving. Ikat is usually of the warp or the weft, although the rare 'double ikat' technique is found in Tenganan (see Gringsing).

Indra – king of the gods

Jalan – street

Jalan Jalan – to walk

Jidur – large cylindrical drums played throughout Lombok

Jukung – see Prahu

Kabupaten – districts (known as regencies during Dutch rule)

Kain – wraparound article of clothing which resembles a sarong

Kaja – Balinese 'north' which is always towards the mountains. The most important shrines are always on the kaja side of a temple.

Kala – demonic face often seen over temple gateways. The kalas' outstretched hands are to stop evil spirits from entering, although they are themselves evil spirits.

Kali – rivulet

Kawi – classical Javanese, the language of poetry

Kawin – married

Kebaya – Chinese, long-sleeved blouse with low neckline and embroidered edges

Kelod – opposite of kaja; the side of a temple oriented away from the mountains and toward the sea

Kemban – woman's breast cloth

Kepala desa – village headman

Kepeng – old Chinese coins with a hole in the centre; these were the everyday currency during the Dutch era and can still be obtained quite readily from shops and antique dealers

Ketupat – a kind of sticky rice cooked in a banana leaf. Balinese Hindus and Wektu-Telus pelt each other with ketupat in a mock war held annually at Lingsar on Lombok – the ceremony is to honour the rainy season.

Kretek – Indonesian clove cigarettes; a very familiar odour in Bali

Kris – traditional dagger, often held to have spiritual or magical powers

Kulkul – the hollow tree-trunk drum used to sound a warning or call meetings

Kuningan – holy day celebrated throughout Bali on the 10th day of the Galungan festival

Labuhan – harbour

Lamak – long, woven palm-leaf strips hung in temples during festivals

Langse – rectangular decorative hangings used in palaces or temples

Leyak – an evil spirit which can assume fantastic forms by the use of black magic

Lontar – type of palm tree; traditional books were written on the dried leaves of lontar

Losmen – small Balinese hotel, often family-run and similar in design to a traditional Balinese house

Mahabharata – one of the great Hindu holy books, tells of the battle between the Pandavas and the Korawas

Majapahit – the last great Hindu dynasty in Java. The Majapahit were pushed out of Java by the rise of Islamic power, and moved into Bali.

Mandi – Indonesian 'bath' consisting of a large water tank from which you ladle water over yourself

Manusa Yadnya – ceremonies which mark the various stages of Balinese life from before birth to after cremation

Mapadik – marriage by request, as opposed to Ngrorod

Meru – multi-roofed shrines in Balinese temples. The name meru comes from the Hindu holy mountain Mahameru

Naga – a mythical snake-like creature

Ngrorod – marriage by elopement; a traditional 'heroic' way of getting married in Bali

Nusa – island

Nyale – worm-like fish caught off Kuta Beach, Lombok; a special ceremony is held each year around February/March in honour of the first catch of the season

Nyepi – major annual festival in the Hindu saka calendar, this is a day of complete stillness and rest in preparation for a night of chasing out evil spirits

Odalan – Balinese 'temple birthday' festival held annually in every temple (ie once every 210 days)

Padmasana – temple shrine, a throne for the sun god Surya

Paduraksa – covered gateway to a temple

Paibon – shrine in a state temple for the royal ancestors

Pak – shortened form of bapak (father)

Palan Palan – slowly

Palinggihs – temple shrines consisting of a simple little throne. Palinggihs are intended as resting places for the gods when they come down for festivals

Pandanus – palm plant used in weaving mats etc

Pande – blacksmiths; they are treated somewhat like a caste in their own right

Pantai – beach

Pantun – ancient Malay poetical verse in rhyming couplets

Pasar – market

Patih – prime minister

Pedanda – high priest

Pekembar – umpire or referee in the traditional Sasak trial of strength known as peresehan

Pemangku – temple guardian and priest for temple rituals, not necessarily of high caste

Pendet – formal offering dance performed at temple festivals

Penjors – long bamboo poles with decorated ends arched over the road or pathway during festivals or ceremonies

Perbekel – government official in charge of a village (desa)

Peresehan – popular form of one-to-one physical combat peculiar to Lombok in which two men fight armed with a small hide shield for protection and a long rattan stave as a weapon

Prahu – traditional Indonesian outrigger

Prasada – see Candi

Pratima – figure of a god used as a 'stand-in' for the actual god's presence during a ceremony

Puputan – a warrior's fight to the death, akin to the suicidal *jauhar* of the rajput warriors of India

Pura – temple

Pura dalem – temple of the dead

Pura desa – temple of the village for everyday functions

Pura puseh – temple of the village founders or fathers, honouring the village's origins

Pura subak – temple of the rice growers association

Puri – palace

Puseh – the place of origin

Rajah – lord or prince

Ramayana – one of the great Hindu holy books, stories from which form the keystone of many Balinese dances and tales

Rangda – the widow-witch who represents evil in Balinese theatre and dance

Rattan – hardy, pliable vine used for handicrafts, furniture and weapons

Rebab – bowed lute

Rudat – traditional Sasak dance, with some Islamic influence

Rumah makan – restaurant; literally 'house to eat'

Sakti – magic power

Sampan – small sailing vessel used primarily for island hops or short journeys

Sanghyang – trance dance in which the dancers impersonate a local village god

Sanghyang Widi – the Balinese supreme being is never actually worshipped as such; one of the 'three in one' or lesser gods stand in

Sasak – native of Lombok

Satria – the second Balinese caste

Sawah – an individual rice field

Sebel – polluted, spiritually unclean

Shiva – the creator and destroyer, one of the three great Hindu gods

Sirih – betel nut, chewed as a mild narcotic

Songket – silver or gold threaded cloth, hand woven using a floating weft technique

Subak – the village association that organises rice terraces and shares out water for irrigation. Each sawah owner must be a member of the subak.

Sudra – the lowest or common caste to which the majority of Balinese belong

Sungai – river

Taman – ornamental garden; literally 'garden with a pond'

Trisakti – the 'three in one' or trinity of Hindu gods: Brahma, Shiva and Vishnu

Uang – money

Vishnu – the preserver, one of the three great Hindu gods

Wantilan – open pavilion used to stage cockfights

Waringin – banyan tree. This large, shady tree, found at many temples, has drooping branches which root to produce new trees.

Warung – food stall, a sort of Indonesian equivalent to a combination corner shop and snack bar

Wayang kulit – leather puppet used in shadow puppet plays

Wayang wong – masked drama playing scenes from the *Ramayana*

Wektu Telu – religion peculiar to Lombok which originated in Bayan and combines many tenets of Islam and aspects of other faiths

Wesia – the military caste and most numerous of the Balinese noble castes

Wihara – monastery

Yeh – water (Balinese)

Index

ABBREVIATIONS

Bali (B)   Lombok (L)

MAPS

Amlapura (B) 199
Ampenan, Mataram,
    Cakranegara & Sweta (L)
    244-245
Bali, East 185
Bali, North 224-225
Bali, South 134
Bali, South-West 208-209
Bangli (B) 203
Candidasa (B) 194-195
Denpasar (B) 126-127
Denpasar to Ubud (B) 161
Gianyar (B) 186

Gili Islands (L) 276-277
Goa Gajah (B) 180
Gunung Batur, Around (B) 215
Jimbaran Bay (B) 155
Klungkung (B) 188
Kuta & Legian (B) 136
Kuta (B) 138
Labuhan Lombok (L) 266
Lake Bratan Area (B) 220
Legian (B) 142
Lendang Nangka (L) 261
Lombok, Central 260
Lombok, North 269

Lombok – South Coast 263
Lovina Beaches (B) 228-229
Negara (B) 210
Nusa Dua (B) 157
Nusa Lembongan (B) 239
Nusa Penida (B) 241
Padangbai (B) 191
Sanur (B) 148
Senggigi Beach (L) 253
Singaraja (B) 226
Ubud & Around (B) 164-165
Ubud (B) 172

TEXT

Map references are in **bold** type

Air Nyet (L) 258
Amlapura (B) 198-200, **199**
    Ujung Water Palace 199
Ampenan (L) 244-252, **244**
    Museum Negeri 247
Anturan (B) 225
Ayung River (B) 169

Bali Barat National Park 234-236
Balina Beach (B) 192-193
Bangko Bangko (L) 252
Bangli (B) 203-204, **203**
    Bukit Demulih 203
    Pura Kehen 203
Banjar (B) 233-234
Banyuwedang Hot Springs (B)
    235
Bat Cave (B) 190
Batu Bolong (L) 254
Batu Koq (L) 268-270
Batuan (B) 162
Batubulan (B) 160-161
Batur (B) 214
Bayan (L) 268
Bebandem (B) 202
Bedugul Leisure Park (B) 219
Bedulu (B) 179-181
    Pura Samuan Tiga 181

Belega (B) 187
Benoa Port (B) 155-156
Benoa Village (B) 156
Besakih (B) 204
    Pura Besakih 204
Blahbatuh (B) 162-163
Blayu (B) 208
Bona (B) 187
Buahan (B) 217
Buitan (B) 192-193
Bukit Dharma (B) 163
Bumgang (L) 264
Bunut Panggan (B) 226

Cakranegara (L) 244-252, **244-245**
    Pura Meru (L) 248
Campuan (B) 168-169
Candidasa (B) 194-198, **194-195**
Candikuning (B) 219
    Pura Ulu Danau 219
Cekek (B) 211
Celuk (B) 161
Celukanbawang (B) 234

Delod Brawah (B) 211
Denpasar (B) 124-132, **126-127**
    Abiankapas 128
    Bali Museum 125-128

Elephant Cave (B) 179, **180**

Gerupak (L) 264
Gianyar (B) 186-187, **186**
Gili Islands (L) 275-279, **276-277**
    Gili Air 278
    Gili Meno 278
    Gili Trawangan 278-279
Gili Nanggu (L) 253-254
Gili Petangan (L) 266
Gili Sulat (L) 266
Gilimanuk (B) 211
Goa Gajah (B) 179, **180**
Goa Karangsari (B) 241-242
Goa Lawah (B) 190
Guang (B) 162
Gumicik (B) 161
Gunung Agung (B) 205-206
Gunung Batukau (B) 221-222
    Pura Luhur 221
Gunung Batur (B) 216-219, **215**
Gunung Kawi (B) 181-182
Gunung Pengsong (L) 252
Gunung Rinjani (L) 271-274

Iseh (B) 202

Jagaraga (B) 236
Jati (B) 183

Jatului (B) 222
Jimbaran Bay (B) 155, **155**
Jungutbatu (B) 238

Kalibukbuk (B) 226
Kapal (B) 207
Kedewatan (B) 169
Kediri (B) 209
Kedisan (B) 216-217
Ketewel (B) 161
Kintamani (B) 214
    Pura Ulun Danu 214
Klungkung (B) 187-190, **188**
    Bale Kambang 188
    Kertha Gosa 187
Kotaraja (L) 259
Krambitan (B) 210
Kuban (B) 217
Kubutambahan (B) 237
    Pura Maduwe Karang 237
Kusamba (B) 190
Kuta (B) 133-147, **136, 138**
Kuta Beach (L) 264-265
Kutri (B) 163

Labuhan Haji (B) 233, (L) 267
Labuhan Lalang (B) 235
Labuhan Lombok (L) 265-266,
    266
Labuhan Pandan (L) 266
Lake Batur (B) 216-218
Lake Bratan (B) 219-221, **220**
Lalang-Linggah (B) 210
Lebih (B) 187
Legian (B) 133-147, **136, 142**
Lembar (L) 252
Lembongan Village (B) 238-239
Lenang (L) 262-264
Lendang Nangka (L) 261, **261**
Lingsar (L) 256-257
Lovina (B) 225-233, **228-229**
Loyok (L) 259-260
Lukluk (B) 207

Marga (B) 208
Mas (B) 162
Mataram (L) 244-252, **244-245**
Mawan (L) 264
Medewi (B) 210
Mengwi (B) 208

Pura Taman Ayun 208

Narmada (L) 256
Negara (B) 211, **210**
Nusa Dua (B) 156-158, **157**
Nusa Lembongan (B) 238-240,
    239
Nusa Penida (B) 240-242, **241**

Pabean (B) 161
Padangbai (B) 190-192, **191**
Payangan (B) 183
Pejaten (B) 210
Pejeng (B) 170, 181
    Pura Pusering Jagat 181
Peliatan (B) 168
Pemaron (B) 225
Penelokan (B) 212-214
Penestanan (B) 169
Penujak (L) 262
Penulisan (B) 216
    Pura Tegeh Koripan 216
Petulu (B) 170
Pringgasela (L) 260
Pulaki (B) 234
Pulau Menjangan (B) 230, 235
Pulau Serangan (B) 154-155
Pulu Lampur (L) 266
Pura Lempuyang (B) 201
Pura Luhur Ulu Watu (B) 159
Pura Masceti (B) 187
Purajati (B) 218

Rambut Siwi (B) 210-211
Rembitan (L) 264
Rendang (B) 202
Rungkang (L) 261-262

Saba (B) 187
Sade (L) 264
Sampalan (B) 241
Sangeh (B) 209
Sangsit (B) 236
Sanur (B) 147-154, **148**
Sawan (B) 236
Sayan (B) 169
Segar Beach (L) 264
Sembalun Bumbung (L) 270-271
Sembalun Lawang (L) 270-71
Sempidi (B) 207

Senaru (L) 270
Senggigi (L) 254-256, **253**
Seririt (B) 234
Serneng (L) 264
Sesaot (L) 258
Sibetan (B) 202
Sidan (B) 187
Silung Blanak (L) 264
Singaraja (B) 223-225, **226**
Sira (L) 268
Siyut (B) 187
Songan (B) 219
Sorga (B) 205
Sukaraja (L) 267
Sukarara (L) 262
Sukawati (B) 161-162
Suranadi (L) 257-258
Sweta (L) 244-252, **244-245**

Tabanan (B) 209
Tampaksiring (B) 181-183
Tanah Lot (B) 207-208
Tanjung Aan (L) 264
Tanjung Luar (L) 267
Tanjung Ringgit (L) 267
Tegalalang (B) 183
Tegenungan Waterfall (B) 163
Teluk Terima (B) 235
Tenganan (B) 193-194
Teranset (L) 266
Tetebatu (L) 260-261
Tirta (B) 217-218
Tirta Empul (B) 182-183
Tirtagangga (B) 200-201
Toyah Bungkah (B) 217-218
Toyapakeh (B) 242
Trunyan (B) 217
Tukad Mungga (B) 225
Tulamben (B) 201-202
Tunjungan (B) 170
Turtle Island (B) 154-155

Ubud (B) 163-178, **164-165, 172**
    Monkey Forest 169
    Museum Neka 167
    Puri Lukisan Museum 167
Ulu Watu (B) 158-159

Yeh Pulu (B) 179
Yeh Sanih (B) 237

Where Can You Find Out.........

HOW to get a Laotian visa in Bangkok?

WHERE to go birdwatching in PNG?

WHAT to expect from the police if you're robbed in Peru?

WHEN you can go to see cow races in Australia?

In the Lonely Planet Newsletter!

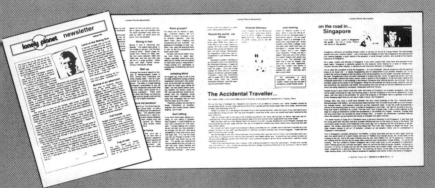

Every issue includes:

- *a letter from Lonely Planet founders Tony and Maureen Wheeler*

- *a letter from an author 'on the road'*

- *the most entertaining or informative reader's letter we've received*

- *the latest news on new and forthcoming releases from Lonely Planet*

- *and all the latest travel news from all over the world*

To receive the FREE quarterly Lonely Planet Newsletter, write to:
Lonely Planet Publications Pty Ltd (A.C.N. 005 607 983)
PO Box 617, Hawthorn, Vic 3122, Australia
Lonely Planet Publications, Inc
PO Box 2001A, Berkeley, CA 94702, USA

Guides to South-East Asia

South-East Asia on a shoestring
The well-known 'yellow bible' for travellers in South-East Asia covers Brunei, Burma, Hong Kong, Indonesia, Macau, Malaysia, Papua New Guinea, the Philippines, Singapore, and Thailand.

Burma - a travel survival kit
Burma is one of Asia's most interesting countries. This book shows how to make the most of a trip around the main triangle route of Rangoon–Mandalay–Pagan, and explores many lesser-known places such as Pegu and Inle Lake.

Malaysia, Singapore & Brunei - a travel survival kit
Three independent nations of amazing geographic and cultural variety — from the national parks, beaches, jungles and rivers of Malaysia, tiny oil-rich Brunei and the urban prosperity and diversity of Singapore.

Philippines - a travel survival kit
The friendly Filipinos, colourful festivals, and superb natural scenery make the Philippines one of the most interesting countries in South-East Asia for adventurous travellers and sun-seekers alike.

Indonesia - a travel survival kit
Some of the most remarkable sights and sounds in South-East Asia can be found amongst the 7000 islands of Indonesia — this book covers the entire archipelago in detail.

Hong Kong, Macau & Canton - a travel survival kit
A comprehensive guide to three fascinating cities linked by history, culture and geography.

Thailand - a travel survival kit
This authoritative guide includes Thai script for all place names and the latest travel details for all regions, including tips in trekking in the remote hills of the Golden Triangle.

Vietnam, Laos & Cambodia - a travel survival kit
This comprehensive guidebook has all the information you'll need on this most beautiful region of Asia – finally opening its doors to the world.

Singapore city guide
Singapore offers a taste of the great Asian cultures in a small, accessible package. This compact guide will help travellers discover the very best that this city of contrasts can offer.

Also available:
Thai phrasebook, *Thai Hill Tribes* phrasebook, *Burmese* phrasebook, *Pilipino* phrasebook and *Indonesia* phrasebook.

Lonely Planet Guidebooks

Lonely Planet guidebooks cover every accessible part of Asia as well as Australia, the Pacific, South America, Africa, the Middle East and parts of North America and Europe. There are four series: *travel survival kits*, covering a country for a range of budgets; *shoestring guides* with compact information for low-budget travel in a major region; *walking guides*; and *phrasebooks*.

Australia & the Pacific
Australia
Bushwalking in Australia
Islands of Australia's Great Barrier Reef
Fiji
Micronesia
New Caledonia
New Zealand
Tramping in New Zealand
Papua New Guinea
Papua New Guinea phrasebook
Rarotonga & the Cook Islands
Samoa
Solomon Islands
Sydney
Tahiti & French Polynesia
Tonga
Vanuatu

South-East Asia
Bali & Lombok
Burma
Burmese phrasebook
Indonesia
Indonesia phrasebook
Malaysia, Singapore & Brunei
Philippines
Pilipino phrasebook
Singapore
South-East Asia on a shoestring
Thailand
Thai phrasebook
Vietnam, Laos & Cambodia

North-East Asia
China
Mandarin Chinese phrasebook
Hong Kong, Macau & Canton
Japan
Japanese phrasebook
Korea
Korean phrasebook
North-East Asia on a shoestring
Taiwan
Tibet
Tibet phrasebook

West Asia
Trekking in Turkey
Turkey
Turkish phrasebook
West Asia on a shoestring

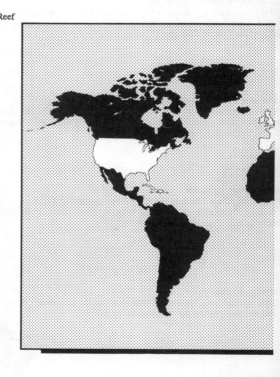

Indian Ocean
Madagascar & Comoros
Maldives & Islands of the East Indian Ocean
Mauritius, Réunion & Seychelles

Mail Order

Lonely Planet guidebooks are distributed worldwide and are sold by good bookshops everywhere. They are also available by mail order from Lonely Planet, so if you have difficulty finding a title please write to us. US and Canadian residents should write to Embarcadero West, 112 Linden St, Oakland CA 94607, USA and residents of other countries to PO Box 617, Hawthorn, Victoria 3122, Australia.

Europe
Eastern Europe on a shoestring
Iceland, Greenland & the Faroe Islands
Trekking in Spain
USSR
Russian phrasebook

Indian Subcontinent
Bangladesh
India
Hindi/Urdu phrasebook
Trekking in the Indian Himalaya
Karakoram Highway
Kashmir, Ladakh & Zanskar
Nepal
Trekking in the Nepal Himalaya
Nepal phrasebook
Pakistan
Sri Lanka
Sri Lanka phrasebook

Africa
Africa on a shoestring
Central Africa
East Africa
Kenya
Swahili phrasebook
Morocco, Algeria & Tunisia
Moroccan Arabic phrasebook
Zimbabwe, Botswana & Namibia
West Africa

North America
Alaska
Canada
Hawaii

Mexico
Baja California
Mexico

South America
Argentina
Bolivia
Brazil
Brazilian phrasebook
Chile & Easter Island
Colombia
Ecuador & the Galápagos Islands
Latin American Spanish phrasebook
Peru
Quechua phrasebook
South America on a shoestring

Central America
Central America on a shoestring
Costa Rica
La Ruta Maya

Middle East
Egypt & the Sudan
Egyptian Arabic phrasebook
Israel
Jordan & Syria
Yemen

The Lonely Planet Story

Lonely Planet published its first book in 1973 in response to the numerous 'How did you do it?' questions Maureen and Tony Wheeler were asked after driving, bussing, hitching, sailing and railing their way from England to Australia.

Written at a kitchen table and hand collated, trimmed and stapled, *Across Asia on the Cheap* became an instant local bestseller, inspiring thoughts of another book.

Eighteen months in South-East Asia resulted in their second guide, *South-East Asia on a shoestring*, which they put together in a backstreet Chinese hotel in Singapore in 1975. The 'yellow bible' as it quickly became known to backpackers around the world, soon became *the* guide to the region. It has sold well over half a million copies and is now in its 7th edition, still retaining its familiar yellow cover.

Today there are over 80 Lonely Planet titles – books that have that same adventurous approach to travel as those early guides; books that 'assume you know how to get your luggage off the carousel' as one reviewer put it.

Although Lonely Planet initially specialised in guides to Asia, they now cover most regions of the world, including the Pacific, South America, Africa, the Middle East and Eastern Europe. The list of *walking guides* and *phrasebooks* (for 'unusual' languages such as Quechua, Swahili, Nepalese and Egyptian Arabic) is also growing rapidly.

The emphasis continues to be on travel for independent travellers. Tony and Maureen still travel for several months of each year and play an active part in the writing, updating and quality control of Lonely Planet's guides.

They have been joined by over 50 authors, 40 staff – mainly editors, cartographers, & designers – at our office in Melbourne, Australia, and another 10 at our US office in Oakland, California. Travellers themselves also make a valuable contribution to the guides through the feedback we receive in thousands of letters each year.

The people at Lonely Planet strongly believe that travellers can make a positive contribution to the countries they visit, both through their appreciation of the countries' culture, wildlife and natural features, and through the money they spend. In addition, the company makes a direct contribution to the countries and regions it covers. Since 1986 a percentage of the income from each book has been donated to ventures such as famine relief in Africa; aid projects in India; agricultural projects in Central America; Greenpeace's efforts to halt French nuclear testing in the Pacific and Amnesty International. In 1991 $68,000 was donated to these causes.

Lonely Planet's basic travel philosophy is summed up in Tony Wheeler's comment, 'Don't worry about whether your trip will work out. Just go!'